Classroom Management

*Models, Applications,
and Cases*

Classroom Management

Models, Applications, and Cases

SECOND EDITION

M. Lee Manning
Old Dominion University

Katherine T. Bucher
Old Dominion University

PEARSON

Merrill
Prentice Hall

Upper Saddle River, New Jersey
Columbus, Ohio

Library of Congress Cataloging-in-Publication Data

Manning, M. Lee.
  Classroom management: models, applications, and cases / M. Lee Manning, Katherine
T. Bucher.—2nd ed.
    p. cm.
  Includes bibliographical references and index.
  ISBN 0-13-170750-7
    1. Classroom management. 2. School discipline. I. Bucher, Katherine Toth, 1947-II.
Title.
LB3013.M327 2007
371.102'4—dc22

2005058679

Vice President and Executive Publisher: Jeffery W. Johnston
Executive Editor: Debra A. Stollenwerk
Assistant Developmental Editor: Elisa Rogers
Editorial Assistant: Mary Morrill
Production Editor: Alexandrina B. Wolf
Production Coordination: Lisa S. Garboski, bookworks
Design Coordinator: Diane C. Lorenzo
Cover Designer: Jason Moore
Cover Image: Corbis
Production Manager: Susan Hannahs
Director of Marketing: David Gesell
Senior Marketing Manager: Darcy Betts Prybella
Marketing Coordinator: Brian Mounts
Photo Coordinator: Monica Merkel

This book was set in Berkeley by Pine Tree Composition. It was printed and bound by Hamilton Printing
Company. The cover was printed by Phoenix Color Corp.

Photo Credits: Sybil Shelton/PH College, p. 3; Rhoda Sidney/PH College, p. 25; Scott Cunningham/
Merrill, pp. 46, 164, 197, 262; Anne Vega/Merrill, pp. 62, 77; Tom Watson/Merrill, pp. 94, 110;
Anthony Magnacca/Merrill, pp. 128, 179, 244; Liz Moore/Merrill, p. 147; Michael Newman/PhotoEdit
Inc., p. 223.

Pearson Prentice Hall™ is a trademark of Pearson Education, Inc.
Pearson® is a registered trademark of Pearson plc
Prentice Hall® is a registered trademark of Pearson Education, Inc.
Merrill® is a registered trademark of Pearson Education, Inc.

Pearson Education Ltd.   Pearson Education Australia Pty. Limited
Pearson Education Singapore Pte. Ltd.   Pearson Education North Asia Ltd.
Pearson Education Canada, Ltd.   Pearson Educación de Mexico, S.A. de C.V.
Pearson Education—Japan   Pearson Education Malaysia Pte. Ltd.

10 9 8 7 6 5 4
ISBN 0-13-170750-7

To my grandchildren, Jada, Abby, and Luke, with the hope they will grow up in a humane and caring world. To their parents, Jennifer and Richard, who are working to make that happen.

MLM

To my husband, Glenn, for his encouragement and understanding; and to the teachers and library media specialists who shared their feelings, experiences, and views about classroom management.

KTB

Preface

THE GROWING CHALLENGES OF CLASSROOM MANAGEMENT

The problems of managing students in classrooms and throughout the school have always challenged teachers and administrators. Our firsthand experiences working in schools and with practicum and student teachers have convinced us that classroom management is a major concern. Although most preservice and in-service teachers appear well-grounded in curricular content and instructional methodology, classroom management continues to be a challenge as educators try to find ways to work with students who lack discipline, disrupt the teaching learning process, limit teachers' effectiveness, and cause others physical and psychological harm. In fact, problems with classroom management have caused some qualified educators to leave the profession.

- The behavior problems that have challenged teachers for centuries are not diminishing. Many students (certainly not all!) talk out of turn, socialize with their friends, goof off when they should be working, walk aimlessly around the classroom, and yell answers without being called upon.

- There are indications that behavior problems are growing more severe. At one time they were more an annoyance than anything else, but now both teachers and students feel threatened by violence and by aggressive behaviors.

- Behavior problems that should have been addressed decades ago (e.g., bullies who prey on weaker students, psychological abusers) are finally being addressed, but it will take some time and a concerted effort by educators to reduce or eliminate them.

- Classroom management models and specific behavior strategies must show an understanding of diversity and the changing composition of contemporary classrooms. For many years, educators used the same classroom management strategies for all students, with little or no regard for students' gender, learning styles and abilities, culture, and other differences.

- Classroom management models need to incorporate instructional management. Rather than just working to make students behave, teachers also need to examine their own instructional and personal behaviors.

In addition to these basic concerns, numerous possible causes contribute to classroom management problems. These include violence in the media, poverty, changing home and family life, easy access to weapons, and court decisions limiting educators' rights. Although we are not downplaying the importance of any of these causes, we believe that the most important thing we can do is to focus on the actions educators can take and help them plan and implement an effective classroom management model.

What about the issue of students bringing guns, knives, and other weapons to school? Current trends and predictions suggest that any definitive answers to these concerns is unlikely in the near future. In fact, recent violent incidents affecting students and educators suggest that the need for exemplary responses to behavior problems will likely grow more acute in the future.

Purpose, Rationale, and Organization of the Text

- Teachers need to understand foundational as well as contemporary classroom management models and theorists.
- Teachers need to be able to use these models to develop their own classroom management model.
- Preservice and in-service teachers will continue to be challenged by behavior problems, with some problems growing more acute (Chapter 1). Behavior problems will not vanish with another generation of students.
- Preservice and inservice teachers need to understand a wide array of classroom management models (Chapters 2–12). Even older theories hold promise for addressing contemporary behavior problems.
- Preservice and in-service teachers need to be familiar with the contemporary safe schools movement (Chapter 13) and learn to apply this information in their own classrooms.
- Preservice and in-service teachers need to understand the philosophical underpinnings of classroom management and to develop their own carefully considered personal philosophy of classroom management (Chapter 14).
- Preservice and in-service teachers need to develop a personal philosophy of classroom management and a comprehensive management (including instructional management) plan that reflects our nation's and schools' increasing diversity.
- Preservice and in-service teachers need to develop a classroom management model that works for them based (Chapter 15) on the philosophy that they have developed.

Classroom Management: Models, Applications, and Cases is divided into 3 parts and 15 chapters:

Part I   Understanding the Need for Classroom Management
Chapter 1 examines classroom management and discipline in contemporary schools, the effects of classroom management problems, and the need to consider student diversity.

Part II   Understanding Classroom Management Models
From the foundational theorists to those still working in the schools, Chapters 2–12 examine the individuals and their ideas, theories, and models which continue to be relevant in contemporary elementary, middle, and high schools.

Part III   Toward a Personal Classroom Management Plan
There is a detailed look at safe schools in Chapter 13. Then, based on the information from Chapters 2–12, we encourage educators to develop a personal philosophy of classroom management (Chapter 14) and to apply that philosophy in workable and effective classroom management practices (Chapter 15).

We examine as many classroom management theorists as possible in order to give preservice and in-service educators a comprehensive overview of models and ideas on which to base their own philosophy and practice. Thus we began, in Chapter 2, with the theorists who contributed to the beginnings of classroom management. Chapters 3–12 provide a collection of the most well-known classroom management theorists whose contributions continue to be widespread and well known. Finally, Chapter 12 gives readers a glance at five contemporary theorists. The theorists in Chapters 3–11 are arranged randomly, not in any assigned order of "significance" or "contribution." Although we personally may like some theories better than others, we have tried to provide an objective examination of each of them, because we believe that they *all* have the potential for helping educators develop their own personal philosophy and model of classroom management.

New in this Edition

In addition to the successful features from the first edition, *Classroom Management: Models, Applications, and Cases* now provides

- A Companion Website for students and faculty at *www.prenhall.com/manning,* containing PowerPoints, Management Tips Extensions, Multiple Choice Questions, Weblinks, and other resources
- Expanded Management Tips
- Extensive update to Chapter 13, "Creating Safe Classrooms and Safe Schools"
- "Reaching Out with Technology" on the Web allows for information updates
- An instructor's manual and test bank are available online through the Prentice Hall Instructor's Resource center at *http://vig.prenhall.com/catalog*

Special Features and Pedagogical Aids

- *Organizing Features*   Each chapter begins with an *Overview* and *Focusing Questions,* which provide an indication of what will be discussed in the chapter. The *Concluding Remarks* in each chapter act as a summary.
- *Key Terms and Glossary*   Key terms are bolded the first time they are used in the chapter and are defined in the glossary.
- *Case Studies*   Chapters 1–12 have one case study each, whereas Chapters 13, 14, and 15 have two, four, and three case studies, respectively. These case studies are actual accounts of classroom management situations with questions.
- *Voices of Educators*   There are two types of Voices of Educators. The first type consists of teachers and administrators responding to specific case studies in Chapters 13, 14, and 15. In the second type, teachers and administrators respond to issues discussed in Chapters 14 and 15. All educators who responded in the Voices sections were given complete freedom to offer their opinions, regardless of whether they reflect the theorists' views or our personal opinions.
- *How Would You React?*   Shorter than the case studies, this feature presents actual situations and asks readers how they would respond.
- *Activities*   This feature appears in each chapter and offers readers the chance to expand some of the ideas presented by the theorist or to consider how the ideas can be implemented in the classroom.
- *Diversity*   Respect for student diversity of all forms is a thread throughout this book. Whenever possible, we consider each model and theorist in terms of diversity. Many of the Activities and How Would You React features examine diversity in management situations. Often, teachers assume students "see" or "perceive" events from middle-class perspectives or from their cultural or gender backgrounds. Research increasingly shows that cultural, gender, and social class differences affect how students perceive management events.

- *Reaching Out with Technology*   Located on the Companion Website at *www .prenhall.com/manning,* this feature uses the Internet to locate additional information on topics and/or theorists.
- *Management Tips*   Although all of the chapters, especially those that discuss management theories, contain ideas for managing a classroom, Chapters 1 through 13 have a special Tips feature, providing practical, teacher-tested ideas on the organization and mechanics of classroom management. These have been categorized into elementary versus secondary divisions to highlight the appropriate level for each tip. Although

these tips may not be a direct part of the theory being discussed, they expand on the concepts. Activities and extensions of the tips are found on the book's Companion Website at *www.prenhall.com/manning,* and are designed to help build a teaching portfolio.
- *Anecdotal Accounts*   Throughout the text, anecdotes bridge the gap between theory and practice and bring the book alive with actual accounts of teachers who have effectively translated research and theory into practice, as well as a few who still have a way to go. We have changed all the names to ensure anonymity.
- *Developing Your Personal Philosophy*   This feature provides activities to help you think about how you can use the theories and information presented in the chapter to develop your own management plan.
- *Suggested Readings*   Four to seven current books and journal readings provide additional information about the material discussed in each chapter.

TEXT SUPPLEMENTS

The Companion Website at *www.prenhall.com/manning* provides instructors and students with many rich and meaningful ways to deepen and expand the information presented in the text. It contains

- Chapter objectives.
- Sample questions so students can "test" their knowledge and comprehension of the material being examined.
- Reaching Out with Technology with additional Internet resources.
- Case Studies.
- Management Tips extensions with additional information and activities.
- Other pedagogical features that will help both instructors and students.
- PowerPoints to help plan and implement instructional experiences.

For instructors, the accompanying Online Instructor's Manual contains:

- A test bank with multiple choice, fill-in-the-blank, and essay questions.
- Teaching suggestions that complement and reflect the test bank.

We hope readers will find the overall organization of *Classroom Management: Models, Applications, and Cases* and its unique pedagogical features helpful as they learn about the various models and theorists and begin the process of developing and applying their personal philosophy of classroom management.

ACKNOWLEDGMENTS

We could not have completed a project of this magnitude without the assistance of a number of individuals. First, we offer our sincere appreciation to the many educators who offered their views throughout the book and in our Voices of Educators sections. Especially we want to thank Laurie Armstrong, Stephanie Banks, Diane Barker, Barbara Bowman, Ronda Clancy, Charlene Fleener, Janet Forbes, Pamela Frazee, Christina Holiday, Cathy Louk, Judith Rea, Valerie Tefft, Melissa (Penny) Van Dyke, and Susan Wilson.

Second, we want to offer our appreciation to Debbie Stollenwerk at Merrill/Prentice Hall for her patience, guidance, and inspiration throughout the writing process, as well as to Elisa Rogers, Mary Morrill, and the staff at Prentice Hall for their help. Last, we are particularly grateful to the following individuals who reviewed the book and offered numerous constructive suggestions: Shirley De Lucia, Capital University; Rey Gomez, Arizona State University; Lucenda McKinney, Gardner-Webb University; and Kristine Servais, North Central College.

M. Lee Manning
Katherine T. Bucher

TEACHER PREP

MERRILL
PRENTICE HALL

Teacher Preparation Classroom

See a demo at
www.prenhall.com/teacherprep/demo

Your Class. Their Careers. Our Future. Will your students be prepared?

We invite you to explore our new, innovative and engaging website and all that it has to offer you, your course, and tomorrow's educators! Organized around the major courses pre-service teachers take, the Teacher Preparation site provides media, student/teacher artifacts, strategies, research articles, and other resources to equip your students with the quality tools needed to excel in their courses and prepare them for their first classroom.

This ultimate on-line education resource is available at no cost, when packaged with a Merrill text, and will provide you and your students access to:

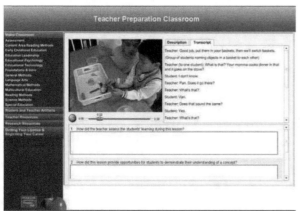

Online Video Library. More than 150 video clips—each tied to a course topic and framed by learning goals and Praxis-type questions—capture real teachers and students working in real classrooms, as well as in-depth interviews with both students and educators.

Student and Teacher Artifacts. More than 200 student and teacher classroom artifacts—each tied to a course topic and framed by learning goals and application questions—provide a wealth of materials and experiences to help make your study to become a professional teacher more concrete and hands-on.

Research Articles. Over 500 articles from ASCD's renowned journal *Educational Leadership*. The site also includes Research Navigator, a searchable database of additional educational journals.

Teaching Strategies. Over 500 strategies and lesson plans for you to use when you become a practicing professional.

Licensure and Career Tools. Resources devoted to helping you pass your licensure exam; learn standards, law, and public policies; plan a teaching portfolio; and succeed in your first year of teaching.

How to ORDER *Teacher Prep* for you and your students:

For students to receive a *Teacher Prep* Access Code with this text, instructors **must** provide a special value pack ISBN number on their textbook order form. To receive this special ISBN, please email **Merrill.marketing@pearsoned.com** and provide the following information:

- Name and Affiliation
- Author/Title/Edition of Merrill text

Upon ordering *Teacher Prep* for their students, instructors will be given a lifetime *Teacher Prep* Access Code.

Brief Contents

Contents

Understanding the Need for Classroom Management

Part 1 consists of chapter 1, "Introducing the Concept of Classroom Management," and describes management and discipline in contemporary schools. Two important points are emphasized. First, teachers should consider the various management models, develop their own philosophies, and then develop their personal classroom management model. Second, educators should understand the safe schools movement, an effort to reduce aggression and violence in elementary, middle, and secondary schools.

In addition to being an introduction to the remaining chapters in *Classroom Management: Models, Applications, and Cases,* chapter 1 addresses inclusion and diversity, important topics that influence management efforts. As with other chapters, readers are encouraged to use technology to learn more about classroom management.

Introducing the Concept of Classroom Management

Focusing Questions

After reading this chapter, you should be able to answer the following questions:

1. What are the major types, causes, and effects of student misbehaviors?

2. How do teachers unknowingly contribute to students' misbehaviors or make existing misbehaviors worse?

3. How does student diversity (cultural, gender, social class, and developmental differences) affect behavior and perspectives of behavior?

4. How does inclusion challenge classroom managers?

5. Why should educators develop a personal philosophy of classroom management, one on which they can base their daily management practices and strategies?

6. What is the safe schools movement, and how can educators combat school violence and work to create safe schools?

7. What are some additional sources of information on classroom management?

Key Terms

Classroom management
Diversity
Inclusion
Safe schools movement
Sense of community
Target behaviors

From the nation's earliest classrooms to the contemporary schools of the 21st century, educators have had the professional responsibility to practice effective classroom management. To do this, educators must manage student behavior, establish safe classrooms, and provide teaching/learning experiences for a diverse student population in an orderly and student-friendly manner. Although educators still deal primarily with relatively minor misbehaviors that interrupt their instructional activities and students' learning, more schools are seeing the need to adopt safe schools policies to deal with or prevent serious misbehaviors. Whether you are a preservice educator (preparing to teach) or an inservice educator (already teaching), you should realize that the classroom management strategies that you develop and implement play a tremendously important role in fostering student learning and providing safe learning environments for all students. Although some schools have potentially fruitful proposals for well-managed and safe schools, it is the individual classroom teacher who makes classroom management efforts work and ultimately provides a safe and productive learning environment for all students.

In this chapter, you will read about the types, extent, and causes of misbehavior in the classroom, the types of diversity found in contemporary classrooms, and the emphasis on providing safe schools for all students and teachers. You will also see that, because management and

3

instruction are linked, both management and instructional planning are necessary. Thus, you will begin to examine your philosophy of teaching and develop a personal management plan.

CLASSROOM MANAGEMENT

The Interstate New Teacher Assessment and Support Consortium (INTASC) has developed a set of standards that identify the knowledge, skills, and attitudes that all educators, especially beginning teachers, should have (*The INTASC Standards*). In addition to understanding their subject matter, educators must also understand diverse learners and student development and must be able to use multiple instructional strategies to motivate learners while creating a learning environment that allows all students to participate fully in both the social and the instructional activities of the classroom. Thus, in this chapter, you will examine the meaning of the term *classroom management* and the relationship between classroom management, instructional strategies, and your specific philosophical beliefs. In doing so, you must strive to develop a rationale for your own management and instructional strategies based on your personal beliefs and on the research and theories provided by experts in the educational field.

Defining Classroom Management

We prefer a broad definition of classroom management—one that encompasses more than just "convincing students to behave." To us, **classroom management** consists of

> strategies for assuring physical and psychological safety in the classroom; techniques for changing student misbehaviors and for teaching self-discipline; methods of assuring an orderly progression of events during the school day; and instructional techniques that contribute to students' positive behaviors.

Connecting Classroom Management to Philosophy and Instruction

As you begin your exploration of classroom management, it important to remember two points. First, an educator's decision about classroom management should be based on the educator's philosophical beliefs. Second, classroom management strategies should be "connected" to instructional practices.

It may surprise you to see that we link classroom management and instruction. The two are not separate entities. Indeed, they must go hand-in-hand with the management plan, providing the setting and support in which good instruction exists. An educator who does not have good management skills will have a difficult time instructing students. Conversely, even a teacher who uses a wide variety of instructional strategies will have problems teaching students without a good management plan to support desired behaviors in the classroom. For example, a teacher who keeps learners on task (e.g., correct developmental level, proper instructional pace, physical and psychological safety, appropriate curricular content, etc.) will be less likely to have students who misbehave. Conversely, teachers who are unprepared and disorganized contribute to students' misbehaviors.

In developing classroom management and instructional strategies, educators need to base their practices on research and educationally sound beliefs. However, they also need to examine their own personal beliefs or philosophies about education and classroom management. Rather than "doing whatever someone else does" or "doing what our teachers did when we were in school," educators need to determine their philosophical beliefs (e.g., their core beliefs about how teachers should "manage" students) and then base their classroom management decisions on these beliefs. For example, teachers need to decide whether they think discipline should be taught or imposed, whether teachers should be democratic or autocratic, and whether punishment works to improve or hinder students' behavior. Teachers should always know *why* they, *personally,* use specific management techniques and strategies.

This does not mean that educators can ignore research on classroom management. Instead it means that each educator can examine the theories and research in a framework of personal beliefs and select the proven strategies that most closely reflect his or her philosophy. In the same way, an educator needs to look at a model of classroom management and see how the theory can be applied to the specific grade levels being taught. Although the theory remains the same, the educator tailors the application to the specific teaching situation.

CLASSROOM MANAGEMENT AND DISCIPLINE IN CONTEMPORARY SCHOOLS

Before we begin an exploration of classroom management theories and models in chapters 2 through 12 of this book and before you begin to develop a personal philosophy of classroom management and consider an actual implementation plan, you need to have a solid grasp of the most common types of misbehaviors, the extent to which students misbehave, and the effects of misbehaviors on teachers as well as on the teaching/learning process.

Types of Student Misbehaviors

Practicing teachers, as well as preservice teachers who have observed in schools, can attest to our belief that the list of misbehaviors is nearly endless. In fact, the Solutions for Handling 117 Misbehaviors Web site (*www.disciplinehelp.com/parent/list.cfm?cause=All*) provides a long list of common misbehaviors ranging from relatively minor off-task behaviors to more serious acts of violence and bullying. Jones (1987) identifies the most common misbehaviors, such as goofing off, walking around the room, and talking and disturbing others.

Although all educators experience some behavior problems, variation occurs with individual schools, grades, and teachers. For example, rural, urban, and suburban schools probably experience different problems, although all classes have some students who misbehave at times. Also, elementary, middle, and high school students demonstrate different behaviors and react differently to classroom management strategies. Although younger students' behavior problems might be bothersome, in most cases these students neither pose a threat nor act violently. However, depending on the individual situation, some of their behaviors need to be addressed because they distract the teacher and other students.

In some cases, educators' actions and decisions contribute to student behavior problems. When educators impose zero-tolerance policies, post strict rules, demand immediate obedience, lack planning and organizational skills to implement effective instruction, and generally frustrate students, students are more prone to test the limits and misbehave.

Extent and Effects of the Problem

One of our university students asked, "Aren't behavior problems unique to each student and each school? How can we make general statements about behavior problems and their effects?" These are perceptive questions, but this student missed several important points:

- Behavior problems challenge all teachers, regardless of the school, grade level, or geographic location.
- Behavior problems differ in frequency and intensity, yet they are similar in type. Although some schools do not experience any violence (albeit the threat continues to loom), all schools have some students who generally goof off and disturb others.
- Behavior problems disturb teachers and students, negatively affect the teaching/learning process, and ultimately hinder academic achievement.

Management Tip 1–1

> ### Learning About Your School
>
> Before you have a discipline problem, you need to learn about the students you will be teaching and about your school's policies for student behavior and disciplinary procedures.
>
> - Review the developmentally appropriate instructional and classroom management strategies for the age group you will teach.
> - Meet with other grade-level, interdisciplinary team members or subject-area teachers to discuss successful management strategies.
> - Meet with assistant principals to learn school policies on acceptable student behavior and management strategies. What problems should a classroom teacher handle and what problems should be referred to others?
> - Meet with parents to learn their behavioral expectations and convey your expectations to them either in person or through a newsletter.
> - Review developmentally appropriate classroom management efforts, e.g, advisor-advisee programs, sense of community, and differentiated instruction.

Please go to *www.prenhall.com/manning* and click on the Management Tips for this chapter to complete management activities and find more information on using student handbooks to prepare for school.

Management Tip 1–1 suggests some strategies all educators can use to learn more about the students in the school where they teach.

Effects on Teachers and Students

Just as the list of behavior problems is nearly endless, the effects of misbehaviors are also limitless. Unfortunately, as a result of classroom management problems, some teachers change professions during their first 2 or 3 years of teaching. They did not realize that just as time and effort must be spent on organizing and implementing instruction, time and effort must be spent on managing behavior (e.g., devising a classroom management program or learning the adopted schoolwide model).

Behavior problems affect both students and teachers. When behavior problems arise, teachers often avoid creative instructional approaches because they have to deal with the increased misbehaviors. Disturbed and distracted, students who want to learn will lose valuable teaching/learning time. Still other students are bullied, threatened, and harassed. Thus, the lack of effective classroom management presents problems for everyone in a school.

> I dread the days when Mr. Pickett brings his class to the library. He doesn't have any control, and the students just bounce off the walls. I was a classroom teacher before I became a library media specialist, so I know exactly what to do to calm the students down and get them working on task. But when I have to spend so much time managing Mr. Pickett's class, the students don't have as much time to complete their research assignment as the other classes do. These aren't bad students; they just need to know the rules and the limits. —A library media specialist.

Causes of Classroom Management Problems

Some teachers might wonder why it is important to know the causes of misbehavior. It might seem that if students misbehave, the teacher should be more concerned with stopping the misbehavior than with looking for the causes. Some misbehaviors do demand immediate attention. However, teachers who look for causes of student misbehavior might have a head start on improving classroom management. As you will read in chapter 4, Dreikurs and Grey (1968) identified four causes or mistaken goals (revenge, attention getting, inadequacy, and power seeking) for student misbehaviors. We accept his ideas, but we also believe that misbehaviors can result from multiple causes and that in addition to personal causes, society in general and families in particular can contribute to the likelihood of a student misbehaving. Thus, when considering misbehaviors, teachers should try to determine the causes and then work to eliminate them rather than focusing only on correction.

> Mr. Filby and his students were disturbed by Whewanna, who constantly interrupted everyone. Often, as Mr. Filby asked a question, Whewanna interrupted with an unrelated question. At other times, she would blurt out the wrong answer or "accidently" drop her books. Mr. Filby constantly admonished her to keep quiet; he put her name on the board, followed up the warnings, and carefully considered punishments. Nothing worked. Whewanna continued to talk out of turn and disturb others. Finally, Ms.

Lubo, another teacher, suggested that warnings and punishments might not be the answer. Ms. Lubo thought the cause of Whewanna's misbehavior might be to gain attention or because she felt inadequate. When Mr. Filby spoke with Whewanna, he found out that she was afraid he would call on her to answer a question she did not know. To help Whewanna, Mr. Filby did extra work with her and made sure he asked her some questions that he knew she could answer. As a result, Whewanna's behavior did improve, not because Mr. Filby inflicted harsh punishments but because he identified and addressed the cause.

Society sometimes contributes to students' misbehaviors. Some students see sarcasm, ridicule, and violence as a way of life or as a means of responding to others. Mimicking behaviors seen on television and in the community, students often act out, use statements heard on television, and resort to aggressive and violent behaviors, such as bringing weapons to school to impress peers or to harm or threaten other students. Although schools always have had fighters and bullies, most schools have been considered safe or immune from serious violence. Now, however, violence plagues some schools and challenges the goals of the safe school movement (the topic of chapter 13).

In other cases, misbehaviors can be rooted in familial causes. Students who experience family disruptions often vent their anger and frustration at school.

Tyrone came to class wearing one blue sock and one brown sock. He was obviously angry and ready to strike out at anyone who mentioned his socks. Finally, he asked Ms. Berganio, his teacher, whether she noticed the different-colored socks. When Ms. Berganio voiced a sympathetic comment and offered to listen, Tyrone poured out the problems he was experiencing at home. As Tyrone learned that Ms. Berganio would be a compassionate yet objective listener, his behavior in class improved.

When students see violent and aggressive behaviors at home, they might begin to consider such behaviors as acceptable methods of dealing with problems. Also, some parents teach inappropriate behaviors. They say to their children, "Don't you take anything off anyone!" or "That teacher can't make you do that—you tell him I said so." Others who do not teach such behavior condone it because they do not want their children to be victimized. Familial causes of misbehavior are often difficult to address because students usually have a strong allegiance to family expectations. In addition, teachers often feel frustrated and unsuccessful as they try to reason with parents who fail to teach appropriate behavior and respect for teachers and others. However, students should be held accountable and responsible for their behaviors, regardless of the cause. How Would You React 1–1 asks you to respond to a mother who encourages aggression. Then Activity 1–1 looks at several misbehaviors and possible causes.

STUDENT DIVERSITY AND CLASSROOM MANAGEMENT

Diversity can be defined as the differences among students that teachers must consider as they develop appropriate classroom management strategies. These differences include (but are not limited to) cultural/intracultural, gender, social class, linguistic, and developmental differences. For teachers, the keys to success are to understand these differences and their effects on behavior and to plan and implement classroom management strategies that accommodate diversities while taking extreme caution to avoid stereotypes.

Cultural, Intracultural, and Gender Differences

All teachers must be aware of cultural and gender diversity and its impact on classroom management. With our nation and schools growing more diverse each year, rapidly increasing cultural diversity is the norm in many parts of the United States as schools continue to be

Responding to Ms. Schiffhauer

Bullying can be a very disruptive behavior that can lead to more serious incidents. However, not all individuals view the same behaviors in the same way. Read the following meeting between a teacher and a parent. Then, respond to the questions following the scenario.

In a parent–teacher conference, Ms. Comeau, a teacher, mentioned to Ms. Schiffhauer that her son Scott demonstrated aggressive and bullying behaviors at school. Ms. Comeau was somewhat surprised to learn that Ms. Schiffhauer encouraged Scott's behavior. "That's the way I want him to be; that's the way I brought him up. No one should take advantage of my Scott. With all that touchy-feely interpersonal relations and self-esteem stuff, you teachers in this school teach boys to be sissies. That's wrong. Scott should take charge and stand up for his rights!" Ms. Schiffhauer refused to listen when Ms. Comeau tried to explain that she was responsible for the welfare of the class, and she could not allow Scott to respond in a manner that

threatened others or caused physical or psychological harm. Ms. Schiffhauer's last words were "Scott has to take up for himself—he's just as good as anyone else."

Working collaboratively in groups of three or four, respond to the following questions:

1. What specific methods might Ms. Comeau use to decrease Scott's aggressive behavior in the classroom?
2. What should Ms. Comeau say or do to help Scott cope with the conflicting messages he is receiving at school and at home?
3. What can Ms. Comeau do to establish a working relationship with Ms. Schiffhauer?
4. What specific methods would you use in your own classroom to address and/or prevent bullying and/or aggressive behaviors?

Activity 1–1

Determining Causes of Misbehavior

For each of the following misbehaviors, identify what you might consider as possible causes of the misbehavior. The first one is completed as an example. How might your responses change if the student were in elementary school? Middle school? High school?

A student refuses to do class work, talks to friends, and plays with things at her desk rather than listening to the lesson.

Possible causes: Feelings of inadequacy, need for attention, more concerned with social aspects of school than with learning.

- A student plays rough and demonstrates other aggressive behaviors.
- A student brings a bag of a white powder to school and shows it to other students.
- A student responds to every request with the comment, "I won't do that and nobody's going to make me."
- A student refuses to wear a coat at recess even though it is cold outside.
- A student has drastic behavior changes and has become antisocial.
- A student throws spitballs at other students during class.

enriched by African Americans, Hispanics, and Asian Americans, just to name the most populous groups. No longer can educators plan classroom management procedures for the majority culture (whatever the majority culture is) and their perspectives of appropriate behavior.

Educators must also address issues of gender diversity. For example, for years, educators have known that male and female students differ in their responses to classroom management methods. However, many teachers have done little to address these differences. Some possible cultural and gender differences are shown in Table 1–1.

Educators must look at several classroom management techniques from cultural and gender perspectives.

- Educators often make eye contact to get students' attention (with the hope that they will correct the inappropriate behavior), yet members of some cultures avoid making eye contact and, in fact, consider the practice rude or insubordinate.
- Educators sometimes stand closer to students (perhaps after eye contact did not work) in an effort to correct misbehaviors, yet some students value their personal space and find this too intrusive.
- Educators sometimes call attention to students and their behaviors. However, students in some cultures feel embarrassed when teachers put their names on the board as a corrective measure. Others even feel uncomfortable with positive recognition, especially when they excel at others' expense or think the recognition places others in a negative light.
- Educators sometimes ask students or groups of students to compete with one another. For example, the students on the right side of the classroom might be asked to compete with those on the left side to see which group can be more successful demonstrating appropriate behavior. This can be a problem for individuals who value cooperation over competition.

In light of these and other cultural differences, individual cultures and individual students must be considered when planning classroom management strategies.

In addition, when working with students from various cultural groups, educators must also consider intracultural differences. It is a fallacy to believe that all members of any given group will act in exactly the same way. Thus, knowing general group preferences is just one part of understanding individual differences.

Linguistic Differences

As educators plan classroom management practices, they often must make accommodations for individuals with linguistic diversity. Unfortunately, many teachers are not adequately prepared to work with and manage diverse English language learners. Curran (2003) noted that educators need to understand and feel comfortable with the natural responses (e.g.,

Table 1-1 Selected Cultural and Gender Differences

Students might have differing perceptions about:
Making eye contact
Standing closer to others
Competing with others
Receiving attention, positive or negative, in front of peers
Behaving appropriately and inappropriately
Working collaboratively toward group goals and working individually toward individual goals

laughter, first language use, and silence) that occur when students who are not completely proficient in a language participate in interactions with proficient language speakers. To assist linguistically diverse students, educators must structure classroom activities and use strategies that will support language acquisition and comprehension of classroom activities. They must also build a strong sense of community in the classroom and foster an appreciation of linguistic diversity (Curran, 2003). In building a **sense of community,** both elementary and secondary educators should strive to create a feeling of togetherness, in which all students, teachers, and administrators know each other, and to create a climate for intellectual development and shared educational purpose.

Socioeconomic Level

If a group of individuals has particular characteristics that are valued by a society, this group will usually enjoy higher status. The reverse is also true. Thus, when speaking of upper and lower classes, we are referring to groups of individuals who either have or do not have qualities in common that are prized by a larger society.

For example, upper classes have wealth, advanced education, professional occupations, and relative freedom from concern about their material needs. Conversely, lower classes live in or on the edge of poverty, have little education, are irregularly employed or employed in jobs requiring little or no training, often require assistance from government welfare agencies, and are constantly concerned with meeting the basic needs of life. Because socioeconomic differences often play a significant role in determining how a person acts, thinks, lives, and relates to others, educators who come from middle and upper classes may have difficulty understanding the social and economic problems facing children and adolescents from lower-socioeconomic homes.

Hodgkinson (2000/2001) maintained that 20% of children in the United States live below the poverty line. Unfortunately, some people look at an individual's socioeconomic class and make judgments about that individual's ambitions, motivations to achieve, and ability to demonstrate acceptable behavior. It is a serious mistake for any educator to make assumptions about expected behavior based on a student's wealth and social class. Teachers should never stereotype by social class and should never assume that students from lower socioeconomic classes have less desire to behave. Just as many learners from higher socioeconomic classes fail to achieve and behave, students from lower socioeconomic classes often demonstrate excellent behavior.

Developmental Differences

Developmental differences between elementary students and secondary students are often easy to detect, and educators do not expect the same misbehaviors from 5- and 6-year-olds as they do from 16- and 17-year-olds. Although these educators may use the same research and classroom management models, they adapt the strategies to suit the general age group. However, more subtle differences exist among students in a particular grade and should be considered when developing classroom management strategies. For example, some seventh-grade students might react positively to certain management strategies, but others in the same grade might react in an immature or perhaps aggressive fashion. How Would You React 1–2 asks you to consider the challenge of understanding differences yet avoiding stereotypes.

Inclusion and the Management of All Students

Simply put, **inclusion** is the policy of educating a learner with special needs in the school, and, whenever possible, in the class that the learner would have attended without the disabling condition. Although inclusion is a relatively new term, the concept of educating students with disabilities has been around for decades. In 1975, Congress passed the Education

How Would You React 1-2

Understanding Differences and Avoiding Stereotypes

There is a fine line between identifying cultural preferences and creating stereotypes. Consider the following scenario and then respond to the questions that follow.

> Mr. Henry, a European American teacher, taught in an urban school that was 98% African and Hispanic American, yet he showed little concern for students' diversities. In fact, he told another teacher that he thought the most effective classroom management strategy was to treat all students the same. Another teacher, Mrs. Hill, casually mentioned cultural differences such as eye contact, physical proximity (standing closer to misbehaving students), expecting student competition, and differing ideas about appropriate and inappropriate behavior. Mr. Henry disagreed and argued against basing classroom management plans on stereotypes. He said, "There are too many intracultural and individual differences for educators to base management strategies on cultural differences or stereotypes. I still think treating all students the same is the best idea."

Working collaboratively in groups of three or four, respond to the following questions:

1. Should teachers modify their classroom management styles to take cultural differences into consideration? Why or why not?
2. What is the difference between cultural preferences and stereotypes?
3. How can a teacher respond to cultural preferences and not create stereotypes?
4. Select one type of diversity mentioned in this chapter and indicate the things from that type of diversity that you would need to take into consideration when developing your own management style. Compare this with the items identified by others in your group or your class.

---

for all Handicapped Children Act, which was renamed the Individuals with Disabilities Education Act (IDEA) in 1990. The intent of IDEA was to provide access to educational services for approximately half of the 8 million students with disabilities who were not receiving a free and appropriate public education.

Inclusion is based upon the belief that all students have a right to be educated in a general education setting with appropriate support services. In addition to benefiting special needs students academically and socially, inclusion will help improve their self-concepts and will help all students learn to accept differences. Additionally, the student role models in the general education classroom will help students with special needs improve their own behavior and social skills.

Thus, educators teach significant numbers of students with special needs in regular classrooms alongside their nondisabled peers. Teachers often feel challenged to provide classroom management strategies that are appropriate for these "inclusive," or disabled, students. In fact, current practices of many schools are at odds with the disciplinary provisions of IDEA. In many instances, educators address problem behaviors with negative consequences that are aimed at eliminating the problem. Unfortunately, this action does not address what the student accomplished by engaging in the behavior (e.g., student disrupts a science class to avoid a difficult academic demand). In addition, the use of punishment to teach students more appropriate behavior can exacerbate an already-difficult situation, especially for students with special needs. Students who lack adequate coping skills often experience feelings of alienation and isolation in schools (Gable, Hendrickson, Tonelson, & Van Acker, 2000).

The disciplinary provisions of IDEA place the emphasis on understanding why the student misbehaves. Then, educators can use this knowledge to reduce future occurrences of the behavior and to promote the use of an alternative behavior that serves the same purpose but that is more socially acceptable or appropriate. General education teachers must work with special educators to address student misconduct that is sufficiently serious to evoke disciplinary action (i.e., suspension or expulsion). Together they can provide positive behavioral interventions, strategies, and supports for students who engage in problem behaviors that either interfere with classroom learning for the student or others, represent a physical danger to the student or others, or involve drugs or weapons (Gable, Hendrickson, Tonelson, & Van Acker, 2000).

Soodak (2003) maintained that the inclusion of children with disabilities in general education classes provides an opportunity for teachers to identify classroom management policies and practices that promote diversity and community. Management strategies that enhance the overall quality of the classroom environment can minimize discipline issues because students feel welcomed, safe, and supported. Educators should create an inclusive community for all students by promoting membership, facilitating friendships, and proving collaborative opportunities for learning and socialization. How Would You React 1–3 allows you to explore the challenges of the inclusion of learners with special needs in a general classroom.

DEVELOPING A PERSONAL CLASSROOM MANAGEMENT MODEL

With the diversity of students in a contemporary classroom and the many needs that they bring to school with them each day, it is important for all educators to examine their beliefs about students and learning, to develop or revisit their philosophy of education, and to review the research and theories about classroom management. The goal is for each educator to develop a personal strategy for classroom management. This should be started long before an educator meets students on the first day of school and should continue, with modifications and refinements, throughout the educator's professional career.

Thus, as you read this book, you should look critically at each model or theory of classroom management. However, developing a personal management model is more complicated than blindly following a given model, theory, or practice. To move from theory and research to a personal philosophy and model of classroom management, you also need to identify student misbehaviors you want to address, review existing models and theories to identify the parts that you believe you would be able to use in your own classroom, and

---

How Would You React 1-3

Addressing Inclusion in a General Classroom

Although inclusion provides many benefits for both students and teachers, some teachers are concerned about the changes that the presence of special education students will bring to their classrooms. Consider the following scenario and then respond to the questions at the end.

Chris Springer was worried about the inclusion of several special education students in her classroom. As she said to Laquisha L'Esperance, the assistant principal, "I'm just not sure about this IDEA. Who thought this up anyway? A bunch of people who have never taught? How can I manage my 28 students and 1 or 2 more children who are disabled? What kinds of modifications will I need to make in my management plan?

Can I expect the same standards of behavior for the students with special needs? Sure, these students need to spend time with other students outside their special education classrooms, but there's got to be a better way."

Working collaboratively in groups of three or four, respond to the following questions:

1. If you were Ms. L'Esperance, how would you respond to Ms. Springer?
2. What modifications to her management plan might Ms. Springer need to make?
3. How can Ms. Springer learn more about inclusion and the regulations of IDEA?

develop a personal classroom management model that works for you. The philosophical beliefs and tenets of your personal model must match your perspectives about the way students learn and behave and the way you will foster learning in your classroom.

Identifying Target Behaviors to Address

Target behaviors are those behaviors that educators decide to address because they violate class or school policy or those that interfere with teachers teaching or students learning. Addressing all misbehaviors is not an efficient use of instructional time. Thus, in developing a philosophy and a model of classroom management, you need to identify the target behaviors in your classroom. Unless the school as a whole has a rule against specific behaviors or unless teachers are working together as a team or working with a group of students on a departmentalized basis, we believe teachers should decide for themselves which misbehaviors to address in their individual classrooms. In this book, we place value on students' diversities, but we maintain that diversity exists among teachers, too. Some misbehaviors bother some teachers and not others. For example, some teachers object to any talking with friends, but others address the misbehavior only if it becomes a serious interruption. Teachers' perceptions of behavior, specific misbehaviors to be addressed, and characteristics of well-managed classrooms should be considered when identifying target misbehaviors. In addition, students have the right to know what those target misbehaviors are and how flexible the teacher is in enforcing the rules. Activity 1–2 focuses on identifying what you consider target misbehaviors.

Unfortunately, individuality in teacher expectations may present a problem when teachers work together in teams or with the same group of students at different times during the day or during the week. How Would You React 1–4 looks at differences among educators serving on the same team.

Activity 1-2

Identifying Target Misbehaviors

To identify a target misbehavior, ask the following questions.

1. Does the behavior disturb me as I conduct instruction and manage the class?
2. Does the behavior disturb students as they engage in the learning process?
3. Does the behavior place students in physical or psychological harm?
4. Does the behavior break a stated school or class rule—one that I have a professional responsibility to enforce?
5. Does the behavior give indications that it might escalate into a larger or more disturbing problem?

What other questions might you ask? Think about some of the misbehaviors you have seen in schools. Use these questions to identify examples of target misbehaviors.

Coping With Differences in Behavior Expectations

Many elementary and middle schools use a team structure, where 2 or more teachers are responsible for the education of a group of students. In an elementary school, there may be a team of 50 students with 2 teachers (one teaching science and math, the other teaching language arts/reading and social studies). A middle school team may have a larger number of both students and teachers, with each teacher responsible for a different subject. Unfortunately, whatever the team structure, problems can arise when team members do not agree on management structures and policies. Consider the following example of a middle school team. Then respond to the questions following the scenario.

Ms. Fontes, Ms. Butterfield, and Mr. Jang taught on the same middle school interdisciplinary team. The differences in their opinions of misbehaviors to be addressed were sufficiently significant that the team was nearly dysfunctional. Ms. Butterfield was a strict disciplinarian who expected immediate obedience to all rules. Ms. Fontes considered each individual misbehavior to determine whether it was a target misbehavior and whether it was one she wanted to address or ignore. "Mr. Jang has no clue about classroom management," Ms. Butterfield said. "He neither knows when students misbehave nor cares." The differences among the teachers' opinions of what constituted misbehavior were so great that students were constantly confused. What was accepted in one classroom was not accepted in the next. Ms. Fontes wanted to discuss the differences, but Ms. Butterfield saw little hope for reaching an agreement.

Working collaboratively in groups of three or four, respond to the following questions:

1. What advice would you give the members of this team?
2. Is it practical for them even to consider having a uniform set of expectations? Is there room for compromise?
3. How would you respond to this situation if these teachers were working in a departmentalized elementary school? In a high school?

Teachers' Contributions to Behavior Problems

As we noted earlier in this chapter, some teachers use instructional and management behaviors that contribute to students' misbehaviors. This is not to say that the students always would have been well behaved if the teachers had been more careful with their teaching techniques. However, the actions of educators, the policies they establish, their instructional expertise, and their beliefs about students have a direct impact on classroom management.

Still, all teachers can take specific steps to set the stage for a successful school year. Management Tip 1–2 offers some general suggestions for both elementary and secondary teachers.

Unfortunately, some teachers believe their classroom management strategies are effective even though they are not. Others are unconscious of the fact that their instructional and management techniques contribute to student misbehavior. It is hoped that these occurrences are rare, but all teachers need to be aware of the instructional and management strategies that they use, periodically assess these strategies, and evaluate their effectiveness. Activity 1–3 gives you an opportunity to identify some teacher behaviors that might contribute to student misbehaviors or that might prevent them. Then, How Would You React 1–5 asks you to make suggestions to Mr. Outsen, who used teaching behaviors that did make student behaviors worse.

Developing Your Own Philosophy and Model

Some schools have adopted a schoolwide classroom management model, such as the Canters' Assertive Discipline. In these situations, teachers usually are required to adhere to the philosophy and mandates of the model. One advantage of a schoolwide model is the consistency that should be found from teacher to teacher. Rather than one teacher being strict and another lenient, students benefit from having teachers with similar expectations. However, all teachers might not enforce all management expectations and strategies equally. Also, problems can result if the philosophical perspectives of the classroom management model do not reflect those of the teachers. In this case, the teachers might need to change their beliefs to coincide with those of the adopted model.

Although schoolwide classroom management models work effectively in some circumstances, we favor allowing teachers to develop their own management philosophy and then build a model that reflects their beliefs. This process is discussed extensively in chapters 14 and 15 and is presented briefly here.

How do you develop a philosophy of classroom management? Bosch (1999) maintains that classroom management must reflect the personality and teaching style of the individual teacher and is a skill that must be learned, practiced, evaluated, and modified to fit the changing situations in contemporary classrooms. Too often, beginning teachers try one management strategy and become discouraged if it does not produce the desired effects immediately. Just as teachers modify and adjust teaching strategies to match students' needs and learning styles, so must teachers modify and adjust their management strategies. In order to develop a plan for classroom management, teachers must identify their own personal and professional strengths and weaknesses and examine and evaluate their instructional practices. Then they should develop a management plan, implement it, and, finally, evaluate and revise that plan (Bosch, 1999). As you think about your philosophy of classroom management, remember that classroom management is not a synonym for discipline. Management looks at the organization and operation of a classroom including classroom arrangement, the individuals in the classroom, the behavior of the teacher and students, the instructional strategies used by the teacher, the interactions of the students and teacher, the atmosphere of the school, and the community in which the school is located (Bosch, 1999).

You can begin to develop your personal philosophy of classroom management by referring to your answers to the questions in Activity 1–2. Then respond to the questions in Developing Your Personal Philosophy. Finally, as you read about the theories and models in chapters 2 through 12, you need to continue to think about these questions and to explore the models and theories and their relationship to your personal beliefs. Finally, in chapters 14 and 15, you will be able to work more intensely on the development of your own philosophy and plan for classroom management.

Just as we do not advocate any one model or theory of classroom management, we do not advocate any specific philosophical position. We believe teachers should develop their own philosophy and then implement classroom management strategies that reflect the philosophy they choose. The Case Study focuses on Ms. LaComba and the management challenges she is not sure she can handle.

Please go to *www.prenhall.com/manning* and click on the Management Tips for this chapter to complete management activities and find more information on adding some first day of school management tips to your teaching portfolio.

Activity 1-3

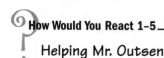

Identifying Effective and Ineffective Teacher Behaviors

Examine each of the following examples. Explain why each might contribute to misbehaviors or help students act appropriately.

Mr. Henson believes that students must obey every rule at all times.

Mr. Sevilla tries to identify the misbehaviors in his classroom that might threaten other students physically or psychologically.

Ms. Whitlock tries to deal immediately with any misbehavior that she believes might escalate.

Ms. Jernigan provides work that is overly challenging or not challenging enough for her students.

Mr. Tow uses teaching techniques that rely on collaboration and encourages students to work cooperatively.

Mr. Lopes gives his class work that frustrates the students or fails to capture their interest.

Ms. Cadle uses positive reinforcement rather than threats or punishments.

Mr. Culliton tries to avoid calling negative attention to students.

Ms. Kabayshi relies on the lecture method and conducts instruction for long periods of time.

Ms. Denosta uses sarcasm and techniques that rely on ridicule and harassment.

Mr. Lezzi is too lenient, and his students have no clear understanding of his expectations, expected behaviors, and the consequences of misbehaving.

Mr. Strempski tries to establish a positive classroom environment where his students feel safe.

Ms. Durant uses teaching methods that rely heavily on competition with a lot of active games in her classroom.

Mr. Sullivan has several zero-tolerance policies that eliminate the need to consider individual students and individual behaviors.

Ms. Toselli allows power struggles to develop with individual students, whereby she and a few students struggle to demonstrate their power to control situations in the classroom.

How Would You React 1-5

Helping Mr. Outsen

The actions of teachers play a part in promoting acceptable behavior in the classroom. Consider the following discussion of the behavior of a high school teacher. Then respond to the questions at the end.

Mr. Outsen thought he should be strict with his ninth-grade students and rely on the lecture method of teaching. "That's the only way they learn and behave," he said, "but they're still pretty rowdy at times." During formal and informal evaluations, Ms. Soriano, the assistant principal, thought Mr. Outsen used instructional and management techniques that contributed to student misbehavior in his classroom. He had 10 or 12 rules, strictly enforced each one, and used numerous threats and bribes to get students to behave. In addition, he never varied from his reliance on lectures. Ms. Soriano pondered what to do. "I don't think Mr. Outsen realizes that his instructional and management techniques make behavior worse. Although I need to discuss the possibility of easing up a little and changing his instructional style, I know he will defend his methods."

Working collaboratively in groups of three or four, respond to the following questions:

1. Do you agree or disagree with Mr. Outsen's belief that lectures are the best instructional strategy for ninth grade?

2. What is your opinion of "He had 10 or 12 rules, strictly enforced each one, and used numerous threats and bribes to get students to behave."

3. What strategies might Mr. Outsen try?

Developing Your Personal Philosophy

Examining Your Beliefs

To form the basis for your personal philosophy of classroom management, answer the following questions to reflect your current beliefs. Later, as you explore the ideas, theories, and models presented in this book, you might want to revise or modify your responses.

1. What is the purpose of education?
2. What is a good teacher, and what is good teaching?
3. What role should a teacher play in a classroom?
4. What should be the goals of a classroom management plan?
5. What misbehaviors do you want students to avoid?
6. What classroom misbehaviors are worth addressing?
7. How can you address diversity in a management plan?
8. What are your personal strengths and weaknesses?
9. What instructional strategies do you prefer to use?
10. Do you believe it is more effective to impose discipline or to teach self-discipline?

On this book's Companion Web Site, you will find a template that you can use to create your own management philosophy.

CASE STUDY
Ms. LaComba's Classroom Management Challenges

Ms. Maribel LaComba, a teacher in an urban school, is in her first year of teaching and faces serious classroom management challenges. As she was glad to explain:

Look, I never wanted to teach fifth grade. I knew these kids would be tough. When I applied for a teaching position, I asked for a third or fourth grade. Then, they called to offer me a fifth-grade job in a school where few teachers want to work. I needed a job and didn't know what else would come along, so I took it. What else was I supposed to do? Now, I am not sure I can control these fifth graders—they are so bad. I always wanted third or fourth grade.

Ms. LaComba did face serious challenges. Some of her students demonstrated relatively minor behaviors, such as goofing off, speaking out of turn, and continually getting out of their seats. She felt she could deal with these behaviors, but she was more concerned about other students who were rowdy and more aggressive. Some students, boys and girls, even bullied others and threatened them, physically and psychologically. What was even more frightening was that the students' behavior seemed to grow worse each week, and they listened to her less and less.

When she tried contacting parents, she met with mixed results. Some parents suggested that she was to blame; others promised to speak to their children, but she doubted they did. Some parents seemed to imply that students always had misbehaved and that teachers just had to deal with the problem.

"I don't know what to do," Ms. LaComba said. "Maybe I can finish out this year, but I'm not sure after that. I have a minor in accounting, so I might just give up teaching."

Questions for consideration

1. Ms. LaComba faced significant challenges that many teachers face. Should she try to find a third-grade teaching position, which was her original plan?
2. Should she give up and pursue an accounting career?
3. Should she ask the administration for more help?
4. How might Ms. LaComba be at fault?
5. If you were in Ms. LaComba's situation, what would you do?
6. After you have read the theories and models in this book, revisit this case study and give Ms. LaComba some specific advice about classroom management techniques she might use.

 You can record your answers to these questions online on this book's Companion Web Site at *www.prenhall.com/manning*.

AGGRESSION, VIOLENCE, AND THE SAFE SCHOOLS MOVEMENT

Educators have always faced the challenge of relatively minor misbehaviors that were disturbing and distracting from the educational process. In addition, educators have always had to deal with bullies. Now, they also face more serious problems of aggression and violence. Guns, knives, and other weapons are found in some schools all too often. Supported by individuals, professional associations, and governmental agencies, the **safe schools movement** places a priority on making schools safe for students and educators by focusing on the problem of violence and proposing possible remedies. Chapter 13 looks at school violence and the safe schools movement in more detail, but this section takes a brief look at the problem and efforts to make schools safe.

The Problem of Aggression and Violence

Mendler and Curwin (1997), the theorists discussed in chapter 7, maintain that although school and societal violence is a sad reality, schools also remain perhaps one of the safest places for children and adolescents. However, violence occurs and deserves to be addressed. Mendler and Curwin identified three forms of violence: bodily (physical injury), esteem (verbal harassment, such as name calling), and property (damage to things one owns). All these breed an atmosphere of hostility and aggression, where it feels and looks better to hurt others than to resolve issues and tolerate others.

Violence has many causes. Some children grow up abused and assume that abuse is a way of life, and others do not have a nurturing family structure. For still other students, the absence of fathers, the increasing depersonalization of communities, and the diminishing role of values and community play a major role (Mendler & Curwin, 1997). Additional causes include gang presence and activity, hate-motivated behavior, and drugs and alcohol (National Education Association, 1998). Other instances of violence can be attributed to bullies, their victims, and loners who feel anonymous or disliked by peers.

The Safe Schools Movement

Understanding the causes of school violence is a viable starting point for ending it, but the challenge is to identify a way to reduce its physical and psychological harm. As the name suggests, the safe schools movement places a priority on making schools safe for students and educators. Rather than the efforts of one organization, the safe schools movement is supported by many people, professional associations, and governmental agencies. As books, articles, and reports on safe schools focus increasingly on the problem of violence and possible remedies, the effort to prevent and reduce school violence gains momentum daily.

The Role of Effective Classroom Management

Teachers might believe that their classroom management methods and strategies are appropriate only for routine misbehaviors—those misbehaviors that disturb students and educators but do not cause physical or psychological harm. They might see violence or aggression as the responsibility of administrators (at the school level and the district level). When we asked about safe schools programs, one teacher said, "Efforts to reduce school violence are made at the school level; the principal has a safe schools plan. I think the associate superintendent sent it to her." Another teacher maintained that it was best to "call the police and get the hoodlums out of here." Such mindsets disavow the role of classroom management in the efforts to reduce school violence. Management Tip 1–3 shows several strategies teachers might take in individual classrooms to promote safe schools.

Each teacher needs to become involved in creating and maintaining safe schools, and educators also need to adopt a collaborative approach to create a safe environment throughout the school. In addition, as teachers develop a classroom management plan, they need to focus on management components that make classrooms safe.

CONCLUDING REMARKS

Although considerable research and writing have focused on classroom management and the various models and theorists, little evidence suggests that educators' classroom management challenges will decrease in the future. For any number of reasons, educators will continue to deal with students who misbehave and interrupt the teaching/learning process. In addition, educators and students will face aggressive, violent, and bullying behaviors. Unfortunately, easy answers and solutions to this violence do not exist. Understanding classroom management challenges is a worthwhile beginning, but the ultimate goal must be to improve student behaviors. One way to attain this goal is for teachers to understand the classroom management theorists and models and then select the ideas that work for them and develop a comprehensive

Management Tip 1–3

Promoting Safe Schools

All teachers need to promote safe schools. Teachers can do the following:

- Model cooperation and collaboration with students and other educators.
- Identify and work with students who have potential for becoming bullies or for demonstrating aggressive behaviors.
- Hold class meetings and help students identify and address possible interpersonal problems before they escalate.
- Work with parents and family members of young children and elementary students who are experiencing academic, social, or behavioral difficulties.
- Help students develop a sense of community, where they learn to be concerned about each other's overall well-being.
- Teach students conflict resolution skills to replace violence and aggressive responses to problems.

Elementary
Work with parents and family members of young children and elementary students who are experiencing academic, social, or behavioral difficulties.

Secondary
Maintain constant vigilance for weapons or any object that students might use as weapons.

classroom management plan. Once teachers accomplish this task, they still will need to implement classroom management strategies that reflect their personal preferences for managing students.

Last, remember that classroom management is a process rather than a product. Educators' perspectives change; students and their behaviors change. Therefore, you will need to improve and revise your management model continually to make classrooms productive and safe learning environments. To help you as you begin your study of classroom management, consult the Internet resources listed in "Reaching Out with Technology" on this book's Companion Web Site, as well as the suggested readings at the end of this book.

 Please go to *www.prenhall.com/manning* and click on the Management Tips for this chapter to complete management activities and find more information on keeping your classroom safe.

Suggested Readings

Blum, R. W. (2005). A case for school connectedness. *Educational Leadership 62* (7), 16–20. Blum examines the role that a positive school climate plays in classroom management.

Boulter, L. (2004). Family-school connection and school violence prevention. *The Negro Educational Review, 55*(1), 27–40. Boulter looks at the social and psychological risk factors that are associated with school violence as well as prevention strategies that involve both the family and the community.

Strain, P. S., & Joseph, G. E. (2004). Engaged supervision to support recommended practices for young children with challenging behavior. *Topics in Early Childhood Special*

 Please go to *www.prenhall.com/manning* and click on Concluding Remarks for this chapter to find more information.

Education, 24(1), 39–50. Writing about young children, these authors maintained that staff members being overwhelmed, overworked, and disrespected are major reasons for recommended practices for providing effective prevention and intervention not being implemented.

Watts, I. E., & Erevelles, N. (2004). These deadly times: Reconceptualizing school violence by using critical race theory and disability studies. *American Educational Research Journal 41* (2), 271–299. The authors look at social conditions as well as political, institutional, and economic structures that impact individual students and may lead to severe misbehaviors.

Weinstein, C. S., Tomlinson-Clarke, S., & Curran, M. (2004). Toward a conception of culturally responsive classroom management. *Journal of Teacher Education, 55*(1), 25–38. The authors examine the importance of cultural in the development of appropriate management strategies.

PART 2

Selected Classroom Management Theorists

Understanding classroom management models and theorists is an excellent first step toward developing your personal philosophy and, eventually, your own classroom management strategies. The challenge is to understand each model or theory and its philosophy, key concepts, strategies, overall effectiveness, and respect for diversity, Then, you can decide whether you want to adopt one of the models or adopt the most applicable aspects of a number of models (usually called an eclectic approach) in an effort to develop a more personal model, one that you believe will work for you. The purpose and goal of this book is to help you do just that—identify workable classroom management strategies and develop your own personal classroom management philosophy. Table 1 provides an overview of the models found in this book and a brief description of each.

As you explore these models in more detail in chapters 2 through 12 of this book, you need to consider specific aspects of each model or theory. Table 2 shows one of the most important aspects, the issue of whether discipline should be taught or imposed.

As you consider the models, you should ask the following questions:

1. Does the model require extensive work and time with record keeping?
2. Does the model require action that some cultures or genders might find offensive or obtrusive?
3. Does the model have a philosophical basis with which I can agree?
4. Does the model require allegiance to one complete model only?
5. Does the model rely on threats, bribes, and coercion?
6. Does the model require the use of praise, rewards, and other devices that shape students' behavior?

Table 1 Selected Classroom Management Theorists and Models: A Brief Overview

Theorist	Model	Basic Beliefs
B. F. Skinner (chapter 2)	**Behavior Modification**	Educators use positive and negative reinforcements or rewards and punishments to modify or shape students' behavior.
Fritz Redl and William Wattenberg (chapter 2)	**Group Life and Classroom Discipline**	Educators encourage students to understand their behavior and actions. Understanding that student behavior differs individually and as a member of a group, educators support students' self-control and use pleasant and unpleasant situations to modify behavior.
William Glasser (chapter 2)	**Choice Theory and Quality Schools**	Schools help satisfy students' psychological needs and add quality to their life. Educators teach, manage, provide caring environments, and conduct class meetings in a way that adds quality to students' lives.
Thomas Gordon (chapter 2)	**Teacher Effectiveness Training**	Educators teach self-discipline, demonstrate active listening, send "I-messages" rather than "you-messages," and teach a six-step conflict resolution program.
Lee Canter and Marlene Canter (chapter 3)	**Assertive Discipline**	Educators and students have rights in the classroom. Educators insist upon responsible behavior and use a hierarchical list of consequences to manage behavior.
Rudolph Dreikurs (chapter 4)	**Democratic Teaching and Management**	Misbehavior results from four major causes (or mistaken goals). Educators use democratic teaching, logical consequences, and encouragement rather than praise.
Haim Ginot (chapter 5)	**Congruent Communication**	Educators demonstrate their best behaviors (harmonious with students' feelings about themselves and their situations) and promote self-discipline as an alternative to punishment.
Jacob Kounin (chapter 6)	**Instructional Management**	Educators use effective instructional behaviors (teaching techniques, movement management, and group focus) to influence student behaviors.
Richard Curwin and Allen Mendler (chapter 7)	**Discipline with Dignity**	Educators protect the dignity of students. Teachers are fair and consider individual situations (as opposed to rigid rules), list rules that make sense to students, and model appropriate behaviors.
Frederic Jones	**Positive Classroom Management**	Positive classroom management procedures affirm students. Educators set limits; build cooperation; and use practical, simple, and easy-to-use strategies.
Barbara Coloroso (chapter 9)	**Inner Discipline**	Students are worth the time and effort it takes to teach them responsible behavior. Educators avoid punishment and evaluative praise. Instead, they model conflict resolution and use natural consequences.
Jerome Freiberg (chapter 10)	**Consistency Management and Cooperative Discipline**	With this schoolwide model, teachers improve behavior, school climate, and academic achievement. Using caring and cooperation, they also teach self-discipline in the classroom.
Forrest Gathercoal (chapter 11)	**Judicious Discipline**	Educators provide behavioral guidelines for property loss and damage, threats to health and safety, and serious disruptions of the educational process. They also demonstrate professional ethics and build a democratic classroom.

Theorist	Model	Basic Beliefs
Linda Albert (chapter 12)	**Cooperative Discipline**	Educators influence rather than control students, helping students connect, contribute, and become capable, educators develop a conduct code that fosters a positive climate in the school.
Carolyn Evertson and Alene Harris (chapter 12)	**Managing Learner-Centered Classrooms**	Educators provide learner-centered classrooms, consider instructional management and behavior management, and begin the school year with clear rules and expectations.
Roger Johnson and David Johnson (chapter 12)	**The Three C's of School and Classroom Discipline**	Teachers stress cooperation, conflict resolution, and civic values. They also use these three C's to address violence, aggression, and physical and psychological abuse, as well as to promote the goals of the safe school movement.
Jane Nelsen, Lynn Lott, and Stephen Glenn (chapter 12)	**Positive Discipline**	Educators emphasize caring, mutual respect, encouragement, and order; teach the skills needed for successful lives; and conduct class meetings.
Alfie Kohn (chapter 12)	**Beyond Discipline**	The new disciplines are no better than the old disciplines. They still emphasize rewards, punishments, and consequences. Educators must consider students from positive perspectives and must believe that they will make correct decisions.

7. Does the model allow me to pick and choose among the strategies that I think will work for me?

As you read these questions, try to identify other questions you might add to the list. Then, as you read each chapter, continue to refer back to these questions and the others that you developed. Finally, refer to these questions as you read chapters 14 and 15.

Table 2 Teaching and Imposing Discipline

Two Types of Discipline

Type One: DISCIPLINE IMPOSED.   Teachers punish (some negative consequence) students for misbehavior.

The teacher thinks or says, "I will discipline Cody to stay in his seat."

Type Two: DISCIPLINE TAUGHT.   Teachers teach students to discipline themselves.

The teacher thinks or says, "I need to teach Cody to discipline himself to stay in his seat."

Building the Foundation: *Skinner; Redl and Wattenberg; Glasser; and Gordon*

Focusing Questions

After reading this chapter, you should be able to answer the following questions:

1. Which major theorists laid the foundation for contemporary classroom management?
2. What are the basics of their theories?
3. What classroom management ideas can be drawn from each model?
4. How has the work of the foundational theorists influenced contemporary theories of classroom management and the movement for safe schools?
5. What are the perceived criticisms of the work of each theorist?
6. What impact do cultural and other forms of student diversity have on each of these theories?

Key Terms

- **Active listening**
- **Choice Theory**
- **Control theory**
- **Corporal punishment**
- **Discipline as self-control**
- **Empathic understanding**
- **Extrinsic bribes**
- **Foundational theorists**
- **Group dynamics**
- **I-messages**
- **Internal motivation**
- **Operant conditioning (or behavior modification)**
- **Pleasure–Pain principle**
- **Positive reinforcement**
- **Problem ownership**
- **Quality School**
- **Reality appraisal**
- **Situational assistance**
- **Supporting self-control**

Since schools came into existence, educators have tried to find the best ways to manage their classrooms and to encourage appropriate student behaviors. This has not been easy. The demands of classroom and behavior management and, more recently, the emphasis on safe schools have tested beginning and experienced classroom teachers and school administrators. They realize that good classroom management and good classroom instruction must go hand in hand, because classroom management can never be used to hide poor teaching. As a result, educators look for methods, strategies, and theories that will help them improve student behaviors in order to make teaching more effective and the overall school day more enjoyable for everyone.

We believe that an understanding of the key concepts of a variety of classroom management theorists will help you develop your own philosophy and techniques of classroom management. No one model will provide all the answers that educators need to manage a classroom effectively and to provide a safe school environment. However, knowledge of these theories allows effective educators to build a management style that combines proactive and reactive elements and that melds instruction and classroom management into a unique, effective style.

In this chapter, we begin our discussion of techniques and theories by exploring some psychological and educational theorists whose work provides the foundation for any discussion of classroom management. Some of these theorists did not address behaviors in a school setting directly; rather, they focused on other psychological aspects of human behavior. Also, writing in the middle of the 20th century, several of the theorists did not have to concern themselves with school violence and the concept of safe schools. Nevertheless, their work provides a significant foundation for the study of classroom management. Included in this group are B. F. Skinner's operant conditioning or behavior modification, Fritz Redl's and William Wattenberg's group dynamics and classroom discipline, William Glasser's Choice Theory, and Thomas Gordon's Discipline as Self-Control. Although these researchers differed in the focus of their work and theories, their contributions continue to influence contemporary classroom management theorists and to offer valuable insights for elementary, middle, and high school educators.

FOUNDATIONAL THEORISTS

Although other scholars and researchers also might be considered foundational theorists in the study of student behavior and classroom management, we selected B. F. Skinner, Fritz Redl and William Wattenberg, William Glasser, and Thomas Gordon to examine. Table 2–1 provides an overview of these theorists and the key concepts that are covered in this chapter.

www.prenhall.com/manning

These individuals and their theories cannot be discussed in detail within the confines of a single chapter; however, "Reaching Out with Technology" on this text's Companion Web Site provides a list of Internet sites where you can find additional information on each of these theorists and their ideas.

Table 2–1 Overview of the Foundational Theorists

Theorist	Model	Key Concepts
B. F. Skinner	Behavior Modification	Operant conditioning
		Positive reinforcement
		Negative reinforcement
Fritz Redl and William Wattenberg	Group Life and Classroom Discipline	Reality appraisal
		Group life in the classroom
		Supporting self-control
		Situational assistance
		Pleasure–pain principle
William Glasser	Choice Theory	Quality schools
		Psychological needs
Thomas Gordon	Discipline as Self-Control	Self-discipline
		Problem ownership
		Active listening
	Teacher Effectiveness	I-Message
	Training	Six-step problem-solving/ conflict resolution

B. F. SKINNER

Biographical Sketch

A leader of 20th-century scientific psychology (Vargas & Chance, 2002), American psychologist Burrhus Frederic Skinner received his doctoral degree in psychology from Harvard in 1931 and taught at the University of Minnesota, Indiana University, and Harvard University. Greatly influenced by American behavioral psychologist John B. Watson and Russian psychologist Ivan Pavlov, Skinner focused his research on the learning process and behavioral psychology, the study of the observable behavior of human beings. He designed the first "baby box," a controlled or managed environmental chamber in which an infant can develop. Selected works by Skinner include *Walden Two* (1948), in which he suggested an ideal planned society based upon principles of learning, and *Beyond Freedom and Dignity* (1971), in which he called for restriction of individual freedoms that hinder the development of a planned society. Neither an authoritarian or a totalitarian (Rutherford, 2000), his experimental research and theoretical work provided new views of language, thinking, problem solving, and creativity (Vargas & Chance, 2002). Overall, his most significant contribution was his theory that proper and immediate reinforcement strengthens the likelihood that appropriate behavior will be repeated.

Overview of Skinner's Theories

Skinner did not work in school classrooms, nor did he describe instructional or general classroom practices to reduce students' behavior problems and to provide safe schools. Still, Skinner suggested that human behavior could be dramatically improved through the use of scientific application of behavioral principles (Ervin, Ehrhardt, & Poling, 2001). His research has influenced the field of classroom management and has become known as **operant conditioning,** or **behavior modification.**

In a series of laboratory experiments, Skinner conditioned rats to press levers and pigeons to play table tennis by rewarding their appropriate behavior with food. Based upon these and other experiments, he reached several conclusions. First, he noted that proper and immediate reinforcement (a favorite food, compliment, or other reward) strengthens the likelihood that appropriate behavior will reoccur. He also found that behavior can be shaped by providing a reinforcing stimulus just after a desired behavior happens. Although constant reinforcement might be necessary to establish a behavior, occasional or intermittent reinforcement can be used to maintain a desired behavior once it is established. Skinner called this process **positive reinforcement.** In contrast, Skinner also researched the power of negative reinforcement, or the removal of something undesirable, in order to stimulate a desired behavior.

Contributions of Skinner's Theories

Skinner placed punishment and motivation in unique perspectives. He felt that when we punish a person for undesirable behavior, we place the responsibility on him or her to learn proper behavior; then, the person can receive credit for behaving in a desired manner. Instead, Skinner thought we should teach proper behavior and offer positive reinforcement (Maag, 2001).

Writing of Skinner, William Wattenberg (1967) explained that the techniques of behavior modification have inspired many teachers, who agree that the proper use of reinforcements has the potential to shape students' behavior. Just as Skinner believed that most learned human behavior is shaped by positive rewards, many teachers believe that students repeat behaviors that are rewarded and stop those undesirable ones that are ignored or not rewarded. Thus, teachers attempt to shape behavior by determining the behaviors they want and by selecting appropriate reinforcers that help students learn to repeat appropriate behaviors. As reinforcement occurs, the likelihood of students repeating the behavior increases.

Reinforcement can take many forms in a classroom. For example, a teacher can reward students who complete their assignments on time by giving them each a token. When students have a set number of tokens, they can redeem them for a desired item such as a "no-homework-tonight pass." (See Management Tip 2–1.) In addition, rather than reprimanding misbehaving students, teachers can praise students who are behaving properly. According to Skinner's theory, the students who are behaving will continue to demonstrate positive behavior, and the students who are misbehaving will desire the positive reinforcement and will begin to behave in an appropriate manner. Employing the principle of negative reinforcement, or the removal of something undesirable to stimulate desired behavior, a teacher can reduce the number of math homework problems for students who correctly complete their work in class. Here the desired effect is to reinforce the behavior of completing in-class work by eliminating or reducing the undesired homework assignment. To be effective, reinforcement for desired behaviors must be proper and immediate.

Skinner also advocated a managed environment such as his baby box. In a classroom, a teacher manages the environment so that it is conducive to positive behavior. A teacher can accomplish this by establishing specific behavioral goals, developing student behavioral contracts, using student input to establish classroom rules, arranging the classroom for optimal student behavior, making behavior expectations clear, and posting some general rules. (See Management Tip 2–2.) The goal is to provide an environment in which the students know what is expected and feel physically and psychologically safe. The classroom then becomes a caring community of learners in which the educational experiences result in some degree of success rather than frustration and failure.

Activity 2–1 provides examples of behaviors that a teacher might praise and types of positive reinforcement that might be used. Then it is your turn to identify examples of each. As you complete this exercise, remember that it is important to consider the chronological age and developmental level of the student before deciding on a type of positive reinforcement. Verbal praise in front of the entire class might prove effective for an elementary student, but it might be ineffective and embarrassing for a middle school or high school student.

★ Management Tip 2–1

Using Rewards

Skinner believed in the use of positive reinforcement to establish, reinforce, and maintain a desired behavior. Many educators use rewards in the classroom to manage student behavior. Following are three suggestions for rewards that have proven effective in classrooms.

Elementary
Some teachers post a chart with the names of all students in a class and reward students for positive behavior (sitting quietly, lining up quickly, walking quietly in the hall, etc.) with a star behind their names. Other teachers make the chart for the entire class by listing the expected behaviors and rewarding group behavior. This "star chart" provides a visual reminder for students.

Secondary
A high school social studies teacher rewards one student each week with a "Friday Sofa Award," which enables the student to sit and work on a comfortable couch that the teacher has placed in the classroom. The teacher also gives the recipient an award certificate ("Encourage Students Successes with Trips to the Couch," 2004). If you do not have room for a couch, try a recliner, bean bag chair, or rocker.

All levels
Some teachers purchase rolls of paper tickets from an office-supply store and reward students for positive behavior (following class rules, turning in homework, etc.) by giving them one or more tickets. Students can redeem their tickets for daily/weekly rewards or save the tickets to go shopping at a store that is set up in the school once each grading period with merchandise supplied by school business partners, found at garage sales and thrift shops, or donated by parents. In some classrooms, misbehavior can result in the loss of tickets. In addition to rewarding positive behavior, this system can teach the value of saving for the future.

Please go to *www.prenhall.com/manning* and click on the Management Tips for this chapter to complete management activities and find more information on using rewards in the classroom.

Application of Skinner's Theories

It is easy to find situations where educators from kindergarten through college can use Skinner's theories in various practical situations. For example, in university classrooms, it can be annoying to the professor and the class members when a student arrives late for class. Instead of lecturing these tardy students, some professors focus on the positive behavior and compliment the punctual students by saying something like, "I understand it is often difficult to be here on time, so I appreciate all of you who make a special effort to arrange your schedules to be here at the beginning of class." Even with college students, this usually works, and most students try to be more punctual.

The following are some additional examples of the applications of Skinner's theories. After reading them, examine the situation in How Would You React 2–1 and use Skinner's theories to solve a problem with a group of seventh-grade students.

> In spite of constant reprimands, Jasper continued to click his ballpoint pen throughout the class. However, when his teacher Jenna Murphy began to ignore Jasper's behavior and to praise the students surrounding Jasper for their good behavior and quiet work habits, Jasper stopped the annoying clicking. When that happened, Ms. Murphy immediately thanked Jasper for his considerate behavior.

> Although it can be difficult to achieve, Alvenia Walker has a goal of zero negative comments to students. Using praise and other forms of positive reinforcement, she constantly scans the class. Looking for students who are behaving, Ms. Walker praises those who follow the class rules, raise their hands before speaking, and demonstrate the caring and considerate behaviors that she believes are important to the overall classroom environment. If students are being physically or verbally abusive, Ms. Walker reacts decisively and properly, yet even in these cases, she continues to be positive and to reinforce positive behavior as much as she can.

Management Tip 2-2

Developing Routines

Managing the classroom environment is an important part of classroom management. Teachers develop routines for

- Collecting and distributing materials
- Keeping track of students
- Jobs in the classroom
- Organizing groups
- Keeping track of attendance and grades
- Keeping records
- Establishing a daily agenda

Here are a few specific suggestions for elementary and secondary routines.

Elementary
Make a detailed list of the day's activities and post it on the board. Include the lessons to be taught, special events, breaks, including lunch, and special classes that some students attend. At the beginning of the day, go over the agenda with the class as an advance organizer for the day. Then, at the end of the day, use the agenda as a summary of the day's work. Students in upper elementary grades can lead the overview instead of the teacher.

Secondary
One recurring task is the collection and distribution of homework and other papers in the classroom. Students are more likely to behave if there is an established procedure for this. Everyone should know and follow these routines with directions left for substitute teachers. Determine

- When homework will be collected (e.g., at the door as students arrive, after students are in their seats and the bell rings, etc.)
- Whether homework is accepted late and if there are any penalties
- How homework will be collected (e.g., placed in a box on the teacher's desk, passed in when students are seated, checked in by the teacher as each student arrives)

Working with a special education inclusion teacher, Sue Beacham developed a behavior contract for LaShawn. LaShawn knows that she can earn points based on her appropriate behavior in Ms. Beacham's class and that the points can be used to "purchase" items at a special school store.

Please go to *www.prenhall.com/manning* and click on the Management Tips for this chapter to complete management activities and find more information on developing routines.

Critique of Skinner's Theories

Because Skinner did not address classroom management in his work, he also did not address the instructional implications of his theory and did not show the relationship between management and instruction. Most effective classroom educators realize the importance of combining effective management with good teaching and believe that it is difficult to have one without the other.

Looking specifically at the behavioral aspects of operant conditioning, not all classroom management theorists agree with Skinner's ideas about rewards. In fact, some believe rewards are counterproductive because they are **extrinsic bribes** rather than **internal motivation**.

Activity 2–1

Providing Positive Reinforcement

1. Teachers can praise positive behaviors when students are working on task, treating others with respect, not bothering or disturbing classmates, or following directions. What are other desired behaviors that you would want to reinforce in your classroom?

2. In addition to verbal praise, teachers frequently reinforce desired behaviors by using tactics such as check marks on a classroom behavior chart, tokens that can be collected and later redeemed for special prizes or privileges, or stickers that provide visual proof of positive behavior. Other teachers use special activities such as extra computer time, the opportunity to work in groups with friends, or classroom duties such as line leader when walking through the halls. What could you use to reinforce appropriate behaviors in your classroom?

As Alfie Kohn (1993, 1997) (a theorist explained in chapter 12) explains, the more people receive rewards for doing something, the more likely it becomes that they will lose the intrinsic motivation to continue the behavior that produced the reward. Thus, when a student works for the extrinsic reward (e.g., homework pass, token, or sticker) rather than the intrinsic reward (i.e., taking self-satisfaction in having appropriate behavior), the intrinsic motivation begins to disappear and the individual learns to perform the behavior solely to get the reward. Other educators believe that students might first be motivated by extrinsic rewards, but they eventually will perform the desired behaviors without the reward or with only an intermittent reward. In other words, as the behavior is shaped, the motivation becomes intrinsic rather than extrinsic. Other criticisms of Skinner's behaviorist theories arise from a general dissatisfaction with any theory that believes punishment is ineffective and that positive reinforcement is better (Staddon, 1995).

How might Skinner's theories fare in our nation's increasingly diverse schools as educators strive to address cultural and gender differences? Several problems might arise. Remember that individuals within any cultural group, socioeconomic class, geographical region, or developmental period can vary significantly. However, different groups can, in general, have certain characteristics that teachers need to consider in the classroom.

Although educators generally believe that competition improves behavior and achievement, the opposite might be true for some cultural groups. For example, Manning and Baruth (2004) explained that some Latinos or Hispanic Americans might avoid any competition or activity that sets them apart from their group. For some Latinos, to stand out among their peers is to place themselves in considerable jeopardy and is to be avoided at all costs. Other people believe competition means that someone has to excel at someone else's expense. Extrinsic rewards such as a homework pass, token, or sticker might be seen as a personal

Keeping Students Quiet in the Halls

In the following scenario, we see a teacher who has difficulty with management. As you read, think about Skinner's views on about operant conditioning and positive reinforcement.

Lars Jensen had problems whenever he took his class through the halls. Whether going to lunch or to the library media center, many of the students walked too fast and talked too loudly, thus disturbing other classes. A few teachers had complained to Lars about the noise, and some went to the principal. Although Lars tried threatening the noisy students, punishing the whole class, and even making the students walk a few feet apart, nothing seemed to work.

Now, using Skinner's ideas, identify some strategies that you think Mr. Jensen would be able to use and explain how Mr. Jensen might be able to apply them. For example, could Mr. Jensen use any positive reinforcements with his class? If so, what specifically could he do? How might his actions vary depending on the grade level of his class?

affront to someone who did not receive one. Also, feminists are concerned that the reward system is unfair to females, who sometimes place value on collaboration rather than competition to receive rewards (Manning & Baruth, 2004).

FRITZ REDL AND WILLIAM W. WATTENBERG

Biographical Sketch

Born in Austria, Fritz Redl earned his doctoral degree at the University of Vienna and completed his training in child analysis. In addition to teaching at the University of Michigan, the University of Chicago, and Wayne State University, Redl also worked as chief of the Child Research branch of the National Institute of Mental Health in Bethesda, Maryland. His keen interest in group therapy projects, particularly the aggressive child, led to his coauthoring several important books, including *Controls From Within* (with David Wineman in 1952). Redl also worked with George Sheviakov on *Discipline for Today's Children and Youth* (Sheviakov & Redl, 1956), which explained his theories of discipline in classroom practice. Speaking in understandable terms, Redl always relied on his direct experiences with young people. He believed that most troubled children had serious emotional problems that could be changed through long-term, intensive interventions. He was adamant about acting as advocates for children, especially those labeled as delinquent, and warned adults to avoid blaming the victim for his or her undesirable behavior (Morse, 2001). At no time should an individual's undesirable behavior be considered a character defect (Maier, 2001).

William Wattenberg grew up in New York City, served in the U.S. Army from 1942 to 1945, and was a faculty member at Teachers College at Columbia University, Northwestern University, and Wayne State University. Wattenberg held memberships in the American Sociological Association, American Psychological Association, National Society for Study of Education, and American Educational Research Association. His writings include *Mental Hygiene in Teaching* with Fritz Redl (1959), as well as *The Adolescent Years* (1955, 1973) and *All Men Are Created Equal* (1967).

Overview of Redl's and Wattenberg's Theories

In *Mental Hygiene in Teaching,* Redl and Wattenberg (1959) offered several theories that have contributed to classroom management concepts and provided the foundational work for many later theorists. Their explanation of **group dynamics** or "group life in the classroom"

(Redl & Wattenberg, 1959, p. 262) has particular relevance to today's educators, who need to understand that individual behavior affects group behavior, and vice versa. In addition, they identified management strategies, including the techniques of supporting self-control, situational assistance, reality appraisal, and the pleasure–pain principle, which educators can use to influence student behavior.

In discussing group dynamics, Redl and Wattenberg (1959) noted that differences occur in the behavior of a student as an individual and the behavior of the same student as a member of a group. Within a group, they found that individuals assume roles, including leader, clown or entertainer, fall guy or blame taker, and instigator. They also identified group actions such as contagious behavior that spreads throughout the group members; scapegoating or blaming a weak or unliked individual; reactions to strangers, which usually cause tension throughout the group; teasing the teacher's pet or showing a negative reaction to a student the group identifies as a teacher's favorite; and group disintegration or the breakup of the group.

Redl and Wattenberg (1959) also identified a number of influence techniques that educators can use to manage behavior in a classroom. Their technique of *supporting self-control* is based on the belief that individuals control their own conduct and that much misbehavior results from a temporary lapse of an individual's control system rather than from a motivation to be disagreeable. Another mainstay of Redl's and Wattenberg's (1959) theories is the concept of appraising reality, or **reality appraisal.** They maintained that students need to appraise reality in an effort to understand whether their actions are guided by intelligence and conscience or by fear or prejudice. To guide students, educators should appeal to students' sense of fairness and also "strengthen their ability to see the consequences of their actions" (Redl & Wattenberg, 1959, p. 358).

Two other influence techniques are the **pleasure–pain principle** and the concept of **situational assistance.** If a student has lost his or her self-control, a teacher steps in with situational assistance to help the student regain control. When using the pleasure–pain principle, the teacher deliberately provides experiences to produce pleasant to unpleasant feelings. In this case, the hope is that a pleasant experience will induce an individual to repeat a desirable behavior, and an unpleasant experience will make the individual want to avoid repeating that unwanted behavior. However, Redl and Wattenberg make it clear that this pleasure–pain principle does not mean that a teacher, in the heat of anger, can lash out at a student. Likewise, pain or punishment should not be in the form of revenge (Redl & Wattenberg, 1959).

Contributions of Redl's and Wattenberg's Theories

With their study of group life, Redl and Wattenberg contributed to our understanding of the ways students function as members of groups within a classroom and the effect that group expectations have on individual group members. A worthwhile project for any teacher is to observe the groups within the classroom, as well as within the total classroom group, in order to identify the roles being played by each of the students. It is also important for a teacher to be aware of group behaviors such as the tension that often accompanies the entrance of a stranger into a room or the hostility over a perceived pet, or favorite, student. A perceptive teacher is aware of the functioning of the class as a whole group, as well as of each smaller group within the classroom, and monitors the actions of each group and its members.

In addition to their work on group dynamics, Redl and Wattenberg (1959) identified many influence principles that are important for educators. Most students want to behave appropriately, but they sometimes need help controlling their actions. Perhaps because they forget, are uncertain about the rules, are bored, or are just tired of sitting, some students lose self-control and need the teacher's assistance. Often this assistance can be minimal and

Educators can support self-control by

1. Using signals such as catching the eye of the student, frowning, or shaking the head,
2. Standing nearer the student and using proximity control,
3. Using humor, not sarcasm, appropriately,
4. Showing interest in the student's work or achievements,
5. Ignoring minor misbehaviors and making a special effort to understand the reasons for misbehaviors.

Educators can provide situational assistance by

1. Making sure students know the classroom routines,
2. Allowing misbehaving students to be alone or providing a "time-out,"
3. Removing seductive objects (games, pictures, comic books, etc.) that draw attention away from the educational task,
4. Planning ahead to eliminate temptations and overstimulation,
5. Helping a student overcome a hurdle or frustrating roadblock.

Figure 2–1 Supporting Self-Control and Providing Situational Assistance

can help students regain or keep from losing their control. At other times, situational assistance requires more action on the part of the educator. Although this assistance can take many forms, Redl and Wattenberg (1959, p. 375) cautioned that **corporal punishment** "can accomplish nothing that cannot be achieved better by some other method." Although this attitude is not unusual today, Redl's and Wattenberg's position probably resulted in considerable criticism when it was stated originally. Figure 2–1 provides several examples of ways teachers can help students control their own actions and provide situational assistance.

In addition to helping students deal with their behavior in an individual situation, educators can use several strategies to help students learn to appraise or understand reality. For example, teachers can use direct appeals and explain to students the connection between their conduct and its consequences. They also can use criticism and encouragement, which can be done in private or within the hearing range of the entire class (not scoldings or tirades but soothing encouragements to help students feel better about the reality of the situation). In addition, educators can clearly define classroom and school limits. One advantage of appraising reality is that these techniques help students develop the values and the feel for reality that should govern their behavior. Activity 2–2 offers you an opportunity to develop some questions that you might ask to encourage students to appraise reality.

Application of Redl's and Wattenberg's Theories

Redl's and Wattenberg's (1959) theories have contributed significantly to classroom management and to ideas about good teaching. Unlike Skinner, who looked only at the psychological aspects of behavior, Redl and Wattenberg focused on aspects of classroom management that have the potential for improving instructional practices as well. Understanding group dynamics, providing situational assistance, and supporting self-control relate to effective management practices and to good teaching. Redl and Wattenberg realized the difficulty of having effective management without good teaching and built upon the connection and relationship between the two.

The following are some examples of ways teachers have followed or disregarded Redl's and Wattenberg's theories. After reading them, use these theories to respond to the situation in How Would You React 2–2.

Activity 2-2

Appraising Reality

Identify the grade levels you teach or want to teach. Then, examine the following questions, think back to your time as a student in those grades, answer each question, and explain how your view of reality at that time in your life shaped your behaviors.

1. How did your behavior influence your feelings about yourself?
2. How did your behavior affect your academic achievement?
3. How did your behavior affect your friends and peers?
4. How did your behavior encourage a group of students or specific individuals to misbehave?
5. How did your behavior break the rules set forth by the teacher and students?
6. What could you have done to improve your behavior and to develop an educational attitude that is more conducive to learning?
7. What could a teacher have done to help you better understand your behavior and change to more positive behaviors?

When Ellen Pandorski began her student teaching, she had a rule that students had to raise their hand to answer one of her questions. That way, she could call on the "right person." However, as the school year progressed, Cory began to answer questions without raising his hand. Because Ms. Pandorski thought the rule violation was a fluke and that Cory, who was an excellent student, had just forgotten, she ignored the rule infraction. Soon, other students began to call out answers, many of which were wrong. Then Ms. Pandorski made another mistake. Knowing Cory usually had the right answer, she allowed him to continue but reprimanded others who called out. Not only did this take time away from instruction, it led other students to resent Cory and call him the teacher's pet. Redl and Wattenberg would have explained the group dynamics of this situation to Ms. Pandorski by stressing that misbehaviors can spread (contagious behavior) once one student initiates the first inappropriate behavior.

How Would You React 2-2

Managing Tammi's Behavior

Redl and Wattenberg had several ideas dealing with group dynamics, supporting self-control, reality appraisal, situational assistance and the pleasure–pain principle. Think about these as you read the following scenario.

Ms. Caprio does not have any problems with Tammi's academic achievement; in fact, Tammi frequently finishes her work before others in her class and it is usually correct. What Ms. Caprio does have a problem with is Tammi's behavior. Because she is one of the first to finish class work, Tammi starts to talk, giggle, and disturb others. Knowing that something must be done about Tammi's behavior, Ms. Caprio has considered giving Tammi more work, calling her parents, or moving her to another part of the classroom.

Which of the ideas of Redl and Wattenburg could Ms. Caprio use with Tammi? Justify your decision and explain how Ms. Caprio could implement these ideas.

In addition, this group resented the favored treatment shown to Cory. Thus, a small management problem grew and impacted the instruction in the classroom.

Gabe Sanchez is a teacher who supports self-control and helps students maintain appropriate behavior. During whole-group instruction, he constantly observes the entire class for signs of misbehavior with a goal, whenever possible, of correcting misbehavior without verbally correcting the student. When Mr. Sanchez notices something, such as a student playing with a game instead of paying attention to the lesson, he catches the student's eye and maintains eye contact for a few moments. Usually, letting the student know that he is aware of the behavior is enough. When it is not, without interrupting his instruction, Mr. Sanchez walks to the student's side and continues talking to the class. This is usually sufficient for the student to put the game away and begin concentrating on the classroom instruction.

Gail Tarron, a ninth-grade Spanish teacher, encourages students to appraise reality in an effort to change their behaviors. After one class, she questioned four girls to get them to realize how their cliquish behaviors affected others in the clique as well as the entire class. Rather than trying to break up the group or seat them in different parts of the classroom, she sought to show them the effects of their behavior on their learning and on other students in the class.

Critique of Redl's and Wattenberg's Theories

In spite of the contributions of Redl's and Wattenberg's theories and the potential they hold for helping teachers manage classrooms, several drawbacks should be mentioned. The proposal that teachers look students in the eye as a means of supporting self-control can be uncomfortable and insulting for students of some cultures, especially those who have been taught that such behavior shows disrespect. For example, some African American children and adolescents and members of some American Indian tribes consider looking an adult or authority figure in the eye to be rude or discourteous (Manning & Baruth, 2004). Thus, for some students in these cultural groups—and possibly others—a teacher looking the student in the eye as a means of supporting self-control could be disconcerting to the student rather than being helpful.

Also, it can be dangerous for a teacher to use physical proximity, such as standing near a student or touching a student on the shoulder, especially when students feel they have been threatened or touched in a harmful manner. In addition, although students in some cultural groups might prefer standing close to others, students of other cultural groups might consider close proximity to be threatening and even insulting.

Another problem is that, although understanding group life in the classroom is important, a teacher might not know appropriate management techniques to use with a group, and a situation can get out of hand.

In one school, a clique of intellectually bright and motivated girls shunned all others, but they significantly influenced the class by spreading rumors. As a group, they were leaders, yet the values they advocated were not always best for the class, nor were they conducive to positive classroom behavior. Although the teacher identified the group dynamics in motion, he did not know how to help the group members realize the negative effects of their behaviors or to encourage them to change.

Redl's and Wattenberg's theories provide an understanding of the girls' roles, but determining the appropriate management actions is difficult and requires considerable skill.

Finally, Redl and Wattenberg wrote prior to the safe schools movement. Schools have always had bullies and fights, but the level of violence faced by educators in the 21st century was not prevalent in the mid-1900s. However, even though Redl and Wattenberg did not address the issue of safety in schools, their theories, such as group life in the classroom, have potential for promoting safe schools.

Thus, even with these criticisms, Redl's and Wattenberg's management theories are sound and support good instructional practices. Providing situational assistance, supporting self-control, and understanding group dynamics are important for classroom management and instruction.

WILLIAM GLASSER

Biographical Sketch

In addition to serving in the U.S. Army, William Glasser worked as a psychiatric consultant with the California Youth Authority in Ventura, California; and as a psychiatrist with the California public schools in Sacramento, Palo Alto, and Los Angeles. He was also the founder and director of the Institute for Reality Therapy. A few of his widely translated books include *Reality Therapy: A New Approach to Psychiatry* (1965), which encouraged the idea of changing from past perspectives to present reality, and *Schools Without Failure* (1969), his first book specifically for teachers. His *Control Theory in the Classroom* (1985) provided foundational work for modern-day classroom management theorists.

Overview of Glasser's Theories

Working primarily with juvenile offenders, William Glasser at first based most of his writings on Freudian psychoanalytic theory, but he later switched to a more behavioral approach that focused on helping people look to present conditions to find solutions to problems. Glasser is well known for his *Reality Therapy* (Glasser, 1965) and **control theory** (Glasser, 1986), but his **Choice Theory** (Glasser, 1997, p. 597) seems to have the most relevance for educators who are interested in classroom management. Glasser (1997) believed that students have specific human needs and motives and should accept responsibility for their behavior. He also changed the terminology from control theory to choice theory because he found "choice theory to be a better and more positive-sounding name" (Glasser, 1997, p. 599).

Choice Theory, according to Glasser (1997), is based upon the belief that the only person whose behavior we can control is our own. The psychology of external control psychology destroys human relationships and prevents individuals from getting along with each other. In contrast, Choice Theory explains that adults and children choose to do everything they do. From birth to death, people behave in specific ways, based upon their "choice" of behavior, or what they think is most appropriate at the time (Clark, 2003). Because the only behavior we can control is our own, it is only the closeness of the relationship that a parent or teacher has with a child that will lead to a change in that student's maladaptive or destructive behavior (Beychok, 2003).

To Glasser, students (as well as all people) are driven by five basic psychological needs: the need for survival, the need to belong, the need for power, the need for freedom, and the need for fun. Once teachers meet these psychological needs, students will choose to demonstrate appropriate behavior. Likewise, when teachers fail to meet students' psychological needs, misbehaviors result. Using coercion or external controls, whether rewards or punishment (such as abuse, violence, criticizing, nagging, or complaining), is harmful because the students are not choosing their behavior; they are changing behavior to get the reward or avoid the punishment. Glasser believes that coercion does not work and should be replaced with Choice Theory.

Glasser's **Quality School** is one that helps students satisfy one or more psychological needs and adds quality to students' lives (Glasser, 1993). Quality is an imprecise term, but "it almost always includes caring for each other, is always useful, has always involved hard work on someone's part, and when we are involved with it, as either a provider or receiver, it always feels good" (Glasser, 1992, p. 37). Other topics discussed by Glasser include class meetings (Glasser, 1969) and his Ten-Step Discipline Guide (Glasser, 1965).

Contributions of Glasser's Theories

Glasser made several contributions to classroom management. In general, he believed that students think rationally, but teachers still need to make and enforce rules and, when necessary, impose appropriate consequences and offer suggestions for inappropriate behavior. However, he moved away from stimulus-response theory (e.g., Skinner's operant conditioning) and spoke against coercion, both in the form of rewards and punishments. He called for educators to make schools into caring places where students experience fun and where they feel a sense of belonging. The suggestions in Activity 2–3 provide a few examples of ways to provide this environment. Although educators can control only their own behavior, they still have the responsibility to help students satisfy their five psychological needs so they will be more likely to choose appropriate behavior. In fact, teachers who implement Choice Theory must always consider students' psychological needs.

According to Glasser, teachers must teach and manage in a way that adds quality to students' lives. In fact, Glasser defined education as "the process through which we discover that learning adds quality to our lives" (1992, p. 39). Furthermore, Glasser (1992, 1997) maintained that quality schools can have positive academic and behavior results. For example, he told how a school with 1,500 suspensions in one year improved so much that the next year suspensions were no longer considered a problem (Glasser, 1997). As educators met more of the students' psychological needs, behavior improved.

Activity 2–3

Developing a Sense of Belonging

The following are a few examples of ways to help students have a sense of belonging. After you read them, identify some additional ways you could help students develop this feeling in your classroom.

1. Allow students to participate in developing class rules and determining acceptable behavior in the classroom.

2. Have the students identify a name for their class or team.

3. Use bulletin boards in the classroom, library, other school locations, or even the walls of the halls to display the work of all students rather than just a selected few.

4. Encourage students to work in groups (e.g., peer tutoring groups or cooperative learning groups) so all students get to know their classmates.

Applications of Glasser's Theories

Glasser's theories can be translated into practical application in several ways. After you read about the following situations, apply Glasser's Choice Theory to the classroom described in How Would You React 2–3.

Perhaps Brenda King considered herself a caring teacher, but her students never knew it. Cold, distant, and aloof, she rarely smiled and abruptly answered students' questions with a lack of enthusiasm and with few words. It appeared that Ms. King thought students would interpret kindness and caring as weaknesses to be exploited. In turn, her students seemed to model themselves after her; they were withdrawn and lacked a cooperative and social spirit that characterized other fourth graders on her hall. Louisa Gonzales, another teacher, took the initiative to suggest to Ms. King that she show a little kindness and a caring attitude. "I know you care," Ms. Gonzales said, "so why don't you show it?" Ms. King took these words to heart. Gradually, as she changed, her students changed. Although Ms. King was never comfortable being too relaxed in the classroom, she did improve, and so did the attitudes and behavior of her students.

An example of the use of Choice Theory can be found in the experiences of Tyrone. Although he was new to the school, could not do the work successfully and was ostracized for a disabling condition, Tyrone still had a strong desire to belong, wanted friendships, and wanted to be liked by his peers. However, he made a choice to misbehave by talking out of turn, speaking sarcastically to the teacher, making cutting remarks about others, and disrupting his classes. Finally, one perceptive teacher realized Tyrone's psychological need to belong and worked with him individually whenever possible to help him see the choices he could make in his life and the results of those choices. In addition to assigning a peer tutor to help Tyrone academically, the teacher worked with other students to help them understand the nature of Tyrone's disability. Soon, Tyrone's behavior began to improve because he chose to change his behavior. As his behavior improved, other students in the class started to change their behavior and their feelings toward him.

As Glasser (1997) suggested, one of students' psychological needs is to enjoy some fun in school. Jermaine Watson was a considerate and gentle man, but he was convinced that an idle mind was the devil's workshop. Therefore, he never let the students in his classes stop working. Everyone always sat in rows and worked on drill sheets. Finally, Mr. Watson's principal convinced him that he probably could accomplish just as much if he let the students have a little fun. In reply to Mr. Watson's question "What kind of fun?" the principal suggested more group work, peer tutoring, opportunities for socialization,

How Would You React 2-3

Having Too Many Rules

Glasser talks about Choice Theory and the psychological needs of students. As you read the following scenario, think about whether or not Glasser's four psychological needs are being met in this classroom.

Shanika Dyar was a teacher who believed in the old adage of not smiling until after Thanksgiving. She had many rules and regulations for behavior in her class. Every move or action was spelled out and posted in the room. In addition to harsh penalties that she handed out for breaking the rules, Ms. Dyar coerced without hesitation, using rewards as well as punishments. She truly believed that she had her class-room management down to a fine art. However, even with her hard-fisted rules, Ms. Dyar still had to deal with students trying to find some way to break or bend a rule. Also, her students often appeared disinterested and showed little enthusiasm.

Relying on the ideas of Glasser, what advice would you offer Ms. Dyar? For example, what would Glasser say about the use of rewards and punishments in Ms. Dyar's classroom? Would he support their use or suggest something else? Do the actions of Ms. Dyar support Glasser's Choice Theory?

role playing, and anything that would allow students to get out of the straight rows and see learning as fun and enjoyable.

Freedom was another psychological need cited by Glasser. Melissa Owens was a practicum student with a cooperating teacher, Lynda Tallman, who had a rigid plan and schedule and refused to offer students any type of freedom. After Ms. Owens asked whether she could implement some teaching methods that would encourage at least a little freedom and even give the students a chance to help make some decisions in the classroom, Ms. Tallman reluctantly agreed. When students were allowed to select the type of project (skit, video, computer slide show, etc.) they would complete at the end of a unit, the entire atmosphere of the classroom began to change, with students appearing happier and behavior problems decreasing.

Critique of Glasser's Theories

Rather than looking only at the psychological aspects of behavior, Glasser looked at the total school environment. His commitment to schools without failure, quality schools, and quality teachers demonstrates his perception of teachers as more than just managers. In his more recent work, Glasser (1992, 1993, 1997) has made the transition from a focus on therapy (e.g., his Reality Therapy) to a more comprehensive school focus on changing student behavior in elementary, middle, and secondary schools and is working to address behavior problems and the safe schools issues faced by most contemporary educators. This lends credence to the belief that good management and good instruction go hand in hand. In addition, many educators agree with Glasser's opposition to coercion and his belief that teachers need to consider students' psychological needs.

In contrast, other educators have raised concerns about Glasser's theory. Although many like his proposal for quality schools, they stress that it might be difficult to implement them on a large-scale basis. Others who have long relied on stimulus-response theories and behavior modification (as Skinner suggested) find that making the switch to Choice Theory takes time and effort. Also, they point out that Glasser's original work focused on juvenile offenders rather than school students who demonstrate more typical problems such as talking, walking around the room, and generally goofing off.

With regard to cultural and gender diversity, Glasser's theories might be offensive to some students. For example, some Asian American cultures teach their children to respect their parents' and teachers' opinions and views rather than adopting their own. Because of this, some students might feel uncomfortable making the significant choices that Glasser's Choice Theory calls for. Also, in some Asian cultures, girls who have been taught to assume subservient roles might feel even more uncomfortable than boys in making choices. However, Asian Americans consist of many different Asian cultures, and teachers need to consider individual Asian American learners before drawing definitive conclusions.

THOMAS GORDON

Biographical Sketch

In addition to his military service in the U.S. Army Air Forces, Thomas Gordon was a faculty member at the University of Chicago, served in various consultant roles, maintained a private psychological practice, and was the president of Effectiveness Training, Inc., in Solana Beach, California. His publications include *Parent Effectiveness Training: The No-Lose Way to Raise Responsible Children* (1970) and *T.E.T.: Teacher Effectiveness Training* (1974). In *Teaching Children Self-Discipline* (1989) and he focused on understanding discipline, the various definitions of the term, and alternatives to disciplining students.

Overview of Gordon's Theories

Thomas Gordon believes that for teachers to be effective, they need skills that include the ability to identify problems and student needs, change the class environment and instructional practices to improve student behavior, send what he called **I-messages,** and listen actively. His emphasis on teaching effectiveness throughout his writing and his call for effective teachers indicates his belief that in order to be a good classroom manager, an educator must have implemented good instructional practices. Also, he believes teachers need to insist upon students engaging in self-discipline. Rather than yelling, screaming, and punishing students to no avail, teachers must realize that they cannot accept responsibility for someone else's behavior. Gordon also believes in the ineffectiveness of rewards and punishments.

Contributions of Gordon's Theories

Please go to
www.prenhall.com/manning
and click on "Reaching Out
with Technology" to find
more information.

Because it is impossible to explain all Gordon's theories in this brief summary, our focus is on selective aspects of his teacher effectiveness training and emphasis on **discipline as self-control.** More complete information can be found in his books and on the Internet sites listed in the "Reaching Out with Technology" section on this chapter's Companion Web Site.

"Who owns the problem?" asked Gordon (1974, p. 46). He maintains that some people will always say that the teachers own the problem because ultimately they are responsible for the classroom. However, Gordon believes the student owns the problem. For example, one daydreaming student does not interfere with the progress of an entire class. Although the teacher should send the message that daydreaming is unacceptable, the student owns the problem rather than the teacher. According to Gordon, educators must get the message to students that the problem rests with them, and they will have to accept responsibility for changing their behavior.

Along with promoting the idea of **problem ownership,** teachers need to engage in **active listening** (Gordon, 1974, p. 63). Students need to know that their teacher genuinely understands their comments, concerns, and behaviors. Teachers who stay silent or only briefly acknowledge students' comments are unlikely to engage in active listening. However, teachers who engage in active listening can better understand behavior problems, help students identify the causes of the misbehavior, and perhaps be more successful in convincing students to accept responsibility or ownership of the problem and in helping determine a solution for the problem.

One of the best ways to correct or prevent misbehaviors is for a teacher to employ what Gordon (1989) called **empathic understanding** in which a teacher learns about individual students and each one's specific needs, interests, and abilities. In this way, a teacher can tailor curricular and instructional decisions toward individual students without sacrificing academic rigor, achievement, productivity, or creativity. Among the causes of students' misbehaviors might be feelings of inadequacy, undesirable home situations, or events in classes earlier in the day, just to name a few. Activity 2–4 identifies some specific activities that teachers can use to provide empathic understanding as a means of improving student behavior and asks you to identify others.

Another important concept in Gordon's theory is the *I-message.* Gordon suggests that when teachers use the word *you,* (1974, p. 136), they focus the message only at the student rather than conveying how the teacher feels. Statements such as "You stop that!" (p. 136) or "You had better quiet down or else!" (p. 136) pose roadblocks to effective management. Instead, teachers need to use I-messages (p. 136) and express how they feel about the behavior or how it affects them. For example, instead of constantly using the word you (p. 136), effective teachers use statements such as "I'm frustrated by all this noise" (p. 137), "I'm really annoyed when people get pushed around in this room" (p. 137), "I have difficulty working in all this clutter," or "I am troubled when I don't receive your homework."

Activity 2-4

Providing Empathic Understanding

Teachers can improve student behavior by

1. Increasing the use of student ideas in instructional interactions,
2. Using more discussion and dialogue with students,
3. Praising students more when appropriate and deserved,
4. Tailoring curricular and instructional decisions for individual students,
5. Placing emphasis on productivity and creativity,
6. Using learning goals that were planned cooperatively by students and teacher,
7. Using more real and genuine teacher talk.

What additional ideas or specific activities can you identify to use empathic understanding in your classroom?

Source: Developed from T. Gordon. (1989). *Teaching children self-discipline: Promoting self-discipline in children.* New York: Penguin, p. 202.

Gordon also believes that teachers need to modify their classroom environments. As Gordon (1974, p. 156) stated, "teachers know from experience, most classrooms unfortunately are designed, constructed, and furnished in ways that make it difficult for students to stay motivated and involved in the learning process." In his books, Gordon offers pages of ways to modify class environments, such as establishing a sense of community, rearranging desks and bookshelves for ease of movement, displaying student work on the walls, and changing instructional approaches. (See Management Tip 2–3.) Creative teachers need to consider their own classrooms and determine the changes that will contribute to improved behavior and attitudes.

Gordon (1974, p. 205) explained how, in a school climate full of rewards and punishments, students "learn the value of winning and looking good." He called this "needing to win, hating to lose." Throughout the day, teachers manipulate students with commendations, grades recorded in teachers' notebooks, special privileges, gold stars, and smiles. Often in a single classroom several students will have notebooks covered with reward stickers, whereas other students have few or no stickers. According to Gordon, such actions result in some students, especially those oriented toward winning, surpassing their peers. The resulting problem is that not all students can win, and only a few come out on top. Students with limited abilities are reminded, directly or indirectly, that they are inadequate, incompetent, below average, and underachievers. To eliminate this, Gordon stresses the importance of providing an environment with less emphasis on winning and losing.

No classroom is without conflicts, and Gordon (1974, p. 228) proposed the following six-step problem-solving process (Figure 2–2) for resolving conflicts. This six-step approach can be used to address almost any problem or conflict, including students who constantly talk, students in cliques, students making too much noise going to lunch, or abusive bullies on the playground. One key is for students to know that the teacher is sincere in working

Figure 2-2 Gordon's
Six-Step Approach

1. Defining the problem
2. Generating possible solutions
3. Evaluating the solutions
4. Deciding which solution is best
5. Determining how to implement the decision
6. Assessing how well the solution solved the problem

Developed from: T. Gordon. (1974). *T.E.T.: Teacher effectiveness training.* New York: Wyden Books, p. 228.

through the six-step approach with the students and that the students also know that they own the problem and they are responsible for the resolution.

Along with the concept of conflict resolution, Gordon also believes that students should be taught self-discipline. In *Teaching Children Self-Discipline: Promoting self-discipline in children* (1989, p. 3), he offered the following definitions. As a noun, the term discipline is understood to mean "behavior and order," such as "discipline in the classroom." The noun form suggests organization, knowing and following rules and procedures, and the consideration of the rights of others. As a verb, the term discipline means "control, punish, penalize, correct, or chastise." Gordon maintained that disciplining (verb) students might be the *least* (italics Gordon's) effective way to get discipline (noun) at home or in the classroom. He further suggested that discipline in the form of punishment produces aggression, hostility, hyperactivity, and violence in students. Ultimately, Gordon believes that discipline should be taught and nurtured rather than imposed upon students. Instead of using rewards and punishments, Gordon (1989) suggested that educators use noncontrolling methods to change a student's behavior with the goal of having the student accept ownership of the problem (i.e., the student's behavior is causing personal problems and possibly problems for the teacher and other students, as well). Figure 2–3 provides a summary of Gordon's ideas to help adults develop noncontrolling behavior.

★ **Management Tip 2-3**

Arranging the Classroom

Like the routines that you use in class, the arrangement of the classroom can help classroom management. In general, you can experiment with a variety of seating arrangements (rows, a circle, a box, U-shape, etc.) until you find the best one for your class. Don't be afraid to change or vary the arrangement throughout the year.

Elementary
Use different seating patterns at desks and on the class rug or carpet. For some activities, assign spaces. For others, allow students to select where they wish to sit.

Secondary
As you arrange the desks in your room, put yourself in the place of your students. Sit in each set and look around for distractions and invasions of personal space.

Application of Gordon's Theories

Some teachers, such as those in the following examples, find Gordon's theories to be effective and relatively easy to implement. After you read these examples, consider Sammy in How Would You React 2–4 and use Gordon's theories to develop a response.

During the first few weeks of school, Paul McGee gives his students an interest inventory, reviews their permanent records, talks with their parents, and interviews each student. He learns as much as he can about students and looks for their challenges and potential problems as well as their strengths on which he can build instruction. Mr. McGee has few behavior problems—mainly, he thinks, because his students know he is interested, caring, and concerned.

When Gloria Currie saw Jermesha enter the room, she could tell that the girl was angry and frustrated. When Ms. Currie asked Jermesha what was wrong, the response was, "Nothing's wrong and I don't want to talk about it." Ms. Currie's only reply was, "OK, but if you feel you need an ear, I have a free period

Please go to
www.prenhall.com/manning
and click on the Management Tips for this chapter to complete management activities and find more information on classroom arrangements and activities for planning your classroom.

Alternative 1	Learn what the student needs (e.g., identify the cause of the behavior).
Alternative 2	Let's make a trade (e.g., encourage students to substitute one behavior for another).
Alternative 3	Modify the environment (e.g., remove temptations and reasons to misbehave).
Alternative 4	Use the confrontive I-message (e.g., use a nonevaluative message that tells the effect of the behaviors on adults).
Alternative 5	Use the preventive I-message (e.g., convey, to the student, a need whose fulfillment requires support and cooperation).
Alternative 6	Shift gears to reduce resistance (e.g., change strategies when I-messages provoke feelings of discomfort, guilt, and denial).
Alternative 7	Apply problem solving (e.g., use the six-step approach).
Alternative 8	Find the primary feeling when angry (e.g., when venting anger in I-messages, consider the source of the anger and change strategies).

Figure 2–3 Steps to Noncontrolling Behavior for Adults

Source: Developed from T. Gordon. (1989). *Teaching children self-discipline: Promoting self-discipline in children.* New York: Penguin, pp. 109–127.

later today." That afternoon, Jermesha found Ms. Currie and shared the problem. With Ms. Currie's help and using Gordon's six-step approach, Jermesha was able to find a way to solve her problem.

Larry Mailhot has a "NO U" policy in his classroom. He encourages his students to focus on sending I-messages, and he tries to model the rule for his students. For example, after he noticed a few of the members of his government class picking on a special education student, he approached the problem and began a class discussion by saying, "I become concerned and annoyed whenever I see someone being bullied by others."

Critique of Gordon's Theories

Gordon's theories contain a number of appealing aspects, including his emphasis on teachers improving their instructional effectiveness, students owning the problem rather than the teacher, the advocacy of positive student–teacher relationships, and the idea of teachers conveying their feelings (e.g., through I-messages) to students. Gordon's emphasis on self-discipline is another plus for teachers, students, and advocates of safe schools. In many cases, teachers will find that most of their theories are workable and effective and that they contribute to instructional effectiveness.

However, Gordon's theories do have several weaknesses. First, teachers have long used you-messages as well as rewards and punishments. That is the way schools have operated

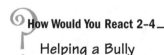

How Would You React 2-4

Helping a Bully

Thomas Gordon has a number of ideas that can be applied to classroom management (refer to Table 2–4). Think about them as you read the following scenario.

Sammy Lombardo continually misbehaves. He does just enough school work to get by, talks about the "reefer" in his bookbag, bullies smaller boys, and disrupts class almost every day. Ms. Vick, one of his teachers, has spoken with him on a number of occasions. When she called Sammy's father to explain the behav-

ior problems, Mr. Lombardo said, "I make him behave at home—you make him behave at school." Then, he hung up the telephone. Although Ms. Vick tried punishments and complaining, nothing seemed to work. "Maybe I'll just have to put up with Sammy's behavior the rest of the year," she said to a colleague.

Which of Gordon's ideas could be applied in Ms. Vick's classroom? Give an example of a way that Ms. Vick could implement one or more of these ideas.

CASE STUDY
"I Hate Your (Obscenity) Guts"

Dennis Shapiro was a first-year teacher in an urban school that had a reputation for having more than its share of behavior problems. A tough taskmaster, perhaps because of the school's reputation, Mr. Shapiro was a firm disciplinarian who tried to address all behavior problems regardless of their severity. Although some teachers in the school admired his demanding authority, others thought he was on an ego trip and always wanted to exert his power. People observing him often felt uncomfortable because they never knew the extent of his strictness.

One day, Mr. Shapiro was teaching a mathematics class. All the students were quiet, but they were not particularly attentive. Some appeared to be listening but were not actively involved; others did not even feign interest. Tyrone Doss, who had a reputation for being quiet and well behaved, had a comic book inside his mathematics book. When Mr. Shapiro asked him to put away the comic book, Tyrone obeyed. However, within 10 minutes, Tyrone had slipped the comic book back into his mathematics book. Again Mr. Shapiro told Tyrone to put the comic book away with the same results. Ten minutes later, Mr. Shapiro firmly told Tyrone to put away the comic book or he would take it.

At this point, Tyrone jumped up and yelled, "I hate your f*****g guts! I ain't gonna put it up, and you ain't gonna take it!"

Unfortunately, we will never know what Mr. Shapiro would have done because just as Tyrone shouted his obscenity and his refusal to obey, the assistant principal walked past the room, heard the commotion, and escorted Tyrone to his office.

Identify what you think were the underlying causes of the incident. Then consider the foundational theorists (Skinner's operant conditioning or behavior modification, Redl's and Wattenberg's group life and supporting self-control, Glasser's noncoercive discipline, and Gordon's self-discipline and problem ownership) discussed in this chapter and suggest how each would have addressed this classroom management situation *before* the incident occurred or *after* it happened. Finally, drawing from all these foundational models, explain how you would have reacted and identify the classroom management strategies you would have employed to deal with it or to prevent it.

 You can record your answers to these questions online on this book's Companion Web Site at *www.prenhall.com/manning*.

for decades, and change will come slowly. Second, Gordon's theories might have less use when serious behaviors (e.g., fights and other acts of violence) break out. I-messages have little relevance when a student is in danger, and a six-step problem-solving approach cannot be implemented when a quick and decisive action is needed. In the long run though, Gordon's theories hold considerable promise for classroom management.

They also hold promise in today's diverse school systems. Gordon's condemnation of rewards and punishments seems appropriate for students in some cultures, who might not

Developing Your Personal Philosophy

Examining the Foundational Theorists

Go back to the ideas mentioned in Activity 1–2 in the previous chapter and examine the foundational theorists in light of these questions. Then, make a chart by listing each theory in a column on the left. Across the page, make three more columns. In each of these columns, list a phrase to stand for one of the following questions:

Similarities: What beliefs of this theorist are similar to the beliefs of the other foundational theorists?

Differences: What beliefs of this theorist are different from the beliefs of the other foundational theorists?

Appeal: What beliefs of this theorist appeal to me?

Finally, as you review each theory, fill in the information on the chart.

want to excel at another's expense. Replacing you-messages with I-messages also seems appropriate for diverse cultural groups. Likewise, most cultural groups will agree with the idea of positive student–teacher relationships, as well as students committing to self-discipline rather than teacher-imposed discipline.

CONCLUDING REMARKS

Chapter 2 provided an overview of the foundational theorists who did the groundwork for many of the effective classroom management practices today. Teachers use Skinner's operant conditioning when they reward positive behavior and fail to reward negative behaviors. They take advantage of Redl's and Wattenberg's theories when they consider the effects of group behavior on individual behavior, and vice versa. Glasser's choice theory is used when teachers conclude that students choose appropriate or inappropriate behavior. Last, the influence of Gordon's work is clear when teachers consider individual student needs and insist that students take ownership of behavior problems. Now that you have had a chance to read about these foundational theorists and their ideas for classroom management, complete the activity in Developing Your Personal Philosophy. Then read and react to the Case Study, which contains the true story of an otherwise well-behaved middle school boy who felt his teacher had pushed him too far.

As we look at the more contemporary theorists in the remainder of this book, remember these foundational theorists and look for their influence in other models. Although no one foundational theorist has all the answers, each has contributed significantly to contemporary classroom management and to safer schools.

Suggested Readings

Davidson, J., & Wood, C. (2004). A conflict resolution model. *Theory into Practice 43*(1), 6–13. The authors present a conflict resolution model that includes the core elements of Thomas Gordon's theory of healthy relationships.

Gaynor, S. T. (2004). Skepticism of caricature: B. F. Skinner turns 100. *Skeptical Inquirer 28*(1), 26–29. Gaynor looks at some misperceptions surrounding B. F. Skinner.

Gordon, T. (1989). *Teaching children self discipline: Promoting self-discipline in children.* New York: Penguin. Gordon's proposal that students are responsible for their own behavior, and, therefore, should acquire self-discipline continues to be relevant for contemporary educators.

Gottlieb, J., & Polirstok, S. (2005). Program to reduce behavioral infractions and referrals to special education. *Children & Schools, 27*(1), 53–57. Behavior modification strategies play a part in reducing referrals and improving academic performance.

Glasser, W. (2002). *Unhappy Teenagers.* New York: HarperCollins. Glasser examines contemporary adolescent problems and the use of Choice Theory as a method to help adolescents deal with their behavior.

Kohn, A. (1993). *Punished by rewards: The trouble with gold stars, incentive plans, A's, praise, and other bribes.* Boston: Houghton-Mifflin. Kohn, also discussed in this book, presents his concerns with rewards.

Olive, E. C. (2004). Practical tools for positive behavior facilitation. *Reclaiming Children and Youth, 13*(1), 43–47. Positive Behavior Facilitation, a management model, explores the differences between behavior management and behavior change.

Wattenberg, W. (1977). The ecology of classroom behavior. *Theory into Practice, 16*(4), 256–261. Wattenberg explains four different theoretical positions that hold potential for improving student behavior and increasing on-task behaviors.

CHAPTER 3

Exploring the Theories of Assertive Discipline: *Lee Canter and Marlene Canter*

Focusing Questions

After reading this chapter, you should be able to answer the following questions:

1. What is Assertive Discipline, what are its major concepts, and what are teachers' roles and responsibilities?

2. What are significant advantages and disadvantages of Assertive Discipline?

3. How can Assertive Discipline be translated into practical application? Do the practical applications reflect a teacher's philosophical and psychological beliefs?

4. How can teachers determine Assertive Discipline's propensity for addressing students' psychological or developmental needs?

5. Does Assertive Discipline have the potential for addressing student misbehaviors in contemporary classrooms? If so, how?

6. How does Assertive Discipline address diversity perspectives, specifically students' diverse cultural, gender, and social class backgrounds?

7. What are some additional sources of information, such as Internet sites, books, and journal articles on Assertive Discipline?

Lee Canter and Marlene Canter (Canter, 1974; Canter & Canter, 1976, 1992) proposed a classroom management model called Assertive Discipline. This limit-setting approach requires teachers to be assertive rather than passive or hostile, to state rules consistently and clearly, to follow through appropriately, to apply positive consequences when students meet behavioral expectations, and to apply negative consequences when students fail to behave appropriately. In this chapter, in addition to exploring the key concepts of Assertive Discipline and some views of its critics, you will read about practical applications and how the model relates to our increasingly multicultural schools.

Key Terms

Assertive style
Behavior modification
Broken-record response
Class rules
Consequences
Discipline hierarchy
Hostile style
Negative consequence
Nonassertive style
Positive reinforcement
Severe clause

LEE AND MARLENE CANTER: BIOGRAPHICAL SKETCH

Assertive Discipline, or the Canter model, is a classroom management model developed by Lee and Marlene Canter. An educator and clinical social worker, Lee Canter has devoted the majority of his professional career to helping educators work more effectively with students with behavioral disorders. Marlene Canter has advanced training in special education. Through their research and personal experiences, the Canters developed Assertive Discipline, a classroom management model in which teachers define and enforce standards for students and classrooms. Their firm, Canter & Associates (Santa Monica, California), offers books, videotapes, multimedia packages, and training (including professional development workshops and graduate-level courses) in discipline and classroom management.

OVERVIEW OF ASSERTIVE DISCIPLINE

To help you understand the Canters' model of classroom management, this section provides a general discussion of its basic concepts, philosophical beliefs, and teacher responsibilities. The next section further explores these basic ideas and shows how they are applied in classroom situations.

Key Concepts

Figure 3–1 provides an overview of the key concepts in the Canters' Assertive Discipline, a classroom management model that highlights consistency, rewards and consequences, and positive relationship building. According to the Canters, when teachers give students clear expectations and consistent follow-through, most students choose appropriate behavior (Canter, 1974; Canter & Canter, 1976, 1992).

Philosophical and Psychological Foundations

The concept of rewards and punishments reflects, in part, B. F. Skinner's **behavior modification** (sometimes called operant conditioning or stimulus-response theory) or the belief that **positive reinforcement** or a reward should follow positive behavior. The Canters also believe that punishment or unpleasant consequences should follow negative behavior, with the unpleasant consequence or penalty system having increasingly severe sanctions. For example, a student who raises his or her hand before answering a question should be rewarded; likewise, the student who blurts out the answer without permission should receive some type of **negative consequence,** with the consequences becoming more serious if the behavior continues. Similarly, teachers should reward students who have their books and learning materials available and who work on task; conversely, they should provide negative consequences for students who continue to be unprepared and waste time.

The Canters identified three response styles, or philosophical stances, that teachers use to manage a classroom. The first, the **nonassertive style,** is usually ineffective and is used by teachers who fail to establish clear standards of behavior or who fail to follow through on threats with appropriate actions. The following are some examples of a teacher using a nonassertive style:

"I've asked you repeatedly to stop talking, and you continue to do it. Please stop."

"Why do you and Bill continue to fight? You've been told time and again to stop it."

Rewards and punishments are effective.

- Both teachers and students have rights in the classroom.
- While giving rewards and punishments, teachers must work toward creating an optimal learning environment.
- Teachers must apply rules and enforce consequences consistently without bias or discrimination.
- Teachers should use a discipline hierarchy with the consequences appropriate for the grade level.
- Rather than using a nonassertive or hostile response style, teachers should be assertive.

Figure 3-1 Key Concepts of Assertive Discipline

"Sarah, the rules are clearly posted on the wall. I don't know why you continue to break them."

In contrast to nonassertive teachers, teachers with a **hostile style** use an aversive approach, shout, and use threats and sarcasm. Although results might be instantaneous, this style has the potential for emotional harm and possible abuse. For example, a hostile teacher might say one of the following:

"Sit down and shut up!"
"Put that comic book away or you'll wish you had!"
"Do that again, Nelson, and see what you get. I've had my fill of you!"

Instead of recommending nonassertive or hostile approaches, the Canters praise teachers with an **assertive style** who clearly and specifically place limits and rewards or consequences on students. Making their expectations known to students, parents, and administrators, assertive teachers not only insist that their expectations be followed but also provide reasonable consequences that are appropriate for the misbehavior for students who choose not to comply with expectations. Likewise, they provide positive consequences for students who do comply. Assertive teachers often use the Canters' **broken-record response** by repeating the same or a similar request for compliance a maximum of three times before invoking the consequence. Although some students like to argue, perhaps to test the teacher's limits, the broken-record technique often works far better than threatening, cajoling, and trying to win students over by saying please. Examples of comments from an assertive teacher include the following:

"We do not ask questions without permission—you must raise your hand."
"Justin, that is your warning for leaning back in the chair. Put the chair down now or you will face a loss of classroom privileges."
"Quentina, you did a good job leading your cooperative learning group."

Teachers' Roles and Responsibilities

In their book *Assertive Discipline: Positive Behavior Management for Today's Classroom,* the Canters called for teachers to help students "take charge" (Canter & Canter, 1992, p. xviii) of the classroom in a firm and positive manner. To help teachers do so, the Canters identified three responsibilities or roles of teachers. In addition to being consistent, teachers must accept the role of giver of rewards and punishments and must be able to hand out rewards and punishments consistently, regardless of the student or the situation. Finally, teachers must be willing to work toward positive interactions with students, in part by creating an optimal learning environment within the classroom. A safe learning environment does not just happen. Instead, students must be taught how to work and socialize together in a comfortable environment (Smith, 2001). Activity 3–1 looks at a few ways to create this environment and then asks you to develop some additional strategies.

APPLYING ASSERTIVE DISCIPLINE

Now that you have an understanding of some of the basic concepts of the Canters' model of classroom management, you can examine these principles in more detail and explore how educators have used them in the classroom.

Activity 3–1

Providing an Optimal Learning Environment

Educators can provide an optimal learning environment by

1. Encouraging students to collaborate, work as teams, and trust each other,
2. Establishing common learning and behavior goals toward which students and teachers can work,
3. Providing curricular content based on the students' cognitive ability and their developmental levels,
4. Helping students understand the relevance of curricular content,
5. Providing an atmosphere of acceptance of students and their diversities,
6. Adopting a genuine student-centered philosophy that addresses students' needs and builds upon learning strengths,
7. Providing a safe learning environment where students feel comfortable voicing opinions,
8. Providing an overall class and school environment that reflects a concern for and a commitment to safe schools and where students and teachers can work without fear of violent acts.

What other ways might teachers use to provide an optimal learning environment and to promote learning and positive behavior? How might this vary with the age of the students? What are some ways that you could develop this type of environment in your classroom?

Rewards and Punishments

In order for Assertive Discipline to work, the Canters suggested that, ideally, an entire school should adopt the model for use in all its classrooms. All teachers and administrators involved with the education of children and adolescents need to adopt the principles of the program (Keiper, 2004). Then, individual teachers can develop a specific behavior plan based on the school model. Consisting of a few simple yet specific rules along with the rewards for following the rules and the consequences of breaking them, this plan should be displayed in the classroom and distributed to parents. Management Tip 3–1 provides more information on rewards. In all cases, teachers must apply the rules and enforce the consequences without bias or discrimination. **Consequences,** or punishments, might include exclusion from certain classroom privileges, time-out, contact with the parent or guardian, referral to an administrator, or detention. It is also important to note that each day begins with a clean slate, which means that consequences accumulated by a student one day are never carried over to the next day.

Teachers can maintain a record of consequences by marking names on a clipboard or adopting whatever manner they consider easiest. In some instances, a name on the clipboard and a series of check marks beside the name for misbehaviors, if necessary, can serve as a visual reminder to a student. However, Canter and Canter (1992) caution that some teachers might use names on the chalkboard as a means of humiliating students.

Discipline Hierarchy

The Canters suggest that teachers use a **discipline hierarchy** that informs students of consequences and the order in which they will be imposed. The following is an example of a discipline hierarchy adapted from *Assertive Discipline: Positive Behavior Management for Today's Classrooms* by the Canters (1992).

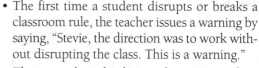

Management Tip 3-1

Establishing Rewards

There are many different types of rewards:

- Social reinforcers
    Words
    Smiles
    Gestures
- Graphic reinforcers
    Star
    Sticker
    Checkmark
- Activity reinforcers
    Free time
    Special game
- Tangible reinforcers
    Bookmark
    Pencils and other supplies
    Certificates

Elementary
The Canters advocate a "marble jar" as a reward. When everything goes well, add a marble to the jar. When the jar is filled, provide the entire class with a reward.

Secondary
Give students a stamp when they are prepared for class each day. To receive the stamp, a student must

- Be on time to class,
- Have supplies, including textbook, notebook, and pen or pencil,
- Have homework completed.

Give each stamp a point value and count a week's worth of stamps as a quiz grade.

- The first time a student disrupts or breaks a classroom rule, the teacher issues a warning by saying, "Stevie, the direction was to work without disrupting the class. This is a warning."
- The second or third time the same student disrupts in the same day, the teacher says, "Stevie, our rule is no talking while working. You have chosen to take a 5-minute time-out at the back table."
- The fourth time the same student disrupts by knocking his books off his desk, the teacher says, "Stevie, you know our rule about classroom disruptions. You have chosen to have your parents notified." In this case, the teacher typically gives the parents a call or sends a note home. As one teacher told the Canters (1992, p. 6): "At recess, we [student and teacher] went to the office. I picked up the phone, handed it to him, and told him to call home and explain to his parents that his behavior had resulted in their being contacted."
- The fifth time the same student disrupts the class in any way, the teacher says, "Stevie, our rule is no class disruptions. You have chosen to go to the office to talk with the principal about your behavior."
- **Severe clause.** The Canters (2001) recognize that in some cases, students demonstrate severe behavior that results in what is known as the severe clause. Students who demonstrate behavior that the teacher considers threatening or severe are sent directly to the principal. This severe clause in the discipline hierarchy is a helpful way to remove students from the classroom if they pose a threat to others. As the Canters (1992, p. 87) explain, when a student becomes angry and begins to hit a classmate, the teacher calmly and assertively says, "There is no fighting in this classroom. You know the rule. You have chosen to go to the principal's office immediately. We will discuss this later."

Please go to *www.prenhall.com/manning* and click on the Management Tips for this chapter to complete management activities and find more information on the use of rewards.

Appropriate Consequences

The Canters (2001) maintain that consequences should be appropriate for the grade level and should reflect the difference in the developmental and psychological levels of the students. Thus, they suggest similar yet slightly different discipline hierarchies for the primary (K–3) and upper elementary (4–6) grades. For example, in grades K–3, a second misbehavior might result in the teacher keeping the child near, but apart from the group, for a short time. Should the child misbehave a third time, the teacher removes the child from the group for a longer period of time. The hierarchy for grades 4 and 5 might be the same, except that a second offense brings 10 minutes away from the group (but near the teacher), and a third offense results in 15 minutes away from the group as the misbehaving student writes in his or her behavior journal. An effective consequence for grades 4–12, this journal provides a place where students write accounts of their misbehavior, reasons for breaking the rule, and alternative actions that they might or should have taken.

For a message to have full effect, the Canters recommend that teachers maintain eye contact. This lets the student know the teacher is in control and is being assertive. As one student said, "We know Ms. Dunn means business when she looks us in the eye." This practice can be effective, but it should be used with caution. In fact, teachers should not insist on eye contact with all students, because students from some cultures might consider eye contact rude or insulting.

Management Tip 3–2 looks at the five steps for teachers practicing assertive discipline.

☆ **Management Tip 3-2**

Practicing Assertive Discipline

The Canters maintain teachers should assertively take charge of classroom management by

- Recognizing and removing roadblocks such as negative expectations based on
  Culture,
  Socioeconomic status,
  Gender,
  Other diversities,
- Practicing assertive responses,
- Setting limits,
- Following through on limits,
- Implementing a system of positive assertions such as
  Personal attention from the teacher,
  Positive notes/phones calls to parents,
  Special awards or privileges,
  Material rewards.

Rights of Students and Teachers

The Canters (Canter, 1974; Canter & Canter, 1976, 1992) believe that students and teachers have rights in the classroom, as shown in Figure 3–2. To ensure these rights, teachers must identify their rules and expectations clearly and follow through with any established consequences for not adhering to them. Noting the connections between classroom instruction and management, the Canters believe that teachers who fail to teach and who deny students opportunities to learn usually have an inability to manage or control the class. Because effective teaching and effective managing go hand in hand, teachers should not be so hounded by behavior problems that their teaching effectiveness is lost. Also, in opposition to those who believe that firm control is stifling and inhumane, the Canters maintain that teachers who act assertively are more effective than nonassertive or hostile teachers.

To the Canters (1992), effective teachers establish an optimal learning environment and use the assertive response style that places limits and rewards (or consequences) on students. However, before limits can be set, students and the classroom teacher need to know what behaviors are expected. The Canters recommend that a teacher, perhaps with the assistance of the students, make and post the **class rules.** (See Management Tip 3–3.) In addition to being age and grade-level appropriate, the rules need to be specific ("Raise your hand before speaking") rather than general or vague ("Be good") and should clearly spell out the behavior expectation ("Keep your hands to yourself").

The following are examples of two assertive and one nonassertive teacher in that order. After reading them, review the situation in How Would You React 3–1.

Please go to *www.prenhall.com/manning* and click on the Management Tips for this chapter to complete management activities and find more information on taking charge of the classroom.

> Luis Kitano reminds her students at the beginning of each lesson: "I expect you to be prepared. That means you should raise your hand before speaking, listen attentively so you will know what to do, and have only your book and notebook on your desk."
>
> Brenda Miller was a teacher in an urban school that was known for its rowdy students. However, Ms. Miller rarely had a problem. Posting her class rules on the wall and

Figure 3–2 Basic
Rights of Students and
Teachers

Students have the right to

   Have an optimal learning environment,

   Have teachers who help them reduce inappropriate behavior,

   Have teachers who provide appropriate support for appropriate behavior,

   Have teachers who do not violate the students' best interests,

   Choose how to behave with the advance knowledge of the consequences that will consistently follow.

Teachers have the right to

   Maintain an optimal learning environment,

   Expect appropriate behavior,

   Expect help from administrators and parents,

   Ensure students' rights and responsibilities are met by a discipline plan that clearly states expectations,
      consistently applies the consequences, and does not violate the best interests of the students.

Source: Developed from L. Canter. (1974). *The ways and hows of working with behavior problems in the classroom.* San Rafael,
CA: Academic Therapy Press; L. Canter & M. Canter. (1976).

Assertive Discipline: A take-charge approach for today's educators. Santa Monica, CA: Lee Canter & Associates; and L. Canter &
M. Canter. (1992). *Assertive Discipline: Positive behavior management for today's classrooms.* Santa Monica, CA: Lee Canter &
Associates.

repeating specific behavior instructions at the beginning of her lessons, she informed
and reminded the students of her expectations and always held them accountable.
Although she never demonstrated hostile behavior, she was always firm. Brenda had
a reputation as a no-nonsense person, but the students liked her because they had a
good environment in which to learn and they knew the limits on their behavior.

How Would You React 3-1

Setting Limits

The Canters believe that effective teachers use an assertive
response style that establishes limits and consequences.
Review the section of this chapter that discusses the roles
and responsibilities of teachers as well as Figure 3–2.
Then read the following scenario and respond to the
questions at the end.

> Throughout his school years, happy-go-lucky Art Brady hated
> to follow rules. Thus, beginning his first year as a teacher, he
> transferred his feelings into his classroom. He believed that
> his fifth-grade students would behave if he allowed them free-
> dom and gave them lots of choices. As Art was fond of say-
> ing, "Students are creative and should be free to express their
> individuality in both schoolwork and behavior." Although he
> conveyed to students that he expected them to act their best,
> he refused to place specific rules on the classroom wall. "That's
> too confining" was all Art would say about it.
>
> By the third month of school, Art's class bordered on chaos.
> Students talked incessantly, walked around the room, and picked

on each other. Art could not conduct instruction, and students
who wanted to learn could not. Teaching became so frustrating
and dissatisfying that Art considered leaving the profession.

Working collaboratively in groups of three or four,
respond to the following questions:

1. According to the Canters, what type of teacher was
   Art Brady?
2. What can he do at this point to gain control of
   his class?
3. What might he do in the future?
4. Would being an assertive teacher stifle creativity in
   the classroom? Why?
5. What rules would you suggest that he use in his
   classroom?
6. How might these rules change if Mr. Brady were
   teaching an eighth-grade class?

Jessica May was a first-year teacher in the same school as Brenda Miller. Unlike Brenda, Jessica seemed to be afraid of her students and was reluctant to establish rules because she thought the students would not like her if she did. Instead, she made empty threats, demonstrated inconsistent behavior, and was the epitome of nonassertiveness. Her favorite phrases included "if that's OK with you, class," "this is the fourth (or any other number) time I've told you to be quiet," and "why can't you behave?" As can be expected, Jessica often questioned whether she wanted to continue teaching.

Not only is it imperative for assertive teachers to establish rules, they must learn to follow through when behaviors exceed these limits or expectations. In addition, teachers should provide positive consequences when students obey rules and meet expectations.

When Chela Little sent her fourth-grade class out to the playground for recess, she clearly told them to stay in back of the school because the kindergarten children were using the front playground to visit the fire truck. Temptation proved too much for five of her students, who ventured around to the front of the school. Rather than resorting to angry statements like "I told you to stay in the back; now, why did you go to the front? You just had to disobey me, didn't you?" Ms. Little assertively and calmly told the five misbehaving students the consequences of their actions: "You were told not to go. That is a check by your names." Then, she told the students who remained in back of the school: "I appreciate your decision not to go to the front. That was a wise choice and you should be commended."

Management Tip 3–3

Developing Rules

General rules might include the following:
- Treat others the way you want to be treated.
- Respect the property of others.
- Be polite/courteous to each other.
- Keep your school clean.

Specific rules might include the following:
- Raise your hand before speaking.
- Ask for permission before leaving your seat.

Elementary

Wash your hands before eating your snack.

Keep your eyes on the teacher when the teacher is talking.

Always be a good listener.

Secondary

Be in your seat with your book and homework on your desk when the class bell rings.

Listen and follow directions.

Leave your seat only with permission from the teacher.

When using rules

Establish the rules,

Set the consequences,

Determine what will happen if the penalty is not completed,

Determine what will happen if the behavior continues,

Teach the rules and consequences to the students.

Please go to *www.prenhall.com/manning* and click on the Management Tips for this chapter to complete management activities and find more information on developing rules.

According to the Canters (1992), assertive discipline requires teachers to be fair and consistent in their actions and not to show prejudice toward any students. This is especially important in contemporary schools, where respect for diversity and the need for effective instruction within a safe school environment are essential. Unfortunately, Jef Unger did not believe in this philosophy.

Jef Unger had many behavior problems in his class that resulted from his lack of consistency. One week he would allow students to walk around the classroom; the next week he would get upset about it. Even in the same day, he would punish Vilay for talking to Stuart when he should be working on his homework but ignore the same behavior when Shavondria talked to Delores. As Jef said, "I know which students are good ones, and Shavondria shouldn't have to follow all the rules. The bad ones, well, when they're like Vilay, I really make them toe the line. And sometimes, when things are going well, I just ignore some misbehaviors. I don't want to break the flow by enforcing rules."

Like Jef Unger, some teachers have preconceived or even negative expectations for a few students. This means that a teacher might make excuses for the behavior of some students while condemning the behavior of others. After reading the following comments, which illustrate an excuse and a negative expectation held by teachers, evaluate the actions of Louisa Del Campo in How Would You React 3–2.

"She's usually a good student but she's been sick. That probably explains why she's been acting up."

"Look at his brothers and sisters. How can you expect any better behavior from him?"

The Canters (1992, p. 58) believe that a system based on positive interactions and positive recognition will "encourage students to continue appropriate behavior." As a result, the students' self-esteem will improve, behavior problems will be reduced, and there will be a positive classroom environment for the teacher and students. It is especially important for this positive recognition to be grade appropriate; for example, verbal praise might be appropriate for a second grader, but something more private probably is better for an older student.

After reading the following examples, consider how you might help the teacher in How Would You React 3–3.

Jamie Bryant and her sister Patti were teachers, but they had different ideas about the use of rewards and punishment in the classroom. For example, Patti, a kindergarten teacher, usually could appeal to her students' desire to satisfy the teacher. However, Jamie, who taught general mathematics in the high school, thought punishments were required to maintain order.

Carmen King, a beginning teacher, had been warned by Isabel Teel, her mentor–teacher, not to smile at students the first few weeks of school. "They'll think they can take advantage of you," Isabel said. Ignoring Isabel's advice, Carmen smiled at the students. Although she was not "trying to become friends with individual students," she built an excellent rapport with the children in her class. She still established rules and let the students know that she expected them to follow the rules, but she also felt that

---

How Would You React 3-2

Acting Like Hoodlums

The Canters believe that teachers must not show prejudice. Instead, they must be fair to all students and be consistent in their actions. Although most teachers follow these beliefs, sometimes they work with others who do not keep an open mind and who rely on stereotypes. Read the following scenario; then respond to the questions.

As Glenda Gonzales entered the teachers' lounge, she heard Louisa Del Campo remark, "All the students from that neighborhood act like hoodlums. I just ignore them in my class most of the time. After all, students from there are just problems waiting to happen." Glenda was sure Louisa was referring to a group of boys and girls who all lived in the same section of town. Sometimes rowdy and often rough looking, they stayed together in school and were in Glenda's and Louisa's middle

school team. Glenda knew these students lived in a lower socioeconomic area where crime statistics were higher than average, but she still shuddered when she heard Louisa's comment. Glenda had two concerns: first was that another member of her teaching team would make such a comment, and second was her concern for the students.

Working collaboratively in groups of three or four, respond to the following questions:

1. What, if anything, should Glenda Gonzales do? How should she handle the situation?

2. Review the key concepts of the Canters' model. If you had these students in your classroom, what strategies from the Canters' model could you try?

How Would You React 3-3_____

Adapting to Eighth Grade

Although a classroom management model may present a number of valid points, the implementation of these points is very important and may vary with the age and developmental level of the students. In the following example, a teacher forgets the level of the students she is teaching.

> Grace Hoffler was earning her teacher's license for grades K–8. After completing her experience in a primary classroom, she moved into a middle school setting. One day, Ms. Hoffler forgot she was teaching an eighth-grade class and said, "I like the way Jonda is doing her work so quietly." The comment would have been appropriate for a student in the primary grades, but

Jonda was embarrassed that she had been singled out in front of the entire class for her appropriate behavior.

Working collaboratively in groups of three or four, respond to the following questions:

1. What are some appropriate ways that Ms. Hoffler could have provided positive recognition for Jonda without embarrassing her?
2. How might Ms. Hoffler adapt her use of positive recognition if she where teaching in a fourth- or fifth-grade class? In a high school?

> positive interactions rather than an adversarial relationship would be beneficial to the students and to her. She was right, and the students worked to be cooperative and to demonstrate positive behavior.

Along with building a classroom based on positive interactions and reinforcement, teachers should develop trust and respect in their classrooms and should also model the behaviors that they want their students to develop. Sometimes, however, situations occur that test the extent of trust and respect in a classroom.

> When Drew Nash confronted one of her sixth-grade students who had broken a class rule, the student pulled a knife out of his desk. Using the broken-record technique, Ms. Nash calmly and matter of factly said, "Stan, put the knife on the desk." Stan did not and the entire class watched to see the actions of Stan and the teacher. Again, Ms. Nash said, "Stan, put the knife on the desk." Stan did not. For a third time, Ms. Nash said, "Stan, put the knife on the desk." This time, Stan placed the knife on the desk. Ms. Nash never raised her voice, never threatened, and never said please.

EFFECTIVENESS OF THE PRACTICAL APPLICATIONS

Although the Canters call for the schoolwide implementation of assertive discipline, this can cause problems because individual teachers often need to determine what works best for them and what supports their instructional styles. What works for one teacher might not be best for another. Although all teachers need classroom management knowledge and skills, teachers also need to determine a plan they feel comfortable with, can implement effectively, and can use with their preferred methods of instruction.

With that said, we still believe that the Canters' assertive discipline model has merit. In most cases, the model can be translated into practical application. In addition to visiting several schools in which the entire school has adopted the model, we have seen many individual teachers use it effectively. Several points that contribute to the model's effectiveness in classroom practice include the emphasis on clear and positive limits and on teachers acting in an assertive rather than nonassertive or hostile manner. One point that might not contribute to its effectiveness, however, is the discipline hierarchy (see pp. 49–50) whereby teachers have to proceed with a step-by-step approach to solve behavior problems. If, for example, the teacher is dealing with one misbehaving student, it is relatively easy to keep track of steps, but what if the teacher has four or five misbehaving students at one time? The teacher easily could become so involved with keeping an account of students' behaviors and using the appropriate consequences that teaching effectiveness diminishes and valuable instructional time is lost.

EVALUATING ASSERTIVE DISCIPLINE

In this book, we want to look at each classroom management model to determine whether it addresses typical student behaviors, its advantages and disadvantages, and whether it teaches or imposes discipline. Although we believe that it is the responsibility of the individual teacher to decide whether a particular model works for him or her, we also believe that it is important, whenever possible, to consider scholarly opinions by experts about each classroom management model and its underlying philosophical bases.

Potential for Addressing Student Misbehaviors

What are the most prevalent types of student misbehaviors? Everyone has seen and heard of acts of violence in schools, but these problems are not encountered on a daily basis by most educators. Instead, most misbehavior includes students sitting idly or talking with friends, disturbing neighborhoods who want to learn and obey rules, and walking around the classroom without permission. Thus, although educators must continue their efforts to promote safe schools and to deal with the violence that is found in many schools, they also must deal with the time wasting that occurs on a regular basis.

Although assertive discipline might have its limitations when two students start fighting or when someone brings a gun to school, the Canters' model can address the routine, but prevalent, time-wasting problems by its emphasis on classroom rules, rewards, and consequences.

> Gerra Price was a student teacher in an elementary school that had adopted Assertive Discipline as its schoolwide model. While teaching a social studies lesson, Ms. Price asked a question. A girl answered without raising her hand. Without speaking, Ms. Price wrote the student's name on a clipboard (that was her first warning) and continued teaching. Assertive Discipline worked in this case; the girl did not speak again without raising her hand and, because Ms. Price never gave a public reprimand, instructional time was not lost.

Although Assertive Discipline's reliance on consistency and clear limits is commendable, teachers need to be aware of two characteristics that could be damaging to students from some cultures. First, although the problems associated with maintaining eye contact have been mentioned, it is worth repeating that students in some cultures have been taught that this action is disrespectful, rude, or threatening. Thus, teachers using Assertive Discipline, just like teachers using any management model, must be aware of and remember to make allowances for cultural differences.

> While reprimanding a student for inappropriate behavior, a principal looked directly in the eye of a ninth grader as he demanded, "You look at me when I talk to you!" The principal assumed the lack of eye contact meant a lack of respect or interest for what he was saying. Instead, the student was being respectful.

Second, problems could arise with Assertive Discipline's system of rewards and punishments. Students in some cultures will feel uncomfortable receiving a reward publicly, especially if it is at the expense of other students. They might not want to excel or stand out from their peers. Students in grades 5 or 6 through 12 also might feel less than honored to receive a reward, especially if it is given in front of the entire group. Likewise, students in some cultures will be distressed and embarrassed even to have a warning. For example, Manning and Baruth (2004) reported that Asian Americans often avoid having attention drawn to themselves, especially if that attention could reflect negatively upon themselves or their families. Thus, teachers must know and consider the students in their classes. To avoid potential problems with this record-keeping technique, a clipboard or some record-keeping book might be more appropriate. Activity 3–2 asks you to suggest other ways diversity might affect the implementation of the Assertive Discipline classroom management model.

Advantages and Disadvantages

Although some writers (Keiper, 2004; Palardy, 1996; Curwin & Mendler, 1988, 1989; Render, Padilla, & Krank, 1989) have questioned various aspects of Assertive Discipline, thousands of educators have attested to its effectiveness in the classroom. Because of the differences in instructional styles among teachers, what one educator sees as an advantage might be a disadvantage to another.

As advantages, some teachers cite the insistence upon consistency and clear limits, with the same classroom rules and discipline hierarchy (e.g., the warnings) applying to all students. Most students like to know how far the teacher will allow their behavior to go.

> Rikki Tiiko liked to wad up his paper into a ball and shoot it to the trash can in a make-believe game of basketball. Steve Hudson, his teacher, chose to ignore the behavior, hoping it would stop. Unfortunately, it did not, and two other students joined the game. Finally, everything escalated to a point where the learning environment was disrupted, and Mr. Hudson had to correct three students instead of one. Rikki and the other students knew the limits, but as Rikki later said, "Mr. Hudson didn't do anything, so we thought it was all right." By setting clear and specific limits, teachers are not acting mean or harsh.

Activity 3–2

Examining the Effects of Diversity

Suggest several ways student diversity in a classroom (e.g., linguistic, cultural, gender, and social class) might affect the implementation of the Assertive Discipline model. What might educators do to adapt Assertive Discipline based on students' differences?

They are, however, setting clear behavior expectations. If Mr. Hudson had set clear limits, he likely could have prevented the escalation. Knowing limits makes most students feel psychologically safe.

In addition, the Canters' model provides sufficient flexibility to address the behavior of elementary, middle, and secondary school students with an emphasis on understanding individual students and meeting their needs whenever possible. The key to successful implementation is for the teacher to determine appropriate behavior, rewards, and consequences for each of the school levels to reflect the students' psychological and developmental maturity levels. Assertive teachers do not damage students' self-esteem with statements such as "How can you be so dense to make the same mistake again? Can't you ever learn one simple rule?" By understanding the psychological and developmental needs of their students, they plan appropriate assertive statements, rewards, and consequences. Management Tip 3–4 looks at a school's mission statement or vision statement as it relates to classroom management, whereas How Would You React 3–4 illustrates a teacher who was not taking the needs of a student into consideration.

Finally, many teachers like the positive approach and the ease of correcting behavior problems (i.e., simply assigning a warning with little disruption to the instructional process). Although verbal threats and nagging are not part of the model, students know that the teacher will act assertively and decisively. The students also know that their behavior affects the teacher's reaction. If they behave appropriately, they get rewarded. If they behave inappropriately, they must endure the consequences.

Realistically speaking, Assertive Discipline could lead to unduly demanding learning environments where teachers do not engage in individual decision making and do not consider the extenuating circumstances of the misbehavior. Just as students have specific rules, teachers have established consequences that must be dealt out consistently without subjective consideration.

Several educators have questioned whether Assertive Discipline teaches or imposes discipline. This topic is discussed in more depth in the next section of this chapter, but it is important to point out that at least two educators regard the imposition of discipline as a disadvantage. J. Michael Palardy (1996, p. 69) maintains that a behavior modification model such as Assertive Discipline "devalues self-discipline as an ultimate goal in favor of management of conduct."

Lee Canter (1988) and Sammie McCormack (1989) have countered these selected criticisms. Canter claims that research supports Assertive Discipline and, in fact, has shown that the model is fair, proven, and does not hurt students. Also, Canter (1989, p. 632) examined the research, explained the fundamentals of Assertive Discipline, and defended the model as a viable means of classroom management without "violating the best interests of the students." Supporting Assertive Discipline, McCormack (1989) maintains that practitioners think the model works, regardless of what the critics report.

Imposing or Teaching Discipline?

Concern always arises among educators about whether a classroom management model imposes or teaches discipline. It is the students' choice whether to misbehave, but some educators believe that as the teacher imposes warnings and punishments, students ultimately learn self-discipline because they do not like the consequences. Others, however, believe that if teachers assign the warnings for misbehavior and the rewards and consequences, the teachers are imposing discipline more than they are teaching discipline.

Some educators, such as J. Michael Palardy (1996), think that the behavior modification in models such as Assertive Discipline emphasizes management of conduct and devalues self-discipline as an ultimate goal. Self-discipline can be achieved only when students search for appropriate methods of meeting all types of personal and social situations. Thus, to foster self-discipline in students, educators need to give students more opportunities to make their own decisions about behavior. Educators also must structure environments in which students learn to hold themselves responsible for the consequences of their behavior. According to Palardy (1996), neither of these responsibilities is considered relevant in classroom management models that emphasize behavior modification.

Consider the following example:

> One day Tim walks around the room, supposedly to discard his trash in the wastebasket. On the way, he disturbs others by knocking one student's books off the desk, hitting another in the back of the head, and asking another to meet him after school. After the teacher assigns a warning, Tim does not walk around again that day. However, the next day, an almost-identical scenario occurs.

Has discipline been taught? Is the teacher just imposing discipline? One might say that if Tim's behavior occurs every day for 2 months and then stops, Tim has learned to discipline himself. Admittedly, a fine line exists; however, Assertive Discipline's insistence upon rewards and consequences will continue to raise the issue of whether students learn self-discipline or merely try to avoid negative consequences.

Underlying Beliefs

As previously suggested, individual teachers should determine what works for them. For example, what works for a 1st-grade teacher probably will not work for an 11th-grade teacher. Also, what works for educators who believe in the authority of the teacher might not work for educators who believe in establishing democratic classrooms. However, regardless of the

Management Tip 3-4

School Vision Statements and Assertive Discipline

Any classroom management program should be reflected in the school's mission statement, sometimes called a vision statement. See Heard Street Discovery Academy's (Worchester Public Schools) opinion of the Canters' Assertive Discipline as well as their mission statement and vision statement at *http://www.wpsweb.com/heard/assertive_discipline.html*. Notice their mission and vision statements do not specifically mention the Canters' Assertive Discipline, but their management program would require several of the Canters' beliefs, such as assertive response styles and student and teacher rights. Other management-related aspects include

- Encouraging learners to achieve their highest potential behaviorally and academically,
- Involving parents, community, and school personnel,
- Accepting and, in fact, valuing diversity,
- Taking pride in oneself and accomplishments,
- Developing a sense of community.

Please go to *www.prenhall.com/manning* and click on the Management Tips for this chapter to complete management activities and find more information on using the Canters' assertive discipline as it relates to a school's mission or vision statement.

How Would You React 3-4

Reviewing Antonio's Day

According to the Canters, it is important to consider the self-esteem of students and to understand their psychological and developmental needs. As you read the following scenario, ask yourself whether the teacher is practicing Assertive Discipline. If she is not, what should she have done differently? How would her response vary if the student was in second grade? Sixth grade? Ninth grade?

> It was the end of a long day for Antonio and Ms. Hunley, his teacher. As Antonio's after-school detention was ending, Ms. Hunley turned to him and said in a friendly way:

> "Well, it sure wasn't your day, was it, Antonio? Boy, you did some dumb things. You gave everybody a good laugh when you came to school with one green and one blue sock. Guess you left your brains in the bed last night, right? When you spilled your soup on you at lunch, you reminded me of a first grader I used to know—a real klutz. Then, you just couldn't stop yapping, could you? You talked all day, didn't you? Try to get your head on right before you come to school tomorrow so you won't seem so stupid. I don't want to waste my time sitting here with you again."

> All this time, Antonio sat silently at his desk.

Developing Your Personal Philosophy

Does Assertive Discipline Reflect Your Beliefs?

If you are considering using the Canters' model in your classroom, ask yourself these questions:

1. Do I see a need (and am I willing) to place clear and specific limits on students' behavior?
2. Do I agree with rewards for appropriate behavior and consequences for inappropriate behavior?
3. Am I able to be consistent with all students and with all situations?
4. Do I believe my students will respond better to intrinsic or extrinsic motivation?
5. Do I see Assertive Discipline as providing too much or just enough structure for me?
6. Do I have the ability and motivation to be as consistent as Assertive Discipline requires?
7. Do I believe all students are capable of behaving appropriately?
8. Am I able to forego all nonassertive and hostile behaviors and adopt only assertive behaviors?
9. Am I willing to treat the symptoms rather than the causes?
10. Am I willing to place less emphasis on self-disciplined and responsible students and more on Assertive Discipline?
11. Am I willing to use tangible rewards such as pencils, treats, or certificates as a means of rewards or positive reinforcers?
12. Am I willing to adopt a program that provides little, if any, teacher discretion in solving behavior problems?

CASE STUDY
Management Problems in the First Grade

Sabrina Price was a first-grade teacher in a suburban school system. She sought the teaching job there because she did not feel she could handle higher grades or the challenges of inner-city schools. As she was preparing for her second year, she thought back to the disaster of her first year and again wondered if she was foolish to attempt a second year. At the end of the last school year, she had almost quit the profession. As Sabrina said:

I couldn't make my students behave. They just would not listen to me! The principal discussed the situation with me on several occasions, but I just didn't know what to do. My first-grade class was often chaotic. No one was ever in danger; but most of the time, the students were loud, ignored my admonitions, walked around the room, played among themselves, yelled to one another, and, generally speaking, just goofed off. I was good at working with small groups, but then the others in the class would make so much noise that no one could concentrate. I know I had students who wanted to learn, but it was too noisy in the room.

Although I tried several techniques, such as bribing them with candy, threatening them, and saying I would call their parents,

nothing seemed to work. Oh sure, some days were better than others and I was able to get them to do their best; but, on other days, I basically just gave up and let them do what they wanted to do.

I want my students to like me; I want to be their friend. But right now, I've got to figure out a way to manage my classroom or I'm leaving teaching at the end of the year, if not before!

Questions for Consideration

1. Can you help Ms. Price prepare for her second year?
2. What would proponents of Canters' Assertive Discipline model suggest Ms. Price do?
3. What would they think was wrong?
4. What actions and changes should she initiate?

 You can record your answers to these questions online on this book's Companion Web Site at *www.prenhall.com/manning*.

classroom management system, teachers must believe the system works, and they must believe it works for them. Developing Your Personal Philosophy provides several questions that you can ask yourself to determine whether Assertive Discipline aligns with your philosophical and psychological beliefs.

CONCLUDING REMARKS

This chapter has provided an overview of the Assertive Discipline Model developed by Lee and Marlene Canter. Additional information about this model and its applications can be found on the Internet sites identified in "Reaching Out With Technology," which is found on this book's Companion Web Site.

Please go to *www.prenhall.com/manning* and click on Concluding Remarks for this chapter to find more information.

The Canters developed their classroom management system based on their observations of successful classroom managers. Through numerous books and journal articles, they have explained every aspect of the model. Several critics have offered their concerns about Assertive Discipline, but many practitioners like it and use the model effectively. Most teachers comment that Assertive Discipline allows them to focus on instructional effectiveness. However, as J. Michael Palardy (1996, p. 67) indicated, Assertive Discipline "is only one of many effective strategies educators can use to foster appropriate school and classroom conduct." Nevertheless, the Canters' Assertive Discipline model seems to hold considerable potential for classroom management.

To review the concepts of the Assertive Discipline model, consider the situation of Sabrina Price in the Case Study. See if you can help Ms. Price prepare for a successful second year of teaching with a classroom management system based on Assertive Discipline.

Suggested Readings

Akin-Little, K. A., & Little, S. G. (2004). Re-examining the overjustification effect. *Journal of Behavioral Education 13*(3), 179–192. This study examined the use and subsequent withdrawal of token reinforcement and the effect on student compliance with classroom rules.

Fielding, M. (2004). Model behaviour: A step-by-step guide to better classroom management. *Child Education, 81*(1), 13. Fielding looks at reward psychology and sanctions for classroom management.

Canter, L. (2002). *Lee Canter's responsible behavior curriculum guide: An instructional approach to successful classroom management.* Los Angeles: Canter & Associates. Management, curriculum, and instruction are complex, with management being enhanced by proper curricular and instructional practices.

Canter, L., & Canter, M. (2001). *Parents on your side: A teacher's guide to creating positive relationships with parents.* Los Angeles: Canter & Associates. As the title implies, Canter explains how teachers can create positive relationships with parents and explains the benefits of these relationships.

Keiper, R. W. (2004). Peacemaking. *Kappa Delta Pi Record, 40*(2), 91. Keiper explains the Peacemaking program—a whole school management program similar to the Canters' program.

CHAPTER 4

Exploring the Theories of Democratic Teaching: *Rudolf Dreikurs*

Focusing Questions

After reading this chapter, you should be able to answer the following questions:

1. What does Dreikurs mean by Democratic Teaching and Management and the belief that democracy is the key to effective classroom management?

2. How was Dreikurs influenced by Alfred Adler's belief that people want to engage in social activities and to relate to other people?

3. What key concepts provide the foundation for Dreikurs's theories?

4. What did Dreikurs mean by encouragement, logical consequences, and the four goals of misbehavior, and how might educators apply these concepts in elementary, middle, and secondary schools?

5. How do Dreikurs's theories of Democratic Teaching contribute to effective instructional practices and to safe schools (and vice versa)?

6. How can educators create democratic classrooms rather than autocratic or permissive classrooms?

7. How and to what extent can Dreikurs's theory of Democratic Teaching and Management meet the individual needs of diverse learners?

Key Terms

Attention getting
Autocratic teacher
Democratic teacher
Encouragement
Feelings of inadequacy
Logical consequences
Permissive teacher
Power seeking
Praise
Revenge

Rudolf Dreikurs called for democratic teaching and management procedures. In his multifaceted theory of classroom management, four aspects stand out: identifying and addressing mistaken goals of misbehavior, acting as democratic rather than autocratic or permissive teachers, using logical consequences rather than punishment, and understanding the difference between praise and encouragement. Unlike the Canter and Canter classroom management model, the Dreikurs model has not been packaged as a marketable program. Nevertheless, his work has had a significant influence on educators and classroom management theory. In this chapter, you will find an overview of Dreikurs's theories and will see how elementary, middle, and secondary educators can use Democratic Teaching and Management to promote positive behavior and the safe schools effort.

RUDOLF DREIKURS: BIOGRAPHICAL SKETCH

Born in Vienna, Austria, Rudolf Dreikurs began the practice of medicine in 1923 and came to the United States in 1937. Influenced by Alfred Adler and considered by many as a preeminent scholar of Adlerian psychotherapy (Carson, 1996), Dreikurs was the founder and medical director of the Community Child Guidance Center of Chicago. Internationally known, Dreikurs spent much of his life as a consultant in public schools, explaining how his theories could be translated into practice for classroom management and discipline. He was also an influential member of several mental health associations, such as the American Society of Adlerian Psychology and the American Psychiatric Association. Many of Dreikurs's books have proved useful to educators and parents, including his *Psychology in the Classroom* (1957), *Children: The Challenge* (1964), and *Encouraging Children to Learn* (1963, with Don Dinkmeyer).

OVERVIEW OF DEMOCRATIC TEACHING AND MANAGEMENT

Dreikurs's theory of Democratic Teaching and Management is based on several key concepts that are essential to understanding his theory. This introductory section provides an overview of some of these concepts, which are discussed in more detail in the next section.

Key Concepts

The four key concepts of Dreikurs's theory are shown in Figure 4–1. Dreikurs believed that when teachers act in a democratic fashion, they demonstrate effective instruction and provide a collaborative learning community where teachers and students work toward common goals. Students should not feel that their self-worth depends on worthy behavior or academic achievement. Thus, as self-esteem and confidence grow, students' misbehaviors should decrease.

Philosophical and Psychological Foundations

Dreikurs based his theory of Democratic Teaching and Management on the beliefs first proposed by Alfred Adler (1927, 1930) in the early 1900s (Pryor & Tollerud, 1999). He believed that people are born with the capacity to develop their social interests and are inherently motivated to relate to and interact with other people. However, this inborn ability to interact in a cooperative way with other people to form a healthy society must be nurtured and developed throughout the childhood years. The school becomes a primary setting for the development of social interest, with adults helping students to belong, feel valued, develop positive self-worth, and not feel discouraged (Pryor & Tollerud, 1999).

Figure 4-1 Key Concepts of Dreikurs's Theory

Mistaken Goals. All misbehavior results when students have one of more of the following "mistaken goals" for their behavior: attention getting, power seeking, revenge, and helplessness (feelings of inadequacy) (Dreikurs, 1968; Dreikers, Grunwald, & Pepper, 1971).

Democratic Teaching. Teachers should be democratic, rather than autocratic ("I told you to do it now; you will do it now") or permissive ("Well, whatever you want to do is all right, I guess. I know you'll do the right thing, won't you?") in their classroom procedures and social interactions with students (Dreikurs, 1968).

Encouragement. Teachers should encourage students (I think you can do the work if you give it a good try") rather than praise students ("You are such a good student—you always do your work just right") (Dinkmeyer & Dreikurs, 1963).

Logical Consequences. Teachers should establish classroom rules and implement logical consequences rather than punishments for broken rules and misbehavior. Punishment should seldom be used and, then, only when all logical consequences have been exhausted (Dreikurs & Grey, 1968).

To establish a nurturing environment within the school, Dreikurs advocated Democratic Teaching and Management. Espousing ideas similar to John Dewey, Dreikurs viewed democracy as an all-around growth of all members of society. For democracy to exist, a clearly defined social vision must be achieved that is characterized by high expectations, high levels of honest encouragement, and an insistence that all people are responsible for others' well-being. Accomplishing this means that all members of society are given a means of gaining acceptance into the social order, as well as the assistance necessary to help them develop the skills needed to do so (Carson, 1996).

Teachers' Roles and Responsibilities

Dreikurs (1968, p. 3) maintained that "In order to be effective, the teacher has to know more than the subject matter." Thus, teachers must develop a democratic classroom and utilize effective instructional strategies that complement Dreikurs's theories. In creating a democratic classroom, a teacher must commit to several beliefs: the belief in the worth and dignity of every person, a belief in the equality of all people, a belief in freedom of decision making, and a belief that people can be trusted to make wise decisions (Dreikurs, 1968). In addition, when dealing with children and young adults, Dreikurs suggested that effective teachers also have the ability to develop positive relationships with parents, the principal, and community members. In doing so, they must feel positive about their own professional accomplishments, especially their ability to teach and instill democratic classroom procedures. Activity 4–1 provides some suggestions for establishing a democratic classroom and asks you to think of others. Then, Management Tip 4–1 has some suggestions for improving relations with parents by developing a parenting skills bookshelf.

Activity 4–1

Implementing Democratic Classrooms

Teachers can develop a democratic classroom by

1. Treating students as individuals and with respect during all teaching and management situations,
2. Modeling respect at all times, such as speaking respectfully, encouraging rather than praising, and avoiding punishments,
3. Developing the self-respect needed to be a professional educator and to respect others,
4. Treating students with dignity, friendliness, firmness, and kindness,
5. Allowing students to help make important class decisions, perhaps allowing a class discussion before a vote,
6. Using instructional methods that meet individual students' learning needs and interests.

Identify the level on which you wish to teach. Then explain how you could use these ideas in your classroom or identify additional ways you could develop your own democratic classroom.

In summary, teachers who are serious about Adlerian principles and Dreikurs's theories should adopt several unique perspectives as they apply his key concepts. First, they need to view students as social beings who want to belong and to find an accepted place in society. Second, instead of simply reacting to students' behaviors by imposing punishments or rewards, they need to identify the goals of these misbehaviors. Then, they need to forego rewards and punishments in favor of logical consequences that result from the misbehaviors. Third, teachers who use democratic procedures must allow and, in fact, encourage students to take an active, participatory role in developing classroom procedures, as well as in making curricular and instructional decisions. Activity 4–2 explores ways to encourage that participation. Finally, extending the ideas of Dreikurs, effective teachers need to use sound instructional strategies and build a sense of community within the classroom. To do so, they probably will not rely solely on Dreikurs's Democratic Teaching model but will understand the complementary nature of management and instruction to build a personal system of classroom management that works for them and their students.

Management Tip 4-1

Developing a Parenting Bookshelf

Work with your library media specialist to develop a parenting skills bookshelf with titles on parenting, reading to children, and study skills.

Overall considerations for selecting "parenting" books include the following:

- Are books "age-appropriate," mainly books that address parenting needs of both elementary and secondary school students?
- Are books current, and do they address contemporary concerns of parents?
- Are reading levels appropriate for parents of varying educational levels?
- Is diversity considered, e.g., the needs of all cultures and social classes?
- Are books available in the parents' native language whenever possible?
- Do books avoid jargon and educational terms that only add to parents' confusion?

Please go to *www.prenhall.com/manning* and click on the Management Tips for this chapter to complete management activities and find more information on developing a parenting bookshelf.

APPLYING DEMOCRATIC TEACHING AND MANAGEMENT

Identifying and Addressing Mistaken Goals

Dreikurs (1957, 1968) proposed that all student misbehavior results when individuals pursue one or more of four mistaken goals: power seeking, revenge, eliminating feelings of inadequacy, and attention getting. The following examples look at these goals and how they might be seen in a classroom.

1. **Attention Getting.**   When students feel they are worthless, they often misbehave to get the attention they want. Dreikurs (1968) maintained that this behavior might be more dominant in young children who feel they have few opportunities to establish their social position through useful contributions or through socially accepted means. When these methods are not effective, students try almost any other method to gain attention. In fact, students even might prefer punishment to being ignored.

    > Ms. Marian Cuffee was an **autocratic teacher** who firmly ruled her class. She demanded silence and obedience the first time she made a request. Robbie, not one of the most motivated students in the class, asked a question—then another, then another, and another. Although the class knew that Ms. Cuffee was growing irritated with the constant stream of questions, Robbie relentlessly continued. Soon, it was clear that Robbie did not have any intention of stopping. Finally, Ms. Cuffee had her fill. She said, "No more questions, Robbie. Now do your work!" Robbie responded, "My mother said I had to ask questions in order to learn, so that's what I'm doing." Ms. Cuffee knew that Robbie would continue his barrage of questions, but she did not know how to stop him effectively. In addition, she realized that the other students in the class were watching attentively to see the outcome. Frustrated and by now impatient, Ms. Cuffee sent Robbie to the office for constantly misbehaving.

Activity 4-2

Encouraging Students to Take Participatory Roles

To encourage the participation of students in a democratic classroom, a teacher can

1. Involve students in making class rules by asking them what rules they want that will contribute to their positive behavior and academic success,

2. Ask students their opinion of logical consequences (i.e., what they think the consequence, instead of an outright punishment, should be for a particular behavior infraction),

3. Ask students how to involve their parents and families in the educational process, especially the classroom management process,

4. Ask students for their ideas for making schools safer for students and teachers.

What other ways might you use to encourage students to assume a participatory role in a classroom?

After Ms. Cuffee determined that Robbie was seeking attention, she should have provided him with more personal attention (e.g., asking a peer tutor to work with him, telling him that she would provide individual assistance, or assigning him to a cooperative learning group). Even sending Robbie on a class errand would have eliminated his bid for attention. In fact, almost anything to give Robbie the attention he wanted would have defused the situation.

2. **Power Seeking.**   Power-seeking students attempt to prove their power by defying the teacher and doing whatever they want. Only when they are the boss of a situation or controlling others will these students feel self-worth. For students who are seeking power, the behavior becomes more defiant and might include disobedience, talking back, or overt resistance (Pryor & Tollerud, 1999).

> Ms. Layla Boxer reprimanded two boys, Emil and Manuel, for horsing around during mathematics class. Emil sat down quietly; Manuel knocked his books off the desk with a thundering crash. The resulting dialogue went as follows:
>
> Ms. Boxer: "Manuel, you pick up those books right now. I know you did that on purpose. Pick them up now and don't do it again."
>
> Manuel: "Emil knocked them off and I ain't picking them up. Tell him to do it. Why do you always tell me to do things?"
>
> Ms. Boxer: "You knocked them off. It's just like you. Now, you pick them up or else."
>
> Manuel: "I ain't picking them up. I didn't do nothing. My mother says you can't make me do anything I don't want to do anyway."
>
> As the conversation continued for another four or five exchanges, the power struggle was in motion: Ms. Boxer made a demand and Manuel refused.

Regardless of the situation, a teacher needs to avoid entering into a power struggle because that will just reinforce the behavior (Pryor & Tollerud, 1999). In dealing with students who are seeking power, most effective teachers will work to prevent power struggles. They think prevention is more effective, and they know that no one wins a power struggle. The teacher might lose face in front of other students, and the power-seeking student's self-worth might diminish even more.

In the previous example, instead of making statements—'Pick up those books right now. I know you did that on purpose. Pick them up now and don't do it again.'—Ms. Boxer might have recognized that Manuel would not have picked them up, regardless of what she demanded. Although she could have asked Manuel more politely to pick up the books, once she suspected a power struggle was about to happen, she should have defused the situation by using an "or" statement, such as "Manuel, either pick up the books now or wait until the break to pick them up." Because Manuel knew he was seeking power, he needed an opportunity to remove himself from the power struggle.

3. **Revenge.**   Students who are seeking revenge want to hurt someone else and believe that revenge is important for their own self-esteem. Students who are focused on revenge can become more vicious and outwardly hostile with time. In order to feel significant and worthy, these students believe they must hurt someone in the same way they believe someone has hurt them. Depending on the age and development of the students involved, their revenge might include stealing, kicking, and intentionally hurting others.

> Mr. Karl Paxton corrected Rachel many times and finally demanded that she sit in the desk nearest him. Rachel protested because the new seat meant she no longer would be near her friends. Trying to avoid a power struggle, Mr. Paxton gave Rachel a choice: "Rachel, you can sit near me or you can go to the assistant principal." Not wanting to go to the assistant principal, Rachel obeyed; however, during her move, she slammed her books, hit one student in the back of the head, and uttered several words that Mr. Paxton did not completely understand. "Well, that's over," Mr. Paxton erroneously thought. However, during the next week, Rachel continued to seek revenge. Her behavior grew worse as she disturbed others, voiced hurtful comments to other students, and was rude to Mr. Paxton. Because she could not move back to her former seat, Rachel wanted to hurt Mr. Paxton and the other students, and revenge seemed like the best option.

In this situation, Mr. Paxton should have asked himself whether moving Rachel to the desk nearest him was the most effective strategy. Were other options available? Was he consistent; that is, would he have moved other students or did he select this punishment just for Rachel? Did having Rachel in front of the class just provide her with more opportunities to get the class's attention?

Moving Rachel to the front of the class was probably a mistake. Instead, Mr. Paxton should have established clear and fair rules that applied to all students in his classroom. In addition, he should have let Rachel know that she was liked by him and other students in the class, and he should have encouraged Rachel to act in a more acceptable manner. However, once the revenge had started, Mr. Paxton should have had a private talk with Rachel to discuss her behavior, possible logical consequences of the behavior, and how she could improve her behavior. Using Dreikurs's encouragement and logical consequences would have been more effective and would have been less likely to convince Rachel of the need to seek revenge.

4. **Feelings of Inadequacy.**   Students who harbor feelings of hopelessness and inferiority might be focused on the goal of inadequacy. These students might just want to

be left alone and might work actively to avoid others (Pryor & Tollerud, 1999). As long as they are left alone, nothing is demanded of them, and their deficiencies, inabilities, and inadequacies might not become obvious (Dreikurs, Grunwald, & Pepper, 1971). They might not even misbehave, but their lack of misbehavior should not keep a teacher from encouraging them to take an active role in classroom activities.

> Rashe was in Ms. Manuelita Allen's class. Regrettably, Ms. Allen had not developed a classroom management system that worked effectively, and although the class was not violent, the students were noisy. So when Rashe sat quietly and passively, Ms. Allen was thankful. Rashe rarely said a word. She did little or no work, but she never misbehaved, and she was never a problem. "If there isn't a problem, I'm not going to make one. At least one student is quiet," Ms. Allen reasoned to herself. Unfortunately, Ms. Allen was unable or unwilling to recognize that a problem did exist. Rashe did not talk to anyone, even at recess, she was not participating in class activities, and she was not developing socialization skills and improving academically.

Rather than being thankful for one behaving student, Ms. Allen should have taken planned and deliberate actions to address Rashe's feelings of inadequacy. Talking with Rashe, her parents, and the guidance counselor would have been worthwhile first steps. Ms. Allen also should have worked to identify Rashe's perceived weaknesses, helped to improve her self-esteem and socialization skills, and encouraged Rashe to participate in learning activities. Ms. Allen's goal should have been to help Rashe develop into a student who felt adequate and able to handle social and academic tasks.

All misbehaviors fall into at least one category of the four mistaken goals, but the challenge always will be to determine which mistaken goal the behavior reflects

How Would You React 4-1

Identifying Mistaken Goals

Dreikurs proposed that all misbehaviors result from the pursuit of one or more of four mistaken goals. Review these goals. Then, consider the following behaviors and identify the mistaken goal(s) shown in each. Using what you know about the psychological and developmental needs of students in the grade noted, suggest a strategy a teacher could use to deal with the behavior in the classroom. See the examples listed in this text with the mistaken goals to help you. How would the strategies change if the student were in a different grade?

1. A kindergartner cries every day and refuses to work.
2. A fifth grader annoys the class and teacher by constantly asking questions of little consequence.
3. A twelfth grader boasts of smoking marijuana the previous night (although the student did not bring any to school).
4. A second grader constantly walks around the room, claiming the movement is for legitimate reasons

(such as getting a book or taking trash to the waste-basket).

5. A seventh grader annoys and disturbs the neighboring students.
6. A sixth grader tries so hard to please that the behavior annoys the teacher and other students.
7. A ninth-grade Latino student feels uncomfortable competing with friends and one day refuses to participate in a competitive activity.
8. A fourth grader always takes control of cooperative learning groups and wants to control the group's direction and activities.
9. An eleventh grader boasts of drinking beer every Friday afternoon and even goes so far as to invite the teacher to share one.
10. An eighth grader with considerable artistic ability makes explicit drawings that most teachers would consider pornographic.

and to identify the appropriate action to take. Also, a behavior might reflect more than one goal (i.e., a behavior might be attention getting and power seeking or nearly any other combination). To identify the cause of the misbehavior, teachers must maintain open lines of communication with all their students. How Would You React 4–1, "Identifying Mistaken Goals," presents several situations and gives you an opportunity to identify the mistaken goal in each.

Using Logical Consequences

The concept of **logical consequences** is another component of Dreikurs's discipline model. However, Dreikurs also believed that prior to providing logical consequences, teachers must establish simple, specific classroom rules. (See

Management Tip 4–2

Developing rules

The importance of classroom rules is a central part of many classroom management theories. They do not replace school division rules or individual school rules.

Rules define

- What behavior the teacher expects,
- What the students should do,
- How the class is conducted or how the day is structured.

Rules may also contain

- Consequences when rules are broken,
- Rewards when rules are followed.

Management Tip 4–2.) Once the rules are established, the teacher can outline a sequence of logical consequences. Finally, after the consequences are established, students are forced to accept responsibility for their own behavior. Some **democratic teachers** even encourage their students to help devise classroom rules and their logical consequences. Dreikurs believed that this practice could help deter discipline problems because the students have worked cooperatively to establish their own rules and procedures (Dreikurs, 1968; Morris, 1996).

After you read the following example, examine the behaviors and logical consequences in Activity 4–3 and suggest some of your own.

Please go to *www.prenhall.com/manning* and click on the Management Tips for this chapter to complete management activities and find more information on developing rules.

> Kristen Martin often asks her students to complete a specific amount of work during mathematics class. Because of the class rules, the students who complete the assignment know they will receive 15 to 20 minutes of free time prior to lunch. The students who do not work diligently to complete the assignment must use their free time to do so. Thus, instead of a harsh punishment, they receive a logical consequence for their actions.

Using Encouragement Rather Than Praise

According to the Dreikurs model, teachers should use more **encouragement** to boost confidence and self-esteem and less **praise,** because students can become dependent on the praise. When praise is used, if students do not or cannot continue the behavior or record of achievement, they begin to think they are of less worth. In essence, the reason for the praise becomes the source of self-worth. When the reason for the praise decreases, the students' feelings of self-worth also drop. As Dinkmeyer and Dreikurs (1963, p. 121) stated, "[p]raise may have a discouraging effect in the long run, since the child may depend on it constantly and never be quite sure whether he will merit another expression of special approval—and get it." As teachers use words of encouragement to demonstrate to students that they believe in them, the encouragement not only boosts students' self-esteem and confidence, but it also keeps students on task and minimizes student disruption (Morris, 1996). After you read the following examples of praise and encouragement, read Activity 4–4 to identify some additional ways to encourage students.

Activity 4–3

Providing Logical Consequences

The following are some misbehaviors and their logical consequences. After reading them, suggest some logical consequences that you would like to use for misbehaviors in your classroom.

Behavior	Logical Consequence
A student writes on a school desk.	The student must clean the desk.
A student destroys another's property.	The student (preferably not the parent) must pay for the property.
A student refuses to complete assignments during class.	The student does the work during recess or before or after school

Praise: "You are a fine student! You finished your math in record time."

Encouragement: "I can tell you've been practicing your math drills and I hope you will continue."

Praise: "You are a whiz with that computer program."

Encouragement: "I can tell you enjoy the challenges of learning to use a new computer program."

Practical Applications of Dreikurs's Theories

Overall, Dreikurs's theories of democratic classroom management have considerable potential for practical application in schools of all levels. To provide positive classrooms where teachers and students work toward a common purpose, teachers can use democratic classroom procedures that help students understand the goals of misbehavior, the effect of logical consequences, and the importance of social interactions. Other practical elements are Dreikurs's ideas about the need for clear limits, rules, and order; the importance of student participation in the development of classroom rules; the development of a spirit of trust and cooperation with a democratic rather than an autocratic teacher; and the use of encouragement (Dreikurs, Grunnwald, & Pepper, 1971).

In the practical application of the goals of misbehaviors, teachers determine whether power seeking, attention getting, revenge, or inadequacy is the cause of student misbehavior. The cause or goal does not justify the behavior, but teachers can work to reduce the need for misbehavior.

A middle school student constantly talked and interrupted the class until his teacher realized he felt inadequate. Once she helped him believe that he could do the work successfully, his behavior improved.

Activity 4–4

Encouraging Students

The following are some examples of ways to encourage students through words and actions. After reading them, identify additional ways that you could encourage rather than praise students in your classroom.

1. Help students find a constructive place in the group, so they will not seek a destructive means of gaining acceptance and feelings of self-worth.
2. Avoid overprotection and indulgence, because these deprive students of the experiences necessary to gain self-confidence in their ability to develop self-discipline.
3. Avoid pointing out to students all their mistakes, so they will not feel overwhelmed in areas to improve.
4. Convey an atmosphere of community, in which class members are willing to assist each other and to feel a sense of social interest in each other.
5. Teach students that they can improve their behavior, even when it is necessary to apply logical consequences.
6. Encourage students to view each day as a new start rather than continually reminding students of past incorrect behaviors.

An autocratic teacher had power-seeking problems until he learned that democratic classroom procedures reduce the need for some students to be power seekers.

Unlike the Canters' Assertive Discipline, democratic teaching and management does not include check marks for misbehavior or a hierarchy of discipline procedures. What it does demand is for effective teachers to have a genuine commitment to democratic classrooms, logical consequences, and the use of encouragement. Use these and other elements of Dreikurs's model to respond to the situation in How Would You React 4–2.

How Would You React 4–2

Refusing to Work

Review Dreikurs's four mistaken goals. Then, read the following scenario and identify the mistaken goal(s) of the student's misbehavior. Finally, review the key concepts (Figure 4–1) from Dreikurs and suggest which of Dreikurs's ideas would be useful for this teacher. Explain why you think this technique would be successful.

Ms. Courtney Brooks, a practicum student, was teaching a mathematics lesson to her class. She had completed her direct instruction and had her students working on the practice problems. All the students were busy except for Carlos, who just sat passively. He was neither misbehaving nor disturbing others, but he did not show any inclination toward doing the work. Ms. Brooks went to Carlos, opened his book and notebook, handed him his pen, and explained what he was supposed to do. As she walked away, Carlos closed his book and notebook and placed his pencil on the desk. Then, for the remainder of the class, he just sat passively. Although Carlos did not disturb anyone, he did not complete the assignment. Ms. Brooks noted that Carlos did not appear to be emotionally upset about anything, but in a discussion with the regular classroom teacher, she learned that Carlos was several grade levels behind others in the class.

EVALUATING DEMOCRATIC TEACHING AND MANAGEMENT

Potential for Addressing Student Misbehaviors

Many teachers believe that Dreikurs's model has the potential for addressing most classroom management problems, including the perennial problem of students who goof off. The model is comprehensive; nearly every behavior problem encountered in schools can be interpreted and addressed using Adlerian principles and Dreikurs's four goals of misbehavior. Although some behavior problems might fit into more than one goal (the challenge for the teacher is to decide the specific goal), we have not seen a behavior that does not fit into at least one of the four categories. Still, managing a classroom requires more than just identifying inappropriate goals of behavior. Teachers also must provide logical consequences for the misbehavior and follow through consistently with their implementation. Dreikurs's principles are based on sound theory, which emphasizes the importance of social interaction. In addition, the model emphasizes the importance of developing understanding, judgment, and responsibility in students by involving them in resolving classroom management problems.

Manning and Baruth (2004) explained that American Indians have a strong cultural belief in sharing. Among some tribes, the concept of sharing is so powerful that people feel free to use others' possessions. The American Indian belief in sharing and other cultures' belief in ownership can result in a difficult situation that many teachers might face. How Would You React 4–3 asks you to consider such a situation in light of Dreikurs's demands that teachers respect their students as well as his emphasis on logical consequences.

Dreikurs's theories also have potential for contributing to the safe schools movement, although he did not mention this in his writings. For example, students who feel inadequate or who have not developed a sense of social interest might resort to violence. When teachers take appropriate actions to reduce students' mistaken goals (e.g., inadequacy and attention getting) and when they help students develop the ability to interact in a cooperative manner, they often can reduce the feelings of hostility that might lead to violence.

Although Dreikurs's proposal of mistaken goals can help teachers understand and correct misbehavior, it is also possible that students from different cultures will respond differently to the identification of their mistaken goals. Due to child-rearing practices that reflect cultural beliefs, students may have been taught, either consciously or unconsciously, to behave in different ways. In other words, because of their cultural backgrounds, students might respond differently to feelings of inadequacy or the need to gain attention. In fact, students in some cultures might not want attention, especially negative attention (Manning & Baruth,

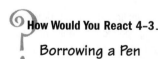

How Would You React 4–3

Borrowing a Pen

Cultural beliefs such as those about ownership can influence students' behavior in the classroom. In the following scenario, how could Mr. Woodley use Dreikurs's principles of respect and democratic ideals to solve this problem? What logical consequences would be appropriate?

Dan Chee, an American Indian student, was obviously accustomed to his cultural tradition of sharing and took a red pen from another student's desk. When the student discovered his pen was missing, he exclaimed, "Someone stole my red pen!" Mr. Woodley, the teacher, was concerned that Dan had taken the pen without asking but was not convinced that Dan had technically stolen the pen. Dan's explanation was that he had only borrowed the pen and that he thought the owner would be willing to share. The incident escalated to a point where distrust developed among the students.

2004). Other students might associate a negative stigma with a power-seeking situation, especially with a teacher they were taught to respect.

Students' misbehaviors differ widely. Some students are openly defiant, and others demonstrate more subtle misbehaviors. Phantom students are those who never misbehave but also never do any schoolwork. To quote one teacher, "These students just fade into the woodwork; they do not actively misbehave, they just do the minimum or do not do the work at all." Other students overtly misbehave and disturb the teacher and others. Regardless of the misbehavior, from phantom to overt, Dreikurs's theories have potential for managing the problem. Students can benefit from democratic classrooms (with the possible exception of the previously mentioned students of culturally different backgrounds), and most students can benefit from understanding their mistaken goals and from the idea of logical consequences for their actions. Knowing that students have a psychological need to belong to a group and to feel valued, a teacher can help these students by encouraging them to interact with others, helping them achieve academic success, and helping them develop their own social interest. How would you respond to the situation in How Would You React 4–4, "Constantly Raising A Hand"?

Students, regardless of their special needs and specific behavior problems, deserve to be understood as individuals. Overall, Dreikurs's basic philosophical beliefs of considering individual students, believing in freedom of student decision making, and trusting people to make wise decisions (Dreikurs, 1968) show that the model is flexible enough to address specific student needs.

Advantages and Disadvantages

Dreikurs's model undoubtedly has several advantages. One is that it promotes respect and communication among teachers and students. With its focus on democratic ideals, it allows students to take responsibility for their own actions, to help establish class rules, and to influence instructional practices. Second, the logical consequences, when used consistently, are a fair and basic element in a discipline plan. Third, Dreikurs's democratic teaching model complements good teaching by providing a caring classroom community, using student-centered instructional techniques, and promoting collaboration between teacher and student.

How Would You React 4–4

Constantly Raising a Hand

Wayne McNeil, a language arts teacher, asked a number of questions during his class. According to the rules Mr. McNeil and his class had developed, students had to raise their hands before giving an answer. One day, Jay raised and blatantly waved his hand in response to every question. "Please call on me, Mr. McNeil," he seemed to be saying. Mr. McNeil and the students (including Jay) knew that he could not call on Jay for every answer. However, Jay made a spectacle of himself raising and waving his hand to answer each question. Finally, Mr. McNeil called on Jay to answer the question. Even though Jay had his hand raised, he said, "I don't know." Mr. McNeil thought, "Why would Jay raise his hand to answer a question when he did not know the answer? What should I do to avoid the blatant hand waving to answer a question?"

Working collaboratively in groups of three or four, respond to the following questions.

1. According to Dreikurs, what is Jay trying to say to Mr. McNeil?
2. What can Mr. McNeil do to help Jay?
3. How different would Mr. McNeil's response be if Jay were an upper elementary student? A primary school student? A middle school student? A high school student?

Fourth, his theories of social interest and the understanding of causes of behavior can contribute to making schools safer for students and teachers.

However, several disadvantages also are associated with the democratic model. It might be difficult for teachers to identify and understand students' reasons for misbehaving. Additionally, even though teachers understand why students misbehave, they might not be able to respond properly and to provide logical consequences for all misbehaviors. Some deep emotional problems that lead to serious feelings of inadequacy or to elaborate plans for revenge might require professional skills beyond those held by classroom teachers or most school counselors and might need resources that are unavailable in many schools. Finally, teachers who are inherently autocratic or permissive might have difficulty adopting democratic perspectives.

Imposing or Teaching Discipline?

Dreikurs believed discipline should be taught rather than imposed. In fact, he stated that "The teaching of discipline is an on-going process, not something to resort to only in times of stress or misbehavior" (Dreikurs, 1968, p. 21). Unfortunately, some educators view discipline as only a punitive measure. To them, discipline means physical punishment, rigid control by rules, or regulations and autocratic authority (Dreikurs, 1968).

Dreikurs's (1968) Democratic Teaching and Management model does provide for the teaching of discipline. For example, as teachers identify mistaken goals, they can teach students to identify those goals.

Taylor can realize that she harasses other students to get attention.

Jason can see that he uses psychological abuse to hide his feelings of inadequacy.

Samantha can understand that her refusal to complete assignments is part of her power-seeking attempt.

Once students learn the reasons for their misbehavior, they are in a better position to learn self-discipline and to apply that discipline themselves.

You might recall that one criticism of the Canters' Assertive Discipline was that teachers are reacting mainly after a student misbehaves. Once students do something wrong, they are given a check mark. Instead, Dreikurs's theory calls for logical consequences for the behavior infraction and for the students to learn the goals of their behavior. Also, rather than traditional punishment, the teacher who follows Dreikurs's model encourages the student to engage in self-discipline and to learn to demonstrate appropriate behavior.

Gartrell (2001) suggested that teachers of young children replace "time-outs" with guidance to develop an encouraging classroom. While maintaining that time-outs probably were first used as alternatives to embarrassment, scolding, and corporal punishment, he maintains that the negatives associated with time-outs call for other strategies. Using ideas that appear to be firmly based in Dreikurs' theories, Gartrell suggests teaching democratic life skills, and building an encouraging classroom.

Underlying Beliefs

For Dreikurs's behavior plan to be effective, educators must subscribe to at least three fundamental concepts. First, they must believe that teachers should be democratic rather than permissive or autocratic. Teachers who believe that students behave better when the teacher is an autocratic dictator will have difficulty with the democratic nature of Dreikurs's theories. Likewise, **permissive teacher**s—those who usually let the students do what they want to do and depend upon their judgment to do what is best for them and other students—also will have problems.

Developing Your Personal Philosophy

Do Democratic Management Practices Reflect Your Beliefs?

Determine how close your management philosophy is to that of Rudolph Dreikurs by answering the following questions:

1. Do I prefer a democratic, permissive, or autocratic classroom?
2. Do I believe students should have a say in the determination of class rules?
3. Do I believe (as Adler and Dreikurs did) that a main condition of positive mental health is social interest or the ability to direct action for the sake of others?
4. Do I have the basic philosophical and/or psychological belief that each person is born with the capacity to develop his or her social interest?
5. Do I believe that for democracy to exist there must be a clearly defined social vision that is characterized by high expectations, high levels of honest encouragement, and an insistence that all people are responsible for others' well-being?
6. Do I believe in the use of encouragement rather than praise and clearly understand the difference between the two?
7. Do I believe in logical consequences (whenever possible) instead of a set punishment for misbehavior in general?

Second, teachers should agree with the concept of logical consequences. "There are not enough logical consequences to go around, and they don't always work, anyway," one teacher said. Any teacher who believes in harsh punishments will not agree with Dreikurs. Also, the teacher who finds it easier to use the same punishment for all behaviors will find fault with the idea of logical consequences.

CASE STUDY
A Struggle to Control a Class

Ms. Candace Gardner, a teacher for 5 years, operated a tight ship. She believed that given the chance, students would misbehave and take advantage of her. In her classroom, Ms. Gardner established the rules, doled out the punishment when students broke rules, and praised students who behaved. "Disciplining students is a strength of mine," she was fond of saying. Ms. Gardner did not feel that students could be trusted to behave on their own. The result was a class full of students who often tested her. Some students wanted to see how far they could go with their misbehavior; others behaved because they feared her punishments and preferred to have her approval and praise. None of the students felt they had any stake in making classroom decisions.

When the principal and the In-Service Planning Committee proposed a series of workshops on classroom management, Ms. Gardner balked. "I already know how to make my class behave. I discipline them by telling them what to do and they do it or face the punishment. What else do I need?"

However, she admitted to herself that a struggle always seemed to exist between the students and her. Instead of working with the students in a sense of community, it seemed that she and the students worked against one another. Ms. Gardner was always adding rules to the class list, making punishments more severe, seeking new ways to praise students who demonstrated positive behavior, and being sure she never let her guard down. "What I'm doing works," she thought, but managing students was a struggle and took a toll on her and the students.

Questions for Consideration

1. What would proponents of Dreikurs's democratic teaching and management think about Ms. Gardner?
2. What would they suggest she do?
3. How could she devise a system that would create more of a sense of democratic community?
4. What could be done to avoid Ms. Gardner's feeling that classroom management was a struggle?

 You can record your answers to these questions online on this book's Companion Web Site at *www.prenhall.com/manning*.

Third, teachers must understand the difference between encouragement and praise and will have to agree with Dreikurs's belief that praise should be avoided in favor of encouragement. A teacher who constantly offers praise even when the praise is not warranted—such as "good job," "fine work," and "you're doing much better"—probably will not see the need for encouragement rather than praise. However, when teachers' philosophical and psychological beliefs reflect Dreikurs's beliefs, they will use encouragement rather than praise. To determine whether you are comfortable accepting Dreikurs's beliefs, complete Developing Your Personal Philosophy.

Sometimes teachers rule with an "iron fist" rather than by developing a sense of democratic community in which students help establish rules and teachers use encouragement and logical consequences. The iron fist technique can lead to power struggles, as well as to negative conditions that can contribute to unsafe schools. The Case Study looks at how one teacher faced a daily struggle managing her students. Additional information on Dreikurs's views and some specific applications of his ideas can be found on this book's Companion Web Site, in "Reaching Out With Technology."

CONCLUDING REMARKS

Please go to www.prenhall.com/manning and click on Concluding Remarks for this chapter to find more information.

Educators in elementary, middle, and secondary schools can implement Dreikurs's democratic classrooms, identify mistaken goals, use logical consequences, and encourage students to behave and achieve. Using Adlerian principles, educators must nurture students' social interest and help children belong, feel valued, develop positive self-worth, and not feel discouraged. Helping children of all ages to feel valued and respected can contribute to improved behavior and to safe schools. Thus, Dreikurs's theories of democratic classrooms can contribute to teaching and management effectiveness.

Suggested Readings

Inlay, L. (2005). Safe schools for the roller coaster years. *Educational Leadership, 62*(7), 41–43. Looking at the changes that occur to adolescents, Inlay relates the use of Dreikurs' ideas in a small middle school.

Lefstein, A. (2002). Thinking power and pedagogy apart—Coping with discipline in progressive school reform. *Teachers College Record, 104*(8), 1627–1655. Lefstein maintained one reason for the failure of the progressive school was the inadequate treatment of pedagogy and classroom control.

Malmgren, K. W., Trezek, B. J., & Paul, P. V. (2005). Models of classroom management as applied to the secondary classroom. *The Clearing House* (In press). Along with models from the Canters and Gordon, this article looks at Dreikurs' model of logical consequences and its use in secondary schools.

Pryor, D. B., & Tollerud, T. R. (1999). Applications of Adlerian principles in school settings. *Professional School Counseling, 2*(4), 299–304. These authors provide an excellent explanation of Adlerian principles and Dreikurs' interpretation for classroom management in contemporary schools.

Richardson, V., & Fallona, C. (2001). Classroom management as method and manner. *Journal of Curriculum Studies, 33*(6), 705–728. These authors describe how two case studies of experienced classroom teachers, whose classroom management approaches differ, appear to meet the overall goals for effective classroom management.

CHAPTER 5

Exploring the Theories of Congruent Communication: *Haim Ginott*

Focusing Questions

After reading this chapter, you should be able to answer the following questions:

1. Why should Ginott's work be termed a theory rather than a model?

2. What is congruent communication, and how does this idea contribute to positive classroom management?

3. What did Ginott mean when he, as a young teacher, said, "I am the decisive element in the classroom" (Ginott, 1972a, p. 15)?

4. What behaviors would Ginott describe as "teachers at their best" and "teachers at their worst"?

5. What are sane messages, and what are some examples?

6. Why does Ginott say that punishment should be avoided, and what does he suggest as an alternative?

7. What are some of Ginott's essential principles, and how can they be implemented effectively?

8. How does diversity affect Ginott's theories of congruent communication?

Key Terms

Appreciative praise
Evaluative praise
I-messages
Sane messages
You-messages

Haim Ginott's theories differ significantly from those of the foundational theorists and from the other classroom management models that we have discussed so far. In fact, he never synthesized his work into a finely developed classroom management model, as did Dreikurs and the Canters. However, the fact that Ginott did not turn his ideas about communication, self-discipline, and appreciative praise into a well-organized classroom management model should not take away from the importance of his theories and the fact that they can be used to complement the models developed by other classroom management theorists.

HAIM GINOTT: BIOGRAPHICAL SKETCH

Born in Tel Aviv, Israel, Haim Ginott received three degrees from Columbia University and worked as a clinical psychologist and as a professor of psychology and psychotherapy. He was a practitioner of what later came to be called parent education. Through his books, newspaper columns, and his role as clinical psychologist on the *Today Show,* he became widely known. In his books *Between Parent and Teenager* (1969) and *Teacher and Child* (1972a), Ginott offered practical guidance and included sample dialogues between adults and children as he tried to help teachers and parents improve their spoken communication with children and young adults.

OVERVIEW OF CONGRUENT COMMUNICATION

Although Ginott did not develop an organized model of classroom management, he had strong ideas about communication, self-discipline, and appreciative praise. Together, these principles have applications in contemporary classrooms.

Key Concepts

Ginott's theory has a number of key concepts, which are shown in Figure 5–1. Together these contribute to the effectiveness of a teacher's management techniques. As you read about Ginott's theories in more detail later in this chapter, you might find additional parts of Ginott's theory that have meaning for you personally and that you might want to add to this list. However, we believe that these concepts summarize the essentials of Ginott's theories.

Philosophical and Psychological Foundations

As you might recall, Skinner's theory was that individuals can condition or shape the behavior of others, and the Canters believed that teachers should assertively inform students of expected behaviors. In contrast, Haim Ginott's theory illustrates a different philosophical and psychological belief, for he thought that the teacher's personal approach creates the "climate" that contributes to students' behavior, whether positive or negative. Consider Ginott's oft-stated philosophy (Ginott, 1972a, p. 15):

> I have come to a frightening conclusion. I am the decisive element in the classroom. It is my personal approach that creates the climate. It is my daily mood that makes the weather. As a teacher I possess tremendous power to make a child's life miserable or joyous. I can be a tool of torture or an instrument of inspiration. I can humiliate or humor, hurt or heal. In all situations it is my response that decides whether a crisis will be escalated or de-escalated, and a child humanized or de-humanized.

Management Tip 5–1 looks at ways that teachers can prepare themselves as a part of classroom management.

According to Ginott's philosophy, a teacher is the influential element in the classroom. Instead of conditioning or shaping students to behave or maintaining a checklist of student infractions, the teacher sets the stage or environment for positive behavior. Although

Figure 5–1 Key Concepts

Teachers should do the following:

- Use congruent communication that is open, harmonious with students' feelings about themselves and their situations, and without sarcasm to send "sane messages" about the situation not the personality or character of the individual.

- Promote self-discipline for both teachers and students and believe that "the essence of discipline is finding effective alternatives to discipline" (Ginott, 1972a, p. 147).

- Accept and acknowledge students and their actions or comments without labeling, arguing, disputing or belittling the individual.

- Avoid evaluative praise, which focuses on a student's character, and use appreciative praise, which focuses on an action or product.

- Avoid sending you-messages and use I-messages to describe how a behavior makes the sender of the message feel.

- Demonstrate their best behaviors or those that contribute to a classroom environment where student cooperation is invited rather than demanded.

proper behavior is still the students' responsibility, the teacher's responsibility is to create the climate or the conditions that contribute to students' proper behavior. Rather than expecting teachers to reach unattainable goals with inadequate tools, Ginott maintains that every teacher deserves effective tools and skills in dealing with children and managing behavior (Roebuck, 2002).

Teachers' Roles and Responsibilities

Thus far in this book, you have seen how various classroom management theorists and models view the roles and responsibilities of teachers. From the work of Skinner came the ideas about teachers conditioning and shaping students' behaviors. The Canters' ideas of teachers as assertive managers focused on identifying expectations as well as rewards and consequences, and Dreikurs thought teachers should seek to understand the goals of student misbehaviors and then respond appropriately. In contrast, Ginott presented a view that, in some ways, reflects the ideas of Redl and Wattenberg (supporting self-control) and Gordon (self-discipline and I-messages). Instead of responding to student

Management Tip 5–1

Preparing Yourself

Ginott talked about the teacher's personal approach, which creates a climate in the classroom. Part of a teacher's preparation includes the professional presence of that individual in a classroom. Too many principals talk about sending a teacher home because he or she was not dressed appropriately or had obvious hygiene problems. Trying to dress like the students, especially in secondary schools, does not promote a professional image and sends the wrong message to students. Remember, you never get a second chance to make a first impression.

Teachers need to

Dress professionally,

Dress appropriately for the grades or subjects they teach,

Have a positive attitude,

Practice good hygiene.

Elementary

Think about the activities that you and your students will be doing on a given day and dress accordingly.

Secondary

Maturing adolescents need to focus on instruction and not on the exposed parts of a teacher's anatomy.

---

behavior (although in all classroom management models, teachers will have to respond to individual behavior at some time), Ginott proposed that teachers should use positive, effective communication to provide a classroom environment that encourages or invites students to behave; demonstrate and model behaviors that invite student cooperation and positive behavior; avoid autocratic behaviors (something Dreikurs also spoke against); and recognize the need to seek alternatives to punishment. The teacher remains sensitive to the needs of students and communicates this sensitivity in words and actions. Thus, teachers who want to promote cooperation with students and harmony in the classroom probably will be successful with Ginott's congruent communication. On the other hand, teachers who feel they have to be autocratic, demand obedience and adherence to their expectations, and use punishments probably will not feel comfortable working with Ginott's theories. How Would You React 5–1 looks at Mr. Holstein and asks you to determine whether he would feel comfortable using Ginott's ideas. Then, Management Tip 5–2 explains how teachers can determine their motivation and ability to use Ginott's congruent communication by maintaining a management journal.

Please go to *www.prenhall.com/manning* and click on the Management Tips for this chapter to complete management activities and find more information on preparing yourself for teaching.

APPLYING CONGRUENT COMMUNICATION

Implementing Practical Applications

Now that you have an overview of Ginott's ideas, we can look at several of them in more detail and apply them to classroom settings. Consider especially how you can use each idea at the level you will be teaching. Although the following 14 applications are taken

How Would You React 5–1

Creating a Classroom Environment

Review Figure 5–1 and the key concepts of Ginott. Keep them in mind as you read the following scenario.

Mr. Holstein, an experienced teacher, had a philosophy of "teachers versus students" and believed that if teachers give students an inch, students will take a mile. His ideas on classroom management were summed up in his favorite saying: "I don't let them get away with a thing, and I don't trust them either." In his classroom, Mr. Holstein lived up to his philosophy, constantly sent you-messages, and berated his students—even the ones who tried to learn and behave. Addressing every misbehavior, he used punishment to get the students' cooperation, and he shouted and yelled. Although he bragged that he had few discipline problems, the fact was that his students were subdued and afraid to misbehave.

How would you describe the environment in Mr. Holstein's classroom? Using Ginott's key concepts (Figure 5–1), determine whether Mr. Holstein's actions support or oppose Ginott's ideas. Would Mr. Holstein be a good candidate for implementing Ginott's theory? What kind of classroom management theory might appeal to Mr. Holstein? Why?

---

primarily from Ginott's *Teacher and Child* (1972a), they are in random order rather than a hierarchy, as the Canters might have suggested in their Assertive Discipline model.

Application 1

Teachers should use clear communication. In Ginott's model, "communication is the key" (Morris, 1996, p. 9). Of primary concern is the communication between teachers and students, in which teachers clearly communicate their expectations in a manner that helps students feel accepted, even when they make a mistake or misbehave. When the lines of communication are kept open, students are able to learn more effectively and behave more appropriately. If teachers show understanding when students make mistakes, the students will be more willing to keep learning. In addition, this open communication promotes autonomy among the students (Morris, 1996).

Application 2

Teachers should use **sane messages.** Teachers who use sane messages address a student's behavior rather than the student's character (Ginott, 1973; Morris, 1996). For example, when Keith walks aimlessly around the room while the teacher is talking, the teacher and other students are disturbed. Instead of using a **you-message** and saying "Keith, for the 15th time, you are walking around again—sit down," the teacher sends a sane **I-message** by calmly saying, "Keith, the other students and I are disturbed when someone walks around during quiet time." Because the teacher addresses the situation (e.g., someone, not just Keith, walking around the room), Keith feels less threatened by the teacher and is more willing to listen to the teacher's request. Also, the tone and sincerity in the teacher's voice when issuing the sane message have an impact on the effectiveness of the message. Teachers should be in control of their emotions when addressing a discipline problem and should not let the problem become a "teacher-versus-student" (Morris, 1996, p. 10) situation.

Application 3

Teachers should refrain from using punishment. Ginott discourages the use of punishment to handle discipline problems. Teachers in contemporary schools realize the legal and emotional dangers associated with physical punishment, but other types of punishment also can be harmful. One of the worst effects of punishment is that it interferes with the development of a student's conscience because it often relieves guilt too easily. For example, if Bernadette feels that she paid for her misbehavior through the punishment, then she might feel free to repeat it (Ginott, 1965). In addition, punishment rarely serves as a means of teaching discipline because once punishment is administered, a student simply might try to avoid future punishment rather than learning self-discipline. By finding a means of teaching discipline other than through the use of punishment, teachers can make discipline in the classroom a learning experience for all students (Morris, 1996).

Application 4

Teachers should ignore common four-letter words rather than making them a public issue. Ginott (1972a) maintained that addressing the problem of the use of a profanity often can be more troublesome than use of the word itself.

> Ginott tells of a teacher who overheard a student say a four-letter word. The teacher even demanded that the student repeat the word so she could be sure what he said. When the teacher ordered the student to leave the room, he said another four-letter word as he left. All this time, the other students in the class watched to see what would happen.

Ginott maintained that a better approach would have been to ignore the word so that it would not have become a major issue. You can try using this idea to respond to the situation in How Would You React 5–2.

Application 5

Teachers should use guidance rather than criticism. When Ms. Conger told Saushanna, "You're so lazy you'll never go to college, and you'll never amount to anything," she violated several of Ginott's principles. Ginott (1973) thought that teachers who use criticism often attack a student's personality and character, possibly use demeaning names, and might predict dire consequences. In his book *Between Parent and Child* (1965), Ginott also maintained that if criticism is used, it always should be constructive so it will point out what needs to be improved and how to do it while omitting negative remarks about the student's personality.

> Ms. Rubio rarely criticizes students for any reason, but she still makes her behavior expectations clear. Her students probably consider her a firm disciplinarian, but they also regard her as positive and likable. She has the unique ability to guide students through their misbehaviors by encouraging them toward appropriate behaviors. For example, on one occasion when Leigh knocked over someone else's books, instead of saying, "Pick up the books; can't you be more careful—you disturbed half the class," Ms. Rubio said, "Perhaps you would like to help pick up the books." Feelings were not hurt, no character was attacked, and no one was embarrassed. The incident was considered an accident (which it was).

Management Tip 5-2

Maintaining a Management Journal

Maintain a daily management journal to determine the success of your behavior management practices. Here are some questions based on Ginott's Congruent Communication that you might consider:

- Did I use
    clear communication,
    sane messages,
    guidance rather than criticism?
- Did I refrain from using punishment?
- Did I handle anger appropriately?

Here are some more specific questions for elementary and secondary teachers.

Elementary

How did I handle behavior situations resulting from elementary students not wanting to leave their parents and homes?

Did I demonstrate clear communication—words, phrases, and voice tones that reflect young children's listening skills and cognitive ability?

Secondary

Did I acknowledge students' developmental concerns—students concerned about their rapid (or too slow) physical development and rapidly expanding social worlds?

Did I show "acceptance and acknowledgment" toward students who chose to go along with peer pressure rather than my rules and expectations?

Please go to *www.prenhall.com/manning* and click on the Management Tips for this chapter to complete management activities and find more information on maintaining a management journal.

How Would You React 5–2

Responding to Profanity

According to Ginott, teachers should not make a public issue out of common four-letter words. However some words are not appropriate for use in school with some schools having serious consequences for students who use them. In the following scenario, is there a way for the teacher to follow Ginott's advice while eliminating a potential problem?

Ms. Neider faced a problem in her fourth-grade class. Although Louisa was not a behavior problem in other ways,

she had a bad habit of talking too much and peppering her conversation with the word sucks. Examples of Louisa's statements included "This school really sucks," "Why do you give us so much homework—this really sucks," and "All these books we have to read suck." Ms. Neider realized her class faced worse problems, but she also did not approve of the word and wanted Louisa to choose a more appropriate one. She was also afraid that Louisa might begin to use other inappropriate words.

Application 6

Teachers should handle their own anger appropriately. Although most teachers are taught or assume that good teachers do not get angry, Ginott maintained that even good teachers get angry (Ginott, 1972b). However, he suggested that anger should be conveyed appropriately and suggested three steps to surviving anger (1965):

1. Accept the fact that the actions of students will make us angry.
2. Realize that we are entitled to our anger without guilt or shame.
3. "Except for one safeguard, we are entitled to express what we feel. We can express our angry feelings *provided* (italics Ginott's) we do not attack the child's personality or character" (pp. 50–51).

Instead of yelling and screaming to convey anger, teachers should give students a warning to change behaviors. Ginott (1965, p. 51) suggested the use of statements such as "I feel annoyed," "I feel irritated," and even "I feel angry." Sometimes just a simple statement like this will be sufficient to stop the student from demonstrating the behavior.

Ginott told the story of Mrs. Brooks, a kindergarten teacher. When she saw 5-year-old Alan throw a stone at his friend, she said loudly, "I saw it. I am indignant and dismayed. Stones are not for throwing at people. People are not for hurting" (Ginott, 1972b, p. 23). This story aptly illustrates anger without attacking the student as an individual.

Application 7

Teachers should show acceptance and acknowledgment with uncritical messages. Communicating acceptance and understanding is a complex art that often is made more difficult by classroom conditions. It is hard to listen to the comments of others and accept what they are saying when we disagree with them. It becomes even more difficult when the individual expressing the opposing viewpoint is a student (Ginott, 1965). For example, Barry might complain that he has too much homework. A teacher can send an accepting and acknowledging, uncritical message by saying: "You seem upset about the homework. It does seem like a lot of work for one day, especially with the unexpected test in chemistry." An unaccepting, critical message would have been, "Don't be ridiculous. When I was your age we had 10 times as much homework. And, if you had been studying your chemistry every night, you wouldn't have anything to worry about. You have only yourself to blame, so stop complaining and get to work or you'll fail."

In communicating with students, the difference between critical and uncritical messages is crucial. In making demands on students, an uncritical message invites cooperation, but a critical message engenders resistance. For example, when a student interrupts a teacher, an uncritical message is "I would like to finish my statement" (Ginott, 1965, p. 95); a critical message is "You are very rude. You are interrupting". Management Tip 5–3 provides examples of times to express acceptance and acknowledgment at the elementary and secondary levels.

Application 8

Teachers should avoid name-calling and labeling students and should avoid "diagnosis and prognosis" (Ginott, 1972a, p. 100). Ginott maintained that labeling or name-calling is taboo in schools. The student who is labeled or called a name begins to feel resentment and to think that the teacher's negative opinion is true. As Ginott (1972a, p. 61) says, "What the teacher says about . . . [a student] has serious consequences." Telling a child he or she is bad does not help that child to improve behavior. Although the problem behavior might be momentarily stopped, the process of halting troublesome behavior has not been supported (Roebuck, 2002)

> ⭐ **Management Tip 5–3**
>
> ## Expressing Acceptance and Acknowledgment
>
> There are a number of times each day that teachers can express acceptance and acknowledgment with uncritical messages. Although elementary teachers can usually express acceptance individually and in front of the class, secondary teachers can best express acceptance individually or on a more private basis.
>
> Most teachers express appreciation, acknowledgment and acceptance when students abide by class routines and obey all rules, but here are some additional times to express appreciation.
>
> **Elementary**
>
> Coming to school
>
> Abiding by the class routines and obeying all rules
>
> Treating smaller and younger children with respect and caring
>
> Behaving properly on the playground, at lunch, and school assemblies
>
> **Secondary**
>
> Coming to class prepared—homework done and with needed books and supplies
>
> Showing accomplishment in academics, athletics, drama, music, and band
>
> Avoiding negative peer pressure

Please go to *www.prenhall.com/manning* and click on the Management Tips for this chapter to complete management activities and find more information on expressing acceptance and acknowledgment.

Ginott (1972a, p. 99) told the story of a teacher disciplining Simon for being late for school. "What's your excuse this time?" When Simon told his story, the teacher answered, "I don't believe a word you said. I know why you are late: You are too lazy to get up on time. I still remember your brother; he too suffered from congenital indolence. If you don't shape up, you know where you'll end up."

One high school physical education teacher had a group of less capable boys who, although well behaved, lacked physical abilities and skills. He called these boys "sissies" and "spastics" without realizing the effects of his hurtful words. Finally, another teacher called the habit to his attention and pointed out the negative effect it was having on the boys.

As Ginott maintained, teachers should not call students names under any circumstances. The psychological results are too devastating and the name-calling usually does not change behaviors.

Application 9

Teachers should avoid sarcasm and ridicule.

"Joel, you're so lazy! You don't bring your books to class. You don't do any work. Why do you come to school anyway? Just to sleep and get lunch?" To make matters even worse, the teacher made this comment in front of the entire class while the student just sat there and endured the teacher's ridicule.

Closely related to the idea of avoiding name-calling is the idea that teachers also should avoid sarcasm and ridicule. Ginott (1972a, p. 66) summed up his position on sarcasm by saying: "Sarcasm is not good for children. It destroys their self-confidence and self-esteem. Like strychnine, it can be fatal. Bitter irony and biting sarcasm only reinforce the traits they attack."

Ginott (1972a, p. 109) gave several examples of caustic comments that teachers need to avoid, such as the following:

"You are relying on your own judgment again. Believe me, it's a poor guide."

"Do you think you can come back to your senses? You have been out of them for quite awhile."

"Must you touch everything? What are you—spastic?"

"You don't need a psychologist; you need a vacuum cleaner. Your mind is cluttered with junk."

We might laugh about such comments when they are made in the abstract, but such devastating comments do not belong in teacher–student communication, even if they are made "in jest." A professional educator must shun sarcastic comments that casually destroy a student's self-esteem (Ginott, 1972a) and that pose a barrier to effective communication (Ginott, 1965). Although we have had several practicum students who felt that they had mastered the art of sarcasm to a point where the recipient would not be harmed, we have a strict "no sarcasm" rule. The effects are potentially too devastating. One student may not be offended (or show any overt signs of distress), but another student might be affected differently.

Application 10

Teachers should strive for brevity when disciplining students.

When Ms. Andrews reprimanded her class, she failed to understand the need for brevity. As she walked around the room, her seemingly endless monologue to the class went as follows:

"You're talking and misbehaving much too much."

"Why do you do this when you know I can't teach when you do?"

"You talk in the hall and in the cafeteria, too."

"Jason, you put down that book! How can you listen to me and look at that book? When I talk to you, you need to listen. Maybe that's why you're one of the worst in the class."

"Now, what are you going to do about all this talking?"

"You're making it so much harder for me to teach."

"Kinesha, why do you talk so much? I just can't understand it."

As Ms. Andrews continued her diatribe, it was obvious that the students were not listening.

Although Ginott says teachers should demonstrate brevity when disciplining students (Ginott, 1972a), many teachers do not understand the need for and the benefits of brevity. Instead of dwelling on the problem and compounding it by her own incessant talking, Ms. Andrews should have used brevity in her corrections and continued her lesson without further interruptions. The students would have known her displeasure and would have been more likely to try to demonstrate appropriate behavior.

Application 11

Teachers always should use *I-messages* instead of *you-messages.* Ginott (1972b, p. 86) believed that you-messages attack students' personality and character. To avoid these personal attacks, a teacher should use I-messages that focus on how the misbehavior makes the teacher feel. "I am annoyed," "I am appalled," and "I am furious" are safer statements than "You are a pest," "Look what you have done," "You are so stupid," and "Who do you think you are?" (Italics are Ginott's.)

The most workable discipline measure is often to ask a student politely to refrain from disturbing the class (whether the misbehavior is talking, walking around the room, or some other infraction). For example, instead of saying "Sundee, stop tapping your pen on the desk. You can find so many ways to disturb the class; you're always getting in trouble," a teacher might say, "I'm bothered when someone keeps tapping a pen on the desk. It makes it difficult for me to concentrate."

In our university classes, we try to take Ginott's advice and use I- rather than you-messages. For example, if we are concerned about the classroom management plan that a preservice elementary school teacher has developed, we will say "I am concerned that fifth-grade students will not see this management plan as sufficiently comprehensive" instead of saying "You did not write a comprehensive management plan—you certainly had time because it was assigned the first day of class. It looks like you just procrastinated until the last minute. What kind of teacher are you going to make?" Even with adults, we find that I-messages are more effective than you-messages. How Would You React 5–3 looks at a parent's remarks in a parent–teacher conference and asks you to consider the comments you would make in response.

Application 12

Teachers, when disciplining, should provide students with a face-saving exit. Students often forget rules or perhaps even inadvertently break a rule. Therefore, Ginott (1972a) believed that students should be provided with a face-saving exit during discipline situations and that teachers should develop a classroom management plan with a focus on teaching discipline rather than humiliating and embarrassing a student. Sometimes students will break a rule only one time and will be appreciative when the teacher gives them an opportunity to agree not to make the same mistake twice. According to Ginott, the teacher should avoid any additional comments and simply accept the student's assertion that "It won't happen again." The student has agreed to the behavior expectations and simultaneously saved face.

How Would You React 5–3

Sending I-messages

Ginott believes that teachers should use I-messages rather than you-messages. However, a problem may arise when a teacher observes another adult using you-messages. Read the following scenario and decide what you would do if placed in a similar situation.

> Mr. and Ms. Madsen and their daughter Silvia were meeting with Mr. Colline, Silvia's teacher. Mr. Colline had just shared his concerns about the work that Silvia was doing in language arts and her behavior in the classroom. Mr. Madsen looked at Sil-

via and said, "Why are you making such bad grades? Can't you behave either? Your mother and I do our best for you and this is the thanks we get—what kind of daughter are you? You just want to come to school to see your friends. Are they as bad as you?"

Assume that you are Mr. Colline. Would you ignore Mr. Madsen's comments? Why? Would you try to explain (or model) more appropriate I-messages? If so, what would you say or do at this point in the conference?

Application 13

Teachers should respect students' privacy and avoid asking prying questions. Although teachers have good intentions, they sometimes pry into students' privacy.

> When Chase walked into the classroom, Ms. DePaulo took one look and saw that something was wrong. In front of the entire class she said, "Why do you look so sad today? Are your mom and dad quarreling again? Why don't you tell me what's wrong? Perhaps I can help."

In this situation, Ms. DePaulo was genuinely concerned about Chase and realized that his emotional state would affect his learning and socialization; however, she invaded Chase's privacy. For any number of reasons, a student might not want to share personal information. Instead of prying needlessly into the student's private life, Ginott (1972a) suggested that the teacher should ask discreetly and succinctly, "Can I be of help?" When Ms. DePaulo saw Chase, a private and simple "I'm available to talk if you want to" would have been sufficient. Chase would have known that Ms. DePaulo was concerned and ready to help without having his privacy violated. How Would You React 5–4 lets you try your hand at reacting to a similar situation.

Application 14

Teachers should provide appreciative praise and avoid evaluative praise. Most teachers use praise to reinforce proper behavior and also to provide students with an indication of their learning progress. In fact, praise has long been considered a means to shape behavior. (Remember Skinner, who recommended positive reinforcement to shape behavior?) However, Ginott divided praise into two types: **evaluative praise**, which is destructive, and **appreciative praise**, which is productive (Ginott, 1972a). Ginott (1965) suggested that parents (and his suggestions also apply to teachers) should follow a single and important rule about praise: Praise should deal only with the student's efforts and accomplishments, *not* (Ginott's italics) with the student's character and personality. To illustrate this, Ginott used the example of a child cleaning the yard. If the child does a good job, the parent can praise how good the yard looks; the leaves have been raked, the trash removed, and the tools arranged. Using appreciative praise, the parent might say, "The yard was so dirty. I didn't believe it could be cleaned

---

How Would You React 5–4

Defusing Anger

Ginott maintains that a teacher should respect students' privacy and not ask personal questions. However, there are times when even an innocent question can produce an unexpected result. Read the following scenario and respond to the questions at the end.

> Mr. Satcher could tell that Arturo was angry or emotionally upset in some way. As Arturo came into class after lunch, he slammed his books on his desk and left no doubt that he was furious. When Mr. Satcher asked, "Arturo, would you like to talk about it," Arturo yelled, "Hell, no—I don't want to talk about it."

1. It would be easy to say that Mr. Satcher should not have asked Arturo a question. However, now that the blow-up has happened, how should Mr. Satcher proceed?

2. Should he confront Arturo publicly about the four-letter word (remember what Ginott said about four-letter words)?

3. Is there a way that Mr. Satcher can help Arturo to find out what is wrong because Arturo's anger is affecting him and the class?

4. What can Mr. Satcher do so that Arturo's anger does not escalate into a fight or more violent behavior later in the day?

in one day" (Ginott, 1965, p. 40). If the parent had used evaluative praise, the focus would have moved from the deed to the child's character and the parent might have said, "You are such a wonderful child" (Ginott, 1965, p. 40).

> Samantha had a perfect score on all her spelling tests and was proud of her accomplishment. Using evaluative praise, a teacher placed a "Great Job" sticker on Samantha's paper and told her, "Samantha, you are such a good student. You've made a 100 on all your spelling tests so far this year. I know your parents are so proud of you! I am, too."

Such evaluative praise places an undue burden on Samantha. If she misses a word on the next test or any future test, Samantha might feel that she is no longer a good student and her parents and the teacher will not be proud of her. Activity 5–1 looks at several additional examples of appreciative praise and evaluative praise.

Effectiveness of Practical Applications

Although Ginott's theories do not constitute a comprehensive model of classroom management and do not provide appropriate actions for addressing the violence affecting our nation's schools, teachers can use Ginott's congruent communication to address the majority of misbehaviors in schools today. In fact, all his key concepts are designed to help teachers develop trust, acknowledge and accept students' feelings, and improve self-esteem. Some might question whether Ginott's ideas are more appropriate for elementary school students rather than middle and secondary school students. How Would You React 5–5 looks at this issue.

Activity 5–1

Using Appreciative Praise and Evaluative Praise

Here are a few examples of appreciative and evaluative praise.

Tyrone, a primary student, does not cry on the field trip.

Appreciative: "Tyrone, I appreciate your fine behavior on the field trip."

Evaluative: "Tyrone, my how you have grown up. You didn't cry on the field trip. You're such a big boy."

Lawree plays the flute with the school band.

Appreciative: "Lawree, I can tell you enjoy playing the flute. You practice a lot, don't you?"

Evaluative: "Lawree, you are a good musician. Keep doing it. I'm glad you're in my class."

Todd plays soccer.

Appreciative: "Todd, thanks for your fine efforts with soccer. You contribute to the team's success."

Evaluative: "Todd, you're a good soccer player. Keep trying. Your teammates are depending on you!"

Yvette is on the debate team.

Appreciative: "Good debate meet yesterday. You work hard at being a good debater."

Evaluative: "Yvette, keep up the good work. So far, so good. Don't let your team members down. It's up to you!"

Now, make up some of your own situations that would be appropriate for the level you hope to teach. Then, meet with other students who plan to teach on the same level. Share the situations and suggest examples of appreciate praise and evaluative praise for each.

How Would You React 5-5

Debating Age Appropriateness

A student in a classroom management class once stated, "I think Ginott's theories are more appropriate and applicable for elementary school students than for middle and secondary school students." Another student partially agreed with her statement, but she thought his theories were also applicable for middle school students. A debate continued among the students, with some saying congruent communication applies to all students and others saying only elementary school (and perhaps middle school) students would respond to Ginott's theories.

Look back at the key concepts in this chapter. What is your position in this debate? Elementary only? Elementary and middle school? All three grade levels? Defend your position with examples of the use of Ginott's theories in appropriate grade levels.

EVALUATING CONGRUENT COMMUNICATION IN A DIVERSE SOCIETY

Do you think Ginott's ideas will be effective in your classroom? At least two aspects deserve evaluation: First, will Ginott's theories serve as a single or cohesive model of classroom management? Second, will Ginott's theories complement other models as you develop your own personal system of classroom management? As you might guess from the discussions in this chapter, we believe that rather than standing alone as a model for classroom management, Ginott's theories hold the most potential when they are used in conjunction with other classroom management models. However, you still need to make your own well-informed decision after careful consideration.

Potential for Addressing Student Misbehaviors

Writing in the early 1970s, Ginott offered his theories prior to the current safe schools movement. Anyone who is acquainted with contemporary schools knows about the violence that is all too common today, especially the extreme cases that make the news. It is important to remember, though, that most behavior problems and disturbances in elementary, middle, and high schools are of lesser magnitude. However, even these lesser disturbances (talking, getting out of one's seat, making noises, etc.) are bothersome, troublesome, and a hindrance to the teaching/learning process. They definitely need to be addressed, which can be done effectively using Ginott's congruent communication and its various applications. Activity 5–2 asks you to consider several misbehaviors to suggest the extent to which Ginott's theories might be effective.

In our increasingly diverse schools, Ginott's theories and their focus on positive treatment, acceptance and acknowledgment, sane messages, and appreciative praise can help teachers promote congruent communication among cultures and between genders. Regardless of their cultural backgrounds, students need positive perceptions of themselves and their cultures. Perhaps because Ginott's theory is a disparate array of ideas rather than an established classroom management model, his ideas can be used to address a number of student differences and the psychological and developmental needs of all students. For example, all students, regardless of their differences and the seriousness of their behavior, need to have their self-esteem and cultural identity enhanced, to feel accepted as individual students, to have a sense of belonging and affection, to believe that teachers have their best interests in mind, and to have their psychosocial and cognitive needs addressed.

Ms. Bariff worked constantly to develop a classroom environment that addressed the developmental needs of her diverse class. "I try to be sure their needs are met, and I want them to feel good about

Activity 5–2

Applying Ginott's Theories to Management Problems

For each of the following situations, indicate whether or not Ginott's theories cover the situation. If so, how do you believe Ginott would advise a teacher to respond?

- An eighth-grade boy yells an obscenity when another student jokingly trips him.
- A second-grade girl cries almost every morning when she comes to school.
- A sixth-grade student walks aimlessly around the room during sustained silent reading time.
- A first-grade student talks constantly and disturbs others.
- A tenth-grade student passes a math test, jumps up, does a victory dance, and yells, "Whoopee!"
- A seventh-grade girl walks to the pencil sharpener without asking; she says she forgot the rule and that she will not do it again.
- Three second-grade students throw pinecones at the other students during recess.
- A fight breaks out between two eighth-grade students.

themselves, other students, and me—that's a good start," she said. As she practiced her beliefs, she worked on self-esteem and positive interpersonal relationships while avoiding sarcasm and you-messages. Quiet and soft-spoken, she was effective at lowering her voice to get students' attention. She had earned the students' respect and was able to reap the benefits of placing her priority on addressing the developmental needs of all her students.

Whether students are in a gifted class, a special needs class, or somewhere in between, Ginott's theories of congruent communication can contribute to their positive behavior. However, individual students may react to Ginott's ideas in different ways. Activity 5–3 asks you to consider a few specific situations.

Advantages and Disadvantages of Ginott's Theories

Ginott's congruent communication theory has advantages and disadvantages that you should consider when determining whether or not to use Ginott's ideas in your personal classroom management model. One distinct advantage is that congruent communication leads to the formation of a positive, friendly rapport between teacher and students and enhances the classroom learning environment. Undoubtedly, positive relationships between students and teachers are a good starting point in any classroom management system; if a teacher models positive and sane messages, the students might do likewise. Remember, though, that the opposite scenario holds true, as well. Students can (and often do) mimic negative teacher behaviors.

Another advantage of Ginott's theory is that when teachers encourage students to take responsibility for their behavior and for developing the self-discipline necessary to behave appropriately, they also are helping students develop positive self-esteem. Finally, Ginott offers specific suggestions for preventing and handling a variety of relatively minor behavior problems. This can be an advantage and a disadvantage. Although teachers can use congruent

Activity 5–3

Reacting to Ginott's Theories

How might students' diversities (e.g., culture, gender, developmental, and social class) affect their reactions to the following ideas of Ginott?

His call for appreciative praise rather than evaluative praise. Might some students misunderstand the teacher's avoidance of evaluative praise (e.g., "She never tells me I'm a good student")?

His insistence that teachers respect privacy and avoid prying. Might students expect teachers to ask personal questions to show an interest in the students (e.g., "He never asks how I'm doing. He's just not interested.")?

His emphasis on I-messages rather than you-messages. Will some students believe that the teacher is not praising them because the praise is not personal?

His insistence that teachers show their own anger appropriately. Will it upset some students if a teacher shows any anger?

communication to handle minor misbehaviors, it is less effective with more serious behavior infractions.

Besides its shortcomings in dealing with severe behavior management problems, Ginott's theory has other disadvantages. His strategies for addressing discipline problems are broad, and the different parts of his theory are not molded into a single model. This lack of a comprehensive and cohesive model is a serious disadvantage and dilutes the effectiveness of Ginott's work (Morris, 1996). Although Ginott's congruent communication has considerable potential when used in conjunction with other models and theories, on its own it lacks the well-thought-out, methodical plan proposed by the Canters' assertive discipline or Dreikurs's democratic teaching. As Morris concluded, the Ginott model has potential for dealing with minor problems but does little to address the goals of the safe schools movement and the guns, knives, and physical violence with which some teachers must contend.

Imposing or Teaching Discipline

In his book *Teacher and Child,* Ginott (1972a, pp. 149–151) included a section called "Self-Discipline" in which he clearly stated his belief that students should learn to discipline themselves. However, he believed that students need a clear definition of acceptable and unacceptable conduct and that they feel more secure when they know the borders of permissible action (Ginott, 1965). He did not believe in punishment though, and thought teachers should teach students self-discipline rather than constantly imposing punishment that "does not deter misconduct" (Ginott, 1972a, p. 151). Ginott (1965) emphasized that teachers who model appropriate behavior can play significant roles in teaching students self-discipline. When adults show clear definitions of acceptable and unacceptable behavior, students can develop inner standards for self-regulation (Ginott, 1965, p. 197). If discipline is used, it should "lead to voluntary acceptance by the child of the need to inhibit and change some of his behavior."

> Ernesto Jamison, a student teacher, constantly had to tell Lamont to stop engaging in minor misbe-
> haviors such as humming to himself and getting up to sharpen his pencil. Finally, Ernesto talked with
> his cooperating teacher about the problem: "I've used about all the punishments I know to use, and
> there's not much else I can do to stop his annoyances. I'll be finished here in 3 weeks, so I guess I
> can put up with anything for that long." His cooperating teacher told Ernesto that he was missing an
> important point in Ginott's theory. Instead of accepting sole responsibility for Lamont's behavior, he
> needed to shift responsibility to Lamont by trying to get him to discipline himself. Following that ad-
> vice, Ernesto stopped all punishments and spoke privately with Lamont about his behavior and how
> it affected others in the classroom. Without being threatening, Ernesto used I-messages to explain
> appropriate behavior. During the next week, he reminded Lamont about how he was supposed to be-
> have and how his improved behavior had positive effects on others' learning and behavior. By the time
> Ernesto finished student teaching, Lamont was not a model student, but he was making a greater ef-
> fort to behave appropriately.

Underlying Beliefs

Whether Ginott's theories reflect a teacher's philosophical and psychological beliefs is a crucial point, because teachers who do not subscribe to the theory of congruent communication will not be successful if they try to implement it. Teachers who say "I don't smile at
students until Thanksgiving," who feel they must be autocratic, and who expect immediate
and strict obedience probably will prefer other methods of managing students. Likewise,
teachers who offer evaluative praise, use you-messages, believe sarcasm works, and rely on
anger to scare students into behaving will not be successful with Ginott's theories.

Even individuals who agree with Ginott's theories might have problems implementing
them. One parent told how, although he supported Ginott's principles, he had difficulty
putting them into actions. When his son neglected to let the dog out, the dog had an acci-
dent on the living room rug. The parent said he was hard pressed to be a "friendly person"
who offers "directions" (Elkind, 1992, p. 222). Instead, he wanted to lash out at his son for
his irresponsibility, even though he knew the negative effects of criticism on young people.
Some teachers will understand this parent's feelings and sympathize with him. Translating
the theories into practice can prove difficult.

Developing Your Personal Philosophy

Does Congruent Communication Reflect Your Beliefs?

Ask yourself the following questions to see if you are ready to incorporate Ginott's ideas
into your classroom management system:

1. Am I willing to examine my own actions and behaviors to determine whether
   they contribute to students' positive and negative behaviors?
2. Can I handle my own feelings of anger and act appropriately?
3. Am I willing to consider and seek alternatives to punishment?
4. Do I feel comfortable sending I- rather than you-messages?
5. Can I use guidance rather than criticism and appreciative praise rather than
   evaluative praise?
6. Can I communicate acceptance and acknowledgment to students?

CASE STUDY
Working With Opposing Philosophies

When Carri Valdez began her student teaching experience at the end of her 4-year program in early childhood education, she was not prepared for the classroom management problems that she had. By the end of her first week, Carri was losing confidence in her decision to become a teacher. She had not had any problems during her earlier practicum experience, perhaps because she was placed in a third-grade class in a school that required all teachers to use the Canters's assertive discipline model, a model that Carri felt comfortable using. Now, in a first-grade class with Mrs. Prager, a teacher who had worked to perfect Ginott's congruent communication ideas, the problems began.

"I don't know what's wrong. The things I thought would work, don't, or Mrs. Prager won't let me use them. After all, what's wrong with telling Angelo that he's a good boy? And why shouldn't I react and punish Bret when he uses a four-letter word? I mean, students learn from punishment, don't they? And I don't understand this whole thing about evaluative and appreciative praise. Praise

is praise, isn't it? The only thing I do know is that if I can't adjust to this congruent communication thing, Mrs. Prager will flunk me in student teaching. My classroom management class taught me about managing instruction but not about Ginott's ideas to manage behavior. What can I do?"

Questions for Consideration

1. How would you help Carri?
2. What suggestions can you give her for using Ginott's ideas?
3. Should she request a transfer to another cooperating teacher who uses a theory of classroom management that is closer to Carri's own philosophy?

 You can record your answers to these questions online on this book's Companion Web Site at *www.prenhall.com/manning*.

We met one teacher who called Ginott's theories "too permissive." "Quite the contrary," we told her. Ginott's theories do not mean that teachers must let students do whatever they want to do. Students must know clear limits set by the professional (Landreth, 2002), how to behave, and how the teacher will respond. Teachers need to model the behavior that they want in their students. Developing Your Personal Philosophy looks at several ways to determine whether you have the philosophical and psychological mind-set to use Ginott's congruent communication theory. Once you have completed it, consider the situation presented in the Case Study.

Please go to *www.prenhall.com/manning* and click on Concluding Remarks for this chapter to find more information.

CONCLUDING REMARKS

Teachers at all grade levels who successfully implement the ideas of Ginott's congruent communication will demonstrate and encourage positive communication, behaviors, and relationships in their classrooms and will establish an environment in which students demonstrate proper behavior. This, in turn, can lead to safe schools and to schools that value and respect diversity. However, Ginott's ideas have their drawbacks. First, congruent communication might not be useful when a fight breaks out or when a student threatens another student with a gun or knife. Also, because Ginott did not synthesize his ideas into a well-defined classroom management model, teachers might have to use his ideas to complement other, more established and developed models of classroom management. You can find additional information about Ginott and his ideas of congruent communication by visiting the Internet sites in "Reaching Out With Technology" on this book's Companion Web Site.

Suggested Readings

Brown, D. R. (2005). The significance of congruent communication in effective classroom management. *The Clearing House* (In press).

Flicker, E. S., & Hoffman, J. A. (2002). Developmental discipline in the early childhood classroom. *Young Children, 57*(5), 82-89. These authors focus on developing discipline with children in the early childhood classroom.

Ginott, H. (1972). *Teacher and child.* New York: Macmillan. In one of the best descriptions of his work, Ginott looks at topics such as teachers at their best and worst, congruent communication, the perils of praise, and alternatives to discipline.

Landreth, G. L. (2002). Therapuetic limit setting in the play therapy relationship. *Professional Psychology: Research and Practice, 33*(6), 529-535. While Landreth's main emphasis is play limit setting during play therapy, the article has implications for elementary and secondary teachers as they propose clear limits.

Manning, M. L., & Bucher, K. T.(2001). Revisiting Ginott's congruent communication after thirty years. *The Clearing House, 74,* 215-218. As the title implies, Manning and Bucher examine Ginott's congruent communication and explain its relevance in contemporary classrooms.

Roebuck, E. (2002). Beat the drum lightly: Reflections on Ginott. *Music Educator's Journal, 88*(5), 40-44, 53. Roebuck explains the principles of positive communication, especially in the focus on teachers and labeling.

CHAPTER 6

Exploring the Theories of Instructional Management: *Jacob Kounin*

Focusing Questions

After reading this chapter, you should be able to answer the following questions:

1. What specifically did Kounin mean by the term instructional management, and why did he think teachers' behaviors contributed to positive student behaviors?

2. What did Kounin mean when he used the following terms to refer to teacher behaviors: withitness, desists, overlapping, and satiation?

3. How did Kounin define the term movement management and related aspects, such as jerkiness, stimulus bound, thrust, dangles, flip-flops, and overdwelling?

4. What suggests that Kounin's Instructional Management teaches or imposes discipline and that his model can address behavior problems in contemporary schools?

5. What did Kounin mean by the term group focus and related terms such as group alerting and accountability?

6. What are several advantages and disadvantages of Kounin's Instructional Management?

7. What is the possibility that Instructional Management can address students' cultural, gender, and social class diversity?

8. Can Kounin's Instructional Management contribute to the effort to make contemporary schools safe?

Key Terms

Accountability
Dangles
Desists
Flip-flops
Fragmentation
(continued)

Jacob Kounin believed that teachers who demonstrate effective instructional behaviors usually have better-behaved students. Testing his theories over two decades of work, he analyzed thousands of hours of tapes of classes on a variety of grade levels and in a variety of neighborhoods and communities (Wattenberg, 1977). Kounin found that teachers who use effective instructional management keep their students focused on learning tasks and minimize behavior problems. In this chapter, we will look at Kounin's classroom Instructional Management model and explore the specific instructional behaviors that he thought contributed to improved student behavior.

JACOB KOUNIN: BIOGRAPHICAL SKETCH

Jacob S. Kounin received degrees from Case Western Reserve University in child and clinical psychology and taught at Wayne State University. With his interest in educational psychology, he was a member of several professional associations including the American Psychological Association and the American Educational Research Association. His book *Discipline and Group Management in Classrooms* (1970) is still widely respected and used to show how effective instructional techniques contribute to classroom management.

OVERVIEW OF INSTRUCTIONAL MANAGEMENT

It is important to understand the major concepts of Kounin's Instructional Management model, as well as its philosophical and psychological foundations. Then you can explore the application of Kounin's theories before you decide whether to adopt his instructional management ideas or use specific aspects that complement other classroom management models.

Key Concepts

Figure 6–1 outlines the key concepts in Kounin's Instructional Management theories. When we apply these concepts to instructional practices later in this chapter, we will explore in more detail the terminology that Kounin developed to discuss instruction and the teacher's behavior in the classroom. An in-depth discussion of Kounin's ideas is contained in his classic work *Discipline and Group Management in Classrooms* (1970).

Philosophical and Psychological Foundations

Kounin's model advances the idea that teachers affect learners' behaviors positively and negatively. Teachers who have clear transitions from one learning activity to another one, who know what is going on in all parts of the classroom at all times, and who know how to maintain instructional momentum will be effective classroom managers. Instead of looking for psychological goals of student misbehavior or developing reward systems, teachers must look at what they do and how those instructional actions and behaviors affect student behavior. William Wattenberg (1977, p. 261), one of the foundational theorists discussed in chapter 2, said of Kounin's model:

> It counteracts mischief by keeping people productively busy. There is minimum reliance on negative experiences, a maximum reliance on activity and psychological alertness.

Teachers' Roles and Responsibilities

According to Kounin, in order to be effective instructors and managers, teachers have to demonstrate appropriate teaching behaviors, maintain appropriate instructional momentum, work toward group focus, and plan a learning environment that is conducive to learning and behavior. His Instructional Management model requires teachers to learn and competently use effective teaching techniques. Although Kounin did not relieve students of their responsibility to behave and achieve self-discipline, he believed that the teacher was primarily responsible for the learners' behaviors. Management Tip 6–1 looks at instructional activities that contribute to classroom management.

Group alerting
Group focus
Jerkiness
Movement management
Overdwelling
Overlapping
Ripple effect
Satiation
Slowdowns
Stimulus bound
Thrust
Truncation
Withitness

- **Teacher Behavior:** Withitness and other teacher behaviors such as desists, overlapping, and satiation have an impact on student behavior.
- **Movement Management:** Pacing and the ebb and flow of instruction are important in the presentation of a lesson and the maintenance of appropriate student behavior in the classroom. Kounin used the terms jerkiness, stimulus bound, thrust, dangles, truncation, flip-flop, slowdowns, overdwelling, and fragmentation to discuss the movement of instruction.
- **Group Focus:** The teacher who uses appropriate instructional strategies and activities can keep the students focused on the lesson and can minimize behavior problems.

Figure 6–1 Key Concepts

Management Tip 6-1

Managing a Classroom with Instructional Activities

Kounin believed that instructional behaviors are a very important part of classroom management. With careful planning, teachers can often use effective instructional activities to prevent behavior problems or to correct misbehaviors.

All teachers can use instructional techniques to promote good student behavior:

- Establish clear procedures.
- Develop lessons that are neither too difficult nor too easy.
- Focus on the entire class, not dwelling too long on one or two students.
- Pace instruction to maintain student interest.
- Provide curricular content and instructional methods that interest and challenge learners.
- Demonstrate appropriate instructional behaviors such as withitness and group alerting, avoiding behaviors such as dangles, fragmentation, and satiation.

Elementary

Model your instruction. When you want students to learn a new skill, be sure that you model the skills for students by working through a sample problem or procedure first and verbalize your thoughts as you complete the procedure.

Use music to designate transitions between lessons and to set a calming tone in the classroom.

Secondary

Know when to have the class take a break or when to change instructional strategy.

During long block classes, build in a 5-minute break so that students can talk quietly, move around the room, visit the restroom, and relax at their seats.

Please go to
www.prenhall.com/manning
and click on the Management Tips for this chapter to complete management activities and find more information on managing a classroom with instructional activities

APPLYING INSTRUCTIONAL MANAGEMENT

Implementing Practical Applications

Using Figure 6–1 and the list of key terms as guides, we can begin to explore, in more detail, the instructional techniques that Kounin thought contributed to appropriate student behavior. The following techniques are grouped according to the general areas of teacher behavior, **movement management,** and group focus.

Withitness

Effective teachers demonstrate **withitness,** which means they are aware of all events, activities, and student behaviors in the classroom and that they convey that knowledge to students. Without hesitation, the "withit" teacher can tell whether behaviors contribute to or take away from learning situations. At the same time, the students know that the withit teacher detects inappropriate behaviors early and accurately (Kounin, 1970). Reflecting the old adage that teachers have "eyes in the backs of their heads," teachers who demonstrate withitness perform more than one task at a time (overlapping) and know all students' actions regardless of the teaching/learning situations.

Teachers who demonstrate withitness are usually skillful at two particular instructional behaviors. First, they know who is causing a disturbance even if that student is one who likes to cause a disturbance and then fade into the background as if having nothing to do with the situation. Second, withit teachers can handle more than one situation at a time and can do it promptly (Gordon, 1997). In addition, they know how to react appropriately.

Bertneta and Jana quietly slipped a magazine back and forth between them as Ms. Anderson taught the lesson. While continuing to teach, Ms. Anderson walked to the girls and took the magazine. Never speaking to the girls and never stopping instruction, Ms. Anderson demonstrated that she knows what is occurring in all parts of the room at all times.

Activity 6–1 suggests other ways teachers can demonstrate withitness and asks you to suggest additional examples.

Desists

Kounin defined **desists** as efforts to stop a misbehavior, such as when a third-grade teacher says, "Gene, please put your feet on the floor instead of on Scott's desk." Gene and all the other students in the class know the expected behavior. Although desists are necessary at

Activity 6–1

Demonstrating Withitness

The following examples demonstrate withitness:

> While helping a student with a problem, a teacher monitors the rest of the class, acknowledges other requests for assistance, handles disruptions, and keeps track of time.
>
> During a discussion, a teacher listens to student answers, watches other students for signs of comprehension or confusion, formulates the next question, and scans the class for possible misbehaviors.
>
> During instruction, the teacher has all needed materials, is prepared to answer relevant questions, and is well prepared.

What other ways can you suggest for teachers to demonstrate withitness? Consider teachers you have had (those who were witit and those who were not). How might you demonstrate withitness in the grades you plan to teach?

times and have the potential for a **ripple effect** (the effect when a teacher corrects one student who is misbehaving and the behavior "ripples" to other students, causing them to behave better), they also can be threatening. In one of his studies, Kounin found that desists resulted in less-relaxed students and reduced feelings of teacher helpfulness and likability (Kounin, 1970).

Kounin also found a relationship between the way teachers issue desists and the impact of those desists on everyone in the class. To be most effective, teachers should ensure that desists are spoken clearly and that they are understood. Firmness and roughness do not impact the effectiveness of desists as much as clarity does (Morris, 1996).

When should you use desists and when should you just take action, as Ms. Anderson, a withit teacher, did in an earlier example in this chapter? That is a good question and one that can be answered only by looking at each individual situation. Depending on the circumstances and the outcomes desired, a teacher must determine quickly whether to handle the misbehavior with a desist or more subtly. How Would You React 6–1 looks at when and how to use desists.

Overlapping

Commenting on Kounin's theories, Wattenberg (1977) maintained that **overlapping** is what teachers do when they have two matters to deal with at the same time (similar to the current idea of multitasking). He also believed that teaching requires "simultaneous multiple stimuli" (p. 259) or working with groups and simultaneously responding to other individuals. In his own writings, Kounin (p. 85) wondered whether a teacher could somehow "attend to both issues simultaneously or does she remain or become interested in one issue only, to the neglect of the other?"

Using Desists

To Kounin, instructional management plays a major role in classroom management. Although there are times when a teacher takes a quiet action while continuing to teach, there are also times when a teacher takes a direct verbal action to stop misbehaviors. Consider each of the following situations. Would you use a desist or a quieter action? Be sure to consider whether your action might result in a beneficial ripple effect or interrupt your instructional momentum. What effect would the grade level have on your response?

- Linda Ann is annoying another student during a lesson. The situation is not dangerous, but both students are distracted.
- A verbal battle breaks out between Ralph and Trevor over the answer to a social studies question.

- Dean and Arrin are quarreling quietly over an insignificant issue, but they are distracting other students who are trying to solve a math problem in their cooperative learning group.
- Everyone in the class seems to be restless after lunch, but Clifton keeps walking to the pencil sharpener again and again.
- A class is noisy during instruction. No one is blatantly misbehaving, but the noise level seems to be getting higher.
- Three students are passing baseball cards around (or the teacher thinks they are baseball cards) while the teacher is trying to teach.
- Two students are vocal in claiming ownership of the same big crayons.

Overlapping is an essential instructional skill because teachers often are expected to engage in more than one activity at a time. For example, a teacher can work with one student or a group of students and at the same time monitor or help another student who is working in another part of the room. Kounin found that teachers who can overlap, or perform more than one task at a time, are better able to demonstrate withitness. Examples of overlapping include a teacher correcting a student's misbehavior and never breaking instructional momentum, a teacher using her hand to acknowledge a student's talking during group time, and a teacher instructing his small group and providing individual assistance to an individual in another group.

Based on Wattenberg (1977), the following are some situations that lead to overlapping:

- An elementary teacher is working with one reading group and a student from another reading group interrupts with a problem.
- A teacher is working with a group of students and a behavior incident occurs in another part of the classroom.
- An administrator interrupts a lesson to discuss a report that is due.

The following are some examples of situations in which teachers successfully use overlapping:

- An elementary teacher distributes drawing materials while explaining the procedures and behaviors she expects.
- A middle school teacher discusses an individual student's problem while monitoring the class on the walk back from lunch.
- A high school teacher acknowledges (e.g., eye contact and proximity) a student's inattention as she continues teaching the social studies lesson.
- A teacher corrects the behavior of a small group while he sees another student in the back of the room take a student's book bag. He motions with his hand to the student that his actions are being monitored.

Regardless of the cause of the interruption, the teacher who can overlap successfully can deal with several issues simultaneously. Also, the students recognize the teacher's ability to handle multiple issues as an indication of awareness and control (withitness).

Satiation

As the term implies, **satiation** occurs when a teacher teaches the same lesson for so long that the students grow tired of the topic. The teacher and students are "doing the same thing over and over" (Kounin, 1970, p. 131). Their interest and enthusiasm wane as the "activity becomes less and less positive then more and more negative" (p. 126). The quality of work decreases, the number of mistakes increases, the activity no longer is an intellectual challenge, and a general breakdown of the activity occurs.

> Mr. Hanna was teaching subordinate clauses to an above-average group of students. After he had clearly explained subordinate clauses and all the students had mastered the topic, about 20 minutes of class time were left. To use the time, Mr. Hanna continued to write sentences on the board and to ask the students to identify the subordinate clause. However, satiation occurred. Students showed signs of lack of enthusiasm, started to talk among themselves, and, generally speaking, started goofing off.

With a little thought and planning, effective teachers can avoid satiation and its accompanying problems. However, once it becomes evident that satiation is occurring, teachers can take several steps to stop it: (1) show a genuine zest and enthusiasm for the topic, (2) make a positive statement about the activity ["This next one is going to be fun; I know you'll enjoy it" (Kounin, 1970, p. 130)], and (3) point out that the activity has a special intellectual challenge ["You're going to need your thinking caps on for the next one, it's tricky" (p. 130)]. Activity 6–2 offers some additional suggestions for avoiding satiation.

Activity 6–2

Avoiding Satiation

The following are some instructional techniques that you can use to avoid satiation. After reading them, identify other instructional strategies you could use to counteract satiation.

- "Read" the class to check for signs of satiation. Look for students who are tired and for signs of growing disinterest.
- Always have additional work available that will extend or enrich the lesson.
- If satiation occurs before mastery, change to another activity that is designed to teach the same material, or break the class into groups.
- Ask higher-level questions that will motivate additional thought about the topic.
- Allow the students to put away their present work and work on independent learning projects or personalized reading programs.

Jerkiness

Jerkiness refers to lack of lesson smoothness and momentum. According to Wattenberg (1977), some teachers demonstrate jerkiness in the way they pace instruction or proceed with the lesson. For example, a teacher might switch from one topic to another without sufficiently notifying the students. In other cases, a teacher might use one activity and then suddenly change to another activity. In this instance, although the learning topic is the same, the change of activities can confuse students and cause them to lose interest and eventually begin to misbehave.

> In the middle of the lesson, Ms. Overton, a teacher, glanced at the fish in the classroom aquarium. She stopped instruction to ask Jesse whether he had fed the fish. The instructional momentum was lost, and the students' interest had to be regained (Wattenberg, 1977).

Once a teacher recognizes the symptoms of jerkiness and its negative effects on students, the problem is relatively easy to address. To maintain an appropriate instructional pace, a teacher should avoid changing the learning topics, avoid asking students questions that do not relate specifically to the lesson (e.g., whether the fish have been fed), and ask students to hold off questions that do not relate specifically to the instructional topic.

Stimulus Bound

Other factors also can affect the momentum of a lesson. When a teacher has the students engaged in a lesson and something else attracts the teacher's attention, that teacher is **stimulus bound.** The instructional focus and momentum are lost while the teacher deals with another issue (e.g., the fish).

> Just as Mr. Liffick started to teach, he noticed that police were in the hall frisking and handcuffing a man. Because of the position of the classroom door, the students could not see what was going on. However, Mr. Liffick clearly was distracted from the lesson he had planned. Knowing that something was going on that was attracting Mr. Liffick's attention, the students began to fidget and turn in their seats, trying to find out what was happening.

Being stimulus bound is a relatively easy problem to avoid. A teacher simply needs to recognize the negative effects and make a genuine commitment to maintaining the instructional focus.

Thrust

A **thrust** consists of a teacher's sudden "bursting in" (Kounin, 1970, p. 100) on students' activities with an order, statement, or question without looking for or being sensitive to the group's readiness to receive the message. An everyday example of a thrust is when someone interrupts a conversation of two or more people without waiting to be noticed. A thrust is similar to a stimulus-bound event except that the stimulus-bound event is started by a stimulus outside the teacher, whereas the thrust is initiated by the intent of the teacher (Kounin, 1970). In both instances, the result is that the teacher and the students lose their instructional pace, jerkiness results, and the conditions become ripe for misbehavior. How Would You React 6–2 asks you to suggest a professional response to a practicum student's thrusts.

Dangles and Truncations

A **dangle** occurs when a teacher starts an activity and then leaves it "hanging in midair" (Kounin, 1970, p. 100) by beginning another activity. Later, the teacher might resume the original activity. A **truncation** is the same as a dangle, except that in a truncation, the teacher does not resume the initiated, then dropped, activity. In other words, a truncation might be described as a longer-lasting dangle (Kounin, 1970). Kounin provided two good examples (p. 101).

How Would You React 6–2

Dealing With Thrusts

As you read the following scenario, think about the effect that a thrust may have on instructional pacing and classroom management. Then respond to the questions at the end.

> Donica Redmon was doing her practicum in a mathematics class. To Mr. Masucci, the teacher, it was evident that Donica did not understand the negative effects of thrusts. As she taught for about 1 hour, he counted 8 to 10 thrusts. During her lesson, Donica made extraneous comments about the situations in the word problems, such as "I've never understood why people would want to drive big cars." Then, after breaking the class into cooperative learning groups, she interrupted their work with comments, such as "Did anyone bring milk jugs for the experiment we're going to do tomorrow?" Finally, she walked around visiting each group and interrupting their work with statements that were unrelated to the lesson, such as "Jill, how is your older sister doing? I went to school with her, you know" and "Wasn't that a great lunch we had in the cafeteria today?" As a result of Donica's comments, students began to talk about things other than the class work they were supposed to be doing, and the level of noise in the room escalated.

1. What effect have Donica's thrusts had on instruction and classroom management?
2. If you were Mr. Masucci, what would you tell Donica?
3. What could Donica do to eliminate thrusts during her instruction?
4. What if Donica says, "I was just being friendly to the students." How should Mr. Masucci explain to Donica the effects of her behavior on the students?

> The students had just completed reading a story in their reading circle. As the teacher got up and walked toward the board, she said something like, "Let's look at these arithmetic problems on the board." Halfway to the board, however, she stopped, turned around, and walked to her desk to look at some papers there. Then, after 10 seconds at her desk, she returned to the problems on the board.

> The students were taking turns reading their answers to the arithmetic problems. After telling Jimmy that his answer to the third question was correct, the teacher looked around and asked Mary to read her answer to number four. As Mary was getting up, the teacher looked around the room and asked, "My now. Let's see. Suzanne isn't here, is she? Does anyone know why Suzanne is absent today?"

Dangles and truncations negatively impact classroom management. Because of the loss of momentum and the lack of smoothness in the instructional pace, students are confused and unsure about what they are supposed to be doing. The result is that they talk, goof off, and do not pay attention to the instruction. As one teacher said, "This is the breeding ground for misbehavior." Confusion reigns due to the teacher's lack of smoothness in the instructional momentum.

Flip-Flops

Flip-flops occur only at transition points, such as when the teacher terminates one activity and begins another and then reverts to the first activity. For example, a teacher says, "All right, let's everybody put away your spelling papers and take your arithmetic books" (Kounin, 1970, p. 101). The students put their spelling papers in their desk and, after most of the students have gotten out their arithmetic books, the teacher asks, "Let's see the hands of the ones who got all their spelling words right" (p. 101). The results of flip-flops are the same as those of dangles and truncations. The teacher confuses students, who then begin to lose their instructional focus and misbehave. Teachers who are good instructional managers realize the importance of smoothness and momentum, and they carefully avoid flip-flops, which confuse learners.

Slowdowns: Overdwelling and Fragmentation

Kounin (1970) maintained that two types of **slowdowns** occur: overdwelling and fragmentation. Both relate to instructional movement and the need for smoothness and consist of those behaviors initiated by teachers that clearly slow down the rate of instructional movement. **Overdwelling** happens when a teacher dwells on corrective behavior longer than needed or on a lesson longer than required for most students' understanding and interest levels (Kounin, 1970).

> Ms. Rentz overdwelled as she corrected behavior. While she was teaching her lesson, Hirooshi wadded up a piece of paper and threw it toward the trash can, his imaginary basketball hoop. Ms. Rentz said, "Hirooshi, don't wad up paper and throw it in the trash like that. You have been told time and time again. Why do you do that? And for the rest of you—I don't like the way you have been behaving lately. La-Toyia, you talk too much and disturb others. Korey, you walk around the room too much. Rosa, well, you know how you are!" All Ms. Rentz had to do was to ignore the paper incident or say "Hirooshi, the others and I are annoyed when someone throws paper in the trash can during a lesson."

> A teacher was explaining how to multiply by twos so that the students would be able to answer the questions in their workbooks as a seatwork assignment. She walked to a large chart that had all the numbers from 1 through 100. In unison, she and the students called out all the odd numbers from one to 99 (Kounin, 1970). The teacher overdwelled and in all likelihood, the students grew disinterested and bored.

Management Tip 6–2 provides some suggestions of activities that can be used in place of overdwelling.

Fragmentation, the other type of slowdown, is produced when a teacher breaks down an activity or behavior into subparts, even though the activity could be performed easily as a single unit or an uninterrupted sequence. For example, the teacher tells each member of a group to do something singly that could be performed by the group as a whole. In this instance, students have to wait for their turn and, while waiting, might begin to talk and engage in other misbehaviors. Kounin also gave the following example of a teacher who focused on subparts rather than a single action. After reading the following example, review Activity 6–3 for other signs of slowdowns.

> Making a transition from spelling to arithmetic, the teacher said, "All right everybody, I want you to close your spelling books. Put away your red pencils. Now close your spelling books. Put your spelling books in your desks. Keep them out of the way." The teacher then waited. After some time she said, "All right now. Take out your arithmetic books and put them on your desk in front of you. That's right, let's keep everything off your desks except your arithmetic books. And let's all sit up straight. We don't want any lazy bones do we? That's fine. Now get your black pens and open your books to page 16" (Kounin, 1970, p. 106).

⭐ **Management Tip 6–2**

Avoiding overdwelling

Teachers are always warned that they need to have backup ideas that they can use any time students finish a lesson in a shorter time than planned. Some suggested activities include

Journal writing,

Free-choice reading from the classroom book collection,

Reading a library book,

Doing homework,

Prepared minilessons that take 10 minutes or less,

Teacher reading a poem or short story aloud,

Listening to an audio book.

Elementary

Assign class jobs so that students have something to do when lessons end early or when they get done with in-class assignments.

Assign jobs to student monitors who will keep everyone on task with their jobs.

Rotate the jobs so that no one becomes bored.

Secondary

Keep a stack of brainteasers on transparencies or worksheets and allow the students to solve them as a class or in small groups.

Please go to *www.prenhall.com/manning* and click on the Management Tips for this chapter to complete management activities and find more information on avoiding overdwelling.

Activity 6-3

Determining Slowdowns

The following are a few questions teachers could ask themselves to eliminate slowdowns in instruction.

Do the students look bored or disinterested?

Has it been too long since I asked questions or made encouraging comments?

Have I been dwelling on the same instructional point for too long?

Are students growing frustrated and disenchanted with the lesson?

How long have I spent on this lesson? Realistically speaking, how much time do I think should have been needed to teach the lesson? Why it is taking me so long? Should I stop the lesson and begin again during the next class (assuming the students still do not know the information)?

How else might you determine whether a slowdown is occurring? What can you do to eliminate overdwelling and fragmentation?

Group Focus

Group focus includes group alerting and group accountability. It occurs when a teacher makes a conscientious attempt to keep the attention of all members of the class at all times. When this happens, the teacher maintains efficient classroom control and reduces student misbehavior (Kounin, 1970).

One aspect of group focus is **group alerting**, which, according to Kounin, refers to the degree to which a teacher attempts to involve all learners in learning tasks, maintain their attention, and keep them "on their toes" (Kounin, 1970, p. 117). When using positive group alerting, teachers create "suspense" (Kounin, 1970, p. 117) before calling on a student to answer a question, keep students in suspense regarding who will be called upon next, call on different students to answer questions, and alert nonperformers that they might be called upon next. Conversely, teachers use negative group alerting methods when they focus attention on the performance of one student instead of the group, prepick a person before asking a question (e.g., putting the name first rather than after a question—"Bill, what is a linking verb?"), and call on students in a predetermined sequence, such as going down rows or the class roll.

Using group **accountability**, the teacher holds the students accountable and responsible for their task performances. To do this, a teacher must know what the students are doing and communicate that knowledge to the students in some observable manner, including the use of record-keeping devices such as checklists and task cards. When students know they are held accountable for their learning and behavior and teachers know each student's progress, student misbehavior decreases. It is important to know about these instructional techniques, but it is also important to know when and how to use them.

Effective teaching behaviors undoubtedly contribute to improved classroom management (and vice versa). One of the authors was observing a practicum student teach a fourth-grade

Management Tip 6–3

Using beginning and ending routines

Kounin believes in consistency in instruction. One way to maintain consistency is to develop routines for many of the common events that happen in a classroom. In chapter 2, we discussed some routines. Another time when routines are necessary is at the beginning and end of the day in elementary school and the beginning and end of class in high school.

Elementary

Have a personal space for each student, such as a cubbie or a crate.

Establish a routine for greeting students each morning and for saying goodbye each afternoon.

Create a special place for parents or guardians to pick up messages if they come to get their children.

Develop a special "take-home" envelope for children to use when they take papers or information home to their parents or guardians.

Secondary

In schools where no lockers are provided or where students have to go outside to portable or temporary classrooms, establish a place for raincoats and umbrellas as well as backpacks and projects.

Establish a procedure that students follow each day when they walk into the class. For example:

- Enter and take your seat quietly.
- Take out your textbook and open to the page indicated on the board.
- Begin working on the assignment listed on the board.

Please go to www.prenhall.com/manning and click on the Management Tips for this chapter to complete management activities and find more information on adding some first-day-of-school management tips to beginning and ending routines.

class. She had done an excellent job of introducing instruction and moving smoothly toward small-group work. Then, she made a serious mistake: She said, "Everyone get an encyclopedia, so you can begin working on your projects." Immediately, about three-fourths of the class hurriedly went to the back of the room for an encyclopedia. Chaos reigned. Management of the class *could* have been maintained if she had said, "The leader of your group should get an encyclopedia." Management Tip 6–3 looks at how elementary and secondary school educators can develop routines to avoid management problems.

Effectiveness of Practical Applications

Teachers have three roles: instructor, manager, and person. Good classroom management occurs when teachers create a positive classroom environment, clear classroom procedures, and clear classroom rules. By identifying behaviors and implementing interventions, teachers are able to make a difference and help students understand the structure of the classroom (Grossman, 2004; Wemlinger, 2004).

Kounin's Instructional Management model has considerable potential to help teachers in the roles of both instructor and manager. To implement the model, teachers can use specific instructional behaviors that are relatively easy to learn and to apply in the classroom. Students behave better when teachers demonstrate withitness and employ techniques such as using desists properly; taking advantage of ripple effects; satiation, jerkiness, thrusts, dangles, and flip-flops; and maintaining a group focus through correct group alerting and accountability. Also, teachers should be able to implement Kounin's theories without a great deal of extra work. In fact, most of these instructional behaviors are second nature for good teachers. For example, all teachers should emphasize academic instruction, expect students to master the curriculum, and allocate most time to curriculum-related activities. In addition, they should maintain an appropriate instructional momentum that contributes to high levels of success.

In addition, Kounin's Instructional Management reflects the philosophy that preventing behavior problems is easier than dealing with them after they occur. For most teachers, it is easier to use Kounin's instructional techniques and prevent misbehaviors than to use the Canters' checklist, Dreikurs's methods to identify the four goals of misbehavior, or Glasser's quality school theories.

EVALUATING INSTRUCTIONAL MANAGEMENT IN A DIVERSE SOCIETY

Like Ginott, Kounin did most of his research in the 1960s and wrote his book *Discipline and Group Management in Classrooms* in 1970. Therefore, in addition to looking at his theories in general, it is important to assess their potential for addressing student misbehaviors in contemporary classrooms. As with all models, you will find that Kounin's Instructional Management model has advantages and disadvantages.

Potential for Addressing Student Misbehaviors

Although a number of external factors (e.g., personal and familial problems, peer pressure, etc.) contribute to student misbehavior, educators, through their instructional actions, can have a powerful influence on students and the teaching/learning environment. By consistently using instructional techniques that promote and encourage learners' best behaviors (i.e., staying on task and not disturbing others), teachers can address common misbehaviors that are experienced in many contemporary schools.

Kounin's Instructional Management model shows respect for all students. Although a problem might occur with developmental differences (e.g., students in elementary school might be affected by Kounin's ripple effect, but middle and secondary students might not be affected as much), no cultural or gender differences (or social class differences) appear to exist that would be affected or that would affect Kounin's prescribed instructional behaviors. With the main focus on what teachers do rather than what students do and the attention to what teachers do to prevent misbehaviors rather than to address them after they have occurred, little corrective attention focuses on the learner.

One instructional technique that addresses the needs of most students is the use of consistency. A teacher should demonstrate withitness and effective instructional movement management and should hold students accountable for their learning and behavior every day rather than sporadically or only on days when the teacher feels the need for control. Most students like consistency because it lets them know the teacher's expectations in terms of maintaining appropriate behavior, staying on task, and being meaningfully engaged in their learning efforts. However, Kounin's objective treatment of all students can be a double-edged sword. Although teachers do not treat students differently, they also do not seek out specific individual differences to address. How Would You React 6–3 looks at Mr. Bixley, a fine teacher, except for his inconsistency.

A teacher who implements Kounin's Instructional Management ideas might prevent students from having the time or inclination to pose serious threats to others' physical and

 **How Would You React 6–3**

Does Inconsistency Work in the Classroom?

According to Kounin, good teachers should be consistent in the practice of good instructional techniques and the avoidance of bad techniques. In the following scenario, you will read about a teacher who did not believe in consistency.

> Teaching fifth grade in a rural school system, Samuel Bixley believed that consistency was negative and contributed to his students' misbehaviors. His theory was to "read" the students (their early morning attitudes and behaviors) on a daily basis and then make a decision about a classroom management plan for the day. "Some days, not much happens; other days, problems exist. That means some days I need to keep a firm hold on things; other days, when students are at their best, I can be more laid back," he said.

1. What are your reactions to Mr. Bixley's idea?

2. How do you think the students feel when an action is ignored one day and brings a stern reprimand or punishment the next? For example, one day students in Mr. Bixley's class were expected to raise their hands before answering questions, but the next day they were allowed to call out the answer as soon as the question was asked. How do you as a student feel about the issue of consistency in instruction?

3. Should a teacher who is consistent also exhibit some flexibility? If so, how could he or she do this?

psychological welfare. If the learners realize the teacher knows what they are doing at all times and in all classroom areas, they are not likely to misbehave unless they are seeking attention or have a serious problem. However, Kounin's Instructional Management model does not address serious behavior problems or specifically promote schools that are safe from serious violence. Although demonstrating withitness when a student shows a gun or knife is better than panicking and not knowing what to do, it does not indicate how to deal with the threat in a way that keeps everyone safe. Also, if a fight breaks out in the hall between classes, demonstrating effective Instructional Management techniques will not solve the problem. Kounin's theories are designed to handle only the routine classroom management problems that teachers must deal with on a daily basis.

Advantages and Disadvantages of Kounin's Theories

Kounin's discipline model has several advantages. You already have read about the effective, practical applications of Kounin's model. In addition to helping the teacher create a withitness image in the classroom, it also helps the teacher handle situational discipline problems. For example, by using a desist to keep one pair of students from talking, the teacher can quiet the whole class (Morris, 1996). Thus, with its easy-to-apply, practical ideas, Kounin's model can be effective in all classrooms.

Kounin's discipline model does, however, have several disadvantages. Students do not necessarily take personal responsibility for their behaviors, nor do they learn a lesson from the use of desists, because the desists are used to stop behaviors immediately rather than to teach a more appropriate way to behave. Furthermore, Kounin's model offers suggestions on preventing behavior problems from occurring in the classroom, but it does not provide strategies to deal with serious problems when they arise (Morris, 1996). Except for keeping students productively busy, it also does little to promote the goals of the safe schools movement.

Imposing or Teaching Discipline

Kounin maintained that teachers should accept responsibility for learning and should demonstrate effective instructional techniques that contribute to positive learner behaviors. Although he likely thought students should develop inner control and ultimately learn self-discipline and how to discipline themselves, his Instructional Management model placed primary responsibility on the teacher. However, he encouraged teachers to develop specific instructional skills to prevent misbehaviors rather than encouraging them to exert control over students. It is regrettable that Kounin did not address the issue of teaching learners to discipline themselves specifically. How Would You React 6–4 asks you to consider Kounin's instructional management and the "discipline imposed/discipline taught" issue.

How Would You React 6-4

Imposing or Teaching Discipline?

In a college class, students were engaged in the following discussion. One student maintained that she did not like Kounin's model because the teacher accepted all the responsibility for discipline. According to her, "The student does nothing—the teacher does it all." Another student disagreed and thought teachers were teaching self-discipline. This student said, "True, the teacher makes most of the effort. The teacher sets up the environment—an ideal environment—but the students are still learning self-discipline."

What do you think? If it were your turn to speak next, what would you say? Does the teacher in Kounin's model do all the work? Is self-discipline being taught?

Underlying Beliefs

Classroom management is more than discipline. With an emphasis on the organization and operation of a classroom, classroom management looks at the behavior of the teacher as well as the students and at the instructional strategies used by teachers as well as the interactions among students and teachers. Teachers who are successful using Kounin's Instructional Management model must believe that their teaching techniques affect learners' behavior. In addition, they must agree that their instruction has the dual purposes of conveying knowledge and serving as a means of influencing behavior. Teachers who feel that their responsibility is to teach and the learners' responsibility is to behave might experience difficulty with Kounin's model. For example, the teacher who teaches and autocratically demands obedience might have a problem seeing a need to influence behavior through teaching. Developing Your Personal Philosophy presents some questions for you to consider as you determine whether or not the ideas of Kounin are congruent with your own classroom management beliefs.

Instead of focusing on instructional behaviors, some teachers might be more comfortable keeping names on a clipboard as the Canters suggested, trying to understand the causes of behavior as Dreikurs recommended, or shaping or conditioning behavior as Skinner recommended. The Case Study tells about a consultant who worked with a school system to implement Kounin's Instructional Management.

CONCLUDING REMARKS

All preservice and inservice teachers can learn Kounin's instructional techniques at least to some degree. Although all teachers might not demonstrate high levels of withitness, most can learn proper desists, how to maintain an appropriate instructional momentum, and the techniques of group alerting and accountability. Kounin's Instructional Management techniques have great potential, especially when they are used in conjunction with another class-

Developing Your Personal Philosophy

Does Instructional Management Reflect Your Beliefs?

In determining the usefulness of Kounin's theories, you can ask yourself several questions:

1. Do I believe that my teaching behaviors are sufficiently powerful to affect learners' behaviors?
2. Can I learn to use Kounin's theories (e.g., specific teacher behaviors, movement management, and group focus) on a consistent basis?
3. Can I effectively implement what I know about jerkiness, stimulus bound, thrust, dangles, truncation, and flip-flops?
4. Do I prefer to watch nearly every move I make or can I just autocratically demand obedience?
5. Am I willing to accept the responsibility for learning all Kounin's instructional methods?
6. Can I remember all of Kounin's techniques and still remember what I am supposed to teach?
7. Do I agree with the philosophy that classroom management includes student behavior and teacher's instructional behaviors?

CASE STUDY
A School Commits to Kounin's Instructional Management

A noted authority on classroom management, Dr. Terence Eubanks was asked to provide consultative services for an urban school division that was known for lower achievement as well as increasing behavior problems. Knowing that he could accomplish little in one in-service session, Dr. Eubanks suggested conducting shorter sessions over a longer period of time. That would allow him to suggest to teachers what they might do and then to follow up and refine their efforts.

When Dr. Eubanks received the preliminary report on the condition of the school system, he was even more concerned than before. Scores were down dramatically, even lower than they had been several years earlier; absenteeism was up; discipline referrals were up; and several schools had experienced serious behavior infractions, including a knifing in a middle school. In spite of this, Dr. Eubanks remained committed to his task and decided that Kounin's Instructional Management had the potential to improve academic achievement as well as students' behavior.

Dr. Eubanks planned his first four sessions as follows:

Session 1: Discussion of the teachers' perceptions of the school system's problems and introductory overview of Kounin's instructional management.

Session 2: Discussion of teacher behaviors, such as withitness, desists, ripple effects, overlapping, and satiation.

Session 3: Discussion of movement management, such as slow-downs, thrusts, dangles, flip-flops, and jerkiness.

Session 4: Discussion of group focus, such as group alerting and group accountability.

Follow-up: He and the various directors and supervisors would visit as many classrooms as they could to determine progress and to assist individual teachers.

After his first session, the teachers were concerned. They felt that learning Kounin's Instructional Management model was the equivalent of learning how to teach all over again. They also thought too much responsibility was placed on them and too little was placed on the students. Although Dr. Eubanks explained that Kounin's techniques were what many good teachers already did (i.e., most already used desists and took advantage of ripple effects, most knew about satiation but did not call it that, and most already knew that an appropriate instructional pace should be maintained), the teachers were still apprehensive. Many expressed concern about the consistency they would have to demonstrate. As one experienced teacher remarked, "That's a lot to keep in mind as we teach."

Questions for Consideration

1. How would you respond if you were a teacher in this school system?

2. Develop a plan for implementing Kounin's ideas in your own classroom. Where would you need to rely on Dr. Eubanks for assistance?

3. Do you believe that a model such as Kounin's can be effective throughout an entire school system?

4. How would you respond to your fellow teachers who were concerned that they would need to "learn to teach all over again?"

 You can record your answers to these questions online on this book's Companion Web Site at *www.prenhall.com/manning*.

Please go to *www.prenhall.com/manning* and click on Concluding Remarks for this chapter to find more information.

room management model that provides for dealing with specific misbehaviors. You can find more information about Kounin's theories in the Internet sources listed in "Reaching Out With Technology" on this book's Companion Web site. As we once heard a teacher say, "The better I am prepared and the better I do in the classroom, the better my students behave." We think Kounin would agree.

Suggested Readings

Bear, G. G. (1998). School discipline in the United States: Prevention, correction and long-term social development. *Educational and Child Psychology, 15*(1), 15–39. Bear reviews strategies used by teachers most effective with classroom management, and specifies those techniques supported by research (e.g., Kounin).

Gordon, R. L. (1997). How novice teachers can succeed with adolescents. *Educational Leadership, 54*(7), 56–58. Gordon has an excellent discussion of withitness and how teachers need to acquire cultural information.

Jeanpierre, B. J. (2004). Two urban elementary science classrooms: The interplay between student interactions and classroom management practices. *Education (Chula Vista, Calif).* *124*(4), 664–675. Research shows that the lack of quality instruction has an effect on classroom management.

Kounin, J. S., & Sherman, L. W. (1979). School environments as behavior settings. *Theory into Practice, 18*(3), 145–151. Kounin and Sherman proposed classrooms have a predictable effect on student behavior and can be manipulated by educators to facilitate learning.

Kounin, J. S. (1970). *Discipline and group management in classrooms.* New York: Holt, Rinehart, and Winston. Kounin's work, although several decades old, continues to be an excellent resource for both preservice and inservice teachers.

CHAPTER 7

Exploring the Theories of Discipline with Dignity: *Richard Curwin and Allen Mendler*

Focusing Questions

After reading this chapter, you should be able to answer the following questions:

1. What seven principles provide a foundation for Curwin's and Mendler's Discipline With Dignity?

2. How do Curwin and Mendler contribute to the discussion of methods of countering school violence, hostility, and aggression?

3. What do Curwin and Mendler mean by dignity, maintaining students' dignity, and maximizing hope?

4. What do Curwin and Mendler mean by the term healthy classrooms?

5. What do Curwin and Mendler mean by the term social contracts, and how do they promote positive behavior?

6. What can teachers do to manage out-of-control students?

Key Terms

Healthy classrooms
Ineffective things
Long-term efforts
Obedience
Responsibility
Short-term efforts
Social contracts
Zero-tolerance policies

Richard Curwin and Allen Mendler proposed Discipline With Dignity, a classroom management model that emphasizes teachers conveying dignity upon students and restoring their hope in democratic, student-centered classrooms. Although their principles reflect some of the ideas of Ginott and Dreikurs, thus far in this book, Curwin and Mendler are the first theorists to address violence, hostility, and aggression in our schools. At the same time, they describe healthy classrooms, where students feel physically and psychologically safe.

RICHARD CURWIN AND ALLEN MENDLER: BIOGRAPHICAL SKETCH

With a doctorate of education from the University of Massachusetts in Amherst, Richard Curwin, a former seventh-grade teacher, joined Allen Mendler, a psychological consultant, educational consultant, and psychotherapist, to found Discipline Associates, a company that provides expertise on classroom management. Both worked with emotionally disturbed and difficult-to-reach students, with Mendler receiving the esteemed Chief Crazy Horse Award for reaching discouraged youth. Their writings include *As Tough as Necessary* (Curwin & Mendler, 1997a), *Taking Charge in the Classroom* (Mendler & Curwin, 1983), *The Discipline Book:*

A Complete Guide to School and Classroom Management (Curwin & Mendler, 1980), *Discipline With Dignity* (Curwin & Mendler, 2001), and *What Do I Do When . . . How to Achieve Discipline with Dignity in the Classroom* (Mendler, 1992).

OVERVIEW OF DISCIPLINE WITH DIGNITY

The classroom management model of Richard Curwin and Allen Mendler is based on democratic, student-centered principles. Before we explore its use in contemporary classroom, there are a number of philosophical and psychological foundations that we must identify.

Key Concepts

Mendler (1992, p. 25) maintains that "most discipline programs incorrectly place their emphases upon strategies and techniques." However, such an approach does not work because all students do not respond the same way or, as Mendler (1992, p. 25) stated, "it is fruitless to expect that any technique will work with all people who present the same symptom." Instead, effective discipline programs should focus on individual students and their specific problem behaviors and on teacher behavior. Thus, Discipline With Dignity is based upon the key concepts shown in Figure 7–1.

Philosophical and Psychological Foundations

The beliefs behind Discipline With Dignity rest on four basic philosophical foundations. First, the model is student centered and emphasizes the student's dignity, self-esteem, and overall well-being. Curwin and Mendler (1997b) wrote that teachers must convey a sense of warmth and make their classrooms welcoming places with basic human touches that encourage acceptable behavior and set the tone for responsible learning. Teachers demonstrate a caring attitude to students as they greet students at the door, share moments of appreciation with them, embrace their interests and concerns, send them a thoughtful note recognizing their efforts, use humor appropriately, and welcome their feedback. Management Tip 7–1 looks at how teachers create a caring environment in their classrooms.

A second foundation is the emphasis on a democratic atmosphere. Curwin and Mendler have long advocated involving students in the process of making classroom rules and guidelines for their behavior and proposing consequences or corrective actions if their rights are violated. In addition, students can also be encouraged to develop expectations for the teacher.

Figure 7–1 Key Concepts of Discipline with Dignity

Curwin and Mendler believe the following:

Classroom management should be student centered, democratic, nonauthoritarian, and responsibility based.

Using the seven basic principles of teacher behavior, teachers should

Work toward long-term behavior changes rather than short-term quick fixes,

Stop doing ineffective things,

Be fair without treating everyone the same way,

Make rules that make sense,

Model what they expect,

Believe that responsibility is more important than obedience,

Treat students with dignity.

☆ **Management Tip 7-1**

Creating a welcoming environment

Curwin and Mendler believe that teachers need to create classrooms that welcome students and convey a sense of warmth. Here are some suggestions for all teachers at the beginning of the school year:

- Have the room neat and clean.
- Organize things—clutter does not set the stage for responsible learning.
- Use storage containers to create a safe, welcoming environment.
- Do not overdecorate.
- Prepare the walls so that you have space for things needed now as well as things to be added later:

  Management plan

  Procedures

  Emergency information

  Assignment alert

  Student showcase

  Special events and schedules

Elementary

Check the number of desks and/or chairs against the number of students in the class to be sure that each student will have a desk on the first day of school. When students arrive the first day, welcome them and help them find their desk by using pictures or name tags on the desks.

Secondary

Be sure the aisles in the room are free for movement and that you can access each part of the room quickly.

Please go to
www.prenhall.com/manning
and click on the Management Tips for this chapter to complete management activities and find more information on creating a welcoming environment.

Responsibility is learned when teachers give students opportunities to make choices and experience consequences (Curwin & Mendler, 1997b).

Related to the previous ideas, a third philosophical foundation of Discipline With Dignity is that teachers need to avoid authoritarian stances. Some teachers demand obedience (what Dreikurs called autocratic) and believe that because they are adults and teachers, students owe them obedience. An autocratic or authoritarian teacher will experience difficulty adhering to student-centered democratic perspectives (Curwin & Mendler, 1997b).

Finally, Discipline With Dignity reflects a responsibility model rather than an obedience model. Emphasis is placed on students accepting responsibility for appropriate behavior rather than adults demanding and receiving obedience. However, because teaching students to accept responsibility might take time, Curwin and Mendler (1997b) believe that emphasis should be placed on long-term behavior improvements rather than short-term fixes.

Teachers' Roles and Responsibilities

With Curwin's and Mendler's Discipline With Dignity model, teachers do not need to keep track of offenses and consequences as the Canters suggested; nor do they have to look for causes of misbehavior as Dreikurs advocated. However, they do have to adopt several roles and accept several responsibilities for successful implementation. First, regardless of the problem or the student behaviors, teachers must be willing to convey dignity, to understand the reasons for conveying dignity, and to genuinely believe that children and adolescents deserve to be treated with dignity. The teacher who thinks student behaviors and teacher behaviors differ because the teacher is an adult and authority figure probably will have problems with Discipline With Dignity, which asks teachers to model the behaviors and attitudes they expect of the students.

Teachers also must consider the effectiveness of their teaching and management behaviors and must be willing to change behaviors that do not work. Along with this, they need to consider whether classroom rules make sense and to help students understand the reasons for the rules. Finally, teachers must accept the belief that long-term behavior changes are preferable to short-term fixes. Instead of seeking a quick fix for a behavior problem, they must look for long-term solutions that convey dignity as well as teach students to develop responsibility for their behavior.

Another teacher role is to make personal and social connections with learners, especially students who demonstrate high-risk behaviors. Mendler (2002) believes that students might be more emotionally healthy if teachers would place as much emphasis on caring for and about others as they do on achieving high scores on high-stakes tests. As a result, students might be less likely to get involved with drugs and gangs or resort to violent behavior. To help students feel valued and cared for, teachers can do fairly simple things to connect with them personally, socially, and academically.

Personal connections include the following:

- Let each student know that he or she is noticed and is as important as the principal, the teacher, or the curriculum.
- Allow students to make decisions for themselves instead of telling them everything and structuring their lives.
- Greet students at the door with a welcoming smile.
- Ask students what they think, believe, want, and expect.
- Make genuine understanding comments to students.
- Sit with students at lunch and let them know you think they are special.

Social connections include the following:

- Focus on the school and classroom as a community of learners who are concerned about each other, help each other, and plan together.
- Involve students through peer and cross-age tutoring.
- Have students bring extra pencils and paper to class so students who forgot will have access to materials.
- Help less-organized students learn organization skills.

Academic connections include the following:

- Value students' thoughts, problem-solving abilities, and the efforts that put forth as they seek to succeed in school.
- Help students avoid feelings of failure by building more on strengths and by minimizing weaknesses.
- Provide opportunities for students to take advantage of brain-compatible learning, learning styles, and multiple intelligences.
- Show appreciation for effort as well as achievement (Mendler, 2002).

APPLYING DISCIPLINE WITH DIGNITY

Please go to *www.prenhall.com/manning* and click on "Reaching Out with Technology" to find more information.

Now that you are familiar with the basic concepts of Curwin's and Mendler's Discipline With Dignity, we can apply them to classroom situations. As with most models, it is difficult to condense all the ideas into a single chapter. Therefore, we encourage you to consult the references and readings at the end of this chapter and Web sites in "Reaching Out with Technology" on this book's Companion Web Site.

Implementing Practical Application

We begin our study of the practical application of Discipline With Dignity by looking at ways to address problem behaviors through dignity, hope, healthy classrooms, social contracts, consequences, and power struggles.

Prerequisite Essentials to Addressing Problem Behaviors

Along with hope and healthy classrooms, dignity is one of the three prerequisite essentials of the classroom management model proposed by Curwin and Mendler. This idea is contained throughout the seven basic principles of teacher behavior (Mendler, 1992).

Activity 7-1

Using Short-Term and Long-Term Efforts to Change Behaviors

- **Rule Infraction:** A third-grade student physically takes another student's lunch box.

  Short-Term: Teacher angrily requires the student to write a sentence 100 times.

  Long-Term: Teacher treats the student with dignity while asking student to return the lunch box and explaining the importance of personal property in the classroom.

- **Rule Infraction:** A sixth-grade student walks around the room, talks out of turn, and is bothersome to other students.

  Short-Term: "Tish, sit down and be quiet. How many times do I have to say the same thing?"

  Long-Term: Meeting with Tish in private, the teacher says, "Tish, the students and I are disturbed when you talk and walk around the room. Let's discuss why you do these things and see whether we can find something constructive for you to do."

- **Rule Infraction:** The teacher overhears a ninth grader use four-letter words while calling Barry, another student, an unkind name.

  Short-Term: "That's the last straw, Hunter. Go straight to the principal's office. That's it for you, young man!"

  Long-Term: "Hunter, I am disturbed when you speak to someone like that. Apologize to Barry and to all those around you who heard the remark. You and I will discuss this during your free period."

Now it is your turn. Drawing on your experiences, identify at least four different classroom management situations. Then, provide a long-term solution to each of them.

Principle 1   *Teachers who practice Discipline With Dignity use **long-term efforts** to change behaviors rather than **short-term efforts**.* You might remember that Curwin and Mendler voiced strong opposition (Curwin & Mendler, 1988; 1989) to the Canters' assertive discipline, which rigidly defines rewards and consequences. Maintaining that such a program is doomed to failure (Mendler, 1992), Mendler thought teachers should look toward long-term behavior changes. In other words, teachers who try only short-term quick fixes often deal with the same problem behaviors and miss an ideal opportunity to teach students self-discipline and long-term behavior changes. Activity 7–1 looks at examples of short-term quick fixes and efforts to promote long-term behavior changes.

Principle 2   *Teachers who practice Discipline With Dignity stop doing **ineffective things**.* It seems incongruous to state that some teachers might need to stop ineffective efforts to change problem behaviors; however, many teachers continue to do things even after all feedback suggests that what they are doing does not work (Mendler, 1992). Perhaps the methods worked with some group of students at some time, but either the students or the behaviors (or both) have changed, and the teacher either does not realize the changes or does not know better classroom management methods to try. Examples of ineffective methods include using "commonsense" methods (p. 28) that do not get students to respond appropriately, using positive reinforcement that often results in students behaving worse, teaching social skills that fail to get students to change behaviors, and sending students to detention when it is clear that being there does not change behaviors. How Would You React 7–1 asks you to consider a classroom situation.

Principle 3   *Teachers who practice discipline with dignity think, "I will be fair, and I won't always treat everyone the same"* (Mendler, 1992, p. 31). Although most teachers have heard

Continuing Misbehavior

Curwin and Mendler believe that teachers need to recognize when they are doing ineffective things and change their methods. As you read the following scenario, identify the teacher's ineffective behavior and decide whether he is treating the misbehaving student with dignity. Then respond to the additional questions at the end.

> "Nathan, I don't know what to do with you," Mr. Deaver said to a second grader. "I've asked you a dozen times to stop hitting Teniko."
>
> Knowing little or no consequence would occur, Nathan hit Teniko again each time Mr. Deaver looked away. Although Nathan considered the whole thing a joke, Teniko found it annoying and painful. Also, each time Nathan hit Teniko, the other students giggled.
>
> Again, Mr. Deaver turned around and asked Nathan to stop. This time, he remarked, "You're just acting like a kindergartner, Nathan. You don't want me to send you back to kindergarten, do you?"

1. What could Mr. Deaver do to stop the problem behavior while still treating Nathan with dignity?
2. What would be the difference in Mr. Deaver's behavior if this were a middle or high school classroom? What strategies would be different? Why?

repeatedly that consistency is the key to effective classroom management, Mendler disagrees and states that students and their behavior problems deserve individual consideration. Because Discipline With Dignity seeks to teach students how to be responsible, it is necessary to tailor the consequences to the individual and to teach students the difference between being fair and treating everyone exactly the same way. Once students understand this concept, a teacher is free to work with each student and take the approaches that best meet that student's needs.

Principle 4   *Teachers who practice Discipline With Dignity make rules that make sense.* Although people break rules for many reasons, rules that are viewed as pointless or unimportant are the least likely to be followed. Instead of school rules being viewed as traps waiting to snare students, they should be considered guidelines needed in order for success to happen. Students who see little value in doing homework are unlikely to do it unless they can see how they will benefit in some way.

Students also deserve an explanation for why rules exist (Mendler, 1992). Instead of "I'm the teacher and you're the student, so you just go by the rule," students should be given explanations such as "The reason for not running in the hall is that someone could fall and get hurt" or "The reason for not calling other students names is that someone's feelings might get hurt." Most students will obey rules for which they see a reason or how it benefits them in some way.

Principle 5   *Teachers who practice Discipline With Dignity model what they expect.* In Mendler's (1992, p. 35) words, "actions speak louder than words." Teachers should let students see them living and abiding by the same rules as students.

> Ms. Carnahan was always prompt in returning homework to the students in her class. "I expect students to do the assigned homework, and I reinforce the importance of completing homework by making sure that I return it the next day, if possible."
>
> Ms. Parker, a student teacher, chewed gum all day long. Although she was secretive about her gum chewing, some students knew she was ignoring a rule that she enforced for the students. Her cooperating teacher reminded Ms. Parker that it was her responsibility to model good behavior for the students and that the gum would have to go.

Activity 7–2 looks at other ways teachers can model appropriate behavior.

Activity 7-2

Modeling Appropriate Behavior

The following examples identify a few ways teachers can model appropriate behavior in the classroom:

1. Speak to students the same way you expect students to speak to you.
2. Do not use critical or harsh remarks to correct student behavior.
3. Obey the same classroom rules you expect students to obey.
4. Meet all deadlines and due dates.
5. Be ready to begin class on time.

What other ways might teachers model appropriate behavior? From your experiences, can you provide examples of teachers modeling appropriate behavior?

Principle 6 *Teachers who practice Discipline With Dignity believe that responsibility is more important than obedience.* The term **obedience** means "do not question and certainly do not be different" (Mendler, 1992, p. 36), but the term *responsibility* means "make the best decision you possibly can with the information you have available" (p. 37). Obedience also implies a hierarchical structure in which one or several powerful individuals dictate the terms of behavior for the masses. Thus, obedience models of discipline have limitations that hinder their effectiveness (Mendler, 1992). Within a **responsibility** model of discipline, students accumulate information, see the options available to them, learn to anticipate consequences, and then choose the path they feel is in the best interest of themselves and others. Because learning responsibility is an ongoing, dynamic process, bad decisions are viewed as opportunities by which students can learn to make better ones. This process also promotes and requires critical thinking. Activity 7–3 looks at some questions suggested by Mendler to help teachers develop discipline techniques that move beyond obedience.

Principle 7 *Teachers who practice Discipline With Dignity always treat students with dignity.* Mendler maintained that the seventh principle is perhaps the most important. Without dignity, students learn to hate school and learning. When teachers attack students' dignity with put-downs, sarcasm, criticism, scolds, and threats, students might follow the rules; however, they also might become angry and resentful. Although teachers should speak to students in a kind and caring manner even when correcting them, treating others with dignity involves more than our manner of speaking. It involves attitudes, body language, tone of voice, and eye contact. Successful educators always convey a basic sense of respect to their students by listening, being open to feedback from students, explaining why they want things done in a certain way, and giving students some say in classroom affairs that affect them (Curwin & Mendler, 1997a).

Activity 7–3

Moving Beyond Obedience

In considering whether discipline techniques move beyond obedience, teachers need to ask:

1. What behaviors occurred after the discipline technique was employed?
2. How does the discipline technique affect motivation for learning?
3. How does the discipline technique affect self-esteem?
4. How does the discipline technique affect the student's dignity?
5. How would I feel if I were at the receiving end of the discipline technique?

Examine several discipline situations that you have observed or in which you have participated. Was obedience or responsibility the driving factor? How could obedience-based responses be changed to become responsibility based?

Source: Developed from Mendler, A. N. (1992). *What do I do when . . . How to achieve discipline with dignity in the classroom.* Bloomington, IN: National Educational Service, p. 38.

Treating others with dignity has to be practiced every day. Teachers cannot have days when they treat students with dignity and other days when they do not. Students, like adults, do not forget easily when they or others have been treated poorly.

Ms. Dela Vega always treated Frank with dignity, yet she did not treat Guy the same way. Hearing the sarcastic comments that Ms. Dela Vega made to Guy, Frank wondered when he would be on the receiving end.

Dignity in discipline often can be accomplished by using privacy, eye contact (with sensitivity to cultural preferences), and proximity when delivering a corrective message to a student. Teachers also should speak comments quietly so that only the student can hear (different from Kounin's ripple effect discussed in the previous chapter). Activity 7–4 provides suggestions for conveying dignity and asks you to suggest others.

In addition to the emphasis on dignity, another prerequisite essential to addressing problem behaviors is that teachers should help students regain hope. Too many students have lost hope in themselves and in schools. They feel they cannot behave appropriately, learn and achieve academically, set realistic goals for their future, and engage in age-appropriate socialization. They believe their efforts toward academic achievement and appropriate behavior will be met only with additional frustration, and they are overwhelmed by their failure to achieve and behave. Some teachers ignore these students, and this only makes the situation worse. Feeling this way and perceiving the teacher's feelings, students either misbehave or just idly sit. Either way, they do not become integral members of the class.

The final prerequisite to addressing problem behaviors is that teachers should ensure **healthy classrooms.** Healthy classrooms do not just happen. Instead, they result from a concerted effort by professional educators who know that healthy classrooms help students

Activity 7–4

Conveying Dignity

Curwin and Mendler think teachers should convey dignity to students, regardless of the grade or developmental level. The following are a few ways you can convey dignity. After reading them, identify other things that you could do in your classroom to treat students with dignity.

1. Listen to the concerns of your students.
2. Be sure that students know that there are clearly defined limits that govern the classroom and that everyone (both students and teacher) is expected to follow them.
3. Help students feel comfortable asking questions and making relevant comments.
4. Foster a spirit of cooperation in the classroom.
5. Let students know they are valued and appreciated even though their problem behaviors are not.
6. Do not use you-messages.
7. Never attack a student's character.

Activity 7–5

Creating Healthy Classrooms for All Students

The following are characteristics of healthy classrooms, where students want to learn and believe they can demonstrate appropriate behavior:

1. Students trust their abilities and their environment.
2. Students see the benefits of improving their behaviors.
3. Students can make real, significant, and meaningful choices.
4. The teacher and students work together to identify what is to be learned and to measure what was learned.
5. Students see the value in what they are learning.
6. Instruction is process and people oriented rather than product and subject oriented.

Suggest other ways classrooms can be made healthy. How could you implement these ideas in your classroom? Can a standards-driven classroom also be a healthy classroom? In what ways do elementary, middle, and high school healthy classrooms differ?

Source: Developed from Mendler, A. N., & Curwin, R. L. (1983). *Taking charge in the classroom: A practical guide to effective discipline.* Reston, VA: Reston Publishing Company.

experience improved self-esteem, achieve higher academic grades, feel physically and psychologically safer, enjoy attending school, demonstrate more cooperative attitudes, and have better interpersonal relationships. Activity 7–5 provides a summary of some characteristics of healthy classrooms and asks you to identify others.

Social Contracts

Curwin and Mendler (2001) maintain that **social contracts** are one of the most effective ways for teachers to take charge of their classrooms and still give students a voice in class decisions. Social contracts are effective because they clearly define acceptable and unacceptable behavior in the classroom or school *before* (italics Mendler's and Curwin's) students misbehave. Without a contract, many good rules and resulting consequences are fully understood by students only after they break the rules. In addition, contracts are effective because they give the students a sense of ownership in what happens in the classroom because they were involved in making the rules. Finally, social contracts spell out an exact procedure for the students and teacher to follow when rules are broken. Management Tip 7–2 provides the steps to follow in developing a social contract.

Mendler and Curwin (1983) tell about a second-grade class that developed a social contract containing 17 rules. Figure 7–2 provides three examples of rules (and consequences) that the class proposed and voted to approve.

Consequences

The social contract depends on the development of effective rules and consequences. The rules clearly state what behavior is expected, and the consequences clarify, in advance, what will happen if the agreed-upon expectations are not met.

A consequence is not a punishment. The goal of punishment is to make rule breakers pay for their misconduct. Punishment has its roots in the philosophy that students will avoid bad behavior to avoid being punished. In addition, punishment offers a release of tension (through a verbal or physical action) for the person giving the punishment. In contrast, consequences directly relate to the rule, and they are logical (see the influence of Dreikurs) and natural. By helping a rule violator learn acceptable behavior from the experience, consequences are instructional rather than punitive. Mendler and Curwin (1983) offered several examples:

> **Management Tip 7-2**
>
> ## Developing a Social Contract
>
> A good contract involves both teacher and students. According to Curwin and Mendler, teachers need to follow these steps to develop a good social contract:
>
> - Teacher identifies the rules that are absolutely necessary to maintain minimal control in the classroom.
> - Teacher proposes other clear and specific rules that are necessary for effective classroom management.
> - Teacher develops consequences for each rule.
> - In small groups, students develop rules for the teacher's behavior.
> - Students develop consequences for each of the teacher's rules.
> - In small groups, students develop rules regarding each other's behavior in class.
> - Students develop consequences if these rules are broken.
> - Class reviews all rules to ensure everyone understands what they mean.
> - The class and teacher decide which of the proposed rules and consequences will become part of the contract.
> - Each student is tested on his or her knowledge of the social contract (a perfect score is required for passing).
>
> *Source:* Developed from Mendler, A. N., & Curwin, R. L. (1983). *Taking charge in the classroom: A practical guide to effective discipline.* Reston, VA: Reston Publishing Company, p. 25.
>
> Figure 7-2 shows a social contract for younger students.

- **Rule:** Students are not for hitting, fighting, or hurting.
  Consequence: Do one nice thing for the victim before the day is over.
  Punishment: Stay after school for 2 hours and sit in silence.
- **Rule:** All trash must be thrown in the wastebasket.
  Consequence: Pick up your trash from the floor.
  Punishment: Apologize to the teacher in front of the entire class.

 Please go to *www.prenhall.com/manning* and click on the Management Tips for this chapter to complete management activities and find more information on developing social contracts as well as a sample contract.

Figure 7–2 Examples
of Rules Proposed by
Second Graders in a
Social Contract

Rules and Consequences for Students

Rule 1: Students do not yell out. They raise their hands and wait to be called upon.

The teacher reminds students to wait and not to yell out.

The teacher will not call on students who yell out.

Rule 2: Instead of fighting, hitting, or pushing in school, students should talk to each other to solve problems.

The teacher reminds students of our rule.

The student will take a time-out.

Rule 3: Do not throw anything in the room. Hand things to each other.

The student must pick up what is thrown.

The student must apologize to others and clean up.

Rules 4–17 dealt with topics such as completing homework, doing work neatly, running in the class or school, sharpening pencils, hanging clothing, taking others' belongings, and copying others' work.

Source: Developed from Mendler, A. N., & Curwin, R. L. (1983). *Taking charge in the classroom: A practical guide to effective discipline.* Reston, VA: Reston Publishing Company, p. 25.

Effective consequences are clear and specific, provide a range of alternative options that allow the teacher to implement a consequence and still treat students as individuals, relate to the rule as much as possible, and teach rather than punish (Mendler & Curwin, 1983). Mendler and Curwin recommend four generic consequences that can be effective for breaking almost any rule.

1. *Reminder of the rule:* "Jef, we raise our hands before speaking. This is your reminder."
2. *A warning:* A warning should be a stern reminder rather than a threat. "Malikah, this is the second time today that you have gotten out of your seat to bother Kristen. This is your warning."
3. *Developing an action plan for improving behavior:* "Malikah, you are out of your seat bothering Kristen. I want you to write for me how you intend to stop breaking this rule. List clearly what you will do when you want to tell Kristen something."
4. *Practicing behavior:* When students do not know how to demonstrate expected behaviors, a teacher can role-play the appropriate behavior first and then have the student repeat it.

Power Struggles

Power struggles, one of Dreikurs's four goals of misbehavior, can present serious problems as teachers and students vie to win a confrontation. Prevention is the best policy, but sometimes teachers are faced with students who refuse to do something the teacher has asked. In some cases, students who engage in power struggles are testing the teacher's resolve by trying to cause embarrassment in the classroom.

- A 4th-grade student refuses to move from one desk to another.
- A 9th-grade student refuses to read aloud in class.
- A 12th-grade student refuses to give up a knife to the principal.

Teachers need to realize that some power struggles are inevitable. Thus, they need to be prepared to deal with them even if it means refusing to engage in the power struggle at all. According to Mendler, most problem moments can be defused through a combination of listening, acknowledging the student's concern, agreeing that there might be truth in the student's accusation, and *deferring* (Mendler's italics) to a private time for continued discussion (Mendler, 1995). Teachers can use an "or" statement to defuse the situation or let the student save face, especially if the power struggle is in front of the class. Another method is to remove the student from the class to avoid having an audience of students.

"Lars, give me the comic book now or after class."

"Rosette, either move to the other desk now or stay in for recess."

"Trey, either stop talking to Sidney or take a time-out."

"Chin Yuan, let's discuss this in the hall."

The ultimate goal is to defuse the situation before it becomes clear that the student will never obey the request or until the student appears angry or violent. Remember, no one wins a power struggle. Always look for a way out of the situation as soon as possible, even if the student has the last word. How Would You React 7–2 recounts a power struggle between a student and teacher.

Violence, Aggression, and Hostility

As you read in chapter 1, many schools have reported an increase in school violence, with attacks on teachers and other students. Without doubt, many teachers must deal with out-of-control students who disrupt the teaching/learning process (Mendler, 1994). These students simply will not become constructive members of the class because they enjoy setting up power struggles, complaining about the teachers' unfairness, constantly making noises, coming to class unprepared, and refusing to take responsibility for their actions. Some schools have reacted by stationing police or private security guards in schools, but their presence creates an atmosphere of a police state and serves to create new tensions (Curwin & Mendler, 1980). Violent and aggressive behavior problems often test teachers' classroom management skills and present problems not addressed by the models and theorists discussed thus far in this book. Management Tip 7–3 examines the stress that teachers may feel and suggests techniques to deal with it.

How Would You React 7–2

Dealing With the "Last-Worder"

Classroom management problems can escalate if teachers and students engage in power struggles. In the following scenario, a teacher is dealing with a "last-worder," or a student who always has to have the last word in all discussions. As you read the scenario, put yourself in the Mrs. Hodges' place. At this point, what should she do to defuse the situation? What should she have done to prevent the problem getting out of hand? Where should she have stopped the power struggle?

Ms. Hodges:	"Doug, I've asked you so many times not to run down the hall."
Doug:	"I was in a hurry. I had to get to my locker."
Ms. Hodges:	"Well, you still shouldn't run in the hall."

Doug:	"I don't see anything wrong with running in the hall. You tell me not to be late for class."
Ms. Hodges:	"I asked you not to run; that's why you shouldn't do it. That's the end of it. Last word."
Doug:	"Everyone else does it."
Ms. Hodges:	"No, Doug, everyone doesn't do it. You name one other student!"
Doug:	"There are two or three. You don't fuss at them for running in the hall. Why do you always pick on me anyway? You don't like me."
Ms. Hodges:	"Doug, you know I like you. That's not the point. I don't want to discuss this anymore."
Doug:	"You don't fuss at anyone else—only me. If I'm late for class, you fuss at me about that, too."

⭐ **Management Tip 7-3**

Dealing with stress

Curwin and Mendler (2001) maintain that the pressures of discipline can lead to stress for teachers with symptoms such as headaches, backaches, fatigue, irritability, and negative thoughts. Here are a few of their tips for reducing stress that can be done in 5 to 10 minutes:

Practice deep-breathing exercises such as sitting in a comfortable chair, close your eyes and breathe in to the count of five, hold it to the count of five and then breathe out to the count of five.

Find a private place in the school (e.g., the school library, a conference room), get into a comfortable position, focus on breathing slowly five times as you clear your mind and close your eyes, and then remember a relaxing or calm place you have been or would like to be. As you focus on that place, put yourself in the picture as you continue to breathe slowly. Stay there for five to ten minutes and then slowly come back to the present.

Smile! Scientists have found that it is hard to be negative while you smile. At the worst, you will have a neutral attitude.

Please go to *www.prenhall.com/manning* and click on the Management Tips for this chapter to complete management activities and find more information on reducing stress.

To deal with the obnoxious, defiant, rebellious, or difficult youth, teachers must remain personally caring despite the angry, hostile behavior (Mendler, 1994) and must continually guard against viewing and responding to troubling students as "worthless ingrates" (Curwin & Mendler, 1997a, p. 14). By reacting with dignity at the very moments in which students are rendering indignities to teachers and students, teachers can send a powerful message that shows capability and strength without brutality. Many explosive students will protect their dignity at all costs, some even with their lives. Thus, they must always know that in school their dignity will be maintained. Teachers must base their strategies and interventions on values rather than on rewards and punishments.

Curwin and Mendler (1997a) identified a number of specific strategies for making schools safer and for working with violent, aggressive, and hostile students. According to them, teachers should learn students' names and then greet them and call them by name often. Using surveys, interest inventories, incomplete sentence forms, and personal interviews, teachers can learn the likes, dislikes, strengths, and weaknesses of their students and can share their joys, frustrations, and concerns. Some teachers might engage in role reversal, where the teacher allows the student to role-play the teacher and the teacher takes the student's role. Older students (especially those who have been behavior problems) can become mentors for younger, disruptive students.

Outside of the school day, teachers should try to attend a school event where one or more of their students (especially the out-of-control or violent and aggressive ones) are likely to be present, greet them personally, and make a special effort to interact. Although Curwin and Mendler advocate the use of touch and other nonverbal messages, we caution that some students might not want to be touched and others might misinterpret the touch.

By teaching to students' diverse learning styles and multiple intelligences, teachers can minimize frustration with learning. In addition, teachers who focus on academic competence can help ensure success, highlight effort and motivation, focus on the positive (especially when it is hard to find), and find times to have fun. The idea is to build a sense of community by modeling and encouraging displays of empathy, whereby students feel that adults are secure, confident, and respectful. Teachers can set clearly defined limits with specific rules and yet not threaten or punish. In fact, students can be encouraged to propose rules for themselves and the teacher, so they will be stakeholders in making the rules work.

Finally, teachers are encouraged to use humor whenever possible, not only to defuse some explosive situations, but to lessen the possibility of a power struggle as well. However, teachers should not use humor that is at the expense of the student. The safest humor is when teachers poke fun at their own imperfections and errors (Mendler & Mendler, 1995). Teachers should allow students to make mistakes but should not let mistakes be too devastating to self-esteem and motivation to learn (Curwin & Mendler, 1997a; Curwin & Mendler, 1980).

How Would You React 7–3

Dealing With an Angry Parent

School safety is a priority in modern classrooms. In the following scenario, a teacher has to make choices in a difficult situation. As you read the following scenario, think what you would do if you were in the same position as this teacher. What obligation does a teacher have to protect his or her class? To protect other teachers? List the options that Mr. Fenrick has and the pros and cons of each. Is there anything that you could adapt from the ideas of Curwin and Mendler to working with an angry parent?

While Mr. Fenrick was teaching his sixth-grade class, he noticed Ms. Johnson, a parent, getting out of her car with something in her hand. He knew that Ms. Johnson had been having difficulty with a fourth-grade teacher who had been the driving force behind a child-neglect claim. Ms. Johnson had to walk past Mr. Fenrick's class, so he looked out of the small window on the door to see what she was carrying. As she approached, he noticed she was angry and had a gun. This old school in a rural area did not have security guards or a security button in the room to press.

These strategies will not make all schools safe, but getting to know students and treating them with respect and dignity will be good starting points. How Would You React 7–3 asks you to apply these strategies to a difficult situation.

Zero-Tolerance Policies

Zero-tolerance policies originally were intended to improve safety by ensuring that all students follow the rules and by sending a strong message to the school community that violent, aggressive behavior will not be tolerated. Developed in the 1990s as part of a larger package of federal school violence-prevention initiatives, they fall into one of three groups: (1) violence prevention and conflict-resolution programs; (2) gun-control laws; and (3) punitive and judicial forms of discipline (Casella, 2003). Although schools need effective policies to protect everyone in the school community, these policies are, according to Curwin and Mendler, inherently unfair because all students are treated alike, regardless of the circumstances.

Eliminating zero-tolerance policies proves difficult, however, because the concept is *simple* to understand, sounds *tough,* and gives the impression of *high standards* (Curwin's and Mendler's italics) for behavior. Instead of zero tolerance, schools need to develop legitimate high standards by refusing to go along with what sounds good and opt instead for what is truly best for children and adolescents (Curwin & Mendler, 1999). Alternatives to zero-tolerance policies include the following (Casella, 2003):

- Peer mediation, student support teams, and other forms of effective conflict resolution
- Character study as part of academic coursework
- Counseling programs for all students
- Inservice programs for teachers about violence prevention
- Student governance councils and interventions in which all students can participate
- In-school suspension accompanied by academic work, tutoring, or community or school service
- Victim services programs
- Discipline contracts that are agreed to and signed by students, parents, and school staff
- Student-developed problem-solving plans

The Case Study looks at a school system that adopted a zero-tolerance policy.

CASE STUDY
A School System With Zero Tolerance

Although the Hanover Public School District did not have serious behavior problems (e.g., physical harm from guns or knives), the administrators adopted a zero-tolerance policy against violent behavior, including substance use and possession of weapons. Decisions no longer were made at the local level; if students had any infraction that violated the zero-tolerance policy, they were suspended from school immediately. A few disruptive students were suspended, but some unexpected results occurred, as well. One student had a 1-inch "charm" of a gun on her key ring and was suspended. Another student was suspended for saying "These teachers piss me off." When another student took a plastic knife out of her lunch box to peel an orange, she was suspended.

The administrators took pride in their zero-tolerance policies. Many disruptive students were out of school, and the educators were not faced with making individual administrative decisions. However, in a meeting, the administrators had to admit that too many students were out of school, thus missing valuable instruction. In addi-

tion, some administrators thought behavior problems had increased since zero tolerance took effect. One brave administrator confided that if he had the authority to make individual school decisions, the student with the gun charm would not have been suspended because the charm was an award for marksmanship in a sporting clays competition.

Questions for Consideration

1. The school system is considering doing away with zero tolerance. What advice would you give the administrators as they reconsider their decision to implement zero tolerance?

2. Draw on the ideas of Curwin and Mendler to offer some alternatives.

 You can record your answers to these questions online on this book's Companion Web Site at *www.prenhall.com/manning*.

Effectiveness of Practical Applications

Many teachers find Curwin's and Mendler's Discipline With Dignity workable in elementary, middle, and secondary classrooms. When caring and conscientious teachers treat students with dignity and strive to help them regain hope in themselves and the educational system, they also work to ensure healthy classrooms and safe schools. Teachers understand the differences between consequences and punishments and realize the need for the former. In addition, by addressing violence, aggression, and hostility, Curwin and Mendler suggest ways to reach out-of-control students as well as ways to teach students alternatives to violence.

EVALUATING DISCIPLINE WITH DIGNITY IN A DIVERSE SOCIETY

Potential for Addressing Student Misbehaviors

With the inclusion of ideas for working with out-of-control students and violent students, the Discipline With Dignity model addresses the problems facing educators in today's schools. Many students likely misbehave and engage in violent or aggressive behaviors because they are seeking attention. They might have lost hope in themselves and their educators. With its emphasis on restoring dignity, helping students regain hope, and making a special effort to learn about individual students, Discipline With Dignity has the potential to address behaviors that are most problematic in today's school systems. In *As Tough as Necessary*, Curwin and Mendler (1997a) provide a comprehensive look at violent, aggressive, and hostile students.

Conveying dignity, developing self-esteem, building hope, and encouraging students to have hope are appropriate strategies for working with all students, regardless of their culture, gender, or social class. However, the suggestion that teachers should use touch and move within close proximity to misbehaving students might result in psychological discomfort for some students. Curwin and Mendler acknowledged this possibility and encouraged teachers to choose other means of managing behavior. Another problem might be that the teacher's lack of authoritarianism and the fact that students sometimes make rules and set consequences for teachers can be discomforting to students who have been taught that teachers are to be placed on a pedestal.

Advantages and Disadvantages of Discipline with Dignity

Discipline With Dignity has several advantages. One is Curwin's and Mendler's proposal that schools are for students and that educators are charged with the responsibility of making sure schools address the individual needs of students. Second, the proposals to instill dignity and help students regain hope are admirable. When educators are genuinely committed to helping students, those students feel good about themselves, their teachers, and their school as a whole and are more likely to demonstrate appropriate behavior. A final advantage is that teachers do not have to keep detailed records of behavior or rule violations.

Disadvantages include the extent to which educators can be expected realistically to instill dignity, especially if they are being threatened in some way. Another disadvantage is that some teachers might have difficulty with the "touchy-feely" nature of Curwin's and Mendler's theories, including the idea of students making rules for themselves and for the teachers and then deciding consequences when the teacher breaks a rule.

Imposing or Teaching Discipline?

Mendler (1992, p. 27) maintained that "effective discipline really means teaching kids how to become responsible." He thought too many children and adolescents have little idea of what being responsible means. Thus, discipline problems are viewed as an opportunity to teach students that they have choices and that they need to adopt and work toward appropriate behavior. Teachers are seen neither as "imposers of discipline" nor as autocratic rulers who demand obedience. A teacher would never say, "Julio, do it because I said so. That's enough reason for you." The teacher would work with Julio to help him understand that he can demonstrate appropriate behavior and that it is in his and the other students' best interest for him to do so.

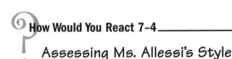

How Would You React 7–4

Assessing Ms. Allessi's Style

Teachers have strong beliefs about the management of their classrooms. Before you read the following scenario, review the key concepts in Figure 7–1 and the essential principles of Curwin and Mendler. Then read the following scenario and respond to the questions at the end.

Ms. Allessi made all the rules in her classroom and conveyed them to the students and their parents. She was not mean, and in fact treated the students fairly by applying the same rules and consequences equally to all students. She kept her psychological distance from the students, because she believed that students should see her as a teacher rather than as a person. When another teacher questioned why Ms. Allessi snacked at her desk throughout the school day but would not

allow students to do the same, Ms. Allessi replied that "There are student rules and teacher rules, and everyone should know the difference." Although she demanded that homework be turned in each day and deducted points for lateness, Ms. Allessi often took 3 or 4 days to grade and return the work. She was fond of saying that she liked to use humor in her classroom, but other teachers thought that the humor was aimed primarily at putting down students.

1. Which, if any, of the key concepts or principles of Curwin and Mendler does Ms. Allessi keep? Which, if any, does she break?
2. What behaviors would she need to change if she wanted to adopt Discipline with Dignity?

Developing Your Personal Philosophy

Does Discipline With Dignity Reflect Your Beliefs?

Ask yourself the following questions to see whether you would like to incorporate the ideas of Discipline With Dignity into your classroom management philosophy:

1. Do I believe that classroom management should be democratic and student centered?
2. Do I believe that it is my job to teach responsibility and hope to my students?
3. Do I believe that it is possible to be fair without treating everyone the same way?
4. Do I believe that I should follow the same rules as the students?
5. Do I feel comfortable conveying dignity to my students?
6. Can I work toward long-term behavioral change rather than quick fixes?

Underlying Beliefs

The ultimate effectiveness of Discipline With Dignity depends upon whether teachers feel comfortable constantly conveying dignity, continually working to restore hope, and distinguishing between punishments and consequences. It is difficult to convey dignity every day, without regard to how obnoxious the students might behave. Undoubtedly, an autocratic teacher would have difficulty implementing this model. How Would You React 7–4 looks at Ms. Allessi and her classroom management beliefs. Then Developing Your Personal Philosophy asks you to consider the ideas of Curwin and Mendler in light of your own beliefs.

CONCLUDING REMARKS

Please go to www.prenhall.com/manning and click on Concluding Remarks for this chapter to find more information.

This chapter has focused in some detail on Curwin's and Mendler's Discipline With Dignity and its call for conveying dignity; restoring hope; providing consequences rather than punishments; and dealing with violent, aggressive, and hostile students. As with other classroom management models, some teachers might be comfortable and successful using the model; others might want to use the concepts of hope and dignity with other classroom management methods. The model can be effective because it rests on sound psychological and philosophical beliefs; the main concept is that students' behavior improves when teachers convey dignity and restore hope. For additional information, you can consult the Internet sites listed in "Reaching Out with Technology" on this book's Companion Web Site.

Suggested Readings

Brown, K. (2005). Terror into triumph: Discipline in the middle grades classroom. *Middle Ground, 9*(1), 31–32. Brown discusses her use of Curwin's ideas as a first-year teacher.

Curwin, R. L. (2003). *Making good choices: Developing responsibility, respect, and self-discipline in grades 4–9.* Thousand Oaks, CA: Corwin Press. Curwin provides practical examples and strategies to help students develop responsibility, respect, and self-discipline.

Frazier, W. M., & Sterling, D. R. (2005). What should my science classroom rules be and how can I get my students to follow them? *The Clearing House, 79*(1), 31–35. The authors look at the difference between classroom rules that students should participate in establishing and the rules needed to maintain safety in school laboratories.

Mendler, A. N. (2002). Connecting with students to limit high-risk behaviors. *Reclaiming Children and Youth, 11*(3), 162–163. Mendler provides practical suggestions for making personal, social, and academic connections with student.

Stanley, P. H., Juhnke, G. A., & Purkey, W. W. (2004). Using an Invitational Theory of Practice to create safe and successful schools. *Journal of Counseling & Development, 82,* 302–309. These authors describe Invitational Theory of Practice as a means of creating and maintaining safe and successful schools.

CHAPTER 8

Exploring the Theories of Positive Classroom Management: *Fredric Jones*

Focusing Questions

After reading this chapter, you should be able to answer the following questions:

1. What does Jones mean by teachers using positive and "cheap" (Jones, 1987a, p. 25) classroom management methods?

2. What are Jones's main objectives on which he bases his positive classroom discipline?

3. What does Jones mean by the "fundamental skills" (Jones, 1987a, p. 3) of classroom management?

4. What are general and specific rules, and how do they play significant roles in teachers' classroom management decisions?

5. What is meant by terms such as limit setting, camping out, PATs, and Grandma's Rule?

6. How does Jones's positive classroom discipline address issues such as diversity and the safe schools movement?

Key Terms

Backup systems
Body language
Cheap
Classroom structures
General rules
Limit setting
Preferred activity time (PAT)
Proximity
Specific rules

Fredric Jones developed his Positive Classroom Management theory to help teachers address an array of student behavior problems by promoting positive behavior, regardless of the grade levels, developmental levels, or diversity of the students. In his book *Positive Classroom Discipline* (Jones, 1987a) and other publications (Jones, 1987b, 1996, 1973, 2000), Jones described students' inappropriate behaviors, suggested specific teacher strategies, and recognized the importance of instructional effectiveness in classroom management. Instead of controlling students, Jones accentuated the positive in all classroom management encounters. This chapter explains his concepts, how they work, how they consider diversity, and how teachers can be successful and effective with Positive Classroom Management.

FREDRIC JONES: BIOGRAPHICAL SKETCH

Fredric Jones has spent more than three decades studying the socialization of children and young adults in home and school environments. Trained as a clinical psychologist, he worked at the Neuropsychiatric Institute at University of California—Los Angeles, where he designed training programs for disabled youth, and at the University of Rochester, where he trained graduate students in family therapy and parent training as well as classroom management and teaching. Dr. Jones also has served as a consultant to individual school districts to implement staff development programs. His books on nonadversarial management procedures include *Positive Classroom Discipline* (1987a), *Positive Classroom Instruction* (1987b), and *Tools for Teaching* (2000).

OVERVIEW OF POSITIVE CLASSROOM MANAGEMENT

Key Concepts

Figure 8–1 lists the key concepts of Jones's (1987a) positive classroom discipline. His main objectives (Jones, 1987a, p. 9) of keeping procedures positive and economical result from his continual research, classroom observation, and teacher training accurately summarize what he believes are the basics of Positive Classroom Management. To Jones, these ideas are feasible, positive, and less time consuming than some of the other theories described in this book, which are "cumbersome" (to use Jones's description on page 9). In essence, teachers treat students with dignity and respect and strive to teach students to do likewise.

Philosophical and Psychological Foundations

"For students to learn, they must enjoy learning" (Jones, 2000, p. 1). "Whether or not lessons come alive and students learn depends upon the teacher's skill" (p. 2) and the teacher's ability to manage the group. Teachers who are able to manage a classroom are "relaxed" (p. 5) and "emotionally warm" (p. 5) as they use Positive Classroom Management, which focuses on three broad areas: instruction, motivation, and discipline (p. 9).

One of the foundations of classroom discipline is cooperation (Jones, 2000). Irresponsible behavior can cause as much stress and lost learning as does goofing off. When responsible students simply do what teachers ask them to do, management becomes much easier and cooperation becomes a matter of routine. What is difficult about cooperation is that it requires a decision on the part of the student. Teachers cannot force students to cooperate. Instead, they have to help students understand that it just makes sense to cooperate with the teacher and other students (*http://www.educationworld.com/a_curr/columnists/jones/jones014.shtml*).

Jones (1987a) also believes that *whole children* (Jones's italics) are at the center stage—the appropriateness of their behavior and their care for themselves, their classmates, their teachers, and their "priceless opportunity to learn" (Jones, 1987a, p. 4). Thus, Jones focuses

Figure 8–1 Key Concepts of Jones's Positive Classroom Management

Fredric Jones believes the following:

1. Classroom management procedures must be

   Positive. They must be gentle, affirm the student, set limits, and build cooperation in the absence of coercion.

   Economical. They must be practical, simple, and easy to use once they are mastered. They must *reduce* (Jones' italics) the teacher's work load (Jones, 1987a, p. 9).

2. There are four groups of fundamental skills of classroom management:

   Developing classroom structures, including rules, procedures, and physical arrangements

   Remaining calm and using body language to set limits

   Teaching students cooperation and responsibility

   Providing backup systems.

3. Time and its allocation are important resources for teachers

not only on the management of behavior, but also on emotions, self-esteem, values, and relationship building, which are, to Jones, the true goals of the classroom management system. By understanding students and mastering instructional and management strategies, teachers can make all young people feel successful in their environment.

Teachers, according to Jones, should strive for positive management techniques that convey dignity (similar to the ideas of Curwin and Mendler in chapter 7), cooperation, and respect and that demonstrate skill, caring, and effort. One of the first lessons teachers must learn about classroom management is that it is emotional. You cannot manage another's behavior until you can manage your own (*http://www.educationworld.com/a_curr/colmunists/jones/jones010.shtml*). Thus, teachers should not assume autocratic roles, demand strict obedience, and threaten or try to control through fear. Instead, they should see students as individuals who are worthy of respect. Teachers also should assume that learners will be responsible and worthy of being treated with dignity.

Dignity and respect can be conveyed in many ways. Activity 8–1 looks at the importance of conveying these feelings to elementary and secondary students.

After you review these ideas and suggest others, examine the situation in How Would You React 8–1. In this example, a student teacher's failure to learn the names of her students went directly against the ideas of conveying dignity and respect.

Teachers' Roles and Responsibilities

Although Jones wrote entire books on teachers' roles in positive classroom discipline and instruction (Jones, 1987a, 1987b, 2000), his ideas about the roles and responsibilities of teachers can be summarized as follows. To build positive classroom discipline, educators should be effective teachers, model appropriate behavior, and use appropriate classroom management methods (Jones, 1987a).

Activity 8–1

Conveying Dignity and Respect

Teachers can convey dignity and respect by

Calling students by their first names,

Treating all students equally as much as possible,

Showing genuine interest in students by asking about hobbies, recreation, music, and entertainment choices,

Striving for cooperative and collaborative endeavors with students and asking them what class rules they think are needed,

Speaking to students in a firm but relaxed tone.

What other ways can you suggest for teachers to convey dignity? For ideas, you can refer to chapter 7 and the work of Curwin and Mendler.

⑨ How Would You React 8-1

‼ Pointing and Saying "Yes, you."

Knowing students' names is an important part of class-room management. In addition to conveying respect and dignity, teachers use names to identify students in various situations. As you read the following scenario, think about how the students in Ms. Creecy's class feel. Then respond to the questions at the end.

> Fayetta Creecy was a student teacher in a seventh-grade social studies class. Her lesson plans were excellent, her teaching skills were good, and she demonstrated good interpersonal skills, except for one aspect. After 3 weeks of observation and 4 weeks of teaching, she still did not know the students' names. Because Ms. Creecy's lessons included lots of questions, she continually had to point to a student and say something like "Yes, you." When asked why she did not know the names of the students, Ms. Creecy replied that she taught four classes of social studies per day and simply could not learn the names.

1. If you were a student in Ms. Creecy's class, how would you feel about her inability to use names to call on students?
2. What effect is her not knowing names having on her management?
3. As an educator, what advice or tips would you give Ms. Creecy to help her learn the names of her students?
4. How would this advice vary if Ms. Creecy had been in a 1st-grade classroom? In a 5th-grade classroom? In an 11th-grade classroom?

At the heart of Jones's theory is the belief that teachers should be exemplary planners and conveyors of positive classroom instruction that helps students want to learn and demonstrate appropriate behavior. In other words, teachers must establish an instructional environment that is conducive to learning and to proper behavior. When students are actively engaged in productive learning activities, they will have legitimate reasons to behave.

To build classroom discipline, teachers also must convey dignity and cooperation. If students feel they are respected as individuals, they will want to reciprocate with similar behaviors. Likewise, when teachers act maturely and competently, students will see them as role models after whom they can pattern their own behavior. Not only do good teachers tell students how to act, they demonstrate appropriate behavior in all their daily routines and interactions.

Finally, good teachers use positive and "cheap" (Jones, 1987a, p. 25) classroom management. By **cheap**, Jones means management techniques that are simple and that require the "least planning, the least effort, the least time and paperwork" (p. 25). Any management system must save time if it is to "truly help the teacher" (Jones, 2000, p. 7). For example, rather than choosing a classroom management plan that requires extensive record keeping and an exhaustive list of rules, teachers should provide simple, positive, and workable rules, routines, and standards. Review the situation in How Would You React 8–2 to see if it meets Jones's criteria for a cheap system.

APPLYING POSITIVE CLASSROOM MANAGEMENT

Jones focuses attention on the type and number of behavior problems that occur in the classroom. In his book *Positive Classroom Discipline* (1987a), he acknowledges the increased violence in schools, the use of guns and knives, and the assaults on teachers and students. However, Jones also maintains that most behaviors are of a lesser degree or what he called *small disruptions* (Jones's italics) (p. 27). These are often the most stressful misbehaviors and can occur almost constantly (*http://www.educationworld.com/a_curr/columnists/jones/jones009.shtml*). For example, Jones (1973) found that in the average class, students are off task between 45%

Developing a System

Before you read the following scenario, refer to Jones' ideas and make a list of some criteria that you could use to identify a cheap classroom management system. Then read about the following and respond to the questions at the end.

It had taken 2 weeks, but Christie Nasta, a first-year teacher, finally had developed an elaborate management plan for her class. "There's no way they can misbehave now," she said to Mr. Panchison, an experienced teacher. "I've spent days thinking of every possible misbehavior and the consequences for each one. Then I created a board for the front of the room with all of my students' names along with a list of penalties and a point system that takes into consideration the severity of each action. With all the reminders and warnings posted throughout the room, no one will get away with anything."

Two weeks later, Ms. Nasta stopped Mr. Panchison in the hall. "Something's wrong," she began. "My new management system seems to limit misbehaviors, but it's taking all my time. I think I'm spending more time watching for misbehaviors than I spend teaching. And keeping track of all the points is a pain. What did I do wrong?"

1. Does Christie Nasta's management system meet your criteria for a cheap system?
2. Based on the ideas of Jones, what advice would you give Ms. Nasta to change her system and make it cheap?

Activity 8-2

Determining Behavior Problems

Observe a group of students in a classroom for 30 minutes to determine their actual behaviors. Make a list of behaviors that you consider inappropriate. Instead of listing general behaviors such as being momentarily off-task, list specific behaviors (talking to classmates for an extended time, walking around the room, playing with a nonclass-related object, etc.) that actually interfere with learning. Where was the teacher when these behaviors occurred? Compare your findings to those Jones listed.

and 55% of the time. In typical elementary or secondary classrooms, whether inner city or suburban, roughly 80% of the disruptions are "talking to neighbors" (Jones, 1987a, p. 27). Students who are of their seats account for another 15%. Thus, Jones found that 95% of classroom disruptions are simply the two most convenient forms of goofing off and taking a break from work. He refers to these as "nickel and dime" misbehaviors (p. 27), which include things such as pencil tapping, note passing, or playing with some object smuggled into class. On average, between 25% and 33% of a class engages in goofing off during any given minute of the day, with students usually generating about 0.6 to 0.8 disruptions per student per minute. The rate of disruptions in typical classrooms escalates when teachers are sitting down at their desk (*http://www.educationworld.com/a_curr/columnists/jones/jones009.shtml*). Even the more serious disruptions that result in office referrals involve student back talk as the primary or secondary teacher complaint in 80% of the cases (Jones, 1996). Activity 8–2 asks you to verify Jones's observations.

Implementing Practical Applications

In *Positive Classroom Discipline* Fredric Jones described the "fundamental skills" (Jones, 1987a, p. 3) of classroom management, or those skills that teachers need to address nickel and dime misbehaviors (p. 27) as well as more violent acts. Some of these skills prevent discipline problems; others remediate them. However, all focus on methods of generating cooperation and appropriate behavior. Jones believes that a thorough understanding of these fundamental skills can help teachers improve classroom discipline and academic achievement. In this section, we have followed the general outline of *Positive Classroom Discipline* and grouped Jones's fundamental skills into four groups: **classroom structures**, limit setting through **body language**, cooperation, and **backup systems**.

Fundamental Skill 1

Effective classroom structures consist of rules, routines, and standards. Jones believes that teachers should set the stage properly with classroom structures so that classroom management and instruction proceed as smoothly as possible or, as Jones said, "make management a matter of routine" (Jones, 1987a, p. 41). What does Jones mean by classroom structures? The term can cover a range of topics from how to arrange the classroom (see Management Tip 8–1 for information on arranging the classroom to maximize management) to how to interact with parents during telephone calls. Structures include the nuts and bolts (p. 41) of getting off on the right foot at the beginning of the school year as well as the management tasks that teachers face continuously throughout the year. Jones believes that structure must take the center stage in classroom management, but he also maintains that it does not receive sufficient attention and in some cases is ignored altogether. Although many things contribute to classroom structure, we want to look at two aspects in more detail: rules and environment.

To examine the concept of classroom rules as a classroom structure, you must consider a number of things such as the nature of the rules, misconceptions about rules, the

Management Tip 8-1

Arranging the Classroom

According to Jones (2000), classroom arrangement helps a teacher use mobility and proximity as part of management. The best room arrangement should

- Allow the teacher to reach any student in the room quickly,
- Provide wide walkways,
- Move the students forward in the room,
- Move the teacher's desk to a corner or the back of the room (Jones, 2000)

All teachers: Jones favors an interior-loop arrangement for the desks in most classrooms with a U-arrangement in computer labs or small classes.

Elementary
Jones notes that "primary teachers might have all of the proximity they need while sitting on the carpet and reading to students at their feet" (Jones, 2000, p. 38). The teacher controls the group by turning toward disruptive students.

Upper elementary and secondary
Jones (2000) suggests using small pieces of masking tape to mark the placement of desks in the classroom. These visual prompts can be colored with markers to provides guides for different class arrangements such as small groups.

Please go to *www.prenhall.com/manning* and click on the Management Tips for this chapter to complete management activities and find more information on arrangements of classrooms.

difference between general and specific rules, ways to teach rules to students, and methods of developing rules. For more detailed information than we can include in this chapter, you should consult Jones's *Positive Classroom Discipline* (1987a).

In that book and other writings, Jones maintains that classroom rules are much more than a list of dos and don'ts. Students in a well-structured classroom know exactly what is expected of them, and they also have been trained and motivated to adhere to the rules. However, a teacher cannot assume that students will agree with and ultimately obey classroom rules. Instead, a teacher must teach the rules, explain the reasons for the rules, and motivate or convince the students that obeying the rules is in their best interests as well as everyone else's.

According to Jones, several myths, misconceptions, or natural defenses about rules exist that teachers need to recognize. Paramount among these are the beliefs shown in Figure 8–2. Believing that all of these are natural defenses, Jones, in his writings, explicates each and explains why he thinks each is a defense. In essence, he believes that all teachers need help with management at some time, regardless of their curriculum, the skills they were born with, the number of years they have been teaching, and the number of students who are misbehaving in a particular class.

It is important that teachers consider their own misconceptions, because these can interfere with a teacher's ability and willingness to insist upon proper classroom behavior. Activity 8–3 asks you to consider your misconceptions or those you might have seen in others.

Jones explains that two types of classroom rules exist: general rules and specific rules. Both play significant roles in teachers' classroom management decisions.

General rules describe teachers' goals and objectives—their hopes and aspirations for classroom management during a coming year. Rather than dictating behavior, they establish a tone in the class and raise expectations briefly until the students have had time to size up the teacher and determine whether the general rules are going to be enforced (Jones, 1987a). Broad guidelines or expressions of the teacher's values are general rules that typically deal with good behavior and good work habits. No best or final set of rules exists, but three guidelines will help you prepare general rules:

1. Do not make any rule you are not willing to enforce every time it is broken.
2. Have a few general rules for behavior and work.
3. Make sure rules are simple, clear, and shared by all students.

In contrast, **specific rules** deal with training a class to do *what* (Jones's italics) you want them to do, *when* (Jones's italics) you want them to do it. For example, during the

Figure 8–2
Misconceptions
about Rules

The following are a number of misconceptions that teachers commonly have about discipline and the use of rules in a classroom (Jones, 1987a).

- A good curriculum means teachers will not have discipline problems.
- Some teachers are born with a gift for good management.
- Some students are truly unmanageable.
- Discipline and rules thwart creativity and spontaneity.
- The longer teachers teach, the better their management will be.
- There are some teachers who do not need help with discipline.
- The only problem is with the class this year.
- Students dislike and resent classroom rules.

Activity 8–3

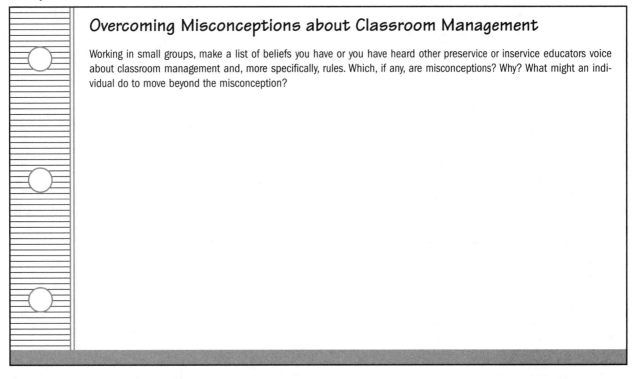

Overcoming Misconceptions about Classroom Management

Working in small groups, make a list of beliefs you have or you have heard other preservice or inservice educators voice about classroom management and, more specifically, rules. Which, if any, are misconceptions? Why? What might an individual do to move beyond the misconception?

first 2 weeks of school, teachers should address rules such as "how to do this" (Jones, 1987a, p. 43) and "how to do that" (p. 43). "Real rules" (Jones, 2000, p. 111) are what the teacher permits rather than what the teacher says the rules are. Thus "classroom rules are ultimately defined by whatever any student can get away with" (p. 112).

Once teachers have decided on their general and specific rules, they need to teach those rules to their students.

> Jones told of a teacher who began the first day of school as follows. Before the students arrived, the teacher had placed on each desk a 3 × 5 card on which the students were to write information about themselves and their parents. As the students arrived, he met each one at the door with a personal greeting. Introducing himself, the teacher shook hands with each student, asked the student's name, handed each student a number (the number corresponded to the seating chart on the board), and directed the student to begin completing the card.

Jones maintains that this teacher's procedure has taught several lessons: (1) my enforcement of the rules begins at the door, (2) I care who you are and that you know who I am, (3) walk, don't run, into my class,(4) take your seat immediately, and (5) begin to work on the assignment before the bell rings.

Teachers cannot assume that "students should know how to behave by this time" (Jones, 1987a, p. 42), that it is foolish to sacrifice instructional time to teach management rules, that teaching rules is a matter of being strict, or that students will understand and obey rules simply because they are posted on the wall. Instead, Jones believes teachers and students benefit when the students know all classroom management expectations. During the first 2 weeks of school, teachers should teach a planned, structured lesson on rules,

Management Tip 8–2

Establishing rules and routines

According to Jones (2000), when teachers do not establish rules and routines, they allow students to establish the agenda and the management plan in the classroom. Teachers should be proactive.

> Arrange the classroom. Have students sit where you want them to sit, not where they want to.
>
> Provide markers to show where the desks belong. Don't let students change the arrangement without your permission.
>
> Get students working right away every day. Let students know that the classroom is where learning takes place.
>
> Use icebreakers to create a community in the classroom. Students should know the name of every other student as well as yours.
>
> List and teach the rules.
>
> Teach the routines you want your students to follow.

Elementary

Before you have your class make that first trip through the halls to the library media center or the music room, practice the routine.

- Explain why it is important to be quiet in the halls.
- Demonstrate and explain hand motions or other visual cues you will use for stop, go, start over, zipped lips, etc.
- Explain lining-up procedures.
- Practice lining up.
- Start the "trip."
- Be ready to go back to the classroom and start over if anyone breaks the silence rule. It may take several tries before everyone gets it right and the group walks in silence (Jones, 2000).

Secondary

Bell work (about 5 minutes) is what students are doing when the class bell rings (Jones, 2000). Standard procedure should be: Come in the class, take your seat, look at the board for the day's bell work, and get started. Tell students who want to socialize that they can remain in the hall. Once in the room, they should be working on their bell work.

Please go to *www.prenhall.com/manning* and click on the Management Tips for this chapter to complete management activities and find more information on establishing rules and routines.

routines, and expected standards. Future instructional time will be enhanced because time will not be wasted dealing with students who break the rules (Jones, 1987a). Management Tip 8–2 provides some additional information about establishing rules and routines in the first weeks of school.

Fundamental Skill 2

Limit setting consists of a set of physical moves performed by the teacher that signal the student to stop specific behaviors. When teachers use the skills of limit setting, they use their bodies to say what their mouths were about to say. This procedure is the opposite of what many teachers do to stop undesired behaviors.

> Seeing that Bianca was talking to Kate during the lesson, Ms. McMichael called out in a loud voice: "Bianca and Kate, stop that talking right now or else you'll be sorry!" At the same time, she scowled and shook her finger at the two girls.

Jones believes that a better alternative is to use body language to correct behavior (Jones, 1987a). As students read a teacher's body language, they learn what they can and cannot get away with. Teachers can use body language to set priorities, demonstrate what is important and what is not important, and reinforce rules (*http://www.educationworld.com/a_curr/columnists/jones/jones011.shtml*).

The objective of limit setting is to *calm the students and get them back on task* (Jones's italics) (Jones, 1987a, p. 86). In addition to stopping undesired behavior, teachers want their own behavior to be contagious. Unlike Ms. McMichael in the previous example, if teachers demonstrate or model calm behavior, they will calm the students. Conversely, if teachers become upset and let their feelings be known, then the students will be upset, too. Unfortunately, when teachers let themselves get upset, students usually become resentful and often do not give their full attention for the remainder of the class period. Real interpersonal power is the power of calm, which allows the teacher and the students to retain their dignity and their sense of volition (Jones, 1987a).

Jones (1996) suggests that teachers should let their students know they mean business (Jones, 1987a, p. 26). Meaning business, however, is done with the body rather than the mouth. Thus, Jones focuses on the use of body language to express thoughts, feelings, and intentions, and to deliver a powerful message (Jones, 1996). The following are some specific uses of body language for classroom management.

Physical **proximity** is a strong deterrent. Teachers can use personal space to correct undesired behaviors. The farther a teacher is from a student, the safer the student usually feels. When the teacher moves closer and into a student's space, the student feels less comfortable. In fact, when a teacher moves within 18 inches of a misbehaving student, the student usually will correct the behavior (Jones, 1987a). A teacher also can engage in camping out, or standing either in front of or behind a student, to encourage the misbehaving or inattentive student to correct the behavior.

> Shonese Barnsdorf often could correct misbehaviors during her lessons without ever speaking a word. When she noticed Tori concentrating on something in her desk rather than on the lesson, Ms. Barnsdorf continued teaching while she moved closer to Tori. Seeing Ms. Barnsdorf approaching, Tori turned her attention to the lesson. Ms. Barnsdorf remained near Tori while she continued teaching. Instructional time was not lost, and Ms. Barnsdorf did not have to announce the offender or the offending behavior publicly.

Proximity should be used with care. Some students can feel threatened and become defensive if they believe the teacher is invading their personal space. When the teacher moves closer and perhaps leans down, she or he can cause discomfort by operating on the edge of the student's personal space. To avoid a potential problem, the teacher can regulate the distance or turn slightly to eliminate a confrontation. By remaining calm, the teacher can have a calming effect on the student (*http://www.educationworld.com/a_curr/columnists/jones/jones013.shtml*).

The strength of calmness is shown through body cues. Teachers should "remember that calm is a strength and upset is a weakness" (Jones, 1996, p. 26). Rather than raising one's voice, Jones (1987a) recommends that teachers use body cues to let students know their behavior is inappropriate. Specifically, teachers can face students, maintain eye contact, employ appropriate facial and body expressions, and say students' names.

Once a student begins to misbehave to an extent that the teacher feels it is necessary to intervene, the teacher should face the student completely and squarely. This action tells the misbehaving student that he or she is the most important person in the classroom at that time and, therefore, must receive the teacher's full attention. It is necessary for the teacher to face the student completely; a gradual or partial turn signals to the student that the teacher has not directed full attention to the problem. By giving partial attention, the teacher conveys, "Hey, give me a break. I'm trying to teach over here" (Jones, 1987a, p. 90). Jones says that the student will not give the teacher a break because a partial gesture has little effect.

Eye contact is another effective tool that teachers can use for classroom management. Jones recommends that a teacher make eye contact with disruptive students and focus on the most disruptive student in a group. To Jones, this eye contact is one of the most "sensitive barometers" (Jones, 1987a, p. 90) of emotional calm or upset on a body. Unwavering eye contact on the teacher's part conveys calmness, which is interpreted as self-confidence. The opposite, failing to look the student in the eye, often is interpreted as meaning the teacher is anxious, uptight, and unsure. When a teacher glances away for only a moment, it tells the student that the teacher is unsure of his or her ability to handle the disruption. It also tells the student that the teacher does not want to stay in the situation. Thus, the student begins to feel more comfortable than the teacher and is unlikely to stop the misbehavior completely, even though the student might offer some insincere smile.

Jones (1987a) admits that some students' cultural backgrounds might prevent them from wanting to make eye contact. For example, Jones maintains that children and adolescents in Asian, Hispanic, and Native American cultures might be reluctant to maintain eye contact in a discipline situation. To do so might convey a sign of disrespect or impudence. In contrast, in many European cultures, eye contact typically is interpreted as a sign of paying attention, and looking away is a sign of disrespect.

Teachers also must use facial and body expressions to let their intentions be known. According to Jones (1987a), every part of the body speaks. Thus, Jones suggests that teachers should smile, especially as they say students' names. In contrast, a frown can stop misbehaviors, but a bland facial expression can convey resignation or can even imply a threat. Often teachers send messages that they are upset because of the difficulty they have hiding their anger and faking relaxation and self-control. Thus, in a difficult discipline situation, even when a teacher slows down and speaks with a relaxed tone, the teacher's facial expressions can give the impression of being upset.

Posture is also important in conveying calm. Jones recommends that teachers keep their hands low because the higher a person's hands are, the more animated or upset the person appears. Arms folded or on a person's hips also convey impatience, a form of being upset. Thus, effective teachers often place their hands in their pockets or at their sides to convey a sense of calmness. Another technique is to place the arms behind the back, because this hides nervous mannerisms (Jones, 1987a).

Good teachers practice patience. However, it is important to point out that patience is not waiting and hoping for the best; it is the relaxed demeanor with which teachers confront the problem while waiting for students to make emotional peace with themselves and return to the learning tasks. Another useful technique for classroom management is for a teacher to say a disruptive student's first name, say it only once, and say it loud enough to be heard. The name should be spoken in a flat or matter-of-fact fashion. A teacher should be "neither sweet nor sour" (Jones, 1987a, p. 93). Because emotions convey feelings and are contagious, Jones thinks teachers will get exactly what they give.

Limit setting allows teachers to learn about themselves. In practicing the skills of relaxation and self-control under pressure, teachers learn how difficult it is to be calm and how easy it is to lose the student's respect during a reprimand. Teachers learn to use the power that is part of their professional role to protect rather than threaten students. When teachers effectively use limit setting, they project a calmness that conveys acceptance of the student without implying acceptance of the behavior. Jones believes that the use of silence, calmness, and genuine patience allows students to confront *themselves* (Jones's italics) rather than the teacher and finally to accept responsibility for their own misbehavior. Also, effective limit setting can reestablish relationships and a sense of reconciliation between student and teacher. In such an atmosphere, students can begin to understand that the teacher is always there for them and cannot be alienated, driven away, or emotionally lost as a result of the student's misbehaviors (Jones, 1987a). How Would You React 8–3 asks you to apply the limit-setting skills to a classroom situation.

Fundamental Skill 3

Responsibility training teaches learners to be responsible for their own actions. Jones (1987a) maintains that the ultimate goal of discipline is to train young people to become self-directing and to be responsible for their own behavior. According to Jones, three conditions must be met for students to demonstrate responsible behavior:

- They have a resource for which they are responsible.
- They have control over the consumption of that resource.
- They must live with the consequences of the consumption of that resource.

The resource to which Jones referred is time rather than stickers or awards. Time is free, is at the teacher's disposal, and can be the universal medium of exchange in the classroom. Teachers allocate students an amount of time, the consumption of which depends

Confronting Bruce

Jones believes in limit setting or using physical moves to send signals to students. As you read the following scenario, think about how you might use limit setting, including calm, physical proximity, facial expressions, and body language in this situation. Then, respond to the questions at the end.

> Everyone in the class was watching and Mr. Tiller knew it. Bruce Maltusi was acting up again, and something had to be done. Unfortunately, Mr. Tiller, a student teacher, did not like conflict and tried to avoid it at all costs. He sometimes told his friends that he was more nervous about conflict situations than his students. Now, however, he couldn't put off the inevitable. Bruce had put down his math book deliberately and started to sort through some baseball cards in his desk. Normally, Mr. Tiller would ignore Bruce and keep teaching. However, he knew from experience that this only would lead to more trouble. Mr. Tiller had to deal with the situation now.

1. How can Mr. Tiller use the practices of limit setting in this situation?

2. What physical moves might he use to get Bruce back on task?

3. What accommodations might Mr. Tiller have to make if the disruptive student had been an American Indian?

4. Role-play with others in the class how you would use your body and voice to set limits in a variety of classroom situations.

---

upon students' behavior. By consumption (Jones, 1987a, p. 158), Jones means "the use of" (i.e., if teachers allocate students an amount of time, then students must decide how to consume the time).

To help teachers manage the resource of time, Jones (1987a, 1987b) developed a system of **preferred activity time (PAT),** which he describes as "embarrassing simplicity" (Jones, 1987a, p. 160). This system of genuine incentives utilizes time as the reinforcer (the bonuses are more PAT; the penalties are less PAT) with group rewards (preferred activity time) and group accountability (one for all and all for one). By the giving and taking of time, teachers can hold the class responsible for the way the time is consumed. For example, if the class does an excellent job of cooperating and being responsible, the teacher can add amounts of PAT. The class can use the PAT time for an activity they enjoy.

> You have 4 minutes to put away your art supplies and get ready for social studies. Left-over time will go to PAT.
>
> I'd like to review for tomorrow's test. Would you like to use 10 minutes of PAT to play your favorite social studies review game or save it for something else?
>
> Everyone worked well and showed responsibility in the cooperative learning groups today. You have earned 5 minutes of PAT.
>
> Thank you for demonstrating that you are mature and responsible juniors when I left the room to escort our guest speaker to Ms. Beecham's room. You have earned 3 minutes of PAT.

Jones (*http://www.educationworld.com/a_curr/columnists/jones/jones015.shtml*) emphasizes that teachers do not lose instructional time with PAT. In fact, in an effort to earn PAT, students will be more willing to start class on time and to make better use of time during transitions. Thus, instructional time is actually increased. Jones offered several general guidelines for using PAT (Figure 8–3), but he reminded teachers PAT might need to be tailored to meet the social maturity of particular students.

PAT is not free time to "kick back" (Jones, 1987a, p. 161), because such an abdication of structure by the teacher usually produces boredom and negation of PAT. PAT is a group

Figure 8–3 Suggested
Guidelines for Providing
PAT

Grade Level	Amount of PAT	Comment
Kindergarten	Use as a break every 15 to 20 minutes.	Keep PAT "cheap" and short.
First Grade	Begin with three PATs in the morning and two in the afternoon. By midyear switch to three PATs—midmorning, end of morning and end of afternoon.	PAT about 10 to 15 minutes.
Second and Third	One PAT before and one after lunch.	Begin to lengthen PATs.
Fourth and Fifth	One PAT a day.	PAT could be as long as 30 minutes.
Middle and High	One PAT each week.	Expand to two a week if needed.

accountability system. Students who misbehave can prevent other students from getting bonuses. Therefore, disruptive students must consider the consequences of their actions on other students, who might receive fewer bonuses.

When giving time, teachers should follow "Grandma's Rule" (Jones, 1987a, p. 153). Grandma's Rule holds students accountable and does not let them have dessert until they finish their vegetables. This means that they do not get their rewards (or incentives) until they demonstrate what the teacher wants. Teachers have to resist pressures to give the reward first and hope the desired behavior will happen later.

In Positive Classroom Discipline, Jones (1987a) gives a far more detailed discussion of his system of Preferred Activity Time than we can discuss here. He believes his PAT system is powerful, simple, economical, and flexible because teachers and students get more of what they want. Teachers want more productive and useful teaching time as well as lower stress and more enjoyment. Similarly, students want more enjoyment, choice of activities, and a productive learning environment. PAT can serve as the main classroom management device and also can serve as a vehicle to which a teacher can attach a myriad of other individualized and specialized time incentive programs. Management Tip 8–3 provides some examples of PAT.

Fundamental Skill 4

Positive Classroom Discipline includes backup systems. Although Jones thinks clear structures, limit setting, and responsibility training will allow teachers to deal successfully with almost any discipline problem, he recognizes that classroom management programs do not come with guarantees. No matter how well designed a management system is, problems can persist, crises can arise, and outrageous behavior can occur. To avoid punishment, teachers must know how to respond in a way that is low key, easy to use, low stress to the teacher, and protective of the student. Therefore, Jones calls for teachers to have a backup system that provides a response to undesirable behaviors.

To Jones (1987a), a backup system is an organization of negative reactions to suppress severe disruptions and provide negative sanctions in discipline management. In Jones's words, "A backup system is a series of responses designed to meet force with force so that the uglier the student's behavior becomes, the deeper he or she digs his or her hole with no escape" (p. 256). An effective backup system is composed of a series of discrete procedures or responses arranged in ascending order so that teachers or administrators can deal effectively with a wide range of unacceptable behaviors in the classroom. These negative sanctions go beyond the mild social sanctions of limit setting and the penalty component of responsibility training. Although negative sanctions are not compatible with a positive approach to discipline, Jones believes that teachers need to understand how to use them properly. Thus, teachers need to understand the importance of knowing what backup systems are, what they are good for, and how they can fail. This idea of failure is important because Jones thinks backup systems frequently fail because they are overused.

Jones provides three levels of backup systems. The first, classroom policy, is the teacher's first line of defense. The action can be private or public, but the intent is to deal with the immediate problem as well as its aftereffects such as embarrassment, resentment, and revenge. Effective teachers avoid going public when at all possible.

> ☆ **Management Tip 8-3**
>
> ### Using Preferred Activity Time (PAT)
>
> Teachers often worry that PAT will take time from instruction. However, Jones (2000, p. 94) maintains that students can use PAT in preferred instructional activities "that the students eagerly look forward to doing."
>
> Allow students to use PAT for the following:
>
> - Art projects
>   Classroom murals to accompany a unit
>   Sketch to accompany a lesson
>   Room decorations
>   Stained class windows
>   Computer art projects
> - Music projects
>   Learning music to accompany a unit or lesson
>   Listening centers
> - Learning games
> - Special-interest centers
> - Computer lab work
> - Extra silent reading time
> - Journal writing
> - Extra-credit work
> - A book talk by the school librarian, with a trip to the library to check out a book

> Mr. Sinashaw had a rule that students could not play with any objects during class. In addition to being posted on the wall, the rule had been discussed at the beginning of the school year. Ignoring the rule, Tyree brought a 2-inch model race car to class and was "driving" it on his desk during social studies. Mr. Sinashaw quietly walked to Tyree's desk and stood beside him, hoping he would put the car away. The model vanished into Tyree's desk and nothing was said. However, about 15 minutes later, Tyree was once again racing the car on his desk. This time, Mr. Sinashaw kept teaching, walked over, took the car, and never said a word. As Mr. Sinashaw later explained, "I wanted to keep this issue private—just between the two of us." At the end of the school day, Mr. Sinashaw returned the car to Tyree and asked him not to bring it back to school. Happy to get the model back, Tyree agreed. Everything was kept between Mr. Sinashaw and Tyree; there was not any embarrassment, resentment, or need for revenge.

The second level, school policy, spells out the due process for dealing with discipline problems that must be handled by teachers and administrators working collaboratively. A well-developed school policy typically consists of a clearly defined hierarchy of negative sanctions for dealing with severe or recurring behavior problems. Such policies tend to be far more explicit at the secondary level than the elementary level and typically are referred to as a "school discipline code" (Jones, 1987a, p. 258) and "hierarchy of consequences" (p. 259).

The following is an example of such a hierarchy:

- Warning
- Conference with the student
- Time-out, being sent to the office, detention
- Conference with the parent
- Conference with teacher, parent, and principal or vice principal
- In-school suspension
- Suspension (1 day)
- Suspension (3 days)
- Expulsion and/or a special program (Jones, 1987a, p. 258)

Please go to *www.prenhall.com/manning* and click on the Management Tips for this chapter to complete management activities and find more information on PAT for both elementary and secondary classrooms.

The third level, law enforcement and the juvenile justice system, is one many teachers and administrators try to avoid; however, with the increasing violence facing educators today, it is one aspect of a backup system that educators might have to use. Sometimes communities construct a buffer between the school system and legal authorities. Often called a family court, this vehicle deals with juvenile offenses rather than with the single issue of guilt or innocence. The judge's recommendation might include psychological testing or therapy, a special remedial program, a rehabilitation program, referral to county agencies such as child protection or social services, some form of restitution to the plaintiff, or even prosecution in juvenile court.

Effectiveness of Practical Applications

Several aspects of Jones's positive classroom discipline contribute to its practical application. Most, with the exception of the accountability measures associated with PAT, can be implemented relatively easily.

First, the concept of limit setting and maintaining physical proximity, portraying calmness, maintaining eye contact, using appropriate bodily expressions, and firmly saying names one time all are implemented easily in a classroom. Body gestures and firm speech can be influential; likewise, a slumping posture and a whiny voice can convey the idea that the teacher is uncomfortable. Without stopping instruction or making misbehaviors public, teachers often can use physical proximity and eye contact to correct behaviors.

Second, Jones wants his system to teach children and adolescents to develop self-discipline. The burden of appropriate behavior is moved from the teacher to the students, who should accept responsibility for their behavior.

Although Jones astutely recognizes the need for backup systems and punitive measures, a third practical aspect is his emphasis on the positive. Teachers practicing Jones's techniques do not threaten, cajole, or coerce. This positive emphasis also can be seen in the belief that the ultimate goal of discipline is to teach learners to discipline themselves.

EVALUATING POSITIVE CLASSROOM MANAGEMENT IN A DIVERSE SOCIETY

Potential for Addressing Student Misbehaviors

Jones basically divided students into three groups as shown in Figure 8–4. Although Jones discussed students based on their instructional habits, instruction and classroom management are closely related. Students in all three groups (admittedly, some more than others) should respond to the management techniques suggested by Jones.

Remember, 80% of office referrals involve student back talk as the teacher complaint (Jones, 1996); roughly 80% of the routine disruptions are "talking to neighbors" (Jones,

Figure 8–4 Three Types of Students

The Self-Starters   These students listen to the directions, follow the instructions, and correctly complete work assignments. They often double-check their assignments for accuracy and neatness; basically, they can do school work without much teacher assistance.
The Most Needy   These students need help; they cannot work alone no matter how hard they try. They appear to try while the teacher is around, but as soon as the teacher leaves, they typically become confused or start fooling around.
The Middle-of-the-Roaders   These students are comfortably falling into a C+ lifestyle; they are not pursuing excellence. They only want to get done and are unwilling to do anything that is not required.

Source: Developed from Jones, F. H. (1987b). *Positive classroom instruction.* New York: McGraw-Hill, p. 36.

1987a, p. 27), and about 15% are students out of their seat. Jones's positive classroom management addresses these nickel and dime misbehaviors (p. 27) through the use of appropriate physical proximity, facial expressions, limit setting, preferred activity time, eye contact, room arrangement, calm, and self-discipline. In addition, Jones recognizes that students can demonstrate more serious behaviors. In those cases, he has an elaborate backup system for repeat misbehavers, as well as a three-tiered plan (e.g., teachers, administrators, and the juvenile justice system) for violent offenders.

Advantages and Disadvantages of Positive Discipline

Advantages of Jones's positive discipline include, first, his emphasis on the positive and on those techniques (e.g., body language, eye contact, and physical proximity) that contribute to discipline being a private rather than a public matter; second, his emphasis on self-discipline and learners accepting responsibility for their behavior; and third, as his book *Positive Classroom Discipline* (1987a) suggests, his fourfold system of prevention (the classroom rules and routines), limit setting, cooperation, and backup systems. Rather than creating a one- or two-step program, Jones recognizes that all students will not respond to a given discipline plan; therefore, alternatives and further steps are needed.

A plus of Jones's theories is that they apply to all age groups and almost all students. Students and their differences are respected, and when students demonstrate inappropriate behaviors, teachers firmly address the behaviors, but they do so in a caring and respectful manner.

A fourth aspect we like can be seen in the following statement: "Our objective, to put it simply, therefore, is to get discipline management off your back! The last thing we want to do is to saddle the teacher with a discipline program that demands the expenditure of a significant amount of time and energy on a daily basis all year long" (Jones, 1987a, p. 26).

Fifth, in his discussion of backup systems. Jones recognizes that some students bring deadly objects to school and might even assault teachers and students. He cannot offer definitive answers (just as no one else can), but he does at least recognize the problem and suggest times when law enforcement officers should be contacted. Sixth, Jones (1987b) sees a close relationship between effective instruction and classroom management.

Jones's theories have a number of advantages, but they include some disadvantages, too. First, although Jones's concept of preferred activity time or PAT sounds useful and he claims implementation is easy, the accountability and record-keeping measures might be cumbersome. In addition, although Jones's concepts can be learned, many details must be handled. To his credit, he describes in his books what teachers should do in specific cases (and then what to do in response to the student's next move); however, such a tremendous amount must be learned that it might take even a conscientious teacher several years to master the techniques. Jones has some excellent ideas though, and positive classroom management has potential for use in all classrooms. Activity 8–4 gives you an opportunity to evaluate Jones's ideas in relation to student needs and to identify how Jones's theories address psychological or developmental needs.

Imposing or Teaching Discipline?

Jones leaves no doubt that his purpose is for children and adolescents to learn self-discipline. In his book *Positive Classroom Discipline,* he says, "The objective of this book, rather than 'law and order,' is the internalization of discipline or self-discipline" (Jones, 1987a, p. 19). Also, Jones says, "Strictly speaking, discipline means to teach, not to punish" (Jones, 1996, p. 42). He maintains that discipline should not be equated with punishment (Chemlynski, 1996). How Would You React 8–4 provides a look at an autocratic teacher.

Activity 8–4

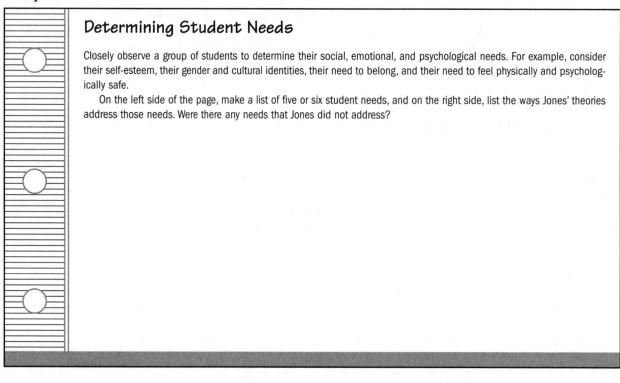

Determining Student Needs

Closely observe a group of students to determine their social, emotional, and psychological needs. For example, consider their self-esteem, their gender and cultural identities, their need to belong, and their need to feel physically and psychologically safe.

On the left side of the page, make a list of five or six student needs, and on the right side, list the ways Jones' theories address those needs. Were there any needs that Jones did not address?

Although Jones suggests a wealth of strategies for managing behavior, he designed them to teach learners to manage themselves. The actions of maintaining eye contact, using physical proximity, and saying names firmly are not designed to be punitive. Instead, they remind students of the teacher's expectations, the class rules and routines, and how their behavior affects others and themselves. Unfortunately, punitive measures sometimes will be needed, and classroom management techniques that work with some students might not work with

How Would You React 8–4

Advising Ms. Muller

Review the key concepts of Jones's positive classroom management found in Figure 8–1 and his fundamental skills. As you read the following scenario, try to determine whether Ms. Muller is following Jones's beliefs. Then respond to the questions at the end.

> Ms. Muller, an eighth-grade teacher, thought she had a group of students who were too immature to learn self-discipline. "I have to accept all the responsibility for disciplining them," she said. "They are simply too immature to behave. I don't know what their teacher did last year!" To make sure they behaved during her lessons, she addressed every problem, no matter how minor. From her podium at the front of the room, she constantly halted the lesson to reprimand individual students.

> When students behaved, she added a star by their name on a chart on the board. Misbehavior brought a check behind a name, with penalties spelled out for various numbers of checks. "Can't give them an inch—they'll take a mile. That's how this group is."

1. Is Ms. Muller correct in assuming that some eighth-grade students are too immature for self-discipline?
2. Using the ideas and fundamental skills of Fredric Jones, give Ms. Muller some specific recommendations of things she can do in her classroom to incorporate the ideas of Positive Classroom Management.

others. However, the positive classroom discipline model is successful in helping many children and adolescents learn to discipline themselves.

Underlying Beliefs

With a focus on teachers who (1) emphasize positive relationships with students, (2) separate discipline and punishment, (3) avoid punitive measures to managing behavior, and (4) walk around the classroom (using proximity and body language) during instruction and practice sessions, Jones's ideas seem to be based on the ways effective teachers manage classes and should meet the philosophical and psychological beliefs of many teachers. On the other hand, Jones's classroom management plan probably will not be well received by a teacher who is more autocratic, believes in punitive measures, feels comfortable when engaging in back talking with students, or thinks students need to be kept under tight control at all times. To determine whether these ideas are congruent with your beliefs, respond to the questions in Developing Your Personal Philosophy.

The Case Study looks at a new elementary teacher who used coercion and bribery to control her students. Because of her stress and dissatisfaction with the management aspects of teaching, she seriously considered leaving the teaching profession. After reading the Case Study, determine how effective Jones's ideas will be for her.

CONCLUDING REMARKS

Calling his plan the "gentle art of classroom discipline" (Jones, 1973, p. 26), Fredric Jones's Positive Classroom Management focuses on cooperation among students and teachers, holds students responsible for their behavior, and suggests specific management behaviors for teachers. He emphasizes body language, eye contact, physical proximity, student self-discipline, classroom rules and routines, limit setting, and backup systems. Because all students will likely respond to a teacher acting in a relaxed, positive, and calm manner, Jones's theories hold promise for teachers working with elementary, middle, and secondary school students— both the students who engage in nickel and dime misbehaviors (Jones, 1987a, p. 27) and those prone to more violent behaviors. For more information than we could present in this chapter, you can consult Jones's works, the suggested reading, or the resources listed in "Reaching Out with Technology" on this book's Companion Web Site.

Please go to *www.prenhall.com/manning* and click on Concluding Remarks for this chapter to find more information.

Developing Your Personal Philosophy

Does Positive Classroom Management Reflect Your Beliefs?

As you consider whether to incorporate the ideas of Frederic Jones into your personal classroom management philosophy, consider the following questions:

1. Do I believe classroom management procedures that are gentle and that build cooperation in the absence of coercion will be effective?
2. Can I remain calm and use body language to set limits?
3. Do I believe that teachers should strive for cooperation and collaboration with students?
4. Do I believe that rules, routines, and standards are necessary for effective management?
5. Do I feel comfortable using a system such as PAT to help students become responsible for their actions?

CASE STUDY
Talking, Walking Around, and Goofing Off

Janice Brisky was a new teacher who was hired in November to teach a class of fifth graders who had had a long-term substitute teacher for 2 months. The students in the class were not bad in the sense that they did not fight or threaten others, but they did display many minor (but still disturbing) behavior problems. They answered out of turn, talked among themselves, goofed off, and walked around the room whenever they pleased. To make matters worse, Ms. Brisky did not seem to know the problems existed (or she intentionally ignored them). She spent nearly all her time sitting at the teacher's desk. Although she had a good lesson plan, it was questionable how many students listened or could listen to her instruction.

When she talked about how things were going in her classroom, Ms. Brisky mentioned that her emphasis was on instruction and that she didn't want to appear to be a strict disciplinarian. "I don't want to keep interrupting my instruction to deal with behavior problems.

The students really aren't 'bad,' so I just ignore things. I guess they're learning, but sometimes it seems that I have to shout to make myself heard over the constant undercurrent of noise. Maybe I should try some management system, but I don't know where to begin. These students need support, not discipline."

Questions for Consideration

1. Develop a plan for Ms. Brisky to implement in her classroom.
2. How might this plan differ if she were teaching a different grade level?

 You can record your answers to these questions online on this book's Companion Web Site at *www.prenhall.com/manning.*

Suggested Readings

Eaton, M. (1997). Positive discipline: Fostering the self-esteem of young children. *Young Children, 52*(6), 43–46. Eaton looks at positive discipline techniques, giving young children choices, and natural and logical consequences.

Jones, F. H. (1987a). *Positive classroom discipline.* New York: McGraw-Hill. Jones in his comprehensive book provides the definitive look at his theory of Positive Classroom Management.

Jones, F. H. (1996). Did not! Did, too! *Learning 24*(6), 24–26. Jones focuses on back talking and effective ways for teachers to deal with this all-too-common problem.

Jones, F. H. (with Jones, P., & Jones, J.). (2000) *Tools for Teaching.* Santa Cruz, CA: Fredric H. Jones & Associates. This is a practical guide for using the ideas of Fred Jones in the classroom.

Schmidt, J. J. (1989). A professional stance for positive discipline—Promoting learning. *NASSP Bulletin, 73,* 14–20. Schmidt offers numerous suggestions for creating effective learning environments and positive discipline.

CHAPTER 9

Exploring the Theories of Inner Discipline: *Barbara Coloroso*

Focusing Questions

After reading this chapter, you should be able to answer the following questions:

1. How does Coloroso's Inner Discipline relate to other classroom management theories and models, such as behaviorist theories?

2. What are the characteristics of jellyfish, brickwall, and backbone teachers?

3. What does Coloroso say about bullying, threats, violence, and aggression—all common problems in contemporary schools?

4. How does Coloroso define the golden rule, and how can teachers best demonstrate this trait?

5. What is meant by the three R's of restitution, resolution, and reconciliation?

6. What are Coloroso's four steps to discipline, and how can educators implement such a discipline procedure?

7. How can teachers avoid destructive words such as "killer statements" (Coloroso, 2000a, p. 146) sarcasm, ridicule, and humiliation?

Barbara Coloroso bases her theory of Inner Discipline on her firm conviction that adults should believe that children and adolescents are worth the effort and time required to teach them responsible behavior. Rather than proposing a packaged management model, Coloroso has a comprehensive array of concepts on how to work with students. Although she most often is considered a commentator on parenting issues, Coloroso has translated many of her ideas into practical applications for teachers. In addition, her books are resources that teachers can suggest when parents appeal for help in disciplining their children.

Key Terms

Assertive confrontation
Backbone teacher
Brickwall teacher
Conflict resolution
Jellyfish teacher
Natural and reasonable consequences
Ownership
Reconciliation
Resolution
Restitution
RSVP Approach

BARBARA COLOROSO: BIOGRAPHICAL SKETCH

Although Barbara Coloroso has impacted the lives of hundreds of parents, teachers, and students around the world, she did not choose education as her first calling in life. At age 17, she joined a convent, where she stayed for 3 years, including 1 year spent in silence. After leaving the convent, she used her background in sociology, special education, philosophy, and theology to develop her own unique view of parenting, which teachers also can adopt. A classroom teacher, university instructor, and seminar leader, Coloroso's major books include *Kids Are Worth It: Giving Your Child the Gift of Inner Discipline* (1994); *Parenting Through*

Crisis: Helping Kids in Times of Loss, Grief, and Change (2000a); and *Parenting With Wit and Wisdom in Times of Chaos and Loss* (2000b).

OVERVIEW OF INNER DISCIPLINE
Key Concepts
Figure 9–1 identifies the key concepts found in the writings of Barbara Coloroso. The next sections of this chapter provide a detailed look at the use of her ideas in a classroom.

Philosophical and Psychological Foundations
Holding children in high esteem, Barbara Coloroso believes in them and knows they are capable achieving. This respect for children underlies her work in a theory she calls inner discipline ("Give Poor Parenting a Time-out," 2002). Coloroso (1994) suggests three philosophical stances that she thinks are essential to teaching Inner Discipline.

1. Kids are worth it. Coloroso believes that children and young adults are worth the efforts that adults exert to teach them Inner Discipline. With dignity and worth as individuals and human beings, they neither have to prove their worth nor earn the attention of adults. Adults do not have to like their appearances, their attitudes, and their behaviors, but adults do need to believe that children and young adults are worth their time, energy, and resources.

2. I will not treat a child in a way I myself would not want to be treated. Coloroso believes that adults should follow the Golden Rule (Coloroso, 1994, p. 14) and treat others as they want to be treated. If teachers feel uncertain about what they are doing to students, they should place themselves in the students' place to see how they would feel. The teacher should ask such questions as: Would I want that done to me? How would I feel if someone did that to me?

3. If it works and leaves a child's and my own dignity intact, do it (Coloroso, 1994, p. 11). Coloroso's third philosophical belief is that efforts to discipline a student should leave the student's and the adult's dignity intact. She maintains that a serious problem with some discipline techniques is that the student's dignity and sense of self-worth are

Figure 9–1 Key Concepts of Inner Discipline

The following are key concepts of the Inner Discipline theory:

- Children and adolescents are worth teachers' and parents' efforts and should be treated with respect and dignity at all times.

- Teachers should always abide by the Golden Rule, being careful to always treat students the way they want to be treated.

- Teachers are either brickwall, jellyfish, or backbone, and their choice affects students and their behavior.

- Students should be taught Inner Discipline rather than being punished physically or being manipulated with destructive words.

- Teachers should accept responsibility for teaching students to accept the ownership of their problems.

- Teachers should use natural consequences as much as possible; when those do not work, reasonable consequences should be used.

- Teachers should avoid punishments, rewards, and threats; use a four-step approach to discipline; and use **assertive confrontation.**

- Restitution, resolution and reconciliation are the three R's of discipline.

sacrificed in the name of behavior management. Manipulative tactics such as rewards, bribes, and threats often make students behave at the expense of their dignity.

Teachers' Roles and Responsibilities

Although the majority of Coloroso's work focuses more on parents than teachers, teachers' roles in Inner Discipline can be identified readily. First, teachers who are effective with Inner Discipline should subscribe to the just-discussed philosophical beliefs of treating others with respect and avoiding humiliation, sarcasm, and ridicule. Teachers also have the responsibility to demonstrate compassion after a student misbehaves (Coloroso, 2000a). Second, effective teachers need to believe in and be willing to teach self-discipline or Inner Discipline rather than believing that the teacher is responsible for disciplining students. Third, teachers need to believe in real-world consequences to discipline and management rather than the intervention of an adult. Fourth, teachers should avoid autocratic behaviors, harshness, and physical punishments. Authoritarian approaches might get students to comply, but they do not help students develop the self-discipline and responsibility that Coloroso advocated (Willis, 1996). The use of Coloroso's Inner Discipline can be learned, but teachers already must possess some of these traits for Inner Discipline to be successful.

APPLYING INNER DISCIPLINE

We do not advocate any one theory of classroom management; in fact, we want you to examine each theory in this book and decide which one (or probably which combination of theories) seems to have the most potential for you. As you read about the major elements of Coloroso's Inner Discipline theory, consider their relation to the behavior problems that elementary and secondary teachers face.

Implementing Practical Applications

The application of Coloroso's Inner Discipline requires consideration of her categories of teachers; her theories on discipline, punishment, and behavior management; and her opinions on the use of words, both harmful and praising.

Three Categories of Teachers

Coloroso places teachers in three categories: *brickwall, jellyfish,* and *backbone* (Coloroso, 1994). The category into which an individual falls affects all interpersonal relationships: student to teacher, teacher to student, teacher to other teachers, student to student, and even the way the teacher relates to the outside world.

A **brickwall teacher** is almost a nonliving entity who restricts and controls others (Coloroso, 1994). This teacher is all powerful; the student is the subordinate. Gray areas do not exist because all class events are clear-cut and in black and white. Placing little trust in students' ability to develop Inner Discipline, the brickwall teacher wields the ultimate power and accepts responsibility for students' behavior rather than teaching Inner Discipline. Operating in an atmosphere of fear, this teacher has a litany of rules; emphasizes punctuality, cleanliness, and order; enforces rules rigidly; tries to break students' wills; emphasizes rituals and rote learning; uses humiliation, rewards, and bribes; relies on competition; and teaches students what to think rather than how to think.

> Mrs. Winchell, a 10th-grade teacher, was called Mrs. Witchell (behind her back) by many of her students. She was the epitome of an autocratic teacher. Making all decisions and rules, and prescribing all punishments, she did not trust her students to accept responsibility for their behavior. As Sean, one of her

students, said: "I guess I'm learning in the witch's class, but I also know I throw up every Sunday night when I think about walking into her room first thing on Monday morning. She seems determined to whip us into shape for the week and thinks we've gotten 'soft' from too much fun on the weekends."

Jellyfish teachers have "no firm parts at all" (Coloroso, 1994, p. 38). They are wishy-washy, are inconsistent about classroom management, and allow anarchy and chaos. Without recognizable structure and rules, they are arbitrary and inconsistent with rules and punishments, use minilectures and put-downs, use threats and bribes, and allow emotions to rule students and their behaviors. They either do not see the need for students to develop Inner Discipline or they fear students might be unreceptive to their insistence upon proper behavior. Students know a jellyfish teacher will make few serious efforts to teach proper behavior.

> Mr. Haney, a first-grade teacher, was a prime example of a jellyfish teacher. He thought first-grade students would behave appropriately without his guidance. As a result, his class was chaos, with students talking incessantly and playing around. It appeared that Mr. Haney did not see the chaos in the room or failed to acknowledge it. His students did not regard him as an assertive adult who had the responsibility to insist and teach proper behavior.

According to Coloroso (1994), **backbone teachers** provide the support and structure necessary for students to realize their uniqueness and to come to know their true selves, something that brickwall teachers suppress and jellyfish teachers ignore. By emphasizing democracy through learned experiences, they advocate creative, constructive, and responsible activity; have simply and clearly defined rules; use **natural and reasonable consequences;** motivate students to be all they can be; and teach students how to think. Teaching students to trust themselves, others, and in their future, backbone teachers help students develop Inner Discipline and, even in the face of adversity and peer pressure, retain faith in themselves and in their own potential (Coloroso, 1994). Teachers need to increase responsibilities as students grow older and give them more opportunities to make decisions. Management Tip 9–1 looks at the use of classroom jobs to develop student responsibility in the classroom. Then, How Would You React 9–1 examines a teacher who faced a dilemma in the classroom.

☆ **Management Tip 9-1**

Developing Responsibility

One way to help students develop responsibility is to assign classroom jobs to students and change the jobs on a scheduled basis. Although some teachers might change jobs every week, others might change them every month or each grading period. Remember to keep the amount of time required for the jobs fairly short and the difficulty level appropriate for the students in your grade level.

Elementary

    Board eraser/cleaner

    Line leader

    Door person

Secondary

    Role taker/attendance keeper

    Time keeper

    Money collector for special programs

All levels

    Greeter to welcome class visitors

    Messenger

    Distributor (of supplies and materials)

    Collector (of supplies, materials, homework)

    Computer assistant

    Cleanup crew (several students hold this job)

Please go to www.prenhall.com/manning and click on the Management Tips for this chapter to complete management activities and find more information on jobs and responsibility in both elementary and secondary classrooms.

Discipline and Behavior Management

To Coloroso, teaching discipline and behavior management is not something that can be packaged as a complete model. Although she offers parents hundreds of tips that have implications for teachers of all levels, her inner discipline theory is not a classroom management

How Would You React 9-1

Helping Ms. Rendell

Before you read the following scenario, review Barbara Coloroso's three types of teachers and make a list of the characteristics of each type. Then as you read the following scenario, try to identify the type of teacher that Ms. Rendell is.

After about 3 weeks of school, Shaniqua Mason, the assistant principal, spoke with Shannon Rendell about the behavior of her fourth-grade students. They were a bit rowdy, and Ms. Mason feared that the situation would worsen as the school year progressed. In her defense, Ms. Rendell replied: "I want my students to like me, not hate me. I remember how I felt when I had a teacher who was mean and always told me what to do. And, I've read about the negative effects of power and con-

trol. Oh sure, I know my students should behave better than they do, but I figured that if I was nice to them and showed them I trusted them, they'd settle down."

1. What type of teacher is Ms. Rendell?
2. Based on the ideas of Coloroso, what advice could you offer Ms. Rendell to develop a classroom management model?
3. What type of teacher should Ms. Rendell try to be?
4. What kinds of things should she do in her classroom to become that teacher?
5. Role-play the interaction between Ms. Rendell and Ms. Mason.

model as the Canters suggested, a list of teacher behaviors as prescribed by Kounin or Gordon, and certainly not a behavior-modification strategy as suggested by Skinner. However, teachers can use many of her ideas when developing or personalizing their own classroom management plan.

Ownership of Problem   One of the key points of Coloroso's Inner Discipline theory is that students accept **ownership** of the problem (Coloroso, 1997). In other words, students learn that they are capable of taking ownership of their behaviors. They also are capable of taking full responsibility for the problems their behaviors create, not because of fear, but because it is the right thing to do. You might remember that Mendler and Curwin (1983) also called for students to accept ownership of the problem, because they thought giving students a sense of ownership for behavior problems in the classroom would result in their accepting more responsibility for solving the problems. Although Mendler and Curwin called for social contracts as a classroom management tool, Coloroso (1994, 1997, 2000a) suggests that students should be taught to develop the Inner Discipline necessary to behave appropriately.

Admittedly, differences about who owns the problem might surface at this point. Parents face at least part ownership of the problem when their son or daughter destroys school property. Similarly, teachers face a problem when their students misbehave so badly that teaching and learning cannot occur. Realistically speaking, it is likely that the school administrator ultimately will hold the teacher responsible for the behavior of students. One key difference might be in the concept of responsibility. The student should accept ownership of the problem, but at least some responsibility lies with the teacher to help the student solve the problem. To Coloroso, the teacher is responsible for teaching students the Inner Discipline to accept ownership of the behavior and the responsibility to take appropriate action to address it. Consider Ms. Modrak in How Would You React 9–2 to determine who has ownership of the problem.

Discipline, Punishment, and Rewards   Although the words sometimes are used interchangeably, Coloroso (1983, 1994) maintains that discipline is not synonymous with punishment. Punishment is adult oriented, imposes power from without, arouses anger and

How Would You React 9-2

Claiming Ownership of a Problem

Barbara Coloroso believes that students must accept ownership of their behaviors. Review the information in this chapter on problem ownership. Then, as you read the following scenario, first decide who owns the behavior problem. If Andy, the student, owns the problem, what are some things that the teacher can do to help Andy?

Ms. Modrak, a seventh-grade teacher, questioned the issue of ownership. A consultant recently visited her school and stated that "the misbehaving student owns the problem. He or she must accept ownership and decide on a responsible action." Although Ms. Modrak liked the consultant's assertion, she thought about Andy, the terror of the seventh grade. He did nearly everything she did not like. He bullied and made verbal threats to other students, acted up in class, constantly thought of reasons to walk around or leave the room ("I just wanted to see if the flowers were blooming yet, Ms. M."), yelled out answers, and nonchalantly goofed off when he should have been working. She asked herself: "Who owns this problem? Is it mine? Is it Andy's? How can it be Andy's if he does not recognize his behavior as a problem and will not agree to any responsible course of action? When Andy disturbs others and me, don't I own the problem?"

resentment, and invites more conflict. It exacerbates wounds rather than healing them by focusing on blame and pain and demonstrates the teacher's ability to control a student. The overriding concerns of punishment include: Which rule was broken? Who did it? What kind of punishment does the student deserve?

Punishment discourages students from acknowledging their actions because they might deny doing the behavior or place blame on anything or anybody other than themselves. When teachers use punishment, good behavior is bought at a terrible price (Coloroso, 2000a, p. 221). Punishment leaves control in the teacher's hands and gives students the message that the teacher is all powerful, accepts responsibility for students' behavior, and negates the need for students to develop Inner Discipline (Coloroso, 1994, 2000a).

In addition, Coloroso (1994) believes teachers should not rely on rewards to promote positive behavior. Punishment brings pain and fear, but rewards also send the wrong message, namely, that kindness and positive behavior can be bought and bartered. Coloroso believes that dangers exist when teachers apply behavior modification to children and adolescents. This technique keeps a student dependent and fearful—dependent on adults for rewards for positive behavior and fearful of punishment for negative behavior. Students who are bribed and rewarded constantly will often start to ask questions such as "What's in it for me?", "What's the payoff?", "Does it count for anything?", and "Did I do it right?" (p. 19).

According to Coloroso (1994), threats are, by their nature, punitive. Adult oriented, they are based on subjective judgment and impose power from without instead of acknowledging the power within students. Arousing anger and resentment and inviting more conflict, threats rob students of their sense of dignity and self-worth.

Faced with threats, domination, manipulation, and control by someone bigger than themselves, students will experience one of three things. First, they will experience fright and will do as they are told out of dependency and fear. In this case, students will obey the teacher only until they are able to get what they need or want. Second, they will fight and attack the teacher or take their anger out on others. Such a response can produce an equal or more severe response from the adult, and the cycle escalates. Third, they will experience flight, meaning they run away mentally or physically. Students whose needs and feelings are dismissed, ignored, punished, or negated begin to believe they are of little or no worth (Coloroso, 1994).

How Would You React 9-3

Using Bribes and Threats

Review Coloroso's beliefs about punishments, threats, and rewards as well as her categories of teachers. Then, as you read the following scenario, identify the category into which Ms. Dorler fits.

> Ms. Dorler, a high school teacher, was heard to say "I know all those theories, but I use whatever I can to get my students to behave—whatever it takes is what I do." Her actions backed up her statement. She used bribes ("For every day everyone co-operates in class this week, I'll shorten Thursday's homework by two questions"), threats ("Peyton, sit down and mind your own business or else"), and intimidation ("Tolbert, I set the rules in this room and you follow them. Do you hear me?").

1. What category of teacher best fits Ms. Dorler?
2. Examine her behavior in light of Coloroso's beliefs about punishments, threats, and rewards.
3. Is she following Coloroso's ideas? If not, how should she change her behavior?

> "As long as Mr. Restino threatens to call my dad, I'll do anything he wants. My dad would whip me for sure if Mr. Restino called him" (a 3rd-grade student).

> "Ms. Allern never found out who did it, but I know that a bunch of the kids in my class broke her car window last weekend. They were bragging about how they planned to get even with her" (an 11th-grade student).

> "Yeah, I know I don't do my work. But when I do, Mr. Rizzo yells at me 'cause I get a lot of the answers wrong. I never do anything right, so why do anything at all? As long as I sit quietly, he ignores me and I can think about what I'll do after school" (a 7th-grade student).

How Would You React 9–3 asks you to consider Ms. Dorler's use of bribes and threats.

The Four Steps of Discipline   According to Coloroso (2000a, 224), the process of discipline does four things that the act of punishment cannot do:

1. It shows students what they should have done.
2. It gives them as much ownership of the problem as they are able to handle.
3. It gives them options for solving the problem.
4. It leaves their dignity intact.

When teachers use the four steps, discipline deals with the reality of the situation rather than the power and control of the adult. Students can change their attitudes and habits that might have led to the misbehavior. This, in turn, leads to a more peaceful classroom.

The Three R's of Discipline   Coloroso (2000a) suggests the three R's of discipline, all of which are incorporated in the four steps just mentioned. These three R's include: *restitution, resolution,* and *reconciliation.* The first R, **restitution,** means fixing what the student did and involves repairing the physical damage (if any) and the personal damage. The second R, **resolution,** includes determining a way not to let the behavior happen again. In other words, how can students accept what they have done and see its implications for a new beginning? The third R, **reconciliation,** is the process of healing with the offender honoring the restitution plan and making a commitment to live up to the resolution.

> Ninth graders Brent and Derek were scuffling in the hall. At first, they were not angry, but their horseplay turned a little rough and Brent became agitated. As Brent turned to hit Derek one last time, Derek

jumped out of the way, and Brent ripped his backpack. The teacher on hall duty observed the incident and had the responsibility to address the situation. She worked the three R's as follows:

Restitution (correcting what was done): Brent and Derek admitted that their horseplay got out of hand, disturbed others, and resulted in a ripped backpack. They were not happy about the situation, but they both accepted ownership and responsibility for the incident. Brent admitted that he started the incident, and although the scuffle started in fun, he was also probably the first one to get mad. Thus, he agreed to take Derek's backpack to be repaired. Brent also agreed to pay up to $10 for the repair; Derek agreed to pay any amount over $10.

Resolution (determining a way to keep the incident from happening again): Both boys agreed that they should not fight, even in fun. They also agreed that if they felt like "horsing around," they would go to the gym for a friendly competition on the mats under the watchful eyes of a physical education assistant. Brent made a commitment to honor his plan of restitution and to rebuild his friendship with Derek.

Reconciliation: They both regretted that the incident got out of hand, and Brent apologized for ripping the backpack. After all, they had been friends since middle school, and the scuffle had begun in fun.

Do all behavior incidents end as successfully as this one? Absolutely not! Brent and Derek had been friends for several years, they shared the blame for the scuffle, and Brent agreed to pay most of the repair costs. However, what if one of the boys or a bystander had been hurt? What if Brent had adamantly refused to pay for the repairs? In those instances, the teacher would have had to intervene more in all three R's. During restitution, the teacher might have to be a stronger advocate for getting someone to pay for the physical damage. During resolution, the teacher might have to help the boys develop a plan of prevention. If Brent had said, "This isn't over yet. Derek started it, but I'll finish it my way," the teacher would face a problem of Brent and Derek finishing the fight that afternoon off the school grounds.

Assertive Confrontation   Coloroso (1983, 1994) maintained that teachers sometimes need to use **assertive confrontation**. However, even in these cases, teachers must use caution to avoid endless arguments that waste a great deal of energy, lead to additional and more heated arguments, and solve nothing. Backbone teachers can serve as a model for students and can show them a way of confronting someone. Coloroso (1994) offers seven rules for a fair fight and a productive, assertive confrontation:

1. When you are angry and upset, speak the message in a straightforward, assertive manner—not aggressively or passively.
2. Tell the other person about your feelings.
3. State your belief but avoid destructive words that attack another person.
4. Give direct feedback. Tell the person the problem and how you feel about the problem.
5. State what you want from the other person.
6. Be open to the other person's perspective on the situation.
7. Negotiate an agreement you can both accept.

All teachers eventually face conflict of some type, either with team members, students, or parents who disagree with educational decisions. Consider How Would You React 9–4 and suggest how you might use Coloroso's assertive confrontation in Ms. Buha's situation.

Conflict Resolution   Conflicts inevitably will occur; thus, Coloroso (1994) believes that teachers need to teach **conflict resolution**. She maintains that students learn how to deal with conflicts in several ways (e.g., from their parents, teachers, peers, and the media). Rather than describing a detailed, step-by-step approach, Coloroso thinks *example* (Coloroso's italics) (1994, p. 131) is one of the best ways to teach conflict resolution. If adults view conflict as a contest,

How Would You React 9-4

Dealing with a Mother

Although Coloroso believes in the four steps of discipline and the three R's of discipline, she also notes that there are times when teachers need to use assertive confrontation. Before reading the following scenario, review her ideas on conflict and confrontation. After reading the scenario, respond to the questions at the end.

> Ms. Buha probably let a situation go too long. Keith, a bully, had been verbally and, in some cases, physically abusive to others in his second-grade class. Ms. Buha kept thinking that class rejection or isolation eventually would tone down Keith's aggressiveness; however, that did not happen. Instead, the principal complained, some parents called, and several other students ended up bruised or crying. When Ms. Buha finally spoke to Keith about his bullying, Keith "blew up."
>
> "You're picking on me, just like the other kids do. I'm bringing my mother to school tomorrow. She knows I'm no bully and she'll tell you so, too."
>
> Sure enough, Keith's mother came to school the next day and defended her son, whom she said, "never has and never will bully anyone."

What should Ms. Buha do? Role-play the situation with other members of your class. Try using Coloroso's seven rules for an assertive confrontation.

---

they probably fight physically and verbally until someone wins and someone loses. If they run from conflict, they probably teach students to avoid conflicts, too. Others seek productive ways to handle conflict, without aggression or passivity, and model this form of conflict resolution.

Consequences: Natural and Reasonable   The concept of *natural and reasonable consequences* is a mainstay of Coloroso's inner discipline theory. Natural consequences involve real-world consequences or interventions and deal with the reality of the situation rather than the power and control of the adult.

> If Francine, a kindergarten child, puts her shoes on the wrong feet, the natural consequence is that her feet will hurt.
>
> If Hersey, a fourth grader, refuses to wear a coat outside, the natural consequence is that he will be cold.
>
> If Juan, an eighth grader, continues to borrow school supplies because he refuses to take responsibility for bringing them to school, eventually others will stop lending things to him.

Coloroso maintains that these consequences are learned without nagging, reminding, or warning. Such consequences teach students about the world around them and that they have positive control over their lives. If natural consequences are not life threatening, Coloroso suggests letting students experience them.

Sometimes natural consequences can be life threatening or morally threatening (e.g., unkind, hurtful, unfair, and dishonest).

- A life-threatening situation: Rolando, a first grader, tries to jump from desk to desk in the classroom.
- A morally threatening situation: Tiffany, a ninth grader, agrees to take a test for a friend.

If the natural consequence is nonexistent or would be inappropriate, Colorosso (1994) recommends that the teacher consider reasonable consequences. Natural consequences just happen, but reasonable consequences require reasoning and planning. A key point in determining reasonable consequences is for the teacher to ask whether the goal is to teach the student or punish the student. Consider whether the statements in Activity 9–1 are reasonable or inappropriate consequences.

Activity 9–1

Identifying Reasonable or Inappropriate Consequences

Explain whether each of the following is a reasonable or inappropriate consequence. For any inappropriate consequences, indicate what a reasonable consequence would be.

1. First grader Dockery leaves his lunch on the school bus and his teacher says, "I am sorry you left your lunch, but missing lunch probably will mean you will not forget it again."
2. Fourth grader Germain rips the teacher's notebook. The teacher says, "Germain, you will need to buy me a new notebook."
3. Sixth grader Dawson forgets to feed the fish in the class fish tank and two tropical fish die. His teacher says, "Just for that, Dawson, you can sit alone next week."
4. Eighth grader Cristin works on her cross-stitch in class after repeatedly being told not to bring it to class again. Her teacher says, "Give me the cross-stitch, and I will keep it for the remainder of the year."

Coloroso calls for an **RSVP approach**—a consequence that is reasonable, simple, valuable (as a learning tool), and practical.

If Woody, a kindergarten student, is engaged in horseplay and breaks a glass, it will not be reasonable to ask him to pick up the small slivers of glass; however, it would be reasonable for him to hold the bag while the teacher picks them up.

Mr. Cohn, a 6th-grade teacher, proposes a long and detailed list of rules and consequences—so detailed that it is not simple for the students to understand and for him to administer.

Temeka, a 9th-grade student, loses a calculator that she borrowed from a friend; a valuable lesson is for her to buy the friend a new and comparable calculator.

Telling Wade, a 12th grader, that he will have to stay after school until he completes his assignment and walk the 8 miles home is not practical; telling him that he will have to stay after school each day until the work is complete and take the late activity bus home is practical.

Management Tip 9–2 provides additional information about conflict resolution.

The Destructiveness of Words   In her writings, Coloroso shows the destructiveness of words (e.g., "She was no good," "He's a lazy bum," and "You're just like your mother") (Coloroso, 2000a, p. 132). She also discusses "killer statements" (p. 146), such as "You are a jerk," that are designed only to attack another person. Sarcasm and ridicule, as well as humiliating and embarrassing statements, also fall into this category.

Teachers need to be aware of the destructiveness of the words they use. Coloroso (1994) maintains that statements such as "Your sister never did anything like that," "You'll never amount to anything," "I figured you would do something stupid like that," "Why don't you just grow up?" and "You call yourself a soccer player?" (pp. 64–65) are designed to hurt, humiliate, and embarrass. Consider the following statements to see the destructiveness of words:

> Talmadge, a kindergartner, wets his pants, and the teacher says, "Grow up! Are you still a baby?"

> Aalise, a 3rd-grade girl, drops her lunch tray on the way to the table, and the teacher says, "How could you be so clumsy? No one else dropped a tray. Just you!"

> Ivo, a 6th-grade boy, scores a D on a test, and the teacher says, "Your sister was a much better student. At least she made B's."

> LoRee, an overweight 8th-grade girl, sits down in a desk, and the teacher says, "Better lose some weight or you might get stuck."

> A 10th-grade class is taking a test, and the teacher says, "Keep your eyes on your own paper. I'll be watching. Don't think I trust any one of you. I bet you'd all cheat if you had the chance."

Although you might think these are exaggerations and that teachers never use words so destructively, sometimes they do. Words might be used destructively for any number of seemingly legitimate reasons, such as teachers thinking they can humiliate or embarrass students into behaving properly. "I took care of him right there in front of the class, and the rest of the students fell in line," we heard one teacher boast.

Interestingly and in keeping with other management theorists such as Ginott and Dreikurs, Coloroso also believes that showing students praise rather than appreciation for efforts has the potential for being destructive. For example, when a child scores a 100 on his mathematics test and you say, "Great, Evan! I knew you were a good student!", what will you say next week when he scores only an 85? The "Great, Evan . . ." statement connected his performance to his dignity and worth as a person. Teachers should be careful to avoid praise that equates students' achievement with their self-esteem. Praise risks the possibility of encouraging students to view mistakes as a negative reflection of themselves. Likewise, to avoid such feelings and to protect their self-esteem, students might blame someone else for the lower grade. Review Figure 9–2 to see some examples of ways teachers can show appreciation rather than praise for students' work and effort. Then consider the statements in Activity 9–2 to determine whether they are potentially destructive or potentially helpful.

Instead of using praise, teachers can ask questions about the grade and the assignment. Whether the grade is an A+ or a D−, students likely will appreciate the teacher's interest in their work. Students might express pleasure with the effort that went into getting the A+ or the disappointment associated with the D−. Students might say how bad they feel about the D− after spending so much time and effort, or they might explain that they could have

---

★ Management Tip 9–2

Resolving Conflicts

Although Coloroso does not describe a detailed approach to conflict resolution, she does talk about using discipline to

- Identify a problem,
- Provide the student with ownership of the problem,
- Identify ways to solve the problem,
- Leave the students' dignity intact (Colorosa, 2002).

One way to do this is to have a student develop an action plan to deal with behavior problems.

1. The student develops the plan and states
   The problem,
   Cause of the problem,
   Possible solutions.
2. The student reviews the plan with teacher and revises it as needed.
3. The student carries out the plan.
4. The student and teacher review the results of the plan.
5. If the plan is not carried out, teacher intervenes and other consequences occur, such as notifying parents or school administration.

Lower Elementary
Have the student develop the plan with the help of others and dictate the plan to a teacher or aide.

Upper elementary and secondary
Have the student write the plan.

Please go to *www.prenhall.com/manning* and click on the Management Tips for this chapter to complete management activities and find more information on resolving conflicts.

Figure 9-2 Showing
Appreciation/Avoiding
Praise

- Gwendolyn, a fifth grader, scores an A on her social studies test.
  Praise: "Gwendolyn, you're a smart girl. Made an A on the test, didn't you?"
  Appreciation: "Gwendolyn, thanks for your fine work on the social studies test."

- First grader Troy goes all day without disturbing others.
  Praise: "Troy, good boy for not disturbing others today. You're a fine person, just like your brother last year."
  Appreciation: "Troy, thanks for not disturbing others today. Both you and they were far more productive."

- Ninth grader Michael has a good performance at the debate tournament.
  Praise: "Mike, great job, you really showed them. I always knew you were a Grade A student."
  Appreciation: Mike, the other debaters and I appreciate your efforts today. Good preparation and performance!"

made a higher grade had they taken the test a little more seriously. With discussion rather than praise, students have little need to make excuses, and in fact, mistakes can be used as learning opportunities (Coloroso, 1994).

In summary, most teachers have always known the destructiveness of statements such as "Boy, was that dumb! You really had to work at failing this test," and "If you don't improve, you'll never amount to anything. Just like your brother, aren't you?" Whether to motivate or to hurt, teachers should never use such statements. However, teachers should remember that praise also can be destructive when the student fails to meet the teacher's expectation. How Would You React 9–5 asks you to consider how you would respond to a teacher who used words destructively.

Activity 9-2

Identifying Potentially Destructive and Potentially Helpful Statements

For each of the following statements, indicate whether the statement is potentially destructive or potentially helpful.

"Samal, you're doing good work, considering that English is your second language."

"Simms, good boy, I knew you could make that soccer goal. Your team members are proud of you."

"Alvenia, I appreciate your fine work on the mathematics test. You improved your average a lot."

"Fine play performance last night, Susan. I know you practiced hard."

"Denise, your handwriting is improving. I am pleased and I know your mom will be, too."

How Would You React 9-5

Delivering Destructive Words

Review Coloroso's ideas on the destructiveness of words and the difference between praise and appreciation. Then, as you read the following scenario, determine whether Mrs. Alberto is "witty" or "destructive" in her use of words.

> Mr. Don Davis, a principal, understood that Mrs. Helen Alberto, a veteran teacher, considered herself a master of words. Mrs. Alberto thought she had a gift of being witty and always knowing just what to say and just the right time to say it. Her comments went from sarcasm ("Julius, you are improving. You're up to 55. Who knows. Someday, you might even pass a test.") to praise (Good job, Meryah, you're a good student. I know I can always depend upon you."). Mr. Davis knew of scores of other destructive comments yet did not know exactly how to handle the delicate situation, especially when Mrs. Alberto thought she was an expert on comments that changed students' behavior.

If Ms. Alberto use of words is destructive, what suggestions would you give to Mr. Davis to use when he talks to Mrs. Alberto? Role-play a meeting between Mr. Davis and Mrs. Alberto in which he confronts the issue.

Bullies and Their Victims

As discussed in chapter 13 of this book, bullying is a serious problem that challenges many teachers and administrators. In the book *The Bully, The Bullied, and the Bystander,* Coloroso (2002) stated that conflict resolution cannot take care of bullies and their victims because their relationship is based on contempt rather than anger. Bullies show disdain or dislike toward someone they consider worthless, inferior or unworthy of respect (Rife, 2004). Although parents often tell their children just to ignore bullies, this does not work because efforts should be on assertive responses (Scelfo, 2003). Coloroso suggests labels (e.g., the bully, the bullied, and the bystander) might be useful to identify certain roles that people play at different times (Liepe-Levinson & Levinson, 2005). However, she cautions that these terms should be used to define how a child is acting at the moment (you're acting like a bully) rather than permanently labeling a child (you're a bully). Management Tip 9-3 looks at Coloroso's antidotes to bullying.

Management Tip 9-3

Dealing with Bullies

Coloroso (2002) maintains that, in order to combat bullies, teachers should be sure that each student

- Develops a strong sense of self,
- Has at least one good friend,
- Belongs to at least one group,
- Can get out of a group when necessary.

In addition Coloroso believes that teachers should do the following:

- Know the school procedures for dealing with bullies
- Listen to students and parents concerns about bullies
- Try not to minimize or explain away the behavior of bullies
- Confront rather than ignore the problem of bullies
- Work with parents and other educators to develop plans to address the problems of bullies
- Know when to involve police or social service agencies in cases of serious abuse as well as racist or sexist bullying

Please go to *www.prenhall.com/manning* and click on the Management Tips for this chapter and chapter 13 to complete management activities and find more information on managing bullies in both elementary and secondary classrooms.

Effectiveness of Practical Applications

Several factors contribute to the effective translation of Coloroso's theory into practice:

1. Coloroso's theories are easy to understand.
2. Special training and staff development are not needed to use them.
3. Teachers do not have to maintain elaborate and time-consuming record-keeping devices.

4. Coloroso's philosophical beliefs (e.g., believing in the worth of students, living by the Golden Rule, and promoting self-esteem) are foundations that most good teachers already have.

5. Teachers can adopt the characteristics of backbone (Coloroso, 1997, p. 44) teachers and become successful managers and teachers.

The only teachers who might have problems with practicing Coloroso's theories are autocratic ones who feel that their students and schools dictate the use of "power and control" messages. Also, some middle and secondary teachers might consider Coloroso's theories to be more appropriate for younger students. However, for high school teachers, Coloroso specifically recommends the programs of the Institute for Affective Skill Development led by Constance Dembrowsky, who has used many of Coloroso's ideas in programs for high school students including students at risk of failing. Techniques such as the Golden Rule, avoiding punishment, avoiding evaluative praise, using the four steps to discipline, using natural consequences, and setting an example for conflict resolution have potential for addressing behaviors of students at all grade levels. In addition, Coloroso offers sufficient details and examples to tell teachers how to move from theory to practice.

EVALUATING INNER DISCIPLINE IN A DIVERSE SOCIETY

With a background in the principle ideas of Barbara Coloroso, we can now evaluate Inner Discipline and its effectiveness in contemporary classrooms.

Potential for Addressing Student Misbehaviors

It seems that Inner Discipline has the potential to address the majority of the problems faced by most teachers such as talking, walking around, and disturbing others, as well as problems resulting from a lack of responsibility and self-esteem. These problems can be addressed by teachers who apply the key concepts of Inner Discipline.

Coloroso does not specifically address students using guns and knives, but she does address the problem of violence in her books *Kids Are Worth It: Giving Your Child the Gift of Inner Discipline* (1994) and *The Bully, The Bullied, and the Bystander* (Coloroso, 2002) and through her emphasis on nonviolent conflict resolution. Our culture is deeply rooted in a win-lose, victim-victor, adversarial approach to conflict, with violence being the tool often used to solve conflicts. Instead of bombarding students with the message that aggression is the way to resolve conflict, educators can teach through example, guidance, and instruction that violence is an immature, irresponsible, and unproductive technique for resolving conflict. Coloroso also maintains that our culture often equates masculinity with violence. Not only is it acceptable for boys to hit, it is sometimes considered a rite of passage to prove their masculinity. Coloroso (2000a) also explains that sometimes students hurt or intimidate others to cover their fears, anxiety, and sadness. Coloroso has some excellent ideas on violence and how students become violent, but she offers little specific direction for addressing violence other than her four steps to discipline and the three R's of discipline. Consider the behaviors in Activity 9–3 and determine the extent to which Inner Discipline will address them.

Coloroso's respect for individual differences can be seen in her call for dignity for all and in the Golden Rule. Teachers who treat all students with dignity and place students in ownership and responsibility situations should not offend any students or their parents. In fact, Coloroso (1994) called for parents to have formal celebrations to recognize cultural customs and to celebrate holidays, holy days, anniversaries, and the first day of

Activity 9–3

Addressing Contemporary Behaviors With Inner Discipline

To what extent would the concepts of Barbara Coloroso's Inner Discipline be helpful in the following situations?

1. Khaliah is goofing off and not listening while the teacher explains a language arts lesson.
2. Latane tells the teacher, "You really can't make me do that. You just say you can."
3. Tyrone bullies most classmates and calls them names.
4. Yoshiro is caught drawing sexually explicit parts on the pictures that are posted in the hall.
5. Clayton becomes angry with the teacher, pulls out a knife, and says, "You stay away from me! You can't do to me what you do to those other #&$*% bastards."

school. This call for respect and recognition of cultural customs should carry over into schools.

Advantages and Disadvantages of Inner Discipline

Significant advantages of Inner Discipline include the following: (1) It is based upon sound psychological and philosophical beliefs, (2) the theories are relatively easy to implement, (3) the four steps of discipline apply to most situations, and (4) it fosters self-discipline.

Significant disadvantages include the following: (1) Coloroso's theories often are viewed as being more useful for parents than teachers, and (2) disagreement might arise over who owns a problem. However, even with these two disadvantages, Coloroso's Inner Discipline has considerable potential as a classroom management theory or as a complement to other models.

Imposing or Teaching Discipline?

Of all the classroom management theorists we have looked at thus far, Coloroso is probably the strongest advocate for student self-discipline. In fact, she is opposed to teachers trying to shape student behavior through behavior modification, punishment, rewards, and bribes. Instead, she thinks teachers should model appropriate behavior and instill in students a desire to discipline themselves by accepting ownership of behavior problems and accepting the responsibility to correct the behavior problem.

Underlying Beliefs

Success with Inner Discipline requires a certain kind of teacher or person. A teacher who feels that adults are superior to students, one who feels that adults can act one way and students another, and one who believes that students should be controlled will be uncomfortable

Developing Your Personal Philosophy

Does Inner Discipline Reflect Your Beliefs?

To determine whether you agree with Coloroso's philosophical and psychological positions, ask yourself the following questions:

1. How important is it for me to hold the power in a classroom and to control the actions of others?
2. Do I genuinely believe that all students are of worth and deserve my time and effort?
3. Do I think teachers always should abide by the Golden Rule (and do I have the capability to)?
4. Do I believe that whether a teacher is a brickwall, jellyfish, or backbone affects students' behaviors?
5. Do I believe in the philosophical perspectives of logical and reasonable consequences, and can I implement them?
6. Do I believe in the importance of maintaining students' dignity?
7. Can I see the difference between destructive words of condemnation and words of praise?
8. Do I view rewards, bribes, and threats as manipulative tactics or necessary realistic classroom procedures?

with Inner Discipline. A teacher must be able to accept the philosophical mindset of modeling expected behavior and living the Golden Rule. Brickwall or jellyfish teachers will experience difficulties as they try to implement Inner Discipline. Developing Your Personal Philosophy asks you to consider your propensity for Coloroso's Inner Discipline.

Now that you have had an opportunity to review the concepts of Inner Discipline, review the Case Study and see whether you can apply Coloroso's ideas.

CASE STUDY
Defusing a Confrontation

"Click. Click, click." Although Candi Hecht was standing at the front of her classroom, she clearly could hear the distracting sound that one of her students was making with a toy "cricket" — the kind students clicked at the basketball games. Although other teachers had reported some problems with the noisemakers, Ms. Hecht had not had to deal with this issue before today. She continued teaching as she walked in the direction of the sound. She was not sure who was making the noise, but it seemed to be coming from the back corner where Isabel Cohoon and Katie Davis sat. Beside them were Olin Raynor, a known troublemaker, and Paul Rodriguez, a new boy in the class. Olin had been on his best behavior since the last parent–teacher conference, and Ms. Hecht wanted to keep it that way. The word was that Olin's dad had a bad temper and that calls from the school could result in physical violence at the Raynor house. However, Olin never had any bruises and nothing had ever been reported to any social services agency. Standing in the back corner, Ms. Hecht finished the lesson and then walked toward the front of the room. "Click. Click, click." Before Ms. Hecht could turn around, Olin was out of his seat, grabbing the front of Paul's shirt, shaking him, and saying: "Stop that damn noise! You aren't going to get me in trouble, you lousy wetback!" As Ms. Hecht started toward the boys, she heard the sound of ripping cloth and Isabel Cohoon screaming.

Questions for Consideration

1. What problems is Ms. Hecht facing?
2. Using Coloroso's ideas, explain what she should do. Look for immediate as well as long-term solutions.

 You can record your answers to these questions online on this book's Companion Web Site at *www.prenhall.com/manning*.

CONCLUDING REMARKS

Please go to www.prenhall.com/manning and click on Concluding Remarks for this chapter to find more information.

Barbara Coloroso wrote mainly for adults wanting to improve their parenting skills, but her Inner Discipline theory can help teachers maintain the order needed for effective teaching and learning. She offers some excellent ideas, such as advocating discipline rather than punishment, following the four steps to discipline, using natural and reasonable consequences, and modeling appropriate behavior. In addition, her Inner Discipline theory requires that teachers treat students with dignity, care, and compassion—aspects that we think all classroom management models need. Regardless of the management procedures that teachers adopt, the interpersonal aspects suggested in Coloroso's Inner Discipline deserve consideration. For additional information, you can consult the Internet resources listed in "Reaching Out with Technology" on the Companion Web Site or read some of Coloroso's own writings or the suggested readings that follow.

Suggested Readings

Coloroso, B.(1994). *Kids are worth it: Giving your child the gift of Inner Discipline.* New York: Morrow. Coloroso provides a detailed examination of how she feels children and adolescents should be taught the gift of Inner Discipline.

Coloroso, B.(1997). Discipline that makes the grade. *Learning, 25*(4), 44–46. In this article for teachers, Coloroso explains what backbone teachers do to make classes and schools successful.

Coloroso, B. (2002). *The bully, the bullied, and the bystander.* New York: Harper-Resource. Coloroso provides an excellent description of the bullying problem and what teachers and parents can do.

Green, L. (2005, February 28). Fighting back against bullies: A recent survey of Sarasota County's schools finds more than half of middle schoolers were bullied. *Sarasota Herald Tribune,* p. BV1. Green describes actual efforts to reduce the bullying problem in middle schools.

Liepe-Levinson, K., & Levinson, M. H. (2005). A general semantics approach to school-age bullying. *ETC: A Review of General Semantics, 62*(1), 4–17. Liepe-Levinson and Levinson discuss the seriousness of bullying and explain Coloroso use of terminology.

CHAPTER 10

Exploring the Theories of Consistency Management: *Jerome Freiberg*

Focusing Questions

After reading this chapter, you should be able to answer the following questions:

1. What is the definition of Consistency Management and Cooperative Discipline (CMCD)?

2. What is the overall goal of CMCD, and what evidence suggests that CMCD has the potential to improve student behavior and academic achievement?

3. How does Freiberg define the term *consistency* in a school and classroom?

4. What are the definitions of the terms 1-minute manager and classroom constitutions?

5. How can CMCD turn tourists into citizens, the terms Freiberg uses to refer to students?

6. What are the five themes of CMCD, and how does each contribute to the goals of effectively managed classrooms?

7. What evidence suggests that CMCD is appropriate for increasingly diverse classrooms?

Key Terms

1-minute student managers
Citizens
Consistency
Constitution
Tourists

Jerome Freiberg's Consistency Management and Cooperative Discipline (CMCD) began as a schoolwide effort designed to improve discipline in inner-city schools. Using terms such as classroom constitutions, 1-minute managers, and tourists, Freiberg designed a program that uses five basic themes to improve behavior, school climate, and academic achievement as well as to teach self-discipline at all grade levels and in schools with diverse populations. This chapter looks at various aspects of Freiberg's CMCD and how the program can be implemented, especially in inner-city and increasingly diverse elementary, middle, and secondary schools.

JEROME FREIBERG: BIOGRAPHICAL SKETCH

H. Jerome Freiberg is a John and Rebecca Moores Scholar and Professor of Education at the University of Houston, where he received the University's Teaching Excellence Award, the College of Education Award for Teaching Excellence, and the College of Education Senior Research Excellence Award. International director and founder of the Consistency Management and Cooperative Discipline Program, Freiberg revised the third edition of *Freedom to Learn* by psychologist Carl Rogers (1994), and coauthored *Universal Teaching Strategies* (2000) with Amy Driscoll. Published in 1999, his book *Beyond Behaviorism: Changing the Classroom*

Management Paradigm contains a comprehensive description and explanation of the Consistency Management and Cooperative Discipline Program.

OVERVIEW OF CONSISTENCY MANAGEMENT AND COOPERATIVE DISCIPLINE

Consistency management was the name given to a program that translated research in classroom management, instructional and school effectiveness, school climate, and staff development into practical classroom and school applications (Freiberg, Prokosch, Treister, Stein, & Opuni, 1989). Ten years later in *Beyond Behaviorism: Changing the Classroom Management Paradigm* (1999), Freiberg expanded the name to consistency management and cooperative discipline (CMCD). Thus, we will use Freiberg's latest terminology throughout this chapter.

Key Concepts

The key concepts of Consistency Management and Cooperative Discipline are shown in Figure 10–1. These ideas provide the foundation for CMCD and for the discussions in the rest of this chapter. Freiberg (1996, 1999) bases his CMCD on the belief that students should be turned from passive into active learners in order to create active classrooms, where cooperation, participation, and support are the cornerstones. Using the terms **tourists** and **citizens**, Freiberg maintains that students who behave as tourists are passive onlookers who lack feelings of genuine participation, and students who behave as citizens are active decision makers who feel they are an integral part of the classroom.

The definition of Consistency Management and Cooperative Discipline continues to evolve through the work of the teachers, students, administrators, and parents who are associated closely with the program (Freiberg, 1999). However, as the name suggests, CMCD has two components. First, the **Consistency** Management component focuses on continuity within a school as well as on classroom and instructional organization and planning by the teacher. Emphasizing the need to prevent misbehaviors rather than intervene later, Freiberg (p. 76) believes that "messages that are changed every year or are inconsistent for every classroom diminish discipline and achievement." Thus, CMCD involves everyone in a school who works with the students, from the administrators and classroom teachers to the library media specialist, physical education teacher, bus driver, and custodian. Everyone must give students the same message about responsibility and self-discipline.

Freiberg's model abandons the behaviorism of Skinner in favor of an approach that emphasizes self-discipline, community building, and social decision making (Weinstein, Tomlinson-Clark, & Curran, 2004). Students behave appropriately, not out of fear of

Figure 10–1 Key Concepts of Consistency Management and Cooperative Discipline

Consistency Management and Cooperative Discipline contains these concepts:

An entire school must develop a continuity of actions and expectations for staff, teachers, and students and must be committed to giving students consistent messages about self-discipline.

Teachers should provide a sense of continuity of actions and expectations that help students learn to become responsible for their actions and to develop self-discipline.

Teachers should strive for person-centered classrooms (emphasizing caring, guidance, and cooperation) rather than teacher-centered classrooms.

Teachers should turn students from tourists to citizens.

Teachers support five themes: prevention, caring, cooperation, organization, and community.

Management Tip 10-1

Providing Leadership to Substitute Teachers

Substitute teachers often face a number of challenges and often do not have the instructional success that the regular classroom teacher would have. The CMCD teacher can create a substitute survival kit. Although the contents will vary based on the grade level and the subject, helpful things include the following:

Lesson plans

Class roll

Seating chart

Description of the management system

List of class rules

Description of daily routines

Names of students and other teachers who can provide assistance

Map of the building

Schedule of special activities

List of students who go to special programs

Elementary

Activities for breaks and rest periods

Specific locations for art, music, physical education, and other special activities

Secondary

Remediation materials for students who might experience academic difficulties.

Name and location of the guidance counselor and assistant principal for discipline.

Please go to www.prenhall.com/manning and click on the Management Tips for this chapter to complete management activities and find more information on providing a survival kit for substitutes.

punishment or desire of reward, but out of sense of personal responsibility. In an individual classroom, whether making seating arrangements, passing out papers, taking attendance, or providing equal opportunity for class participation, the teacher becomes the instructional leader who creates a consistent, supportive, flexible, and caring environment in which everyone (teacher and students) participates and learns. The teacher "leads" her or his team members toward management efforts that promote learning and psychological and physical well-being. The teacher even prepares her or his substitute teacher to meet the responsibilities of the class. Management Tip 10–1 suggests ways to provide leadership to substitute teachers.

Second, the Cooperative Discipline component expands the leadership role in the classroom from the teacher to the student. It gives *all* (Freiberg's italics) (Freiberg, 1999) students the opportunity to become leaders. With multiple chances for leadership in small and large ways, students gain the experiences necessary to become self-disciplined. As partners and stakeholders in the classroom, students can create a classroom **constitution** (or *compact*) or accept responsibility for tasks that teachers usually do. In addition, this student responsibility also includes knowing what to do when the teacher is absent, how to solve disputes, how to prevent problems, and how to work cooperatively in groups. Rather than being the sole responsibility of a single teacher, teaching and learning become a collaborative effort that extends throughout the entire school and remains consistent as a student moves through the grades.

The overall goal of the CMCD program is to create a warm and supportive, but firm and orderly, classroom environment in an urban setting (Freiberg et al., 1989). Freiberg has a carefully prepared staff development program that is provided to all teachers in schools that adopt the CMCD model and that helps them work with all aspects of CMCD. When a school district adopts the CMCD model, the first year of the program is implemented at the elementary school level, with the second and third years implemented at the middle and high schools, respectively. This provides a consistent framework throughout the school district. Interestingly, Freiberg requires at least a 70% vote of the professional staff to accept the CMCD model before a school can adopt the CMCD program (*www.ed.gov/pubs/ToolsforSchools/cmcd.html*).

Philosophical and Psychological Foundations

Several ideas form the philosophy of CMCD. Primary is the belief espoused by Rogers and Freiberg (1994) that teachers must shift from a teacher-centered classroom, in which the teacher assumes full responsibility for leadership, to a person-centered one, in which the teacher and students share leadership responsibility. Working together, the teacher and students develop rules, a classroom constitution, or a compact. These might vary from classroom to classroom within a school, but they should reflect the standards identified by the school as a whole. Freiberg believes that once students help develop the rules, it is difficult for them to disobey the rules. Thus, because of the emphasis on shared responsibility among students and teachers for classroom discipline, classrooms become communities of ownership (Fashola & Slavin, 1998). Instead of punishing students for misbehaviors or rewarding them for appropriate behaviors, teachers who use CMCD expect students to discipline themselves. This means that teachers are not solely responsible for classroom management. In addition, representatives of community and business groups come to the classroom and work with the students and the teacher to provide a variety of learning experiences rather than having the class rely solely on the teacher. In turn, these learning opportunities help students demonstrate appropriate behaviors. Activity 10–1 looks at some classroom characteristics and asks you to determine whether each is person centered or teacher centered.

The CMCD program also is based upon the belief that students need a reasonable degree of freedom in the classroom. However, Freiberg et al. (1989) caution that a basic distinction exists between freedom and license. In a classroom with freedom, the climate is one of mutual respect in which students and teachers share and build responsibilities. In contrast, chaos, disrespect, and a lack of focus are signs of a classroom with license.

The philosophical belief that students can assume leadership roles, develop self-discipline, take advantage of various partnerships designed to enrich their educational experiences, and use freedom to make decisions and choices shows Freiberg's move away

Activity 10-1

Identifying a Person-Centered Classroom

Identify which of the following characteristics describe a person-centered classroom and which describe a teacher-centered one. What other expressions might you use to describe a person-centered classroom?

1. The teacher shows genuine interest for individual students and knows things such as names, birthdays and other celebration days, reading interests, and hobbies.
2. Before the first day of school, the teacher posts a list of rules for classroom behavior.
3. Students have a wide variety of significant and meaningful class jobs.
4. The teacher tries to provide educational experiences that students believe are worthwhile and beneficial.
5. The teacher allows students to work collaboratively with friends.
6. The teacher has identified consequences for each misbehavior and applies them equally to all students regardless of the individual differences among the students.

from Skinner's behaviorism. This move is reflected in the title of his 1999 book, *Beyond Behaviorism: Changing the Classroom Management Paradigm*. As Weinstein stated (p. 199), the "movement away from behavioral approaches is especially understandable given the value of individualism and the suspicion of control that are so deeply rooted in American society."

Teachers' Roles and Responsibilities

As with all classroom management plans, CMCD requires teachers to adopt several roles and accept several responsibilities. At the core is the need for teachers to examine their own values regarding student behavior and behavior management, to understand how they are communicating those values to students, and to determine whether those values have meaning for the students. In so doing, the teachers provide strategies to promote positive role models, help students achieve self-discipline, and enjoy reasonable freedom in class-rooms through a person-centered leadership style rather than a strict, teacher-centered style (Freiberg et al., 1989; Freiberg, 1999).

To be successful with CMCD, teachers also must be consistent. Freiberg et al. (1989, p. 379) explained that the term *consistency* should not be confused with rigidity. Consistency provides a sense of continuity of actions and expectations for students and teachers. However, every action that might, on the surface, seem consistent does not reflect the ideas of CMCD. Just because an action is repeated again and again does not mean that the action fits with the philosophy of the CMCD model. Activity 10–2 asks you to consider several examples of consistency to determine which ones reflect Freiberg's theory.

Activity 10–2

Remaining Consistent

Which of the following instances are examples of Freiberg's concept of consistency? Explain your reasoning for each.

1. Ms. Perry maintains consistency by rewarding her students with a sticker every time they answer a question correctly.
2. Mr. Titra maintains a consistent procedure whenever he asks the student homework monitor to collect and return homework.
3. On the first day of school, Ms. Pennington tells her class that she has a firm and consistent rule: "Leave your home-work at home and you get a zero for the day—no excuses."
4. Ten minutes before the end of each art lesson, the student timekeeper in Mr. Devore's class consistently announces, "It is time to clean up and store supplies as we always do."
5. Ms. Simenson, a science teacher, developed a rule that she consistently applies: "If you talk during lab, I will deduct 10 points from your lab grade—no exceptions."
6. Ms. Condra says, "We will use the same organizational pattern for this report as we have done for all of our other reports this year.

APPLYING CONSISTENCY MANAGEMENT AND COOPERATIVE DISCIPLINE

When teachers use Freiberg's CMCD, they must adopt five basic themes, use a progressively ordered sequence of disciplinary management, teach students to become 1-minute managers, and allow students to assume more leadership in the classroom.

Implementing Practical Applications

Figure 10–2 provides an overview of Freiberg's five themes of CMCD, which are discussed in more detail next.

Theme 1

CMCD teachers work to prevent classroom management problems. Freiberg (1999) believes that 80% or more of classroom management is problem prevention rather than problem intervention. In many cases, discipline problems reflect a breakdown in a prevention plan or a lack of inclusion by the students into the classroom environment. To prevent or minimize future discipline problems, teachers can plan classroom rules as well as consistent and appropriate rewards and punishments for students' adherence or lack of adherence to them (Freiberg et al., 1989). Then, during the first weeks of the year, they can provide students with opportunities to begin to develop self-discipline and set standards for their own behavior. Working from a list of five or six rules identified by the teacher, students can develop the rules more fully and add rules of their own. A teacher could also ask students to come up with the initial list of rules, but Freiberg believes the students' rules and the teacher's rules would be almost identical (Willis, 1996). Freiberg (1996) also believes that consistency without rigidity in the classroom and throughout the school helps raise expectations for behavior and learning.

> Before the school year began, Ronald Morales worked with the other teachers and staff in his school to identify the school climate they wanted and the six general rules they would enforce throughout the school. Then he planned the physical layout of his room, the routines he would follow, and the jobs that he felt he could assign to students. During the first weeks of school, he worked with the students to develop a class constitution that stated the rights of everyone in the classroom, the rules they would follow, and a grievance procedure for any complaints. Mr. Morales was pleased to see that the students took an active role in identifying the things they felt would make the classroom a place where they could learn and feel safe.

Although a class constitution can take many forms, it usually lists the rights of the students and the rules for learning and helps students gain a sense of ownership and pride in their class and their school (Freiberg et al., 1989, p. 380). Teachers should guide students

Figure 10-2 Five Themes of Consistency Management and Cooperative Discipline

Prevention	Focus on problem prevention rather than problem solving and reduce the need for intervention.
Caring	Let students know that teachers care by developing a caring environment.
Cooperation	Move students from tourists to citizens and help them assume ownership, and responsibility for self-discipline.
Organization	Share the responsibility for classroom organization to build ownership and increase valuable teaching and learning time.
Community	Build teams, involve the community, and link the school with the home.

Source: Developed from *Consistency Management and Cooperative Discipline. http://www.ed.gov/pubs/ToolsforSchools/cmed.html.*

in the development of the constitution to be sure it is a set of positive rules and objectives that have meaning for the students. For example, in one fifth-grade Magna Carta that Freiberg (1996, p. 33) cites, the students listed the following rights: "feel safe, complain to the grievance committee . . . , ask questions, speak freely, have friends, not be put down, . . . get help, . . . and be treated kindly." Even though a class constitution or Magna Carta is developed at the beginning of the year, Freiberg (1999) cautions that it should not be considered a fixed document. Rather, it can be reviewed and revised as conditions in the classroom change. How Would You React 10–1 looks at a teacher who is having difficulty developing a classroom constitution.

Theme 2

CMCD teachers provide a caring environment where students know teachers care for them. As you read in the Magna Carta example under Theme 1, students want to know that the teachers care about them. Thus, teachers should listen to students, reflect on what they say, trust them, and respect them while also helping students learn proper behavior. Freiberg (1996) believes that how much the teacher cares is more important to students than how much the teacher knows. One prime example of this is all adults and students in a school should be positive models for caring. Another example of caring is how well the teacher works to get students to care for each other. CMCD teacher will teach students that words can be as harmful as actions. Activity 10–3 shows some activities that can create a caring school environment and asks you to identify others.

Theme 3

CMCD teachers cooperate with students to help them develop a feeling of ownership, to become involved, and to have opportunities for self-discipline. In a cooperative classroom, students and teachers help each other, share responsibilities, work together, plan, and participate. The result is that students develop a sense of ownership and involvement, and that they have more opportunities for self-discipline (Freiberg, 1999).

> Freiberg shares the story of Sergio, a student from an inner-city middle school. One day when his teacher was absent and the substitute did not show up, Sergio wrote in his journal: "I feel lucky today because the day has just started and we have already been trusted in something we have never been trusted on,

---

How Would You React 10–1

Creating a Constitution

Review Freiberg's comments about a class constitution and the step used to develop one. Then read the following scenario and respond to the questions at the end.

> Fred Rainey thought he was a true believer and advocate of Freiberg's CMCD, but he was having trouble getting his class to develop a constitution. "I talked a little about the U.S. Constitution and how it protects the freedoms and liberties of all citizens. Then I let the students come up with ideas, but all they wanted was things like no homework, free ice cream, and the right to talk to their friends whenever they wanted to. Well, that won't work, so I drew up a constitution myself and pre-

sented it to the class. They weren't enthusiastic about it, but what else could I do?"

1. What choices does Mr. Rainey have?
2. Is it necessary for the students to write their constitution?
3. How should he introduce the idea of a constitution to his class?
4. How will that introduction vary by the grade level Fred teaches?
5. What procedures should he use?

Activity 10–3

Creating a Caring School Environment

The following are some activities that can create a caring environment in the classroom and the entire school. After reading them, identify other ways that educators can show they care about students.

1. When administrators visit classrooms to read stories, teach lessons, and share their own experiences, students begin to see them as more than disciplinarians (Freiberg, 1996).
2. Each month, library media specialists can feature new displays of student work in the library and can arrange for students to decorate showcases to show their hobbies and interests.
3. Individual birthdays can be celebrated in the classroom on the date they occur, and a whole school celebration can be held each month for all students and staff with birthdays during the summer. This is a common practice in elementary schools, but it rarely occurs in the secondary schools (Freiberg, 1999).

being alone. It is 8:15 and everything is cool. Nothing is even wrong . . ." (p. 83). In the class, one student took attendance and sent the list to the office. Another student led the homework review and began the scheduled classroom presentations. The students were on-task and on schedule when the substitute arrived. As citizens rather than tourists, they were prepared to take responsibility for the classroom.

Theme 4

CMCD teachers work with students to organize the classroom to increase teaching and learning time and to help students build ownership and self-discipline. In CMCD schools, classroom organization is a mutual responsibility of the students and the teachers. Thus, students assume classroom management positions, become **1-minute student managers** (Freiberg, 1996, p. 34), and free the teacher for instructional activities by assuming responsibility for routine classroom tasks. Freiberg found that students were enthusiastic about contributing to the smooth operation of the class (Latham, 1998).

At the beginning, jobs can be identified by the teacher, but students also should be involved in revising the list. Although teachers in the primary grades often select students for classroom management positions, in grades 3 through 12, many teachers have students complete applications for specific jobs. These applications are reviewed, interviews sometimes are held, and students are selected for positions based on their interests and skills. By rotating the jobs every 4 to 6 weeks, all students, not just a select few, are able to hold management positions in the classroom. Freiberg (1999) found that the use of 1-minute student managers gave teachers an average of 14 to 30 minutes (or more) of additional teaching time each day. It is important to remember that student managers do not receive any external rewards. Rather, students work for the intrinsic reward of contributing to the organization and smooth operation of the class.

Learning Students' Backgrounds

Freiberg (2002, p. 30) maintains that it is important for teachers to "have a knowledge of students' cultural backgrounds to develop skills for cross-cultural interaction." Specifically, teachers must learn about the following:

- Family background and structure
- Educational background
- Interpersonal relationship styles
- Use of discipline in the home and culture
- Cultural concepts of time and space
- Religious beliefs and restrictions
- Food customs and preferences
- Health and hygiene
- Traditions, history, and holidays of the culture

Please go to *www.prenhall.com/manning* and click on the Management Tips for this chapter to complete management activities and find questions that teachers can ask to learn more about diverse cultures.

Theme 5

CMCD teachers involve parents and community members in school activities and try to link the school with the home. With the diverse makeup of today's families and communities, teachers need to use a variety of flexible approaches to reach out to families and community members. Management Tip 10–2 explains ways to learn about students' backgrounds. When students see adults other than the school staff in the school, they are exposed to additional positive role models who validate the importance of education (Freiberg, 1999).

> Knowing the benefits for her students, Erika Pisani worked hard to involve parents and community members in her class activities. When she realized that many of her students came from families where the adults worked during the day, she used postcards to send positive notes home on a regular basis. Working with her school's community partner, the crew of a Navy ship, she invited some sailors to come to her class and talk about the rules they had to follow in their jobs. Ms. Pisani hoped this would help her students see the importance of classroom rules. She was also glad to see that her school was going to continue the monthly "partners day" in the lunchroom, where family members (a parent, uncle, cousin, or sibling) or someone from the Navy would have lunch with each student each month. It seemed to help some of the students to see that an adult was interested in them.

How Would You React 10–2 offers Ms. Romanski's different perspective and asks what you might do.

In addition to the five themes that you just read about, Freiberg (1996, 1999) has many other ideas for developing a CMCD school, most of which are covered in the extensive

Voting for Privacy

Community and parental involvement is a basic part of CMCD. however, not all teachers seem comfortable with it. Read the following scenario and then respond to the questions at the end.

> Ms. Romanski was a teacher in a school with an excellent reputation and tremendous parental and community involvement. However, even the principal admitted that perhaps the school had too much support. Although the principal was reluctant to express his views, Ms. Romanski had no problem making her beliefs clear. "Absolutely, we have too much involvement at this school. Parents and community members are always walking down the hall, poking their noses in our business, and telling us how to do things. With the parent volunteers and senior citizen volunteers constantly popping in and out of my room, there are no jobs left for the students to do. I don't know about this CMCD thing, but any more community involvement and I will not get anything done."

1. Think back to Freiberg's comments. Is this what he means by community involvement?
2. Can you have too much parental/community involvement in a school?
3. What advice would you give Ms. Romanski and the principal of this school?

staff-development programs that are provided exclusively to CMCD schools. These intensive programs begin in the spring of the year preceding the implementation of CMCD and continue throughout the first and second years of implementation, with special sessions for new teachers. An attempt is made to time the staff development to the needs of the students and teachers.

We cannot include information from all the workshops in this chapter, but we do want to discuss briefly one other CMCD idea. Freiberg et al. (1989) suggest that CMCD teachers use a system of progressively ordered disciplinary management to help students. Realizing that students will not abandon disruptive behaviors automatically, teachers need to prepare students to assume responsibility for self-discipline and classroom management. This might take extra planning and work with students in the beginning, but the long-term dividend is worth the effort. Even when the plan is in place, teachers still need to have a disciplinary management plan that will help students regain self-control. Thus, when a problem begins to develop, a teacher can start with a subtle intervention, such as the use of nonverbal eye contact. If the student continues to break a class rule, the teacher might need to use more overt interventions, such as standing next to the disruptive student or revoking the student's privileges. This progressive sequence of management applies to students who disregard the class constitution as well as to those who disobey other rules.

Effectiveness of Practical Applications

The concepts incorporated in CMCD lend themselves to practical implementation. When applying the five themes, teachers work to prevent behavior problems, use 1-minute managers and class constitutions, and teach self-discipline. In addition to being useful and relatively easy to implement, these ideas do not place burdensome demands on teachers for detailed record keeping, identifying "psychological causes" of misbehavior, and memorizing elaborate teaching behaviors to respond to specific student misbehaviors. However, to be successful with Freiberg's CMCD, teachers have to maintain consistency with their expectations and behaviors. Management Tip 10–3 provides information from a first-year teacher who, after attending a Freiberg workshop, analyzed her teaching.

⭐ Management Tip 10-3

Analyzing Instruction for Management

Freiberg (2002, p. 59) believes that self-assessment is a "crucial component of instructional change" and helps new teachers develop a repertoire of instructional strategies which contribute to classroom management. He suggests that new teachers audio- or videotape a class and analyze the lesson. They should ask the following:

- How did I begin the lesson?
- Did I gain the students' attention?
- Did I make the objectives clear to the students?
- Did I involve all of the students in the lesson?
- How did I give directions?
- Did I make sure all students understood the directions?
- What strategies did I use to make sure all students were on-task and learning?
- What types of questions did I ask?
- Did I allow an adequate amount of time for students to answer?
- How did I move throughout the classroom?
- Did I favor or ignore any students?
- Did I provide adequate time for student questions?

EVALUATING CONSISTENCY MANAGEMENT AND COOPERATIVE DISCIPLINE IN A DIVERSE SOCIETY

Potential for Addressing Student Misbehaviors

Freiberg's CMCD has considerable potential for addressing nonviolent (but still disturbing) as well as violent student behaviors in contemporary classrooms. Freiberg (2002, p. 58) wrote that when classes are poorly managed, "disorder and chaos steal time from learning and

Please go to *www.prenhall.com/manning* and click on the Management Tips for this chapter to complete management activities and find additional information on self-assessment.

How Would You React 10-3

Helping Tiwanda

Review the key concepts (Figure 10–1) and themes (Figure 10–2) of CMCD. Then read the following scenario.

Tiwanda was not a violent student. Good natured and usually a pleasure to be around, she just did not have a lot of interest in schoolwork. Instead, she looked for other things to do so she could avoid working on her assignments. During independent practice time, she said, "No problem—I'll do this at home tonight." However, she never did. Other times she just sat and did nothing. When questioned, Tiwanda would say, "What's the point in studying? I'll just get to high school, get pregnant, and get on welfare like my mom and my sister. So why should I worry about school? I'll never graduate anyway."

1. Consider each of the five themes of CMCD. How would each of them apply to Tiwanda's situation?
2. What would Freiberg say about Tiwanda?
3. Using Freiberg's ideas, give her teacher some suggestions to help Tiwanda.

exhaust the teacher." Poor management can lead to student discipline problems. In addition, student misbehavior often discourages teachers from using the interactive instructional approaches (e.g., cooperative learning, learning centers, projects and experiments) that foster student achievement and active learning. CMCD has the potential to reduce these problem behaviors as students realize they have ownership in the school and the individual classroom and as they develop the self-discipline to behave appropriately. The CMCD model does not resolve every problem that students bring to the classroom, but Freiberg (1999) believes that it will prevent many of the behavior problems facing contemporary educators. In addition, CMCD, with its framework of schools adapting to individual needs and its themes of prevention, caring, cooperation, organization, and community, can be used successfully to address the needs of all students, rather than only those with specific behavior problems (Fashola & Slavin, 1998). How Would You React 10–3 asks you to apply the model to a student who is goofing off.

CMCD also has proved successful with behavior problems that require disciplinary referrals (Freiberg et al., 1989; Freiberg, 1999, 2000). The reasoning is that students who feel a sense of community and know the teacher cares for them will not see a need for violent behaviors. In one at-risk, urban elementary school that adopted CMCD, disciplinary referrals for its 276 students dropped from 109 in the year before implementation to 19 the next year, with suspensions decreasing from 24 to 0 (Freiberg et al., 1989). In two rural intermediate schools, discipline referrals decreased 40% to 60% in 3 years (Freiberg, 1996). We believe CMCD has and can continue to reduce disciplinary referrals, but we are less sure what a teacher using CMCD will do when a student brings a gun or knife to school and threatens to use it. However, in all fairness, other classroom management programs that we have looked at in this text thus far have not offered solutions to this problem either. Freiberg's CMCD has the potential for creating a school climate that should lessen the possibility of acts of violence.

Freiberg's CMCD has been evaluated primarily with inner-city schools in Houston, Texas, and is used in urban schools in Chicago and Norfolk, Virginia, as well as some rural schools. In schools with many African American and Latino students, student behavior and academic achievement have improved (Fashola & Slavin, 1998). The program has proven its effectiveness with boys and girls, as well as with students of various cultures and social classes. How Would You React 10–4 asks for your response to a teacher who questioned the use of CMCD in her suburban school.

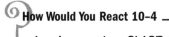

Implementing CMCD in a Diverse Suburban School

The following comments were made by a teacher in a suburban, middle-class community:

> Oh, I know all about Freiberg's CMCD. I read about his model in a book, but CMCD doesn't apply to us. He did his work in rural and inner-city, at-risk schools. Our students have self-discipline and leadership skills, so we don't need to bother with that 1-minute manager or class constitution stuff. Plus, look at his effectiveness studies. All of them were done with inner-city students. There is simply nothing to suggest that CMCD is needed or that it will work in our school. We simply don't have those kinds of problems.

1. Is this teacher right or wrong? Why?
2. Are there parts of CMCD that apply to all schools?

Advantages and Disadvantages of CMCD

All classroom management theories have their advantages and disadvantages, which teachers must consider when deciding whether to use the model singularly or as a complement to another model. CMCD is no exception to this.

Advantages include CMCD's emphasis on preventing behavior problems, teaching self-discipline, incorporating the five themes, using progressively ordered disciplinary management, improving behavior and academic achievement, and providing students with significant leadership roles in the classroom. In addition, Freiberg's (1999, 2000) research suggests that his program does what it claims to do, including improving teacher and student attendance, fostering positive school and classroom climates, providing significant gains in student learning as measured by standardized national tests, increasing time for teachers to teach, and dramatically reducing school violence. As Fashola and Slavin (1998) suggest, CMCD can be a stand-alone model or can complement other classroom management models—even models directed at improving curriculum and instruction.

Evaluating the use of classroom rules and their role in effective instruction, Latham (1998) maintained that the results of the CMCD program are encouraging. Citing Freiberg's (1996) work in inner-city elementary schools, he noted that 3 years after program implementation, participating students had outdistanced students from comparison schools by an average of three quarters of a year's achievement on state and national criterion-referenced tests and had significantly higher scores in student involvement, academic self-concept, task orientation, student and teacher expectations, and achievement motivation (Latham, 1998; Freiberg, 1996).

Admittedly, disadvantages are difficult to suggest because Freiberg has proposed a workable and effective program. One possible disadvantage is that teachers must adhere to the person-centered philosophical position and must maintain consistency. A teacher who sends students inconsistent messages, believes in an autocratic management style, or follows a strict behaviorist approach probably will not be successful with CMCD. Another disadvantage is that the CMCD model must be purchased as a complete package by an entire school with at least 70% of the teachers voting for its adoption, because CMCD is not designed to be adopted by a single teacher or group of teachers in a school. The cost for the required staff development could be prohibitive for some schools. How Would You React 10–5 asks you to consider Ms. Myer, a skeptic of CMCD.

Imposing or Teaching Discipline?

Because the goal of CMCD is to create a democratic, productive learning environment that builds students' self-discipline, Freiberg makes it clear that teachers should teach, not impose discipline (Freiberg, 1996, 1999, 2000). Specifically, the cooperative discipline component

Rejecting CMCD

When asked why she voted against CMCD for her school, Ms. Myer said:

> My class is too bad for me to try to use some person-centered approach. Look, I do my best with this difficult group. But, I don't think they would respond to Freiberg's caring, concern, and cooperation. They'd probably run over me and take advantage of me if they had a chance. Look what they did to their teacher last year. Drove her to quit teaching, that's what they did. Sure, CMCD looks good on paper, but implementing it is a big question mark. No, I think I'll keep this bunch under control and keep my job.

1. Does Ms. Myer have a valid point?
2. What might you tell her to convince her to reconsider CMCD?

of CMCD emphasizes significant leadership roles for students in decision making and in management of a classroom (Freiberg, 1999).

Freiberg (2000) maintains that an emphasis on compliance rather than self-discipline leads to dissatisfied teachers and students. Instead of bribing students with rewards and punishments, teachers should provide opportunities for students to become leaders. As Freiberg (1999, p. 12) wrote: "In the person-centered learning environment there is discipline—*self-discipline*" (Freiberg's italics). Objecting to rewards and punishments that shape students' behavior, Freiberg believes that self-discipline in a person-centered classroom will eliminate the need to use behavioristic approaches.

Underlying Beliefs

Developing Your Personal Philosophy identifies some questions you can answer to determine your propensity toward CMCD. Realistically, teachers probably will not like the CMCD program if they believe teachers control discipline and consider students to be passive learners (Freiberg, 1999). However, teachers who are person centered should, as Freiberg (1999, 2000) suggests, like the CMCD program.

One consideration is whether it is better to have a separate management plan for each classroom or a single plan for the whole school. The Case Study tells about a secondary school advisory committee debating whether to have a schoolwide management plan and, if so,

Developing Your Personal Philosophy

Subscribing to CMCD

Respond to the following questions to examine your philosophical and psychological beliefs and their relation to CMCD.

1. Do I agree with person-centered philosophies, and would I feel comfortable implementing them in my classroom?
2. Do I agree with the five themes, and how would I design my classroom and instruction to reflect them?
3. Do I agree that students should be assigned classroom jobs that teachers traditionally have done? What jobs would I feel comfortable assigning to my students?
4. Do I believe students can and will develop self-discipline? Am I prepared to help them do this?

CASE STUDY
Selecting a Management Approach

Grover Cleveland High School was an inner-city secondary school that had gained a reputation for its high number of discipline referrals and for its students' rowdy behavior. At the beginning of the year, the principal asked for volunteers to help determine whether or not the faculty should adopt a schoolwide classroom management program. Committee members knew they faced at least two major obstacles. First, although all teachers agreed that student behavior was bad, some cringed at the thought of any schoolwide management or discipline plan. "Classroom management and discipline is my responsibility and my choice; no one should tell me how to run my classroom," social studies teacher Brad Dayag declared. Second, the committee knew that reaching a decision on a specific classroom management model would be controversial, take considerable time, and perhaps be impossible.

The committee members were right; there were problems. Mr. Dayag, as well as several other teachers, met with the committee to voice their concerns about any schoolwide effort. Unfortunately, this issue was not settled to the dissenters' satisfaction because several committee members spoke as though the decision to adopt such a plan already had been made. The committee also heard other concerns. Jackie Dela Ossa summarized the feeling of many teachers when she said:

Let's just assume we adopt one management plan, and I say adopt because the administration has probably already made the decision without consulting us first. Which one will we adopt? How will we know what's best for our school? You know, we have a unique school here.

As the committee continued to meet, they examined many plans, including the Canters's Assertive Discipline, Dreikurs's four goals of misbehavior, Kounin's teacher effectiveness, Curwin's and Mendler's Discipline With Dignity, Jones's Positive Classroom Discipline, Coloroso's

Inner Discipline, and Freiberg's CMCD. Rather than discussing the strengths and weaknesses of each theory or model, the committee just talked randomly about tidbits of information they knew or had heard from other teachers. No one on the committee had sufficient knowledge of a classroom management model to talk intelligently about it.

Finally, at one meeting, an exasperated teacher made a suggestion. "Midyear break is almost here. Why don't we wait until next semester to meet again? That will give us time to think about specific models. Plus, it will give the teachers who don't like a schoolwide effort time to settle down." The committee agreed and scheduled their next meeting for the following semester. After a semester of talk and debate, the committee had almost nothing to show for its work.

Questions for Consideration

1. How should the committee respond to the teachers who objected to a schoolwide management plan?
2. What should they do to make more progress?
3. Suppose you were asked to make a presentation to this committee about CMCD and your recommendation for its use at Grover Cleveland High. What major points would you include in your presentation?
4. Did you notice that the teachers always spoke about selecting a specific classroom management model, but no one ever suggested choosing a combination of models? Assuming that a member thinks more than one management model or theory should be adopted, how should this person state his or her opinion?

 You can record your answers to these questions online on this book's Companion Web Site at *www.prenhall.com/manning*.

which theory or model to adopt. Refer to the notes you have been making about your philosophical beliefs to respond to the questions.

CONCLUDING REMARKS

Using CMCD, elementary, middle, and high school teachers can show caring and concern for their students and can develop cooperative attitudes. With its emphasis on students assuming responsibility for self-discipline and accepting leadership positions within the classroom, CMCD offers opportunities for improved student behaviors and increased academic achievement. As students move from tourist to citizen roles, they become an integral part of the classroom community.

 Please go to *www.prenhall.com/manning* and click on Concluding Remarks for this chapter to find more information.

As with other classroom management models, you will have to make your own decision about using CMCD to manage behavior. You can find additional information about CMCD by visiting the Web sites in "Reaching Out with Technology" or checking some of the suggested readings. Also, you will need to decide whether to implement the program alone or in conjunction with other programs. We think Freiberg's CMCD has potential for improving student behavior and academic achievement in contemporary schools, but no model exists in a vacuum. We encourage you to consider CMCD along with other classroom management models to determine what you think will work best in your classroom. On this book's Companion Web Site, you will find Internet sites with more information about CMCD.

Suggested Readings

Freiberg, H. J. (1996). From tourists to citizens. *Educational Leadership, 54*(1), 32–36. Freiberg provides a detailed look at the five themes of his CMCD.

Freiberg, H. J. (1999). Consistency Management and Cooperative Discipline: From tourists to citizens in the classroom. In H. J. Freiberg (Ed.), *Beyond behaviorism: Changing the classroom management paradigm* (pp. 75–97). Boston: Allyn and Bacon. This highly recommended edited book examines CMCD as well as several other classroom management models.

Freiberg, H. J. (2002). Essential skills for new teachers. *Educational Leadership, 59*(6), 56–60. Freiberg describes professional development for new teachers based on organizing (which includes classroom management), instructing, and assessing.

Weinstein, C. S., Tomlinson-Clark, S., & Curran, M. (2004). Toward a conception of culturally responsive classroom management. *Journal of Teacher Education, 55*(1), 25–38. These authors look at the increasing diversity of classrooms and call for culturally responsive classroom management practices.

CHAPTER 11

Exploring the Theories of Judicious Discipline: *Forrest Gathercoal*

Focusing Questions

After reading this chapter, you should be able to answer the following questions:

1. How does Gathercoal propose creating a democratic school community that is based upon the Bill of Rights, the first 10 amendments to the U.S. Constitution?

2. What does Gathercoal say about Judicious Discipline being a scaffold or framework for management strategies rather than an independent model designed to be used alone (e.g., the Canters' Assertive Discipline or Dreikurs's Social Discipline)?

3. Why does Gathercoal advocate a democratic rather than autocratic school community?

4. What discipline practices should be avoided when implementing Judicious Discipline?

5. What does Gathercoal mean by judicious consequences, and how might they be implemented?

6. What is meant by the terms front loading (P. Gathercoal & Crowell, 2000, p. 174) and democratic class meetings?

7. What are several concerns about the effectiveness of Judicious Discipline?

8. How successful is Judicious Discipline with students who are diverse and who have special needs?

Forrest Gathercoal based his theory of Judicious Discipline on the belief that educators should develop democratic classrooms in which students know that their constitutional rights of freedom, justice, and equality will be protected. Explaining that Judicious Discipline should be considered a scaffold or framework rather than a management model, Gathercoal suggested that Judicious Discipline can successfully complement other classroom management models. This chapter looks at Gathercoal's Judicious Discipline, identifies educators' roles, explains procedures for practical application, and evaluates the theory's propensity for addressing schools' increasing diversity, as well as for meeting the goals of the safe schools movement.

FORREST GATHERCOAL: BIOGRAPHICAL SKETCH

Forrest Gathercoal taught law to educators at Oregon State University in Corvallis. Before receiving his law degree, he had experience as a classroom teacher, coach, and high school vice principal in the public schools. Forrest Gathercoal is the author of *Judicious Discipline* (2001) and has led workshops on Judicious Discipline across the nation.

Key Terms

Class meetings

Code of ethics

Compelling state interests

Democratic classrooms

Front loading

Judicious consequences

Justice

OVERVIEW OF JUDICIOUS DISCIPLINE

Educators who want to use Gathercoal's Judicious Discipline as a framework to complement other classroom management models need to accept the philosophical foundations and basic tenets of the theory, namely, that Judicious Discipline is based upon the U.S. Bill of Rights. This section looks in more detail at the philosophical underpinnings of Judicious Discipline and examines specific roles that teachers need to adopt to use the theory successfully.

Key Concepts

Judicious Discipline, as a classroom management style, is based on the synthesis of professional ethics, effective educational practices, and student constitutional rights. It requires that students accept responsibility for their actions, and it also asks educators to create an environment that respects the citizenship rights of students (F. Gathercoal, 2001). Figure 11–1 provides an overview of the basic concepts of Judicious Discipline.

Philosophical and Psychological Foundations

According to F. Gathercoal (2001), it is more difficult to try to remember rules than it is to accept and abide by a moral and ethical code that consists of a few principles that guide behavior. Therefore, Gathercoal based his Judicious Discipline on the uncomplicated yet workable rule that students may do whatever they wish in a classroom until their behavior interferes with the rights of others. When teachers apply this philosophy in an evenhanded manner to student conduct and avoid capricious reactions to every new situation, fad, or change in lifestyle, they teach and respect students' constitutional rights to freedom, justice, and equality. Such a position acknowledges individual differences among students and recognizes the need for an educational environment free from disruptive forces.

Just as the values of freedom, justice, and equality have formed the basis of our nation's constitution, they also form the basis of Judicious Discipline. Freedom does not, however, mean that students have license to do as they please. It means they have freedom to think and act on behalf of their own self-interests, but only if those individual interests are balanced with the welfare needs of other members of the larger community. Management Tip 11–1 explains ways to prepare for emergencies that can happen in any classroom community.

Justice is concerned primarily with due process and deals with basic government fairness. Students in schools have the same right to fair and reasonable rules as citizens in the nation have to be governed by fair and reasonable laws.

Figure 11–1 Key Concepts

1. Based on the U.S. Bill of Rights, Judicious Discipline is a citizenship approach that teaches students about the rights and responsibilities needed to live and learn in a democratic society (P. Gathercoal & Crowell, 2000).

2. Educators should always practice professional ethics by modeling acceptable standards of moral and proper conduct and by acting in the best interests of students (F. Gathercoal, 2001).

3. Students and educators should cooperatively develop behavioral guidelines for their own teaching and learning based upon four interests: property loss and damage; threat to health and safety; legitimate educational purpose; and serious disruption of the educational process (P. Gathercoal & Crowell, 2000; F. Gathercoal, 2001).

4. Educators should use judicious consequences rather than rewards and punishments (F. Gathercoal, 2001).

5. Educators should consider students' constitutional rights and provide consequences based upon individual situations (F. Gathercoal, 2001).

6. In the same way that citizens' rights in the community and overall society should not be violated, teachers need to ensure that students' rights in schools are not violated.

Equality does not mean that all students possess the same abilities, interests, and talents. Although all people might not achieve the same goals or perform at the same level in their schools, they each have the opportunity to succeed. This opportunity is a constitutional right that must be given equally to all individuals (F. Gathercoal, 2001).

Teachers' Roles and Responsibilities

As with all classroom management theories (although you must remember that Gathercoal believes that Judicious Discipline must be used with other models), educators have specific roles and responsibilities when implementing Judicious Discipline. First, teachers must introduce students to the rights encompassed in the concepts of freedom, justice, and equality. This process includes creating a democratic school environment in which everyone teaches and models these three values.

Second, teachers have the responsibility to create an equitable learning environment in which every student has the opportunity to be successful. In the professional and ethical relationships they establish with everyone in the school, teachers must model the values of a democratic society (McEwan, P. Gathercoal, & Nimmo, 1999).

Third, educators should teach students to be leaders. Student leadership is a vital part of a student's school experiences and will lead to positive outcomes for the class, school, and society as a whole. Individual teachers need to adapt their teaching styles and management expectations in order to teach and model leadership skills to students (Flecknoe, 2004).

Finally, teachers have a responsibility to develop **democratic classrooms** in which students know that their human rights are secure (F. Gathercoal, 2001). For example, teachers should use rules and consequences to build a sense of community and keep students in schools. Serving as professional mentors and establishing and maintaining a co-dependent relationship with students, teachers who use Judicious Discipline in their classrooms empower their students to want to behave, to develop a sense of character, and to respect the rights of others (P. Gathercoal & Crowell, 2000). How Would You React 11–1 profiles Ms. Yoder and her ideas about student rights in the classroom.

Management Tip 11-1

Gaining Attention

Sometimes students show too much freedom when they talk in class. Teachers need appropriate techniques to get the immediate attention of students. Strategies include the following:

Turn the lights on and off.

Turn the lights off and wait for the class to become quiet before turning the lights on again.

Ring a bell or sound a gong.

Raise your hand and have students raise their hands as they become quiet.

Count down from 5 to 1—by 1 the room should be quiet.

Remember, with any procedure, you need to do the following:

Explain the procedure.

- When I turn the lights on and off, I expect you to stop talking immediately, turn and face me, give me your full attention, and wait quietly for directions.

Demonstrate the procedure.

Practice the procedure.

Provide intermittent practice with encouragement until students have mastered the procedure.

Elementary

Some teachers use music or creative dramatics to quiet students and to shift between activities. A certain piece of music can signal time to end an activity and sit quietly. To calm students after a busy activity, have them pretend they are walking quietly through a forest or a garden.

Please go to *www.prenhall.com/manning* and click on the Management Tips for this chapter to complete management activities and find additional information on gaining attention.

APPLYING JUDICIOUS DISCIPLINE

How difficult is it to implement Judicious Discipline? Can the basic values of freedom, justice, and equality form the foundation of classroom management? To what extent does Judicious Discipline address students' psychological or developmental needs? You will find Gathercoal's answers in this section.

Questioning Student Rights

Review the philosophical and psychological beliefs that a teacher should have in order to use Judicious Discipline. Then read the following scenario and determine whether this teacher seems to have the beliefs that would allow her to be successful with this management approach. What would Gathercoal say about her idea that students' rights are given up at the classroom door?

Ms. Yoder questioned the concept that students have constitutional rights in schools. "How far do we have to go with all

this? How about my constitutional rights? Why do the students get all the rights and we teachers don't get any? In fact, if students don't know their rights in my classroom, why should I tell them? I have a classroom to run, you know. And I can't spend my time wondering if someone's rights are being violated. I know what needs to be done and I tell my students to do it. What could be simpler?"

Implementing Practical Applications

When implementing Judicious Discipline, educators need to focus on professional ethics, a constitutional perspective to school rules with judicious consequences, and the development of a democratic school community. In addition, because Judicious Discipline is designed to complement more refined management models, teachers need to decide what to use as their primary classroom management model.

It is also important for teachers to realize that Judicious Discipline is a **front-loading** (P. Gathercoal & Crowell, 2000, p. 174) framework. This means that educators develop and teach rules and expectations for behavior through class discussions, group activities that are designed to create rules based on constitutional concepts, and **class meetings** in which classroom conflicts are resolved peacefully in a democratic forum (Landau & P. Gathercoal, 2000). Front loading also means that one of the first things that happens in a classroom is that students develop a class set of expected behaviors. To help them get started, teachers have to focus on the Bill of Rights and the legal **compelling interests** that are discussed later in this chapter. Then, the students must help define what these concepts mean in various teaching and learning situations.

Demonstrating Professional Ethics

Educators usually pass along their professional ethics through their daily interactions with students. Although these interactions encompass a wide array of behaviors, F. Gathercoal (2001) emphasized the need for a teacher's personal code of ethics, student centeredness in all interactions with students, positive ethical practices, and the avoidance of negative disciplinary practices.

Statement of Ethics   F. Gathercoal (2001) suggested that all educators draft and post their personal statement, or **code of ethics.** This allows students and other teachers to see the ethics by which the educator tries to live. Reflected in the statement should be an indication of acceptable standards of student conduct and the belief that an educator should act in the best interests of students. Before you read further in this chapter, complete Activity 11–1, which asks you to explore your own ideas of acceptable conduct.

Student Centeredness   F. Gathercoal (1997, 2001) believes that teachers' professional ethical beliefs should show their commitment to "student centeredness." For example, when students make mistakes, educators should say "Tell me about it" (1997, p. 31) or "What do

Activity 11-1

Developing a Code of Ethics

Suggest five or six ethical practices and acceptable standards of student or teacher conduct that you would include in your personal code of ethics. For example, you might state that a teacher should never call a student derogatory names or should not punish an entire class for the actions of a few. You also could state that you expect students to treat each other with respect.

After you read Gathercoal's ideas in this chapter, revisit your statements. In what ways do they reflect his beliefs? How are they different?

you think needs to be learned here?" (1997, p. 31). Every interaction with misbehaving students should center on the resolution of the problem by helping the students grow and recover from mistakes (2001). Rather than using educator-centered approaches in which teachers establish power through a system of rewards and punishments, student-centered educators share their power and authority with students. By modeling responsible behavior and by empowering students to make their own decisions, educators help students think independently, act responsibly, and develop the values of cooperation and mutual respect. With practice, educators can develop a "mindset of professional responsibility" (1997, p. 33) in which behavior problems are relatively unimportant compared to the educational and developmental needs of students.

Ethical Practices   All educators, either consciously or unconsciously, believe in some fundamental moral principles that guide them through their daily activities. Several factors affect their ethical practices: the way they were raised, their educational training, and their daily interactions with students and other educators. Figure 11–2 shows seven positive ethical practices that Gathercoal considered appropriate for all educators, especially educators who consider themselves to be student centered.

In contrast, Figure 11–3 looks at discipline practices that Gathercoal believes should be avoided. After you read both these figures, complete Activity 11–2.

Unfortunately, a difference often exists between what a person says is an ethical thing to do and what that person does when an ethical dilemma occurs. In the real world, time constraints, unforeseen situational factors, and spur-of-the-moment emotions come into play. Until you experience a situation, you never can be sure exactly how you will behave. Thus, in a classroom, educators consistently must try to use the same ethical behavior so that

Figure 11–2 Positive
Ethical Practices

Educators should

1. Encourage and model an eagerness for learning and teaching,
2. Model responsible professional behavior,
3. Manifest appropriate personal behaviors,
4. Focus their efforts on motivation, encouragement, and building students' self-esteem,
5. Accept the reality that students behave in ways they truly believe at that time are in their own best interests,
6. Develop judicious rules and consequences that accept students as citizens,
7. Feel challenged by the problems in education and be proud they are in a position to help students.

Source: Developed from Gathercoal, F. (2001). *Judicious discipline* (5th ed). San Francisco: Caddo Gap Press.

students feel secure and know what they can expect. Over time, students will gain confidence and come to believe that their teachers always will act in the students' best interests (F. Gathercoal, 2001).

Adopting a Constitutional Perspective to School Discipline

F. Gathercoal (1998, 2001) and Wolfgang (1995) explained that Judicious Discipline followers must adopt a constitutional perspective to school rules and create an environment that respects the citizenship rights of students, especially the fundamental human values of freedom, justice, and equality that are contained in the Bill of Rights of the U.S. Constitution. However, respecting students' constitutional rights and providing them with considerable freedom does not mean that students are free to misbehave or that they have the freedom to do as they please. Rather, it means that students have the freedom to think and act on behalf of their self-interests as long as those actions are balanced against the welfare needs of the larger community (F. Gathercoal, 1998). Educators have a professional responsibility to "sustain a balance between the individual and the state's interests in our public schools" (F. Gathercoal, 1997, p. 68).

Figure 11–3 Discipline
Practices to Avoid

Educators should

1. Never demean students,
2. Never judge or lecture students on their behavior,
3. Never compare students,
4. Never demand respect,
5. Never fear an apology,
6. Never accuse students of not trying,
7. Never ask misbehaving students "Why?" (p. 45),
8. Never get into a power struggle,
9. Never flaunt the fact they are the educators and the children or young adults are mere students,
10. Never become defensive or lose control of their feelings.
11. Never use fear and intimidation to control students,
12. Never say "If I let you do it, I will have to let everyone else do it" (p. 47),
13. Never say "You will thank me someday" (p. 48) as a rationale for a decision,
14. Never say that being consistent means treating all students alike.

Source: Developed from Gathercoal, F. (1997). *Judicious Discipline* (4th ed). San Francisco: Caddo Gap Press.

Activity 11-2

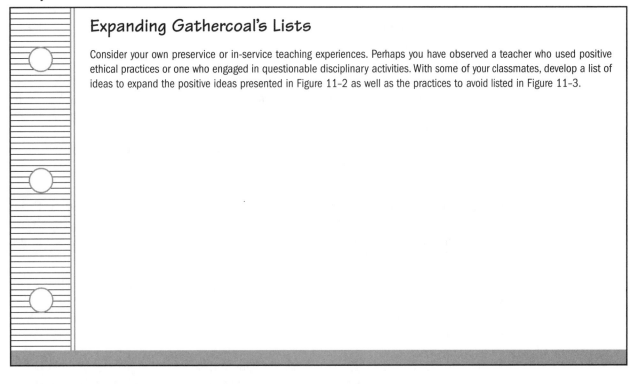

Expanding Gathercoal's Lists

Consider your own preservice or in-service teaching experiences. Perhaps you have observed a teacher who used positive ethical practices or one who engaged in questionable disciplinary activities. With some of your classmates, develop a list of ideas to expand the positive ideas presented in Figure 11-2 as well as the practices to avoid listed in Figure 11-3.

Constitutional Rights   In the United States, the key provisions for individual rights are contained in the Bill of Rights, particularly the 1st, 4th, and 14th Amendments (Wolfgang, 1995), which are shown in Figure 11–4.

Keeping these rights in mind, teachers constantly have to answer questions such as the following:

- Do students have the right to publish and distribute any material they wish on school grounds?
- Can Brooke refuse to complete specific assigned readings based on her religious beliefs?

- The First Amendment: Congress shall make no law respecting an establishment of religion, or prohibiting the free exercise thereof; or abridging the freedom of speech, or of the press; or the people peacefully to assemble, and to petition the Government for a redress of grievances.

- The Fourth Amendment: The right of the people to be secure in their persons, houses, papers, and effects, against unreasonable searches and seizures, shall not be violated, and no Warrants shall issue, but upon probable cause, supported by Oath or affirmation, and particularly describing the placed to be searched, and the persons or things to be seized.

- The Fourteenth Amendment: All persons born or naturalized in the United States, and subject to the jurisdiction thereof, are citizens of the United States and of the State wherein they reside. No State shall make or enforce any law which shall abridge the privileges or immunities of citizens of the United States; nor shall any State deprive any person of life, liberty, or property, without the due process of law; nor deny to any person within its jurisdiction the equal protection of the laws.

Figure 11-4
Selections From the Bill of Rights

- Can Lamont wear clothing that is prohibited in the school handbook but is an expression of his religious faith?
- Can Samit and Davisha be excused from school for religious practices without losing the opportunity to learn?
- Can I search students' property, including lockers, purses, pockets, or vehicles in the parking lot?
- Unless I grant her a due process hearing, can I discipline Lesa by putting her in the hall or other isolated area or can the principal suspend or expel her, thereby depriving Lesa of the right to be educated?
- Can I lower Rahjean's grade, described by Gathercoal as a student's "property" (Wolfgang, 1995, p. 128), because he was late to class?

Compelling State Interest   In addition to relying on the Bill of Rights, Judicious Discipline offers four compelling interests of any state as the basis for classroom rules: health and safety, property loss and damage, legitimate educational purpose, and serious disruption. These interests translate into class rules such as, "Be safe. Protect our property. Do your best work. Respect the needs of others" (Landau & P. Gathercoal, 2000, p. 454). Broad in scope, these four rules address any management issue that might arise at any grade level or in any setting.

Other examples of these compelling interests as the basis for classroom rules include the following:

Property Loss or Damage. No one has the right to destroy the property of another person or school property; therefore, educators have a responsibility to prevent the destruction of property (F. Gathercoal, 2001).
  - "Elaine, be sure you're wearing appropriate shoes on the gym floor."
  - "Class, please clean up your work area and return the microscopes to their storage cases."

Legitimate Educational Purpose. Educational rules and consequences should help students succeed in school and should address issues such as plagiarism, classroom and homework assignments, grading practices, and special or advanced placement (F. Gathercoal, 2001).
  - All school-aged children and young adults must attend school.
  - "Hanson, homework is due at the beginning of each class. The rule is that late work will not be graded without a valid absentee pass from the school office."

Threat to Health and Safety. Educators are responsible for protecting students' physical safety, as well as their psychological and emotional health. (includes the development of rules on playgrounds, in science labs, during physical education, and even in hallways.
  - "Larisha, remember that all students must wear protective eyewear when working in the industrial technology labs."
  - "Noell, the rule is that students should not run in the halls or stairways."
      Management Tip 11–2 includes some suggestions to prepare for serious disruptions in your classroom.

Serious Disruption of the Educational Process. School officials have the legal authority and the professional responsibility to deny student rights if those rights seriously disrupt educational activities. According to the courts, to be serious, a disruption "must materially and/or substantially interfere with the requirements of appropriate discipline in the operation of the public schools" (F. Gathercoal, 1997, p. 72).

- School Rule 11: Students cannot wear gang colors or symbols at school.
- School Rule 3: Students cannot have knives of any type in school or on the school grounds.

Building a Democratic School Community

Democratic and autocratic classrooms approach rules from two entirely different philosophical perspectives. In democratic classrooms, rules are based on the concept that students are free but that their behaviors must show respect for others and their welfare. In autocratic classrooms, rules begin with student responsibilities, and privileges are earned through good behavior (F. Gathercoal, 2001).

F. Gathercoal (2001) calls for a democratic classroom community that creates a freedom of movement and nurtures qualities such as confidence, trust, and conscientiousness. Most educators, however, fear losing control over their students and are reluctant to embrace democratic methods. Gathercoal, though, does not equate a democratic classroom with a permissive environment. Instead, democratic classrooms are led by teachers who recognize and establish the principles of human rights (Bill of Rights), counterbalanced with the four compelling state interests that we outlined in the previous section of this chapter.

The rationale for a democratic classroom is simple. Students need democratic models operating in their daily lives, as well as opportunities to exercise their democratic rights and responsibilities (P. Gathercoal, 2000, April). Too many educators believe that discipline is achieved through rules; presumably, the longer the list of rules is, the better discipline will be (F. Gathercoal, 1990). However, in a democratic classroom, school rules should be kept to a minimum and should be based on the four compelling state interests. In addition, students should be involved in the rule-making process and should learn that there is an appropriate time, place, and manner for exercising their individual rights. When students develop class rules within a democratic structure, the class owns the expectations (P. Gathercoal & Crowell, 2000) and the students learn the skills required to be responsible and self-motivated (McEwan, 2000). Activity 11–3 provides several other ways to build a democratic learning community.

Providing Judicious Consequences

Educators use consequences to encourage, persuade, and if necessary, coerce, students to behave. In many cases students behave only when they think they cannot get away with misbehaviors. However, older students are capable of behaving well not only because of the consequences for misbehavior, but also because they accept the values that make them exhibit the proper behavior (P. Gathercoal & Nimmo, 2001; Grossman, 2005).

☆ **Management Tip 11-2**

Preparing for Emergencies

Before school begins, learn emergency procedures and drills:

> Fire
> Intrusions and lockdowns
> Earthquakes
> Medical emergencies
> Tornado

In emergencies you might need quick access to your class roll.

> Reduce the roll using a copier and put it on bright colored paper.
> Laminate the result.
> Put the roll in an envelope on a bulletin board near the door.

Elementary
Along with the roll, put a list of special classes that students visit throughout the day.

Secondary
Use different-colored paper for each class of the day.

Activity 11-3

Building a Democratic Learning Community

The following are a few characteristics of a democratic classroom:

1. Fewer, not more, rules exist.
2. Students help make the rules.
3. Students know that freedom exists in the classroom but that it also requires responsibility.
4. Students understand their rights and respect the rights of others.

What other characteristics might you see in a democratic classroom? How do these differ from the characteristics of an autocratic classroom? Drawing on your experiences, can you provide examples of activities that occurred in a democratic classroom?

When it is necessary to have consequence for misbehaviors, Judicious Discipline calls for the adoption of **judicious consequences.** Specifically, an "eye for an eye" (F. Gathercoal, 1998, p. 208) type of punishment or a "me against them" (F. Gathercoal, 1997, p. 111) mentality is replaced by a more professional relationship and the use of individual consequences that keep in mind the student's best interests and what the student can learn from the incident.

Two Important Aspects   Two important principles of judicious consequences are that (1) the consequence must be commensurate with the violation; and (2) the consequence must be compatible with the needs and interests of the student and the school community. According to F. Gathercoal (1990), the term *commensurate* (p. 22) means that the consequence must be consistent with and flow logically from the student's misbehavior. The term *compatible* (p. 22) recognizes the student's need for personal self-worth and academic achievement, as well as the effect of the student's behavior on the school or classroom.

Developing the Question   According to F. Gathercoal (2001), when a misbehavior occurs, the first words a teacher speaks to a student should be in the form of a question. By avoiding accusatory statements and lectures, teachers send the message that they are working in the students' best interests and give the students power in the relationship. Questions also can prompt students to open up and discuss the problem, not by defending who they are but by talking about what they have done. Instead of asking "Why?" teachers need to ask questions such as these (F. Gathercoal, 1997, p. 116):

"Is there something I can do to help?"
"What happened?"
"Would you like to talk about it?"

If students are willing to discuss their behavior, they are beginning to accept ownership of the problem, and, if properly handled, should become accountable for their actions (F. Gathercoal, 1997, 2001). In contrast, students who do not respond immediately to questions or who refuse to discuss the situation might need more time to process their feelings. When giving a student more time to think about a misbehavior, a teacher might say: "I see that you would rather not discuss this now. Maybe we can get together later, when we both have had time to think about it" (1997, p. 118). How Would You React 11–2 asks you to give Ms. Michaelais some advice about a professional response to a misbehavior.

Shaping Consequences   When students break the rules, teachers need to consider two important things: (1) What needs to be done? (2) What needs to be learned? "What needs to be done" (F. Gathercoal, 1998, p. 210) usually involves restitution and apology. On the other hand, "what needs to be learned" (p. 210) looks at changing future goals and attitudes, such as the immorality of taking another student's possessions or the dangers of running in the hall. As they work toward equitable solutions to these questions, students must believe that their feelings and opinions are valued and that the teacher wants to help them rather than dish out punishment.

Individualizing Consequences   "Never think that being consistent means treating all students alike," cautioned F. Gathercoal (1997, p. 48). Consistency is a mainstay in many classroom management theories, but Gathercoal has a different conception of its use. In fact, he believes that consequences for misbehavior should be individualized, should not be designed to punish students, and should consider individual differences among students in order to meet the emotional and learning needs of students. Students who misbehave simply might have different ways of learning from their mistakes and, as a result, might need different consequences (F. Gathercoal 1997; 1998).

To determine those consequences, teachers need to understand the real nature of the problem and to account for individual differences. F. Gathercoal (1998) provided the following example: When two boys vandalized a wall and were asked by school officials to clean up the wall, the first replied that he would clean the wall right after school. The other one

---

How Would You React 11-2 _____

Responding Professionally

Before you read the following scenario, reread the sections of this chapter that discuss professional ethics and Judicious Consequences. According to Gathercoal, how should teachers demonstrate professional ethics? Then read the scenario and respond to the questions at the end.

The problem occurred in the hall as Charmaine Michaelais, a fifth-grade teacher, was taking her class to the school library. Unfortunately, several teachers were standing in the hall and saw the misbehavior. Thus, Ms. Michaelais took the incident as a personal affront. After getting the class under control, she turned to her colleagues, shook her head, and said, "I do my best for them; I use the latest management techniques that are touted as respecting student dignity and self-esteem. And what do I get? Misbehavior in the hallway for all to see!" Wheeling around, Ms. Michaelais spoke loudly to her class: "Why do you act like that? You don't deserve to be treated with respect; you deserve the same thing you give others: sarcasm and threats. Let me show you who's in charge here."

1. Is Ms. Michaelais demonstrating ethical behavior?
2. How could Ms. Michaelais provide a professional response to her class?
3. How could she use Judicious Consequences in this situation?
4. What consequences would be appropriate?

angrily responded that cleaning the wall was not his job and he would not do it. Gathercoal maintained that the problem is different for both students and, therefore, the consequences should not be the same. In the case of the first student, cleaning the wall probably will be considered an act of making amends rather than punishment. In the case of the second student, a more serious problem has emerged, and the act of cleaning the wall becomes secondary to the more serious problem (F. Gathercoal 1997; 1998).

Class Meetings

Several authors (P. Gathercoal, 2000, April; Browning, Davis, & Resta, 2000) propose class meetings as a means of giving students a voice in class decisions, as well as helping students resolve interpersonal conflicts. In **class meetings**, students can deal with undesired behaviors or arrive at peaceful conflict resolution (Bertone, Meard, Flavier, Euzet, & Durand, 2002). In addition, democratic class meetings are an essential part of the effective operation of Judicious Discipline classrooms. By providing excellent opportunities for developing and discussing goals, expectations, and relationships, they contribute to the sharing of power and to the avoidance of power struggles because all students have opportunities to express their concerns. When students feel that they have power in class operations, they are less likely to misbehave (P. Gathercoal, 2000, April). Class meetings also can help students learn skills, such as conflict resolution, that they can use during all aspects of their lives.

In his presentation at the American Educational Research Association meeting, Paul Gathercoal (2000, April) explained the key elements of democratic meetings. In advance of the meetings, the teacher should determine who can call a class meeting and when the meetings should be held. Some teachers allow a student to call a meeting at any time, and others have specific times and places for the meetings. The idea is to give students a sense of significance and some power and control over events in the classroom. At the meeting, the room should be arranged so that everyone can see everyone else. A circle is an arrangement that provides a feeling of community and that encourages positive and productive communication.

During the meeting, certain rules apply. First, everyone must agree that names will never be used during the class meetings. Using names casts an accusatory finger at the person being named and has the effect of putting that person on the defense. Instead, teachers should suggest that all speakers say, "a person who acts in this way. . . ." This general statement protects individuals in the class and allows them to participate in the discussion about behavior and not about personalities. Everyone also should agree to stay on the topic and to keep family concerns out of the discussions.

Although Judicious Discipline promotes democratic classrooms, P. Gathercoal (2000, April) believes that the teacher should lead the class meeting. When teachers give students leadership roles, the class meeting sometimes digresses. Often, empowering class officers propagates popularity contests and competition. In addition, a rule should be established that students are not required to participate in the discussion.

Students and teacher should maintain a class meeting journal. Each class meeting begins with journal writing, or, for younger students, drawing in a journal. A prompt for the writing or drawing might be a question such as "Does anyone have concerns, clarifications, or problem areas they would like to discuss?" This type of broad statement encourages everyone to write.

During democratic class meetings, teachers should encourage students to set goals for themselves and to determine how they will attain those goals (Landau & P. Gathercoal, 2000). It is important that the teacher and each student set his or her own goals and that no one ever sets a goal for someone else. A teacher can suggest a goal (e.g., "What do you think about setting a goal like . . .?"), but setting a goal for someone else brings about a co-dependent rather than a mentoring relationship. Teachers also should not ask students to share their goals and should warn students to be careful about sharing goals.

Class meetings can be a helpful means of letting students feel a part of the classroom and the decision-making process. One sixth-grade classroom meeting we observed dealt with the problem of students treating others with respect. Although the teacher was a master, she did experience some students behaving rudely to each other. She called and methodically conducted the class meeting. Students raised their hands to speak, voiced perceptive comments, and reached a consensus that all students should be treated with respect. Another class meeting was a group of second graders discussing "bullies and bullying." The teacher distributed some age-appropriate information on the problem and students discussed reasons for children bullying and how bullying made victims feel. This excellent discussion resulted because the teacher was proficient at class meetings and letting students reveal how they felt. Management Tip 11–3 looks at class meetings, especially in light of F. Gathercoal's Judicious Discipline.

Holding democratic class meetings takes time, and some teachers might question their importance and effectiveness. How Would You React 11–3 tells about the skepticism of Mr. Choudhuri.

Effectiveness of the Practical Applications

Judicious Discipline has been tested in Minnesota, Michigan, and Oregon to determine its usefulness in practical situations. In these states, the use of Judicious Discipline coupled with class meetings promoted good citizenship and safe, productive learning environments (Landau & P. Gathercoal, 2000). Teachers found positive results, primarily in reducing fighting and other angry outbursts. In addition, the consistent use of class meetings based on the framework of rights and responsibilities provided students with an opportunity to discuss issues of concern peacefully. In Oregon, the framework successfully allowed students to practice goal setting and to have authentic input into classroom management.

> **Management Tip 11-3**
>
> ### Planning Class Meetings
>
> Teachers and students can use class meetings to deal with nearly any problem facing the class.
>> Possible topics for class meetings include
>>
>> treating others with respect,
>>
>> understanding bullies and their victims,
>>
>> class rules,
>>
>> concerns about class and school expectations,
>>
>> behavior during group work,
>>
>> behavior at lunch or on field trips,
>>
>> understanding reasons for misbehavior,
>>
>> developing communication skills,
>>
>> practicing role playing, and
>>
>> focusing on nonpunitive solutions to problems.

Please go to *www.prenhall.com/manning* and click on the Management Tips for this chapter to complete management activities and find additional information on class meetings.

EVALUATING JUDICIOUS DISCIPLINE

All classroom management models and theories should undergo close scrutiny to assess their potential for addressing common misbehaviors, their advantages and disadvantages, and their views about teaching or imposing discipline. Although Judicious Discipline is not a refined classroom management model, its use as a framework means it should be evaluated.

Potential for Addressing Student Misbehaviors

When used in conjunction with another, more refined classroom management model, Judicious Discipline has the potential to address many of the problems facing schools today.

How Would You React 11-3

Holding a Class Meeting

Reread the section of this chapter on class meetings and make a list of the benefits as well as the problems that teachers would need to anticipate. Then, read the following scenario and respond to the questions at the end.

When Mr. Choudhuri, a secondary American history teacher, walked into the teacher's lounge, he threw up his hands and said, "I've had it with class meetings. They take time, and I'm not sure that's time well spent. Today was a great example! Garth and Dorene got into a 'he said, she said' shouting argument and Carrie, our class president, couldn't do anything.

Then Piper accused Travis of wasting time and getting the class in trouble with the substitute last week. When I tried to ask the students to tell me some of their goals for the rest of the semester, all they said were things like 'get out of school.' Why should I even bother with class meetings?"

1. According to Gathercoal, what are the benefits of class meetings?
2. If you were a teacher in the lounge, what could you tell Mr. Choudhuri about planning and holding class meetings?

As you have read in other chapters of this book, few fights or acts of physical violence occur in most schools. Instead, students disrupt classes by talking out of turn and to each other, by walking around the room without a justified reason, and by neither listening to the teacher nor engaging in learning. These misbehaviors are not dangerous or threatening, but they are annoying and disturbing to the teacher as well as to other students. Through Judicious Discipline, students can learn how their behavior infringes on the rights of others to learn (and vice versa), and a teacher can move management issues away from a struggle between student and teacher for classroom control and toward a method by which two people can work together to resolve a conflict.

When students believe that teachers respect their rights, students should feel they are an integral part of the class organization. This should promote self-esteem, provide a sense of physical and psychological security, and improve socialization skills. Although perceptive educators would not teach the four compelling state interests to younger elementary students as they would to secondary students, they can teach the basic concepts of respect for others' rights.

Some educators maintain that special needs students (e.g., emotionally disturbed) are not capable of responding in appropriate ways to the knowledge that certain rights and responsibilities are expected of them by society. Therefore, these educators believe that Judicious Discipline will not work in inclusion classrooms. In contrast, McEwan, P. Gathercoal, and Nimmo (1999) believe that the framework is particularly well suited to serving the needs of all students because students in a Judicious Discipline classroom use the language of human rights and responsibilities for decision making and understand the values that sustain a peaceful and equitable learning environment. F. Gathercoal (1998) told of a middle school special education teacher of emotionally/behaviorally disturbed students. After adopting Judicious Discipline, she had an excellent year. In addition to receiving more respect, she found that power struggles had decreased, and she believed that her students understood the concepts of Judicious Discipline. How Would You React 11–4 allows you to respond to a teacher who is not completely convinced that Judicious Discipline can be effective.

All educators have a responsibility to provide safe schools. This requires taking sensible steps to protect students and other individuals in the school (McEwan, 2000) and to deal with the serious problems of physical violence and the use of knives, guns, and other weapons. Although Judicious Discipline does not specifically provide a response for such acts of violence, the philosophical concepts embedded in its framework can be a sensible beginning

Applying Judicious Discipline in an Inclusion Classroom

Before reading the following scenario, review the basic concepts of Judicious Discipline (See Figures 11–1, 11–2, and 11–3. Then read the scenario and respond to the questions at the end.

> When asked if she saw any potential for using Judicious Discipline in her inclusion classroom, Erin Ruffin replied, "All this sounds good, but what exactly do I do when Jason walks around the room and talks to all his friends? I can teach constitutional rights, but what if Andria and Todd do not respect others' rights? Judicious Discipline does not tell me what to do when Kawanti answers out of turn. And, I'm not sure Nancie, one of my inclusion students, can understand the concept of rights and responsibilities. I think I need a more specific model, one that will tell me how to address all behavior situations."

1. Respond to Ms. Ruffin's concerns. Which of the concepts (Figure 1) would apply in her classroom?
2. Which of the behaviors in Figures 11–2 and 11–3 could she use in her classroom?
3. What things is Judicious Discipline not designed to do?
4. In what ways will she need to rely on another classroom management system?
5. Reviewing the other models and theories discussed in this book, suggest things she might use with Judicious Discipline.

point. For example, Judicious Discipline does little when a student pulls a knife and threatens another student, but its front-loading characteristics can help students learn to respect others and thus diminish the chances of a fight occurring.

Once students have actually fought, it can be difficult for a teacher to individualize consequences because so many educators believe that regardless of the circumstances, all students in a fight should be suspended from school. This show of force is supposed to send a message that the school will not condone fighting. Thus, educators who try to avoid suspending students often are accused of being "too soft" (F. Gathercoal, 1997, p. 125). However, F. Gathercoal (1997, 2001) maintains that educators must consider students' dilemmas (peer pressure, the saving of face, and the perceived need to hold one's ground) when they try to curb fighting. Further, he believes that although fights should not be condoned, educators need to commit to keeping the students in school. As an alternative to suspension, he suggests providing students with professional assistance such as counseling, mentoring, and peer mediation programs.

Gathercoal says little about diversity (except for students with special needs), but several of his assertions illustrate his firm belief that all people should be treated with respect: "educators . . . teaching and respecting their students' constitutional rights" (F. Gathercoal, 1997, pp. 9–10), and "teach(ing) students . . . accountability, self-efficacy, tolerance, cooperation, and mutual respect" (p. 10). No aspects of Judicious Discipline should offend any cultural group, either gender, or any social class group.

Advantages and Disadvantages of Judicious Discipline

Like any other classroom management model, Judicious Discipline has advantages and disadvantages that educators need to consider when deciding whether to adopt the model as part of their classroom management strategy. In support of the model, Paul Gathercoal (2000, April) maintained that teachers using Judicious Discipline

Experience less frustration and/or less work-related stress,

Feel more respected by other educators and by students,

Perceive a sense of professionalism,

Consider Judicious Discipline to be legal, ethical, and educationally sound,

Believe their students are provided with a "language of civility," to use to discuss, mediate, reconcile, and solve social problems.

In addition, Judicious Discipline provides a legal basis for establishing rules, procedures, and policies; provides guidelines for due process; and gives an overall legal construction for broader discipline policy issues (Wolfgang, 1995). Older students can be told that the rights they have in school come primarily from the 1st, 4th, and 14th Amendments, and younger students can be taught that they have the right to be themselves (Landau & P. Gathercoal, 2000).

Judicious Discipline has several disadvantages, including the fact that it does not deal with the daily problems of limit setting and confronting misbehaving students, and it might take considerable time to implement if every teacher needs to teach constitutional rights and go through a rule-developing process (Wolfgang, 1995). In addition, teachers who are concerned that students and parents will complain that "You're not treating all students the same" (F. Gathercoal, 1990, p. 23) will be reluctant to individualize the consequences for rule breaking.

Imposing or Teaching Discipline?

F. Gathercoal's (1997, p. 9) assertion that "You may do what you want in this classroom until it interferes with the rights of others" implies that he wants students to accept responsibility for learning self-discipline rather than have the teacher impose strict rules and consequences. When teachers create an environment that respects the citizenship rights of students, students will learn and experience a model of discipline that emphasizes personal responsibility (F. Gathercoal, 2001). In addition, after students learn the four compelling state interests, they might come to realize that a long list of rules and punishments is unnecessary as long as they respect the rights of others.

Underlying Beliefs

Before adopting the ideas in Judicious Discipline, educators need to consider whether the theory reflects their own philosophical and psychological beliefs. First, they need to ask themselves whether they agree with the idea of constitutional rights for students. Educators who

How Would You React 11-5

Using Judicious Discipline in the Primary Grades

Before reading the following scenario, review the basic concepts of Judicious Discipline (See Figures 11–1, 11–2, and 11–3. Then read the scenario and respond to the questions at the end.

Emilio Fischer wondered if he could use Judicious Discipline in the primary grades. "Students in the upper elementary grades can understand their rights as well as those amendments, but in the primary grades, I'm not sure. How can I explain all those concepts to second or third graders? I don't

think they're ready to understand the concepts associated with Judicious Discipline."

1. Do you agree with Mr. Fischer?
2. Are there any of Gathercoal's ideas that would be useful in an elementary school?
3. What about his ideas of demonstrating ethical practices and building a community?
4. What role can Judicious Discipline play in the primary grades?

Developing Your Personal Philosophy

> **Considering Judicious Discipline**
>
> Think about your philosophical and psychological beliefs. Then answer the following questions.
>
> 1. Do I genuinely believe students have constitutional rights (especially 1st-, 4th-, and 14th-Amendment rights) in classrooms?
> 2. Do I believe that students will behave better in democratic classrooms where they experience freedom and responsibility?
> 3. Am I willing to transfer some of my power to the students?
> 4. Am I willing to abide by decisions reached in democratic class meetings?
> 5. Do I think students are sufficiently developed and mature to handle the freedoms associated with their constitutional rights?
> 6. How can I implement Judicious Discipline in my own classroom?

favor autocratic positions might not agree with such perspectives, and some educators might not want to teach students about personal freedoms. Second, some educators will not want to risk individualizing the consequences for rule breaking. Considering such an approach to be unfair, they might question why Tally should receive different consequences than Kashana if they both do the same thing.

Third, teachers who think rewards and punishments work (and actually teach students) might have a philosophical disagreement with F. Gathercoal's (2001) position that rewards and punishments result in co-dependent relationships between students and the teacher. Finally, an educator who wants to use Judicious Discipline must be able to trust students, teach students the concepts of rights and responsibilities, and act in ways consistent with civil responsibility. To consider whether you might adopt the ideas of Judicious Discipline, respond to the questions in Developing Your Personal Philosophy. Then react to the use of Judicious Discipline in the lower grades in How Would You React 11–5.

The decision to adopt a classroom management model or theory is a major consideration for any teacher. The Case Study looks at Mr. Penmark and Ms. Dantzeler and their debate about Judicious Discipline.

CONCLUDING REMARKS

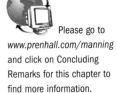

Please go to *www.prenhall.com/manning* and click on Concluding Remarks for this chapter to find more information.

Judicious Discipline has the potential for being a valuable framework to complement other more refined classroom management models. With an emphasis on teachers demonstrating professional ethics, adopting a constitutional perspective to school rules, building a democratic school community, and providing judicious consequences, this framework holds students accountable for their actions. It also holds educators accountable for creating an environment that respects students' citizenship rights. Teaching students their constitutional rights and teaching them to respect others' constitutional rights can contribute to the development of a democratic school environment where students and teachers respect each other. You can learn more about Judicious Discipline by visiting some of the Internet sites listed in "Reaching Out with Technology" on this book's Companion Web Site.

CASE STUDY
A Decision to Implement Judicious Discipline

One June afternoon, Phil Penmark, a seventh-grade math teacher, was surprised when Lysbet Dantzeler, an eighth-grade science teacher, stopped by his room with a copy of Gathercoal's Judicious Discipline in her hand. Phil had been using Judicious Discipline as a basis for his classroom management model for several years, and he and Lysbet had had several heated discussions about its use in the diverse classrooms of Linear Middle School.

Before Phil could say anything, Lysbet held up her hand. "No, I'm not a convert!" she said. "But I've been a teacher long enough to see the writing on the wall. School gossip has it that Dr. Herr would like everyone to consider putting Judicious Discipline in place in their classrooms. You know Dr. Herr—he doesn't want to flex his muscles as principal if he can get us all to cooperate some other way. So he's talking to all the teams about the great results you and the other teachers on the Lion Team have been having with JD."

Phil shook his head. "Sure we've had some great success with it, but you and I have had the debate before, Lysbet. I remember the day you stood in the faculty cafeteria and told me quite clearly that . . ."

Lysbet cut him off. "You don't have to remind me! I think I muttered something about teaching science, not social studies. Then I probably said I was not hired to teach students about their constitutional rights. I probably ended up with the statement that the time it takes to teach the amendments and hold class meetings would take time away from science, and that's what I'm being paid to teach!"

"Yep, that pretty much sums it up," Phil replied. "Oh, you also said something about teaching a diverse class and how ridiculous it was to expect kids who speak very little English or who are at risk of failing to understand and care about constitutional rights and amendments and all that legalese."

"You really did listen, didn't you?" Lysbet sighed. "Well, now it looks like I'm going to have to eat my words. But I'm still not convinced that it will work. There's nothing you or this book can tell me about using JD to stop a fight. This Gathercoal doesn't even believe in suspending fighters. And he thinks I should use judicious consequences, whatever that means, by individualizing consequences. Oh, I can just see that. Our team is 73% minorities. If I treat a white kid one way and a Hispanic kid another way, I'll be setting myself up for a visit from a lawyer."

Seeing Lysbet's dismay, Phil broke in. "If you're not in favor of JD, why come to me? I really don't feel like arguing its philosophical and psychological points with you today."

Lysbet took a deep breath. "Well, I really respect you as a colleague. And, as I said before, Dr. Herr started me thinking. Maybe there is something to JD after all. But, Phil, I'm scared. I've been a good teacher for 10 years and I have my management system down pat. If I have to change to this Judicious Discipline, how should I do it? Is there something I can do this summer to get ready to implement it next fall? If I give students their rights, will I have any rights left?"

Questions to Consider

1. Help Phil Penmark respond to Lysbet Dantzeler's concerns. What steps can she take to incorporate the concepts of Judicious Discipline into her classroom?

2. What can Phil say to relieve the concerns that Lysbet has?

 You can record your answers to these questions online on this book's Companion Web Site at *www.prenhall.com/manning*.

Suggested Readings

Bickmore, K. (2004). Discipline for Democracy? School districts' management of conflict and social exclusion. *Theory and Research in Social Education, 32*(1), 75–97. Bickmore looks at six urban Canadian schools' classroom management and citizenship education.

Gathercoal, F. (1990). Judicious Discipline. *The Education Digest, 55*(6), 20–24. Gathercoal provides a succinct description of Judicious Discipline and provides excellent information on judicious consequences.

Gathercoal, F. (2001). *Judicious Discipline* (5th ed.). San Francisco: Caddo Gap Press. Gathercoal provides a detailed and comprehensive examination of Judicious Discipline—required reading for those who want additional information on this framework.

Gathercoal, P., & Crowell, R. (2000). Judicious Discipline. *Kappa Delta Pi Record, 36*(4), 173–177. This article focuses on character education and how Judicious Discipline teaches character.

Landau, B. M., & Gathercoal, P. (2000). Creating peaceful classrooms: Judicious Discipline and class meetings. *Phi Delta Kappan, 81*(6), 450–454. Barbara Landau and Paul Gathercoal provide an excellent discussion of democratic class meetings.

CHAPTER 12

Introducing Additional Theorists: *Albert; Evertson and Harris; Johnson and Johnson; Nelsen, Lott, and Glenn; and Kohn*

Focusing Questions

After reading this chapter, you should be able to answer the following questions:

1. How did Rudolf Dreikurs influence Linda Albert's Cooperative Discipline as well as Nelsen's, Lott's, and Glenn's Positive Discipline?

2. What does Albert mean by the terms capable, connect, and contribute?

3. What do Evertson and Harris mean by the terms minor interventions, moderate interventions, and more extensive interventions?

4. How do Evertson and Harris suggest teachers plan for the beginning of the school year?

5. What do Johnson and Johnson mean by the Three C's of Classroom Management?

6. What do Johnson and Johnson think was one answer to the increasing violence facing our schools?

7. What do Nelsen, Lott, and Glenn mean by the significant seven (e.g., the three empowering perceptions and the four essential skills)?

8. What do Nelsen, Lott, and Glenn mean by the terms barriers and builders?

9. Why does Kohn think the New Disciplines do not differ significantly from the older discipline models?

10. What does Kohn mean when he says he wants educators to move beyond rules to students making decisions and beyond compliance to community?

INTRODUCTION

After reading about the foundational theorists of classroom management in chapter 2, you have had an opportunity to explore individual classroom management theorists and models in chapters 3 through 11. Now, in chapter 12, we conclude our review by looking at Linda Albert's Cooperative Discipline; Carolyn Evertson's and Alene Harris's Managing Learning-Centered Classrooms; David Johnson's and Roger Johnson's Three C's of School and Classroom Management; Jane Nelsen's, Lynn Lott's, and Stephen Glenn's Positive Discipline, and Alfie Kohn's Beyond Discipline. Like the other theorists presented in this book, each of them adds to our repertoire of ideas and techniques for understanding students, managing classrooms, and promoting safe schools.

ADDITIONAL THEORISTS

When writing this book, we realized that it would be impossible to explore all classroom management theories in detail. Thus, we combined the foundational theorists into a single chapter. Now, having reviewed

Key Terms

Linda Albert
Autocratic teacher
Capable
Code of conduct
Connect
Contribute
Democratic teacher
Influence
Permissive teacher
Evertson and Harris
Advance preparation
Interventions
Johnson and Johnson
Civic values
Conflict resolution
Cooperation
Cooperative learning
Nelsen, Lott, and Glenn
Barriers
Builders
Class meetings
Empowering perceptions
Essential skills
Significant Seven
Alfie Kohn
Communities
New Disciplines

Please go to
www.prenhall.com/manning
and click on Concluding
Remarks for this chapter to
find more information.

Table 12–1 Overview of Additional Theorists

Theorist	Model	Key Concepts
Linda Albert	Cooperative Discipline	Shared responsibility Encouragement Influence
Carolyn Evertson and Alene Harris	Managing Learning-Centered Classrooms	Instructional management and behavior management
David Johnson and Roger Johnson	Three C's of School and Classroom Management	Cooperation Conflict resolution Civic values
Jane Nelsen, Lynn Lott, and Stephen Glenn	Positive Discipline	Respect Opportunities to learn life skills
Alfie Kohn	Beyond Discipline	Learner-centered Community

the major classroom management theories, we conclude our discussion by examining a number of important current theorists. Table 12–1 shows the theorists, their models, and the key concepts that we will examine in this chapter. Although our discussion will provide only an overview of their ideas, we encourage you to use the information in the Suggested Readings and "Reaching Out with Technology" on this book's Companion Web Site to explore these and other contemporary theorists in more detail.

Linda Albert: Cooperative Discipline

Biographical Sketch

A nationally syndicated columnist, author, public speaker, former classroom teacher, and professor of education, Linda Albert has focused on issues such as coping with disruptive and inappropriate behavior, reducing violence, overcoming academic and developmental difficulties, and reducing substance abuse. With a master's degree in education and a doctorate in psychology, she has written a number of books, including *Cooperative Discipline Implementation Guide* (1996) and *Coping with Kids and School* (1984). Featured in a number of videos, she has appeared on television shows such as the *Today Show* and *CNN Cable News* (*www.teachersworkshop.com/twshop/albert.html*).

Overview of Albert's Theories

In Cooperative Discipline, Linda Albert encourages teachers to **influence** the behavior of individual students. She emphasizes that "students choose their behavior, and we have power to influence—not control—their choices" (Albert, 1995, p. 43). Using the four goals of misbehavior (attention, power, revenge, and inadequacy, or the fear of failure) identified by Rudolph Dreikurs (discussed in chapter 4) as a basis for Cooperative Discipline, she encourages teachers to work with parents and students to help students with the three C's: *connecting* to the teacher and other students, *contributing* to the class, and feeling *capable* of successful behavior and academic work. Noting that a teacher can have either a **permissive** (hands-off), **autocratic** (hands-on), or **democratic** (hands-joined) classroom management style, Albert believes that a teacher's greatest assets are good self-control and the use of encouragement to help students face daily challenges, have appropriate behavior, and be successful in school.

Contributions of Albert's Theories

With an emphasis on influence, cooperation, and a positive approach to classroom management, Albert (1995) maintains that once teachers identify the cause of a misbehavior, they should try to influence a student's choice of behavior. One way to do that is through the use of encouragement. Albert believes that some discipline programs, such as control theories or zero-tolerance policies, fail to show teachers how to keep misbehavior from recurring and can even make behavior problems worse. Cooperative Discipline assumes that students will misbehave again unless teachers use encouragement techniques that build self-esteem and strengthen the student's motivation to cooperate and learn.

Neither time-consuming nor difficult to learn, encouragement strategies include the three C's: capable, connect, and contribute. According to Albert, students must feel **capable** of completing their work in a satisfactory manner. To assist students, teachers can create an environment in which students can make mistakes without fear of punishment or embarrassment; build confidence by focusing on improvement and on past successes; and make learning objectives reachable for all students. By accepting all students regardless of their behavior, listening to students, showing interest in their activities outside of school, showing appreciation, and using positive statements about a student's good behavior and abilities, teachers help students **connect** and develop positive relationships with teachers and classmates. Finally, teachers can help students learn how they can **contribute** to the welfare of the class and feel that they make a difference. Techniques to foster this sense of contribution include involving students in maintaining the classroom, holding class meetings, asking for suggestions when decisions need to be made, using cooperative learning groups, and encouraging peer tutoring (Albert, 1995).

Albert also cautions against the use of several teacher techniques that often backfire. She tells teachers not to raise their voices, yell, insist on having the last word, use sarcasm, attack a student's character, plead or bribe, back a student into a corner, use physical force, act superior, or bring up unrelated events (Albert, 1989).

One unique aspect of Albert's theories is that she suggests ways teachers can talk to parents to inspire parents' cooperation. In doing so, she encourages teachers to choose their words carefully and use objective language and nonjudgmental terms. In addition, teachers should keep complaints to a minimum by selecting examples of misbehavior rather than naming a student's every transgression. When a teacher is negative, parents may feel no obligation to cooperate with that teacher. Avoiding predictions of future failures, teachers should never make parents think their child is incorrigible or unable to succeed in school. Instead, teachers should present a specific plan and help parents understand that chances for success are good. Although it might be difficult, teachers should avoid taking parents' defensiveness personally and should ask parents to help with something that is possible rather than impossible (Albert, 1997). Management Tip 12–1 provides ways to encourage cooperation with parents.

Management Tip 12–1

Developing Parents' Cooperation

When you meet with a number of different parents, it may be difficult to remember what you said to each and what they said to you. Teachers should do the following:

Document conversations with parents or guardians.

Keep a notebook with a page for each family or each student.

Note if a student lives with more than one family during the year.

Use a form that includes

- Whom you talked to,
- How you talked to them—in person, telephone, e-mail, etc.,
- The date,
- A summary of the conversation,
- Agreed-upon actions to be taken.

Record the times you tried to contact the parent or guardian but were unsuccessful.

Record the date and the message that you left on an answering machine or with another person.

Keep all e-mail contacts with the parents or guardians.

Please go to *www.prenhall.com/manning* and click on the Management Tips for this chapter to complete management activities and find additional information on communications with parents.

Practical Application of Albert's Theories

Linda Albert's theories can be applied in many practical ways. For example, in her discussion of the four causes of misbehavior, she identifies ways to address each of them (Albert, 1995).

Attention
- Use eye contact to let the student know you are aware of his or her misbehavior.
- Move closer to the student while continuing to teach.
- Ask a direct question or use the student's name while continuing the lesson.
- Give specific praise to a nearby student who is on-task.

Power
- Avoid direct confrontation by agreeing with the student or changing the subject.
- Acknowledge the student's power and state your actions: "You're right, I can't make you finish the math problems, but I'll be collecting the assignment at the end of class" (Albert, 1995, p. 44).
- Change the activity, do something unexpected, or initiate another class discussion on a topic of interest.
- Use time-out by giving a choice: "You may sit quietly, keep your hands and feet to yourself, and complete the assignment, or you may go to time-out in Mr. Weber's room. You decide" (Albert, 1995, p. 44).

Revenge
- Revoke a privilege: "Rita, you will not be able to play on the swings today."
- Build a caring relationship and use affirmative statements to say "You're okay, but your choice of behavior is not" (Albert, 1995, p. 44).
- Require the return, repair, or replacement of damaged articles.
- Involve school personnel or parents if necessary.

Avoidance of Failure
- Acknowledge the difficulty of the assigned task, but remind the student of past successes.
- Modify instruction and materials.
- Teach the student to say "I can" instead of "I can't" by recognizing achievements.
- Provide peer tutors or ask the student to help someone else, perhaps a younger student, to build self-confidence.

Teachers also can apply Albert's ideas on the use of influence over control in the classroom. After you read the following examples, complete Activity 12–1.

Influence: Seeing Luchee, a third grader, talking to another student, Mr. Palmbo said, "Luchee, your talking is disturbing others. Please be considerate."
Control: Mr. Palmbo said, "Luchee, you're talking. Take a time-out."

Influence: When Ms. Alvett believed that Mark, a senior, cheated on an assignment, she talked to him privately and encouraged him to do his own work.
Control: Standing at the front of the room, Ms. Alvett announced to the class, "Someone didn't feel like completing the class poetry assignment so he copied another student's paper, didn't he, Mark?"

When fostering a climate for learning and teaching, educators use encouragement, intervention, and collaboration to influence students. They also can help students develop a **code of conduct** such as the one shown in Figure 12–1. Although the students are affected by

Activity 12-1

Providing Influence Rather Than Control

In each of the following situations, explain how a teacher might help a student behave by providing influence rather than control.

- Alysha, a ninth grader, smells like smoke right after a restroom break.
- Harry, a kindergartner, throws his crayons across the room.
- Carlos, a fifth grader, leans forward and raps Mike on the head with his ruler.
- When the teacher asks Louisa why she is crying, Louisa replies that Juan called her a "fat retard."

heredity, environment, and experiences, they can choose their behavior. Thus, they need to feel that they belong in the classroom and that they are important, worthwhile, and valued. How Would You React 12–1 asks you to consider Rashan, a misbehaving student.

Critique of Albert's Theories

All classroom management models or theories should take into account our schools' increasing diversity and should recognize that students might react differently to teachers' management techniques. Fortunately, the four goals of misbehavior originally posed by Dreikurs and now a focus of Albert's Cooperative Discipline apply equally to students of all cultures, backgrounds, and abilities. All students need encouragement (a mainstay of Albert's model), and all students need to feel they are capable, connected, and contributing to the school community.

Figure 12-1 Sample Code of Conduct

I am: Respectful—Responsible—Safe—Prepared.

I will not keep anyone from learning or teaching.

I will cooperate with others in the school community.

I will respect: Myself—Others—The environment.

Source: Developed from *http://campus.kcc.edu/faculty/dfyfee/albert.html.*

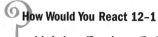

Helping Rashan Behave

Before reading the following scenario, review Albert's ideas on the causes of misbehaviors, sharing responsibility and providing influence. Then respond to the questions at the end.

> Rashan was a constant behavior problem. He was neither violent nor hurtful, but he wasted time and bothered others. He never refused to do classwork, but he rarely finished it. Instead, he talked to others and the teacher, walked around the room, went to the wastebasket, or sharpened his pencils. Although Rashan often said "I"ll get this done today—before school's out. I can do most of it," he rarely finished an assignment. Unfortunately, he also disturbed others so some of them did not finish either. His teacher wondered what to do.

1. Using Albert's and Dreikurs's ideas, identify the possible causes of Rashan's misbehavior.
2. What might Rashan's teacher do to address the specific cause or causes?
3. How could the teacher use influence rather than control to help Rashan?

Carolyn Evertson and Alene Harris: Managing Learning-Centered Classrooms

Biographical Sketch

Carolyn Evertson and Alene Harris have worked together on the Classroom Organization and Management Program (COMP), a management system developed by Evertson. Harris serves as the project coordinator and national trainer for COMP and is the program's codirector and national trainer (*www.comp.org/*). In addition, Evertson has written extensively on the social context of classrooms, and teacher education and professional development. Her books include *Classroom Management for Elementary Teachers* (with Edmund Emmer and M. E. Worsham, 2000), *Classroom Management for Middle and High School Teachers* (with Edmund Emmer and M. E. Worsham, 2000), *Student Characteristics and Teaching* (with Jere Brophy, 1981), and *Learning From Teaching* (with Jere Brophy, 1976).

Overview of Evertson's and Harris's Theories

Evertson's and Harris's COMP helps teachers develop a management framework and a supportive learning environment in which students learn to take responsibility for their decisions, actions, and learning (Evertson & Harris, 1992). Like Jacob Kounin (discussed in chapter 6), who focused on strategies such as withitness, overlapping, smoothness, and momentum, Evertson and Harris (1992) see management in broader terms than many classroom management theorists and focus on instructional as well as behavior management. They advocate learner-centered classrooms that support academic achievement and appropriate behavior.

Contributions of Evertson's and Harris's Theories

Evertson and Harris have made several contributions to the field of classroom management, including the focus on teachers' instructional behaviors, different interventions for different misbehaviors, and *advanced planning* or *preparation* for the first of the year. Like Kounin, they insist that teachers' behaviors influence students' behaviors. Teachers who are most effective with classroom management consider the effects of their own behaviors and understand the complex relationships between instructional management and classroom management.

In addition, according to Evertson and Harris, specific student misbehaviors call for different types of **interventions:** *minor* interventions, *moderate* interventions, and more *extensive* interventions. Thus, instead of having the same punishments for all misbehaviors, teachers must determine quickly the severity of the behavior offense and then determine the needed intervention.

Finally, Evertson and Harris believe that teachers should plan the beginning of the year carefully, so that students will know the rules and expectations on the first day. Teachers who choose to wait to see what the students are like often find it difficult to manage students. In addition, it can be hard to change behaviors after the first couple of days because students who find that certain behaviors are permissible at the beginning of school might be reluctant to change these behaviors later.

Practical Application of Evertson's and Harris's Theories

The following sections show the practicalities of Evertson's and Harris's ideas.

Specific Instructional Behaviors   Like Kounin, Evertson and Harris suggest specific behaviors that effective classroom managers demonstrate. First, good managers conserve instruction time by planning activities and tasks to fit the learning materials; by setting and conveying procedural and academic expectations; and by appropriately sequencing, pacing, monitoring, and providing feedback for student work (Evertson & Harris, 1992). Second, teachers should deal with student misbehavior promptly and consistently. Teachers who deal quickly with misbehavior prevent it from becoming more widespread (Evertson, Emmer, Sanford, & Clements, 1983). Third, teachers who are effective managers use group strategies and lesson formats with high levels of student involvement and low levels of misbehavior (Evertson & Harris, 1992).

Advance Preparation   One key to organizing and managing classrooms for effective instruction is **advance preparation** and planning from the first day of school (Evertson, 1989). To help students know classroom expectations from the beginning, teachers should arrange classroom space and supplies, plan and teach classroom rules and procedures, develop accountability measures for work and behavior, establish consequences and incentives, choose activities for the beginning of the year, and communicate their expectations clearly (Evertson, 1987). This management plan should be maintained throughout the school year, with teachers monitoring and providing feedback about student behavior and academic work, modeling and reinforcing appropriate behavior consistently, intervening to restore order when necessary, and managing special classroom groups while conducting instruction and maintaining momentum (Evertson, Emmer, & Worsham, 2000). When teachers are careful about advanced preparation and planning, there is improved student task engagement, less inappropriate behavior, a smoother transition between activities, and generally higher academic performance (Evertson, 1987; Evertson & Harris, 1992).

> Bret Curtis, a middle school teacher, made phone calls or scheduled meetings with students and parents during the first weeks of school to explain the school and district expectations for behavior.

> The week before school started, Brenda Hensby, an elementary school teacher, arranged the furniture in her classroom, put up new bulletin boards, and made sure she had the supplies she needed.

> On the first day of class, Charlene Orenduff, a high school teacher, posted the following rule and discussed what it meant with her class: "Any inappropriate behavior in this room will be dealt with quickly, fairly, and consistently."

Effective Communication   Effective classroom management also is based on effective communication between the teacher and the students. This includes letting students know how they can participate in class. Thus, during a lesson, a teacher not only presents information but also dictates to the students who can participate, as well as when and how (Evertson, 1987).

- "Remember to raise your hand if you know the answer."
- "I will only call on students to read if they are seated quietly with their book open to the proper page."
- "Since you all should have the answers to the homework problems, I will call on students at random. You do not need to raise your hands."

Addressing Undesirable Behaviors   Although a carefully planned classroom management system will not stop all misbehaviors, teachers usually can handle undesirable behaviors with minor intervention techniques such as using physical proximity, maintaining eye contact, reminding students of appropriate behavior, providing needed assistance, telling students to stop the behavior, and using an I-message. More serious misbehaviors require moderate interventions, such as withholding a privilege or desired activity, isolating or removing a student, using a penalty, or assigning detention. In extreme situations, more extensive interventions are necessary. These include the use of a five-step problem-solving procedure (shown in Figure 12–2), peer *mediation/conflict resolution,* a conference with the parents or guardian, or the development of an individual behavior contract with the student (Evertson, Emmer, & Worsham, 2000).

How Would You React 12–2 asks you to consider Ms. Ruiz and the misbehavior problems that result from "dead times" during transitions and class instruction.

Because punishment neither teaches desirable behavior nor instills a desire to behave, it is, perhaps, best used as part of a planned response to repeated behavior. Evertson and Harris believe this holds true for all discipline programs, even Teacher Effectiveness Training (discussed in chapter 2) and Assertive Discipline (discussed in chapter 3). These systems provide methods of dealing with threats to classroom order, according to Evertson and Harris, but they fail to address preventive and supportive functions for effective management and discipline (Evertson & Harris, 1992).

Critique of Evertson's and Harris's Theories

Evertson and Harris (1992, p. 59) maintain that "the need for effective classroom management burgeons" as schools deal with diverse populations of students with differing needs and modes of learning. Thus, their focus on learner-centered classrooms contributes to the well-being of all students and should not offend students' cultural backgrounds and other diversities. For example, all students will be influenced positively by teachers who use appropriate

Figure 12–2 A Five-Step Problem-Solving Procedure

To deal with a misbehavior, teachers should work through the following steps:

1. Use a nonverbal clue.
2. Ask the student to obey the rule.
3. Give the student the choice to obey the rule or develop a plan.
4. Move the student to another part of the room.
5. Send the student to another location to complete the plan.

Source: Developed from Evertson, C., Emmer, E. T., & Worsham, M. E. (2000). *Classroom management for elementary teachers* (5th ed.). Boston: Allyn and Bacon.

How Would You React 12-2

Eliminating Misbehaviors During "Dead Times"

Review Evertson's and Harris's ideas about the influence of instructional behaviors on classroom management and the need for advance preparation and effective communication. Then read the following scenario and respond to the questions at the end.

Danielle Ruiz, an elementary teacher, has taught for 3 years and continues to experience a problem: She allows her instruction to drift into "dead times." When she does, a few of the students in the class begin to act up. The longer the dead time lasts, the more students misbehave. Some of the dead times are intentional. ("The students need a break; my not doing anything for awhile gives them a little rest," she often says.) At other times, she just has too many things going on at once or she cannot find the instructional materials she needs. Either way, the situation results in the students having dead time, which in turn results in them misbehaving.

1. What is causing the misbehaviors in this classroom?

2. Is there really a need for dead time in a classroom? If not, what should Ms. Ruiz do to eliminate it?

3. If some dead time is desirable, what should Ms. Ruiz do to prevent misbehaviors during it?

instructional behaviors, base specific interventions on the severity of the misbehavior, and plan the beginning of the school year. Students, regardless of their diversities, should appreciate knowing the teacher's expectations for academic achievement and behavior. In addition, they should appreciate having a teacher who is committed to effective teaching behaviors.

David Johnson and Roger Johnson: Three C's of School and Classroom Management

Biographical Sketch

David W. Johnson and Roger T. Johnson have developed a management system known as the Three C's of School and Classroom Management. The author of more than 350 research articles and book chapters and more than 40 books (most coauthored with R. Johnson), David W. Johnson is a psychotherapist and has served as an organizational consultant to schools and businesses throughout the world, specializing in such areas as management training, team building, ethnic relations, conflict resolution, interpersonal and group skills training, and drug abuse prevention. Roger T. Johnson is an authority on inquiry teaching in science and has extensive public school experience, including teaching in kindergarten through eighth grade in self-contained classrooms, open schools, nongraded situations, cottage schools, and departmentalized schools (*www.clcrc.com/pages/rj.html*).

Overview of the Johnsons' Theories

As David W. Johnson and Roger T. Johnson (1987b) point out, educators in today's schools face the problems of student violence, damaged school property, and physical and psychological abuse. Johnson and Johnson believe that by focusing on the three C's of **cooperation**, **conflict resolution**, and **civic values**, educators can help make schools safer places for students and teachers. Cooperation, as the term implies, calls for cooperative efforts of students, teachers, administrators, and community members to work toward mutual goals. As part of cooperation, the Johnsons emphasize cooperative learning. If and when conflicts arise in cooperative communities, conflict resolution allows the participants to solve problems. This means that conflict resolution training is required for all members of the school community. When the school community shares common civic values that guide all decision making, cooperative communities can be established and can solve conflicts constructively (Johnson & Johnson, 1999).

Contributions of the Johnsons' Theories

Although the Johnsons do not focus on managing students through an array of rules, consequences, rewards, and punishments, they offer some excellent ideas that should lead to a safer learning environment and help students see a need to behave appropriately.

Noting that violent and aggressive behaviors often result in property damage as well as physical and psychological damage to students and teachers, the Johnsons, more than any other management theorists in this book, address these problems and the need for safe schools. Thus, they have proposed the three C's as a basis not only for classroom management but also to ensure safer schools and to provide environments that are conducive to learning. This expectation that students will adhere to civic values is reminiscent of Gathercoal's Judicious Discipline (discussed in chapter 11). Realistically, the Johnsons admit that no matter how hard teachers try to promote the three C's, conflict will arise occasionally. Therefore, they propose conflict resolution as a means to address problems.

As part of the emphasis on cooperation, the Johnsons advocate the use of **cooperative learning,** which they define as "the instructional use of small groups so that students work together to maximize their own and each other's learning" (Johnson & Johnson, 1999, p. 125). Believing that classroom management is "enhanced by keeping students engaged constructively in learning from the moment they enter the classroom until the time they leave" (p. 125), they agree that cooperative learning is one of the best methods of achieving this objective. Traditionally, the American school system has been based on competition, with students encouraged to compete for grades and teachers' time. Unfortunately, any competition results in winners and losers and also can lead to misbehavior and ill feelings. That is one reason the Johnsons propose cooperative learning as a way to help students learn to work together toward agreed upon goals (Johnson & Johnson, 1987b, 1999).

The Teaching Students to be Peacemakers Program (TSP Program) is part of the Johnsons' (Johnson & Johnson, 2004) conflict-resolution program. Training students to resolve conflicts and to make their schools safe places to learn, TSP exposes students to positive role models for constructive conflict management and teaches the procedures and skills required to manage conflicts constructively. According to Johnson and Johnson (2004), teachers should use a conflict-resolution program to help students from kindergarten though high school learn how to mediate conflicts. The goals are to

Build a positive school and classroom climate,

Help students and faculty have positive attitudes toward the resolution of conflicts,

Understand the importance of goals and relationships in conflict resolution,

Ensure that all students, regardless of cultural background, can use conflict resolution strategies,

Help students and educators practice the "negotiation and mediation procedures" (p. 69) until they can be applied automatically in a conflict,

"Create a schoolwide discipline program" that empowers students to control their own behaviors.

Practical Application of the Johnsons' Theories

Any examination of the practical applications of the Johnsons' theories must focus on the use of the three C's in the classroom.

The First C: Cooperation   The first of the three C's is *cooperation,* including cooperative learning. In addition to demonstrating cooperative attitudes and working cooperatively with others throughout the school day and throughout the school community, educators can emphasize cooperation by doing the following:

- Involving parents and community members in genuinely meaningful school activities
- Modeling cooperative attitudes in all interactions including those with students, parents, administrators, and other teachers
- Communicating effectively with all people involved in the education process
- Working to understand the positions and motivations of others and striving to clarify misperceptions
- Developing a sense of trust so students will respond to the requests and needs of others
- Perceiving conflicts as mutual problems so everyone eventually will benefit from their resolution (Johnson & Johnson, 1999)

Because cooperative learning is a major component of the first C, the Johnsons have developed the Learning Together cooperative learning method, which consists of five basic elements: positive interdependence (students believe they are responsible for their learning as well as their group's learning), face-to-face interaction (students explain their learning and help others with assignments), individual accountability (students demonstrate mastery of material), social skills (students communicate effectively, build and maintain trust, and resolve conflicts), and group processing (groups periodically assess their progress and how to improve effectiveness) (Johnson & Johnson, 1987, 1989/1990). In addition to laying the foundation for safe schools, cooperative learning provides other benefits, as shown in Figure 12–3.

The Johnsons also maintain that cooperative learning works with and contributes to the welfare of diverse students such as gifted students (Johnson & Johnson, 1993), learning disabled students (Putnam, Markovchick, Johnson & Johnson, 1996), mentally disabled students (Johnson & Johnson, 1989), and students from culturally pluralistic backgrounds (Johnson & Johnson, 1989, 1999). How Would You React 12–3 asks you to consider Ms. Beeber's opinions about cooperative learning. Then, Management Tip 12–2 focuses on cooperative learning and how to make it most useful.

The Second C: Conflict Resolution   The Johnsons have worked on programs for understanding violence (Johnson & Johnson, 1995a) and for conflict resolution (Johnson & Johnson, 1995b). Although most schools have established violence-prevention programs to deal with the increasing level of violence among students, the Johnsons believe that many of these programs do not result in long-term changes in violent behavior. In order to be effective, programs must go beyond violence prevention and must include conflict-resolution training. This does not mean the elimination of all conflicts. In fact, some conflicts can have positive outcomes, and academic controversy can increase learning.

Figure 12–3 Benefits of Cooperative Learning

Cooperative learning

Ensures that all students are meaningful and actively involved in learning,

Ensures that students achieve up to their potential and experience psychological success so they are motivated to continue,

Promotes caring and committed relationships for every student,

Provides an arena in which students develop the interdependence and small-group skills needed to work effectively with diverse peers,

Provides students with opportunities to work together to discuss and possibly solve personal problems,

Provides an arena for students in which they can feel a sense of meaning, pride, and esteem by helping and assisting each other; contributes to cooperation among educators working in the school.

Source: Developed from Johnson, D., & Johnson, R. (1999). The three C's of school and classroom management. In H. Jerome Freiberg (ed.), *Beyond behaviorism: Changing the classroom management paradigm* (pp. 119–144). Boston: Allyn and Bacon.

Doubting the Use of Cooperative Learning

Review the benefits of cooperative learning groups and the Johnsons' ideas about the use of groups with diverse learners. Then read the following scenario and respond to the questions at the end.

As a preservice teacher, Sandi Beeber was not sure about the effectiveness of using cooperative learning with diverse students. "Ok, I know it works with regular students, those who are on working on grade level. But I'm not sure about more diverse students. What about learning disabled students? Just how much can they contribute to or get out of a group? And gifted students like to compete. Cooperative learning takes away half of their fun! And it probably slows them down, too. Then there are those students who like to goof off. With a cooperative learning group, they'll just wait for someone else to do the work. Nope, I don't see how cooperative learning helps diverse classes of students and I don't see how it helps classroom management."

1. Using the ideas of the Johnsons, respond to each of Sandi Beeber's concerns.
2. Can cooperative learning groups work with a diverse population of students?
3. What accommodations might she have to make?

"I know I'll get a better grade on the science test than you will," Dwayne said to his friend Omar.

"Class, I seem to hear different opinions about whether the treaty was fair. Let's debate the issue."

However, educators need to work to create a cooperative context in which the entire school becomes a learning community with a decrease in school at-risk factors (Johnson & Johnson, 1995a).

"Letha, I see you've finished your homework. Will you help me by going over the problems with Rebecca?"

Teachers can model the use of conflict resolution to solve problems and diffuse potential violence. The following example, developed from Johnson and Johnson (1999), illustrates the six steps of conflict resolution, which are discussed in more detail in chapter 13 of this book.

When Chip McFarland, a teacher, found Angelo and Darold arguing in the hall, he was afraid they would resort to violence. Drawing on his conflict resolution training, he acted as follows:

"Angelo and Darold, come with me to the library seminar room and let's explore what's happening. This is a shared problem and I want you to take turns explaining the situation to me" (describe what you want, using good communication skills and defining the conflict as a specific mutual problem). "I expect you both to be honest (communicate and describe your feelings openly and clearly) and to listen to what the other person is saying" (describe the reasons for your wants and feelings, while expressing cooperative intentions and listening carefully). "Remember, I'll expect you to summarize the problem from each other's perspective" (take the person's perspective and summarize your understanding of what he or she wants, how the other person feels, and the reasons underlying both). "After that, we'll come up with at least three ways to solve this problem" (invent three optional plans to resolve the conflict that maximize joint benefits). "I know you'll choose the right solution for both of you" (choose one and formalize the agreement with a handshake).

The Third C: Civic Values   Johnson and Johnson (1987b, 1999) maintain that to create a community, its members must share common goals and values that help define appropriate behavior. A community cannot exist if its members have a variety of different value systems, believe only in their own self-interests, or have no values at all.

One school adopted caring, respect, and responsibility as its core values, which were translated into the civic values of integrity, courage, compassion, commitment, appreciation of diversity, and responsibility. The civic values were posted on the walls of all classrooms, reflected in the literature used by the teachers, and discussed in class meetings (Johnson & Johnson, 1987b).

Although the Johnsons think civic values ideally should apply to the entire school, they can be used in individual classrooms. Activity 12–2 asks you to consider the civic values that you want in your classroom.

Critique of the Johnsons' Theories

The Johnsons' Three C's theory and their cooperative learning ideas reflect an appreciation for the diversity found in schools. In fact, Johnson and Johnson have written about cooperative learning and culturally pluralistic schools and their belief that pluralism and diversity create opportunities that can have positive or negative outcomes, depending largely on whether learning situations are structured competitively, individualistically, or cooperatively (Johnson & Johnson, 1989). Students of diverse cultures should not be offended when teachers emphasize cooperation. In addition, conflict resolution has an objective, step-by-step approach that treats all students fairly. With cooperation and conflict resolution, students should believe that their teacher works in their best interest. Likewise, the emphasis on civic values (e.g., caring, respect, and responsibility) (Johnson & Johnson, 1987b) should not cause distress to any students.

Management Tip 12–2

Using Cooperative Groups

There are number of different strategies that teachers can use to establish cooperative learning groups. In most classrooms, it is ideal to vary the composition of the groups so that everyone has an opportunity to work with everyone else in the class.

- Randomly pass out to the class one of the following:
  Colored craft sticks
  Colored 3 × 5 cards
  Playing cards
- Use a group chart with student names at the top and side. Whenever two students work together, put a small check in the appropriate box. Allow two students to work with each other only a set number of times each grading period. The checks in the boxes do the record keeping.

Elementary
Buy sets of animal stickers and use them on 3 × 5 cards.

Secondary

Cut an illustration in sections. The people who have matching pieces are in one group.

Have students fill out information cards; then shuffle these each time you need cooperative groups.

Please go to *www.prenhall.com/manning* and click on the Management Tips for this chapter to complete management activities and find additional information on cooperative learning groups.

Jane Nelsen, Lynn Lott, and Stephen Glenn: Positive Discipline

Biographical Sketch

Jane Nelsen, Lynn Lott, and Stephen Glenn coauthored *Positive Discipline in the Classroom* (1997). Nelson is an education specialist, and she and Lott are therapists in marriage, family, and child counseling. A diplomate in Adlerian psychology, Lott has appeared on television shows including the *Phil Donahue Show, The Home Show,* and the *Today Show* (*www.positivediscipline.com/Lynn_Lott/index.html*).

Glenn has worked in education, human services, juvenile justice, and family psychology. A consultant on training, education, alcoholism, and drug abuse, he has been honored by the White House as one of the nation's most outstanding family life and prevention professionals (*www.lecturemanagement.com/profiles/glen_stephen.html*).

Overview of Nelsen's, Lott's, and Glenn's Theories

Nelsen, Lott, and Glenn (1997) envision schools where young people are treated with respect, will not be humiliated when they fail, and will have the opportunity to learn in a safe

Activity 12–2

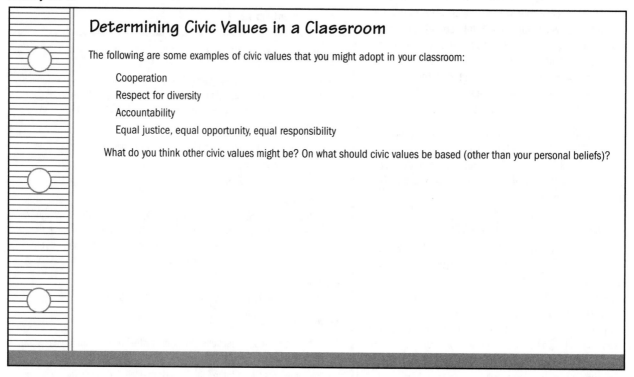

Determining Civic Values in a Classroom

The following are some examples of civic values that you might adopt in your classroom:

    Cooperation
    Respect for diversity
    Accountability
    Equal justice, equal opportunity, equal responsibility

What do you think other civic values might be? On what should civic values be based (other than your personal beliefs)?

environment, with a focus on cooperation rather than competition. In these schools, teachers will provide an environment that inspires excitement about life and learning, because fear and feelings of inadequacy and discouragement are not part of the learning environment. A sense of mutual respect becomes the norm. These dream schools nurture self-esteem, mutual respect, and academic performance and give students the skills and attitudes that will help them be happy, contributing members of society. Influenced by Rudolf Dreikurs (discussed in chapter 4) and his four goals of misbehavior, Nelsen, Lott, and Glenn place considerable priority on understanding why students behave as they do and suggest that any form of punishment or permissiveness is disrespectful and discouraging and should be avoided.

Contributions of Nelsen's, Lott's, and Glenn's Theories

Nelsen, Lott, and Glenn (1997) offer several contributions to classroom management. One is their belief that teachers should emphasize caring, mutual respect, encouragement, and order in today's classrooms. Explaining **barriers** (disrespectful and discouraging behaviors) and **builders** (respectful and encouraging behaviors), they go beyond academics and encourage teachers to teach the skills that students will need for successful lives in schools and in society.

Like Johnson and Johnson, Nelson, Lott, and Glenn recognize the harmful effects of vandalism and violence and maintain that class meetings can lessen these problems. Their eight building blocks of **class meetings** can contribute to effective class meetings and help in a variety of classroom management situations (e.g., understanding reasons for misbehavior, developing communication skills, practicing role playing, and focusing on non-punitive solutions).

Practical Application of Nelsen's, Lott's, and Glenn's Theories

Nelson, Lott, and Glenn have a number of ideas on positive discipline, but due to limited space, we can explain only three of them.

The Significant Seven   Nelsen, Lott, and Glenn (1997) identify the **Significant Seven,** those three **empowering perceptions** and four **essential skills** that all teachers should convey upon students. They explain the perceptions and skills as follows:

Three Empowering Perceptions

1. *Perceptions of personal capabilities:* Teachers create a safe climate where students can experiment with learning and behavior without judgments about success or failure.

"Alisha, I know you can do this problem."

2. *Perceptions of significance in primary relationships:* Teachers listen to the feelings, thoughts, and ideas of students and take them seriously.

"Kraig, you contributed some great ideas to our discussion today."

3. *Perceptions of the personal power of influence in life:* Teachers give students the opportunity to contribute in useful ways and help them accept their power to create positive and negative environments.

"Akemi, would you be the leader for the group that is decorating our classroom for parent visitation night?"

Four Essential Skills

1. *Intrapersonal skills:* Students have opportunities to gain understanding of their emotions and behaviors by hearing feedback from their classmates. They learn to be accountable for their actions and the results of their behavior.

"I was upset when Cam went on and on about how bad my hair looks today. I thought he was my friend!"

2. *Interpersonal skills:* Students can develop interpersonal skills through dialogue and sharing, listening and empathizing, cooperation, negotiation, and conflict resolution.

"Jamila, I know how it feels when you try so hard and don't get an A. That happened to me on the last test."

3. *Systemic skills:* Students respond to the limits and consequences of everyday life with responsibility, adaptability, flexibility, and integrity because they do not experience punishment or disapproval.

"I'm sorry, Mr. Nazif. I bumped Carmen's desk by mistake. I'll pick up her things."

4. *Judgment skills:* Students develop judgment skills when they have opportunities and encouragement to practice making decisions in an environment that emphasizes learning from mistakes rather than "paying" for mistakes through punishment (Nelsen, Lott, & Glenn, 1997, p. 9).

"I guess it would have been better, Ms. Talbott, to start over with the volcano project than try to repair the old one. But at least you let us try."

Barriers and Builders   Although respect and encouragement are two basic ingredients for building positive relationships, Nelsen, Lott, and Glenn (1997) maintain that educators often create barriers to their use. They identified five barriers that teachers use with students that show disrespect and discouragement and five builders that show respect and encouragement. Instead of assuming they know what students think and feel without asking them (Barrier 1: Assuming), educators should check with students (Builder 1: Checking) to learn their unique perceptions and capabilities and to discover how students are maturing in their ability to deal with problems and issues.

Rather than doing things for students (Barrier 2: Rescuing/Explaining), educators should allow them to learn from their own experiences (Builder 2: Exploring) and to help each other learn to make choices. Teachers often direct students to do things in disrespectful ways (Barrier 3: Directing) that reinforce dependency, eliminate initiative and cooperation, and encourage passive-aggressive behavior. As an alternative, educators should allow students to be involved in the planning and problem-solving activities that help them become self-directed (Builder 3: Inviting/Encouraging).

Sometimes, when teachers expect students to do certain things (Barrier 4: Expecting), the potential becomes the standard, and students are judged for falling short. If educators demand too much too soon, they can discourage students. Nelson, Lott, and Glenn encourage teachers to celebrate the direction of a student's maturity or potential (Builder 4: Celebrating).

Finally, "adultisms" (p. 24) (Barrier 5: Adultisms) occur when educators forget that students are not mature adults and expect them to act and think like adults. Instead, educators should interact with students to understand the differences in how people perceive things (Builder 5: Respecting). Such respect also contributes to a climate of acceptance that encourages growth and effective communication (Nelsen, Lott, & Glenn, 1997). Activity 12–3 presents some situations and asks whether each is a barrier or a builder.

Activity 12–3

Identifying Barriers and Builders

For each of the following, identify whether the situation describes a barrier or a builder. Turn each barrier into a builder.

1. "Gabriel, what suggestions do you have for hanging the mobiles in the classroom?"
2. "Well, Victor, you're never going to get the grades that your brother did."
3. "Joan, let me do that. It's too difficult for you to do. You're just in seventh grade."
4. "Fiona, you have experience overcoming a problem like that. Can you help Deshawn?"
5. "Melissa, clean out your desk now! It's a mess."
6. "I expected more mature behavior from you, Aalise. When are you going to grow up?"
7. "Roy, can you think of a way to arrange your locker so that you can find the things you need for class?

The Eight Building Blocks of Class Meetings

Nelsen, Lott, and Glenn (1997, p. 3) explained the "incredible benefits of class meetings for teachers and students," including involving students in their education, teaching them to think for themselves, and eliminating most problems with students who act out. Because space will not allow a detailed discussion of class meetings, Management Tip 12–3 provides Nelsen's, Lott's, and Glenn's eight building blocks for effective class meetings.

Even elementary students can use class meetings to clarify rules, resolve interpersonal conflicts, engage in collective problem solving, and create a peaceful atmosphere in the classroom (Angell, 2004). How Would You React 12–4 asks you to consider a teacher's skepticism about class meetings.

Critique of Nelsen's, Lott's, and Glenn's Theories

Although Nelsen, Lott, and Glenn do not focus extensively on diversity, the tenets of Positive Discipline demonstrate respect for diversity in their emphasis on respecting others, conveying mutual respect, and encouraging students to become productive in and out of the classroom. Students should appreciate the "positiveness" of the program, with teachers conveying acceptance, dignity, and encouragement because they truly care about students. In addition, the use of class meetings accentuates the emphasis on mutual respect and confidence in students.

Alfie Kohn: Beyond Discipline

Biographical Sketch

An educator and widely respected speaker on human behavior and social theory, Alfie Kohn has appeared on *Donahue*, National Public Radio, the *Today Show,* and more than 200 other television and radio programs. Since his book *No Contest: The Case Against Competition* (1986)

Management Tip 12-3

Holding Effective Class Meetings

According to Nelsen, Lott, and Glenn, teachers should use the following ideas for planning and conducting a class meeting:

- Form a circle.
- Practice compliments and appreciations.
- Create an agenda.
- Develop communication skills.
- Learn about separate realities (there is more than one way; it does not have to be "my" [p. 64] way).
- Recognize the four reasons people do what they do (remember Dreikurs's four mistaken goals of misbehavior).
- Practice role-playing and brainstorming.
- Focus on nonpunitive solutions.

Source: Developed from Nelsen, J., Lott, L., & Glenn, H. S. (1997). *Positive discipline in the classroom.* Rocklin, CA: Prima.

Please go to *www.prenhall.com/manning* and click on the Management Tips for this chapter to complete management activities and find additional information on class meetings.

How Would You React 12-4

Planning for Class Meetings

Kelli Selby decided that she would hold class meetings this year. However, she knew that good class meetings do not just happen. She knew that her class would include students with a wide range of abilities—perhaps gifted students, perhaps some who had learning disabilities. What she was unsure about was how to begin the process.

Review the ideas of Nelsen, Lott, and Glenn about effective class meetings. You might also want to look at what Forrest Gathercoal (discussed in chapter 11) said about class meetings. Then, list three suggestions you would give Ms. Selby in planning her first class meeting. Meet with a group of other students in your class who hope to teach on the same level as you do. As a group, develop a list of suggestions for planning class meetings and develop an agenda for the first three meetings.

received the American Psychological Association's Award for Excellence in the Media, Kohn has become a leading critic of competition in schools. His latest books include *What Does It Mean to Be Well Educated: And More Essays on Standards, Grading, and Other Follies* (2004b).

Overview of Kohn's Theories

Rather than advancing a model or a well-defined theory of classroom management, Alfie Kohn challenges some commonly accepted beliefs about students and discipline and encourages educators to move beyond traditional concepts of classroom management. Although behavior modification approaches may force students to behave in a particular way, they do not promote "a dedication to, or an understanding of, that behavior" (Kohn, 2004a, p. 185). Even the **New Disciplines** such as Canter's and Canter's Assertive Discipline, Driekurs's Democratic Teaching, Curwin's and Mendler's Discipline with Dignity, and Kounin's Instructional Management do not represent a real departure from the theories and models they claim to replace. To Kohn, most are driven by a negative set of beliefs in which it is difficult to distinguish the so-called logical consequences from the old-fashioned punishments. He sees disciplinary techniques such as rewards, bribes, threats, coercion, and punishment as instruments for controlling people. Instead, he maintains that educators need to move beyond rules to a point where they ask what children need, how those needs can be met (Kohn, 1996a), and how educators can help students decide for themselves how best to behave. His ideas of "deep modeling (Kohn, 2004a, p. 186) encourage teachers to help children see what is behind or beneath ethical decisions.

Contributions of Kohn's Theories

Kohn does not provide a well-defined model of classroom management. Rather, he focuses on four areas: a criticism of the New Disciplines, ideas about the nature of students, suggested alternatives to punishments and rewards, and ideas on community. Looking at the *New Disciplines,* he maintains that they "suggest a subtler, somewhat nicer way by which we can continue to do things *to* (Kohn's italics) children—as distinct from working *with* (Kohn's italics) them in a democratic environment to promote their social and moral development" (Kohn, 1996a, p. 38). You may remember reading some of his specific comments in chapter 2 of this book.

Examining the nature of students, Kohn (1996a) maintains that people usually consider only the dark side of students' human nature. However, these cynical feelings about competitive, lazy, and aggressive students are not real. Rather than being selfish and self-centered, students are decent, able to feel the pain of others, and prepared to relieve that pain. Drawing on the work of Deci and Ryan (1990), Kohn (1996a) believes that educators must provide for three universal human needs: autonomy, relatedness, and competence. Students who are autonomous have self-determination or the ability to make decisions rather than being the victim of things outside of their control. When they are related, students have a connection to others and a sense of affirmation and belonging. Finally, students want to be competent, to learn new things, to acquire skills, and to put them to use. Activity 12–4 asks you to consider additional needs of students.

Kohn believes that "schools will not become inviting, productive places for learning until we have dispensed with bribes and threats altogether" (Kohn, 1996a, p. 36). Making students suffer in order to alter their future behavior might result in temporary compliance, but this approach probably will not help students become ethical and compassionate decision makers. Rather than promoting reason, punishment damages relationships between teachers and students and tends to generate anger, defiance, and a desire for revenge. In an

Activity 12-4

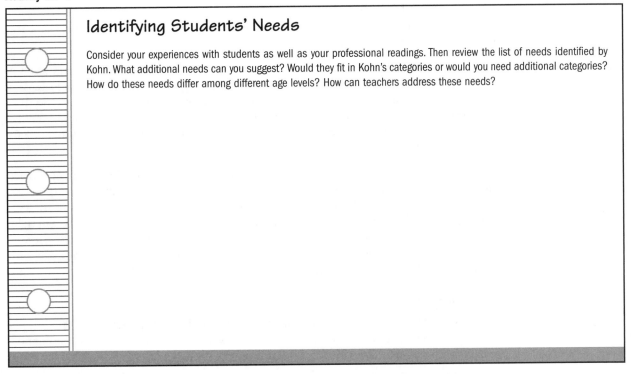

Identifying Students' Needs

Consider your experiences with students as well as your professional readings. Then review the list of needs identified by Kohn. What additional needs can you suggest? Would they fit in Kohn's categories or would you need additional categories? How do these needs differ among different age levels? How can teachers address these needs?

interview (Brandt, 1995), Kohn reported that although some people call punishments "consequences" and even add the word logical, the results remain the same. Logical consequences are only a kinder way of doing things to children rather than working with them.

Many teachers who see the harmful effects of punishing students turn to using rewards. However, Kohn claims that "manipulating student behavior with either punishment or rewards is not only unnecessary but counterproductive" (Kohn, 1993, p. 783). Rewards (e.g., A's, awards, stars, stickers, praise, and privileges) and their use elicit only temporary compliance in many cases (Kohn, 1994). Not only are extrinsic rewards ineffective at producing lasting change in attitudes or behaviors (Kohn, 1993), they fail to help children become caring, responsible people or lifelong, self-directed learners (Kohn, 1994).

Kohn links his focus on learning and the classroom environment to an emphasis on positive behaviors and believes in learner-centered classrooms in which the climate or environment is "often guided by a certain set of values, a vision of what school *ought* (Kohn's italics) to be like" (Kohn, 1996b, p. 54). In these rooms, teachers work collaboratively with students, encourage students to make decisions, and use student interests and questions to drive much of the curriculum. Promoting deep understanding, teachers should build on students' natural curiosity and desire to become competent and should help students become proficient learners (Kohn, 1997, September 3). To produce not only good students but good people, teachers need to focus on promoting positive behaviors rather than on curbing negative ones as a way to eliminate troublesome or even violent conduct (Kohn, 1997, September 3).

Kohn (1996a; 1997, September 3), a leading critic of competition in schools, argues that it is inherently destructive for students to compete for grades or for good behavior rewards. In fact, competition means someone has to lose or fail in order that others can win. Thus, teachers should not expect students to compete with each other to see which ones or which groups demonstrate the best behavior; neither should discipline become a competition or contest between the teacher and the students.

Instead of competition, Kohn emphasizes **communities,** but he also recognizes the difficulty with defining the term.

> In saying that a classroom or school is a "community," then, I mean that it is a place in which students feel cared about and are encouraged to care about each other. They experience a sense of being valued and respected; the children matter to one another and to the teacher. They have come to think in the plural: They feel connected to one another; they are part of an "us." And, as a result of all this, they feel safe in their classes, not only physically but emotionally. (Kohn, 1996a, p. 101–102).

Kohn bases much of his writing on "community" on the Child Development Project, based in Oakland, California, which has profoundly influenced his thinking about schools. In this project, he concluded that the stronger the community feeling is, the more students reported liking school and the more they saw learning as something valuable in its own right. These students also tended to be more concerned about others and more skilled at resolving conflict than those who did not feel like part of a community. In addition, he concluded that the positive effects were particularly pronounced in schools with low-income students.

Practical Application of Kohn's Theories

Although he does not focus on practical applications, Kohn does present many philosophical issues for educators to resolve. First, Kohn (1996a, p. 2) proposed several "profoundly negative theories" that teachers need to face.

> "If the teacher isn't in control of the classroom, the most likely result is chaos" (Kohn, 1996a, p. 2).

> "Children need to be told exactly what the adult expects of them, as well as what will happen if they don't do what they're told" (Kohn, 1996a, p. 2).

Both of these assumptions are staples of the classroom management field. To Kohn, teachers who agree with them believe that disaster will occur if students are not given precise instructions on how to behave. They imply that requests and explanations never suffice and that reasonable expectations will not be honored without threats of punishment.

> "At the heart of all moral education is the need to help people control their impulses" (Kohn, 1996a, p. 2).

> "You need to give positive reinforcement to a child who does something nice if you want him to keep acting that way" Kohn, 1996a, p. 3).

This common defense of praise seems to imply that the only reason a student would ever demonstrate kindness is to be rewarded with an adult's approval. If qualities like generosity must be propped up by verbal rewards, they must be unnatural, which suggests that students who are left on their own are only concerned about themselves (Kohn, 1996a).

In addition to questioning rewards, Kohn opposes rules for behavior. Instead, he believes that students should be given the freedom and responsibility to move beyond rules to a point where they can decide appropriate behavior for themselves. Kohn maintains that teachers who rely on rules turn children into lawyers who scan for loopholes and narrow the discussion to technicalities when a problem occurs. These teachers also become police officers— a role that is at odds with being facilitators of learning. Finally, rules usually include a punitive consequence for breaking them, something that Kohn does not support (Kohn, 1996a). How Would You React 12–5 considers this issue of rules.

⌖ **How Would You React 12-5**

Eliminating Rules

In contrast to many other theorists mentioned in this book, Kohn is not in favor of rules for behavior. He also does not favor rewards for behavior. Make a list of the theorists that you have studied in this book. Which favor rewards? Which favor rules? Then, read the following scenario and respond to the questions at the end.

Phillip Naylor was a high school student teacher. In a discussion at a weekly seminar, he said, "Kohn's opinions on rules might make sense for early childhood students, but they certainly do not apply to the high school where I teach. Listen, these students are tough with a capital T—they argue, threaten

others, and fight. What will happen if I tell them the class does not have or need rules? What we need are strict and specific rules—ones we can enforce."

1. React to Mr. Naylor's comments.
2. How do you feel about Kohn's beliefs about rules?
3. How do you feel about his beliefs about rewards and punishments? Do you believe that they would be effective in classrooms today?

For another perspective, try reading Brant's (1995) book *Punished by Rewards: A Conversation With Alfie Kohn.*

Kohn (1995) told of times when things in his classroom did not go well. Reflecting on those times, he now realizes that the problem was not with the students. Instead, the problem was with his curriculum, textbooks, worksheets, and diet of disconnected facts and skills. Unfortunately, most discipline plans offer an array of techniques to manipulate student behavior. Many educators find these strategies convenient and take for granted that the fault lies solely with the student. Kohn, on the other hand, believes that when students misbehave, a teacher should focus not only on the students, but also on what they are being asked to do. Also, when a student is off-task, the teacher should ask "What is the task" instead of "How do I get this student back on task?" Threats and bribes might produce a short-term change in behavior, but they cannot help students develop a commitment to positive values.

In examining contemporary problems, Kohn (1999) recognizes the violence facing schools today and places most of the blame on structural problems related to secondary education. He believes that instead of taking more constructive approaches, educators try to curb violence by telling students what to wear, subjecting them to drug tests, and announcing zero-tolerance policies. When punishment proves ineffective, then it is wrongly assumed that the answer is more punishment.

Critique of Kohn's Theories

Kohn's Beyond Discipline respects diversity. All cultures, all social classes, and both genders should appreciate caring teachers who have a positive view of children. In addition, Kohn's ideas do not require punishment, threats, bribes, rules, and other forms of compliance. Undue attention will not be given to individual students and their misbehaviors. Also, Kohn's emphasis on the three universal human needs (autonomy, relatedness, and competence) of all individuals should help students succeed. Kohn expects teachers to have a desire to develop caring, compassionate, and ethical students, regardless of their specific differences.

Considering the Five Theories

Now that you have examined these five additional classroom management theories, you can begin to integrate some of their ideas into your personal philosophy by completing the activity in Developing Your Personal Philosophy.

You can learn more about each of the theorists discussed in this chapter by consulting the Internet sources identified in "Reaching Out with Technology" on this book's Companion Web

Developing Your Personal Philosophy

> ### Considering Additional Theorists
>
> Just as you did in chapter 2, make a chart by listing each theory on the left. Across the page, make three additional columns. In each of the columns, list a phrase to stand for one of the following questions:
>
> - *Similarities:* What beliefs of this theorist are similar to the beliefs of the other foundational theorists?
> - *Differences:* What beliefs of this theorist are different from the beliefs of the other foundational theorists?
> - *Appeal:* What beliefs of this theorist appeal to me?
>
> Next, review the theories in this chapter and complete the chart.

Site. After looking at a few of these sites, consider the problem identified in the Case Study and explain how the work of these contemporary theorists can be used to help teachers.

CONCLUDING REMARKS

Please go to *www.prenhall.com/manning* and click on Concluding Remarks for this chapter to find more information.

Although more contemporary classroom management theorists exist than can be included in this chapter, those presented are making valuable contributions to the classroom management field. You have read about Albert's idea that teachers should insist on students accepting responsibility for their own behavior; Evertson's and Harris's theory that management includes classroom management and instructional management; the Johnsons' proposal of the three C's, as well as their work on safe schools; Nelsen's, Lott's, and Glenn's emphasis on the positive and caring; and Kohn's call to move beyond discipline. Now, the challenge is for you to decide whether to implement one of these theories singularly, coupled with one of the other contemporary theories, or with one of the models discussed in chapters 2 through 11.

Suggested Readings

Albert, L. (1995). Discipline: Is it a dirty word? *Learning 24*(2), 43–46. Albert discusses strategies for the four goals of misbehavior, ways to encourage students, and ways to address the three C's: capable, connect, and contribute.

Albert, L. (1997). Solutions to four behavior nightmares. *Instructor, 107*(1), 59–61. Albert identifies why students misbehave and suggests appropriate behavior management strategies.

Buchs, C., Butera, F., Mugny, G., Darnon, C. (2004). Conflict elaboration and cognitive outcomes. *Theory into Practice, 43*(1), 23–30. The authors discuss the work of the Johnsons in cooperation and conflict resolution.

Evertson, C., Emmer, E. T., & Worsham, M. E. (2000). *Classroom management for elementary teachers* (5th ed.). Boston: Allyn & Bacon. Evertson and her colleagues provide an excellent discussion of how to address minor interventions, moderate interventions, and more extensive interventions.

CASE STUDY
A Need to "Calm" and "Tame" the Students

Cassandra Bracken, a consultant, was asked to visit Park Place Middle School to look for ways "to calm the students, to tame them down a little"—to use the superintendent's exact words. The school did not have the serious problems of students' bringing guns or knives to school, but too much rowdy behavior was occurring. Students were noisy, rude to each other, and, generally speaking, lived in an atmosphere of hostility. After Dr. Bracken heard the administrators' concerns, she decided to talk with some teachers and students.

Ms. Stancill, an eighth-grade teacher, remarked, "I've about had my fill of this. Not only don't these students listen to me, they don't respect me, other students, or themselves. I don't even think some of them know how to behave."

Ms. Zeichner, a sixth-grade teacher, agreed to some extent that the students lacked proper behavior, but she did not think the situation was as serious as Ms. Stancill did. "True, they're bad, but aren't most middle schoolers just a bundle of hormones and emotions?" she asked.

Ms. Omerto, the library media specialist, voiced her comments. "I think the school administration has made the situation worse. The situation was bad to begin with, but the administration has kept adding on more and more rules. Now, I can't even keep up with all the regulations, and the students are worse than ever."

Dr. Bracken also interviewed some students who were more than willing to share their opinions. "We're not too bad; it could be a lot worse," remarked Gema. "We like to joke each other, but most of us like it. Yeah, those Goths and Nerds might not like it, but they want to be left alone anyway. That's fine with me." Although some peer pressure might have been occurring, most of the students seemed to concur. One student, however, spoke out. "If you won't use names, I want to say something." When Dr. Bracken agreed to anonymity, the student said, "They run this place like a prison—too many rules; they treat us like babies. Now there's 'zero tolerance' for this and for that. I feel that if I crack a joke someone will take it the wrong way and I'll be expelled. This school never was much fun—now, it's not fun at all. I'm just waiting to get out of here."

That night in her hotel room, Dr. Bracken started jotting down some ideas for her report. Although she knew that she would need time to think about the situation, she wanted to have a positive impact in her remarks to the faculty the next day. Specifically, she wanted to call attention to some of the contemporary classroom management theories and let the faculty know that models have been created to address some of the problems at Park Place.

Questions to Consider

Consider what you know about the contemporary theorists covered in this chapter.

1. How can their ideas be used to help "calm down and tame the students"?

2. Can the school administrators loosen their rules, eliminate zero-tolerance policies, and convince students to accept responsibility for their own behaviors?

3. How can Dr. Bracken help the teachers examine their own teaching behaviors to determine whether their behaviors contribute to student problems?

4. Is it possible to develop cooperation, a sense of community, and an acceptance of civic values at a school such as Park Place?

5. Will positive discipline and a climate of respect, encouragement, and dignity solve the problems that the educators at Park Place are experiencing?

6. Think about all the models and theorists in this book. What should Dr. Bracken suggest?

 You can record your answers to these questions online on this book's Companion Web Site at *www.prenhall.com/manning*.

Johnson, D. W., & Johnson, R. T. (2004). Implementing the "Teaching Students to be Peacemakers Program." *Theory into Practice, 43*(1), 68–79. The Johnsons describe in considerable detail the procedures of the "Teaching Students to be Peacemakers Program."

Johnson, D., & McLeod, S. (2004/2005). Get answers: Using student response systems to see students' thinking. *Learning and Leading with Technology, 32*(4), 18–23. These authors explain student response systems that enable teachers to conduct ongoing formative assessments—systems that allow teachers to ask questions, receive student answers, and display the results electronically.

Kohn, A. (1996). *Beyond discipline: From compliance to community.* Alexandria, VA: Association for Supervision and Curriculum Development. Kohn explains his problems with behaviorism and the New Disciplines and proposes how educators can move from compliance to a sense of community.

Kohn, A. (1999). Constant frustration and occasional violence: The legacy of American high schools. *American School Board Journal, 186*(9), 20–24. Kohn looks at the problem of violence in secondary schools and explains the structural causes of problems.

Kohn, A. (2004). Safety from the inside out: Rethinking traditional approaches. *Educational Horizons, 83*(1), 33–41. Kohn maintains educators look at the wrong aspects (e.g., technical fixes and skills) of school safety and suggests we should rethink several traditional approaches about school safety.

Nelsen, J., Lott, L., & Glenn, H. S. (1997). *Positive discipline in the classroom.* Rocklin, CA: Prima. Nelsen, Lott, and Glenn provide a clear explanation of positive discipline in this book, which we highly recommend.

PART 3

Toward a Personal Classroom Management Plan

Part III includes chapters 13, 14, and 15. Chapter 13, "Creating Safe Classrooms and Safe Schools," focuses on aggression, violence, bullying, and the various classroom prevention and intervention efforts. Educators should find this chapter interesting because schools need to be psychologically and physically safe for both students and educators. Students should not fear attending school, and teachers should be able to teach in a safe, caring environment that is conducive to academic achievement.

Chapter 14 asks readers to develop their own personal classroom management philosophy. Then, chapter 15 deals with taking one's personal philosophical beliefs and moving to practical application. Readers now have an understanding of the various classroom management models discussed in chapters 2–12. Readers also understand the importance of classes and schools being safe for both students and teachers. With these understandings, preservice and in-service teachers can identify their philosophical beliefs and begin to move toward actual classroom management practices, ones that are effective for individual teachers. We have tried to present classroom management models and theories in an objective and unbiased manner. We have also encouraged readers to consider each model and, then, make their own decisions about classroom management. Chapters 14 and 15 provide readers with an ideal opportunity to identify their philosophical beliefs and plan actual management practices that they think will work for them.

CHAPTER 13

Creating Safe Classrooms and Safe Schools

Focusing Questions

After reading this chapter, you should be able to answer the following questions:

1. How do violence and bullying in classrooms challenge educators in their efforts to have safe learning environments?

2. How can teachers, parents, and students contribute to the physical and psychological safety of classrooms?

3. What should teachers know about zero-tolerance policies, environmental design, and security technologies?

4. Should teachers "profile" students for violent behavior?

5. What are some early warning signs of physical and psychological violence?

6. What do selected classroom management theorists in this book say about ways to promote safe schools?

7. What are peer mediation and conflict resolution and how do they work?

8. What are some additional sources of information on this challenge facing teachers who want their classes to be physically and psychologically safe?

Key Terms

Bullying
Conflict resolution
Direct bullying
Environmental design
Indirect bullying
Peer mediation
Profiling
Safe school
School-based risk factors
Security technologies
Violence
Warning signs
Written intervention plans
Zero tolerance

In chapter 1, we briefly discussed the violence that is affecting our schools, as well as the goals of the safe schools movement. Unless educators take deliberate and effective measures to curb it, classroom violence and bullying are likely to continue to be problems. It would take several books rather than a single chapter to explore fully the reasons for violence and the headline-making incidents that have occurred across our country. However, in this chapter we want to review the most prevalent forms of violence, look at various prevention and intervention methods, and examine how selected classroom management theorists can contribute to the movement to have safe classrooms and schools for students and educators.

CHALLENGES TO SAFE CLASSROOMS

According to Ronald D. Stephens (Mabie, 2003):

> A **safe school** is a place where the business of education can be conducted in a welcoming environment free of intimidation, violence, and fear. Such a setting provides an educational climate that fosters a spirit of acceptance and care for every child. It is a place free of bullying where behavior expectations are clearly communicated, consistently enforced and fairly applied (Mabie, 2003, p. 157).

Although a number of things can threaten the physical and psychological safety of students and teachers, two of the most commonplace threats are **violence** and **bullying.** It is tempting to place bullying in the violence category, but some students have been the victims of bullies for so long that we think bullying deserves individual attention.

Classroom Violence

Ranging from threats of physical violence to physical assaults and homicide, *violence* in classrooms has caused many parents, teachers, and administrators to rethink their beliefs about school safety. They raise questions such as: Are classrooms physically and psychologically safe places for students to learn and teachers to teach? By what means can we determine whether schools are safe? What can teachers, administrators, and parents do to make classrooms safe?

Today, there is conflicting information about school safety. Some people (Merrow, 2004) contend schools are safe, and children are more likely to be victims of crime when they are away from school than when they are at school (Schaefer-Schiumo & Patraka, 2003). However, *Crime and Safety in America's Public Schools* (National Center for Education Statistics, 2003) offered some disturbing information.

- Serious crimes committed in schools include rape, sexual battery other than rape, physical attacks or fights with and without a weapon, and robberies with and without a weapon.
- 71% of public elementary and secondary schools experienced at least one violent incident.
- 36% of public schools reported at least one violent incident to police or other law enforcement personnel.
- 22% of public schools experienced at least one serious violent incident (e.g., rape, physical attacks or fights with a weapon, etc.), for a total of 61,000 violent incidents (National Center for Education Statistics, 2003).

Other researchers found the following:

- Boys are victimized physically twice as often as girls, especially in elementary school (Schroeder, 2005).
- Girl crime is surging as physical violence once associated only with boys occurrs increasingly in girl fights (*Behind the Surge in Girl Crime,* 2004).

In addition to violent crimes, bullying and harassment occur all too often and cause students to be reluctant to attend school. Also, when teachers are afraid to enforce classroom management policies, unsafe conditions can arise.

Although there are differing opinions about school safety, all elementary and secondary educators can probably agree on two issues.

1. Schools need to be safe for students and teachers. They should not be afraid to attend school, to travel back and forth to school, and to attend all school activities. This safety includes the elimination of aggravated assaults, threats of violence, and bullying.
2. President George W. Bush's "No Child Left Behind" (NCLB) initiatives aimed at keeping schools safe and orderly ("NCLB Policies Leave Safe, Orderly Schools Behind," 2005) have increased the interest of all individuals in maintaining safe schools. Under NCLB, parents have the right to take their children elsewhere if their school is deemed unsafe. This gives educators an added impetus to maintain a safe and secure environment (Mabie, 2003; School-Safety Rankings—or Just Black Marks, 2003).

Two aspects of school safety continue to challenge educators. First, all classrooms face the threat of some violence. Second, the goal should be for classrooms and schools to be safe for all students and educators. Although individual teachers are limited in what they can do to make their classrooms safe, their decision on a classroom management model or their choice of management strategies and practices can have significant effects on the classroom climate, as well as on student decisions about whether to solve disputes through conflict resolution or the use of deadly weapons.

Causes of School Violence

The causes of violence vary considerably, but the National Education Association (NEA, 1998) maintains that most serious violence can be linked to three phenomena: gang presence and activity, hate-motivated behavior, and drugs. Figure 13–1 provides a brief overview of these activities. In addition, some school conditions, often called **school-based risk factors,** contribute to violence and aggression. Things such as poor design of school space, overcrowding, lack of caring, insensitivity toward multicultural factors, student alienation, rejection of at-risk students by teachers and peers, anger and resentment at school routines, and demands for conformity can lead to problems.

Bullying

Bullying is such a serious problem that it needs to be addressed as a separate safety issue.

- On the average an act of bullying occurs every 7 minutes.
- Each bullying episode lasts 37 seconds.
- 15% of all children are regularly bullied.
- Most bullying takes place at school where there is little or no supervision.
- Boys bully both boys and girls; girls bully girls.
- Boys engage in more bullying behavior and are victims of bullies more frequently than girls.
- The victims are often blamed for the treatment (Ditzhazy & Burton, 2003).

One junior high school reported that an average of 43% of the discipline reports over 2 years involved bullying (Walsh & Reina, 2004). On all levels, many students are concerned and

Figure 13–1 Causes of Violence

Gang presence and activity: Gangs are organized groups whose distinctive language and dress identify their members. Even though only a small number of students belong to gangs, they are an important force because of their involvement with drugs and weapons and their fights over turf.

Hate-motivated behavior: Hate groups often target specific types of students in school, such as ethnic, racial, and religious groups; gays, lesbians, and bisexuals; and females.

Drugs: Drugs lead to violence because of drug sales, fights over turf, and the violent or erratic behavior of some students who are on drugs.

Source: Developed from National Education Association. (1998). *NEA action sheet: Safe schools.* Washington, DC: Author.

Figure 13-2
Categories of Bullying

> *Physical bullying* includes punching, poking, strangling, hair pulling, beating, biting, and excessive tickling.
>
> *Verbal bullying* includes acts such as hurtful name calling, teasing, and gossip.
>
> *Emotional bullying* includes rejecting; terrorizing; extorting; defaming; humiliating; blackmailing; rating/ranking of personal characteristics such as race, disability, ethnicity, or perceived sexual orientation; manipulating friendships; isolating; ostracizing; and peer pressure.
>
> *Sexual bullying* includes many of the actions listed above as well as exhibitionism, voyeurism, sexual propositioning, sexual harassment, and abuse involving actual physical contact and sexual assault.

Source: U.S. Department of Education. (1998a). *Preventing bullying: A manual for schools and communities.* Washington, DC: Author.

anxious about being bullied, witnessing others being bullied, or fearing they will be the next victims (Newman-Carlson & Horne, 2004).

There are two categories of **bullying. Direct bullying** consists of teasing, taunting, threatening, hitting, and stealing. **Indirect bullying** can cause a student to be socially isolated through exclusion. Whether direct or indirect, the key component of bullying is that the physical or psychological intimidation occurs repeatedly over time to create an ongoing pattern of harassment and abuse. These bullying acts are not intentionally provoked by the victims. In fact, for such acts to be defined as bullying, an imbalance of real or perceived power must exist between the bully and the victim. Boys typically engage in direct bullying methods, but girls who bully are more apt to utilize subtle strategies such as spreading rumors and enforcing social isolation (Ditzhazy & Burton, 2003). Figure 13–2 shows how the U.S. Department of Education (1998a) categorizes bullying.

Bullies like to feel that they are strong and superior and that they have power over others. More than just teasing someone, some bullies use violence, intimidation, and various hostile tactics. Stories about bullies abound: the fourth-grade bully who regularly trips other students, the second-grade bully who makes girls cry, and the eighth-grade bully who preys on students walking home from school. Figure 13–3 provides an overview of the characteristics of bullies.

Although direct bullying seems to increase through the elementary grades, peak in middle school, and decline during the high school years (Dake, Price, & Telljohann, 2003), indirect verbal abuse appears to remain constant. School size, racial composition, and school

Figure 13-3
Characteristics of Bullies

Bullies

- Seem to have a need to feel powerful and in control,
- Appear to derive satisfaction from inflicting injury and suffering on others,
- Seem to have little empathy for their victims,
- Often defend their actions by saying victims provoke them in some way,
- Often come from homes where physical punishment is prevalent and where children are taught to strike back physically as a way of handling problems,
- Seem to have parents who lack involvement and warmth,
- Are often defiant and oppositional toward adults, antisocial, and apt to break rules,
- Appear to have little anxiety and usually possess strong self-esteem.

Source: Developed from Banks (1997), Batsche & Knoff (1994), and Olweus (1993).

Figure 13–4
Characteristics of Victims
of Bullies

Victims of bullies

- Are typically anxious, insecure, cautious, and suffer from low self-esteem,
- Rarely defend themselves or retaliate when confronted by students who bully them,
- May lack social skills and friends and are often socially isolated,
- Are close to their parents and may have parents who are overprotective,
- Tend to be physically weaker than their peers.

Source: Developed from Banks (1997), Batsche & Knoff (1994), and Olweus (1993).

setting (e.g., rural, suburban, and urban) do not seem to be distinguishing factors in predicting the occurrence of bullying. Figure 13–4 looks at characteristics of victims of bullies.

Teachers should not assume that bullying is a normal part of childhood. Getting teased, picked on, and pushed around should not be part of growing up for any student. Victims often fear school and consider classrooms as unhappy and unsafe places. In fact, one estimate is that 160,000 children miss school each day because of fear (Newman-Carlson & Horne, 2004). When students are bullied, they become isolated from their peers, who do not want to lose status by associating with them or do not want to increase the risk of being bullied themselves. Being bullied leads to depression and low self-esteem—problems that can be carried into adulthood (Crothers & Levinson, 2004). With miserable school lives, students who are bullied eventually might decide that the only way to retaliate is to resort to violence. Unfortunately, some teachers feel they lack adequate skills and training to intervene in bullying situations; some feel that addressing bullying will result in these behaviors becoming more subtle; and some teachers seem not to notice that bullying occurs and has harmful and long-term effects (Newman-Carlson & Horne, 2004).

CLASSROOM PREVENTION AND INTERVENTION EFFORTS: TEACHERS' EFFORTS

Prevention and intervention efforts for bullying and school violence can take many forms, including instilling a positive school culture, using new technologies, imposing zero-tolerance policies, providing staff development, profiling students to identify possible offenders, and developing written intervention plans. In this section, we will look at some prevention and intervention efforts that classroom teachers can implement and explore some serious questions about the effectiveness of some of them.

Positive School and Classroom Culture

Emotional and verbal violence can be just as damaging as physical violence, although its effects might not be as visible. To combat violence in any form, Plucker (2000) recommends the use of respect and constructive communication. One way to develop respect and communication is to create a positive school climate.

School climate or culture consists of a number of factors, including the attitudes, feelings, and behaviors of all individuals within the school (Hernandez & Seem, 2004). Included are specific factors such as how teachers and students speak to one another, how teachers view students' mistakes, and how students speak and treat one another. Educators must help students feel they belong, have opportunities to make real choices, use communication to prevent violence, and know the consequences of their actions (Plucker, 2000). In part, the positiveness of the school environment depends on the teachers' classroom management philosophies and strategies. Alfie Kohn (2004) maintains that a reliance upon old-fashioned discipline, with threats of punishments for offenders, not only distracts from dealing with the real causes of aggression, but in effect models bullying and power for students. Teachers and administrators often make conditions worse by adding harsher punishments. They sometimes use "negative behaviors" in the hope of getting students to stop "negative behaviors." When this does not work, teachers and administrators use even harsher forces—in other words, they are modeling the same behaviors they are trying to stop.

What, then, is included in a positive school and class culture? What does the "ideal" actually consist of? Management Tip 13–1 offers a checklist of essentials of a positive school culture. A protective culture stresses inclusionary values and practices, strong student bonding to the educative environment and the schooling process, high levels of student participation and parent involvement, and provision of opportunities for skill development and social development (Trends and issues: School safety and violence prevention, n.d.). Activity 13–1 looks at several ways to promote a positive school and class learning environment.

Efforts to Curb Bullying

Although understanding bullying and its effects are essential steps in reducing the problem, it is even more important that teachers take deliberate steps to eliminate the problem. No student should be bullied at school or on the way to and from school; similarly, no student should dread being bullied.

For bullying to be reduced:

Management Tip 13–1

Identifying the school climate

Based on the work of Gunzelmann (2004), here are a few questions to ask to determine whether a school has a positive climate:

1. Is there a strong administration that is open to criticism, complaints and suggestions?
2. Do the students want to attend school?
3. Do the students see the school as a place for belonging and achievement?
4. Are violence and bullying tolerated or are there specific measures for prevention and intervention?
5. Are students and teachers optimistic?
6. Is testing kept in perspective to the total goals of the curriculum?
7. Are small classes the norm?
8. Are behavioral problems handled quickly and respectfully?
9. Do the educators communicate with and listen to the parents?
10. Are there high expectations for behavior and achievement?
11. Are students taught to achieve the high expectations?
12. Do teachers enjoy teaching and working with students?

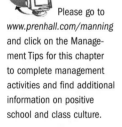

Please go to *www.prenhall.com/manning* and click on the Management Tips for this chapter to complete management activities and find additional information on positive school and class culture.

- Teachers and students should be warm, positive, and caring.
- Teachers should set firm limits on acceptable behavior.
- Teachers should be consistent in applying nonhostile and nonphysical sanctions on offenders.
- Teachers should be authoritative but not authoritarian (Ditzhazy & Burton, 2003).

To assist teachers in their efforts, building-level administrators can use a student questionnaire to determine the nature and extent of bullying problems. Then, at an in-service day, teachers can review findings from the questionnaire, discuss problems of bullying, and plan violence-prevention efforts. It might be wise to form a bullying-prevention coordinating committee of teachers, administrators, counselors, and other school staff to plan and monitor intervention programs. Teachers might decide simply to increase supervision in areas where bullying frequently occurs. If a formal program is planned, parents can become involved, and schoolwide events such as a closed-circuit television show or an assembly can be used to launch the program.

Administrators can help teachers combat the problem of bullies in other ways, too. First, they need to be sure that students are supervised on the playgrounds and in classrooms, hallways, rest rooms, cafeterias, and areas where bullying might occur. By conducting

Activity 13-1

Promoting Positive Learning Environments

After reading the following general examples of ways teachers can promote positive learning environments, identify other, more specific measures you could use in the grade levels that you teach or would like to teach.

1. Focus educational efforts and classroom management on both cognitive and psychosocial domains.
2. Provide times for students to have positive socialization that is appropriate for the age group.
3. Provide age-appropriate discussions on drug abuse, sex, and violence.
4. Teach students how to think and act in school and class situations.
5. Teach socialization skills to students who are fearful in social situations.
6. Teach conflict resolution skills to solve problems among students.

What else might you to do promote positive learning environments?

---

schoolwide assemblies, posting and publicizing clear behavior standards, developing rules against bullying, and consistently and fairly enforcing these rules, administrators can raise awareness about the problems of bullying.

Teachers also can foster mutual understanding of and appreciation for differences in others by providing prevention and intervention classroom activities that are designed to build self-esteem and by spotlighting special talents, hobbies, interests, and abilities of all students. They can teach cooperation by assigning projects that require collaboration. At regularly scheduled classroom meetings, students and teachers can discuss the problem and the harm that bullying does, define what constitutes bullying, establish classroom rules against bullying, and engage in role playing and artistic activities that focus on prevention. It might be necessary to develop a classroom plan to ensure that students know what to do when they observe a bully–victim confrontation. Individual students might need to have opportunities to talk about bullying and might need support or protection. Creating a buddy system, whereby students have a particular friend or older buddy on whom they can depend and with whom they share class schedule information and plans for the day, is one alternative. All educators should always listen receptively to parents who report bullying and follow up by investigating reported circumstances.

When bullying is observed, it is important to take immediate action. This means confronting bullies in private, because challenging bullies in front of their peers might enhance their status and lead to further aggression. Notify parents of victims and bullies when a confrontation occurs, seek to resolve the problem expeditiously, and refer victims and aggressors to counseling whenever appropriate.

Students can also be encouraged to take appropriate actions when they witness or experience bullying. For instance, depending on the situation and their level of comfort, students

Helping Galon

Review the section in the chapter on bullying, including the measures that a teacher could take to decrease bullying. Then, as you read the following scenario, identify the type of bullying that is being done. Finally, respond to the questions at the end.

Galon, a 14-year-old boy, was almost the stereotypical victim. Skinny, with thick glasses, he read profusely and was a social isolate—in some ways by choice. He was bullied nearly every day. Some students laughed at him, one threw a lizard on him, and another put chewing gum in his hair during algebra class. Although all of the teachers in his middle school team knew of Galon's plight, none of them took any action. Finally, the principal told Galon that he would suspend the person who put the chewing gum in his hair. The problem was that Galon had not seen the person who did it. Despite the fact that all Galon had to do was find one person who would tell him the bully's name, he was unsuccessful in his search.

1. If you were the teacher in this school, what could you do to help Galon?
2. Should he be expected to solve this problem by himself?
3. Are these instances of bullying just part of the natural process of growing up?

can be encouraged to seek immediate help from an adult; report bullying/victimization incidents; speak up and offer support to the victim when they see the person being bullied; express disapproval of bullying behavior by not joining in the laughter, teasing, or spreading of rumors or gossip; and attempt to defuse problem situations either single-handedly or in a group. When problems arise, a confidential reporting system allows students to report incidents and to record the details of the bullying. How Would You React 13–1 asks you to apply some of these suggestions to the situation of Galon, a middle school student. Then Management Tip 13–2 provides principles of prevention and intervention for addressing bullying.

Environmental Design

Although teachers have little influence over **environmental design**, they should know how school design contributes to safe classrooms and schools. Most educational facilities were not designed with environmental safety in mind. However, now that safety has become a high priority in schools, Crime Prevention Through Environmental Design (CPTED) offers principles for creating a safe school environment (Schneider, 2001a).

Unfortunately, conventional security measures emphasize prohibited behavior and are largely fear based. For example, a school that uses security guards and metal detectors might become more secure, but it also might fail to address underlying problems leading to violence and might reinforce fear. In contrast, CPTED focuses on desired behavior and uses posted rules and theme-oriented artwork to reinforce a prosocial curriculum, student art displays to build a sense of pride, altered seating arrangements to encourage supportive group interactions, or changes in scheduling to avoid conflict in the halls.

CPTED advocates a number of things, including natural surveillance or the practice of keeping an eye on the whole school environment. This means eliminating solid walls, providing windows, and pruning shrubbery. CPTED also stresses natural access control, in which educators determine who can or cannot enter a facility. Converting several unsupervised, unlocked entrances into locked, alarmed, emergency exits is one way to improve access control. Finally, establishing territoriality cultivates a sense of belonging and provides some control over the environment. With things such as school uniforms, schools not only build a sense of pride, but they also make it easy to distinguish between students and nonstudents (Schneider, 2001a).

There are specific things teachers can do to make their classrooms safer. For example, teachers can stand at the classroom door as students enter (which is always a good idea anyway) to identify troubled or potentially dangerous students, post rules requiring respect and civility, watch for signs of weapons, teach students exit drills in the case of dangerous situations, and arrange the room so all students can be seen at all times. Also, teachers can watch for social isolates—those students who feel bullied, ignored, disliked, and neglected.

New Technologies

Although teachers can do little on their own to implement new technologies, they still should be aware of the available *safety technologies* so they can be active and vocal participants on school-safety committees. At times, it might be necessary to consider technological solutions to school security, including the use of "smart" cards, metal detectors, alarm systems, and surveillance equipment (Schneider, 2001b). However, before selecting high-tech security solutions, school officials should think carefully about the possible (and unintended) consequences of using **security technologies.** In addition to reinforcing fear and undermining the social ecology of the school, they could be a mismatch for the school's problems and could be expensive when costs for maintenance, repairs, and upgrades are considered.

In some schools, smart cards are used to control access. Issued primarily to teachers, these cards can be tailored to an individual's needs and can be canceled instantly in case they are lost or stolen. The cards are swiped through a slot (swipe cards) or held close to a reader (proximity cards). With these cards, people can be given access to an area only on certain days or during specified hours. In addition, parking-lot access can be controlled to allow students to enter and exit freely only before or after school.

Metal-detector wands provide a relatively inexpensive way for security personnel or other staff to check for metal weapons. Detection portals, which students can walk through, are much more expensive. With either system, the effectiveness of metal-detection equipment has received mixed reviews because most schools have many entry points. At least two security personnel must be at each entry point to scan incoming students, take students aside who trigger the alarm, monitor the remaining students, and respond to found weapons. In addition, the use of any monitoring equipment requires the staggering of students' arrival at school to allow sufficient time for processing.

Alarm systems are used in schools to detect intruders after hours or in controlled areas and to signal emergency personnel when immediate help is needed. Staff can trigger panic buttons in emergencies, such as when an unauthorized or armed individual is seen entering the building.

Management Tip 13–2

Preventing Bullies

According to Feinberg (2003), you can work with other educators in your building to address bullying by doing several things.

Lay the Groundwork

Learn what other schools in your district are doing.

Assess the extent of the problem in your school.

Volunteer to work on a team that involves the school community.

Build a Schoolwide Foundation

Develop a code of conduct for students and staff.

Establish and consistently enforce consequences for bullying.

Build students' sense of responsibility for the school community.

Distinguish between ratting and reporting.

Train all school personnel.

Increase adult supervision.

Conduct schoolwide bullying-prevention activities.

Make Early Interventions

Teach specific skills and values in your classroom.

Teach conflict-resolution skills.

Meet with parents and discuss your efforts to reduce bullying.

Provide Individual Interventions

Establish a protocol for intervening or investigating a bullying incident.

Reinforce alternative behaviors.

Work with parents on parenting style and family issues.

Address bullying to and from school.

Please go to *www.prenhall.com/manning* and click on the Management Tips for this chapter to complete management activities and find additional information on bullying.

The greatest strength of closed-circuit television (CCTV) cameras is their use to identify suspects after the fact. Although they can deter some criminal activity, cameras can be targeted by vandals. In addition, premeditated crimes can be planned to avoid the cameras, or offenders can wear disguises to obscure their identities. One drawback to the use of fake cameras is the possibility that students will assume they can rely on a certain level of security, when in fact that is not the case (Schneider, 2001b).

Zero Tolerance

More than 90% of U.S. public schools have some type of **zero-tolerance** policy. Unfortunately, some believe that these policies are neither effective nor implemented in a manner that is child centered or equitable (Verdugo, 2002). Educators have a responsibility to review the pros and cons of zero tolerance and decide for themselves whether this policy is the most effective way to prevent school violence.

The demand for zero-tolerance policies began when Congress passed the Gun-Free Schools Act of 1994, which required states to legislate zero-tolerance laws or risk losing federal funding (Casella, 2003). As a result, various states and school districts developed policies to combat weapons, drugs, violence, and antisocial behavior and to reflect local needs. In doing so, some administrators began to treat all behaviors, minor and major, with equal severity to make clear to everyone that policies would be enforced. Today, almost all schools have zero-tolerance policies for firearms (94%) and weapons other than firearms (91%). Eighty-seven percent of schools have zero-tolerance policies for alcohol, and 88% have policies for drugs. Most schools have zero-tolerance policies for violence and tobacco (79% each) (McAndrews, 2001).

Unfortunately, zero tolerance has been viewed as a "cure-all" for all school violence. Although the Gun-Free Schools Act provided for a case-by-case consideration, some administrators simply use the established consequences rather than considering students' behaviors on an individual basis. Examples of consequences of zero tolerance include the following:

- A student was suspended from school for violating the absence policy in one of his classes.
- A student was suspended because he talked a suicidal friend into giving him the knife with which she threatened to kill herself.
- A student received a suspension for wearing a "Tweetie Bird" that could be categorized as a weapon (Stanley, Juhnke, & Purkey, 2004).
- A student was expelled for having a plastic knife to spread cheese on her crackers at lunch.
- A student was expelled when he had a plastic toy gun on his key chain.

Supporters of zero tolerance maintain that violence in school has become lethal and must be addressed in a firm manner. Thus, they believe these policies are one method (other efforts include peer mediation and conflict resolution programs) to prevent school violence and to provide consequences for those engaging in specific, undesired behaviors. Social and behavioral psychologists suggest that students will become conditioned to the new rules and learn to accept higher expectations placed upon their behavior (Casella, 2003).

Critics of zero tolerance maintain that the approach affects a disproportionate number of students at risk, as well as students who are poor and minority. Allowing little or no room for administrators' discretion or students' due-process rights, the policies impose punishments for behaviors that are not actually dangerous, e.g., the plastic knife incident or a gun charm on a key ring.

If school districts decide to include zero-tolerance policies in their effort to make schools safe, the polices should be developed with state departments of education, juvenile justice, teachers, and parents. Educators should tailor the policy to local schools; clearly define what constitutes a weapon, a drug, or an act of misbehavior; specify clear consequences for misbehavior; allow flexibility; and consider alternatives (McAndrews, 2001).

Profiling Students

When using student profiles, educators use checklists of behaviors and personal character-istics associated with youth who have perpetuated violence to predict an individual stu-dent's potential for acting out in a violent manner. If a student shows a large number of the characteristics on the checklist, the assumption is that this student is at risk of committing violence. It is not surprising that student **profiling** is a controversial topic. Some people see student profiling as a promising tool, but others consider the practice to be an ill-conceived response to violence in classrooms (Lumsden, 2000).

One central issue surrounding profiling is whether teachers should attempt to make pre-dictions about an individual student's propensity for future violence, because that task has been difficult even for mental health professionals. In addition, the reliability of student-profiling checklists is a concern. For example, all professionals cannot agree upon a single list of behavioral warning signs. Even the warning-sign lists (such as *Early Warning, Timely Response: A Guide to Safe Schools*) published by the U.S. Department of Education (1998b) were not intended to be used for profiling purposes. If a list eventually can be developed, a final con-cern centers on what to do with the profiling results, who will see the profiles, and whether the profiles unfairly single out and stigmatize students for further isolation (Lumsden, 2000).

Warning Signs of Violence

To prevent violent behavior, educators need to be trained to look for **warning signs** of poten-tially dangerous students (Brunner and Lewis, 2005). Although students who have specific char-acteristics should not be stigmatized as potentially violent offenders based simply on a checklist of behaviors, emotional and behavioral early warning signs can indicate that the potential for violence to self and others exists. Before you read further, complete Activity 13–2 on designing

Activity 13–2

Reviewing Classroom Security

Think about your classes in child/adolescent development and psychology. Then, working with a group of your classmates, identify some characteristics that you believe might be early warning signs of a potential for violent behavior. Once you have completed your list, return to the section of this chapter on early warning signs and continue reading. After you complete the section, compare your list of characteristics with those developed by the U.S. Department of Education (1998b) and Schaefer-Schiumo & Patraka (2003).

CASE STUDY 13–1
Developing a "Safe Schools" Plan

During the past 2 years, several acts of violence had occurred at the high school in the middle-sized Cozzens Area School District. In addition to a fight that sent several students and one teacher to the hospital with minor cuts, one student brought a gun to school in a book bag, and another student threatened a teacher with an ice pick. The violence had escalated in the past month when a middle school student pulled out a knife and slashed the parka of another student who was in her way. Although the increased number of suspensions showed that school administrators were trying to address the problem, everyone felt that something more needed to be done.

Thus, the issue was on the school board agenda for its March meeting. Parents and educators spoke with parents, voicing their concerns that they wanted their children to be feel safe while at school and wanted guns and knives out of the school. Teachers wanted metal detectors at all doors and asked to have potentially violent students expelled. After listening to the speakers, the school board discussed various options. Finally, the school board asked the superintendent to develop a written Safe Schools plan by no later than the June meeting, along with a time line for implementation.

The next day, the superintendent and his administrative team met to discuss the Safe Schools plan and how to proceed with its development. Various questions came up: Did they want to do an assessment of the types and severity of the violence? Were more professional development in-services needed? How had other school districts successfully dealt with the problem of violence? Did their plan need mea-surable objectives and goals or were global statements enough? Should their plan include the local police or other law enforcement officers? Should they consider an alternative school for troubled students? Should they look to one or more classroom management models, or was this beyond the content of most models? What legal aspects did they have to consider (e.g., keeping students safe while not violating their rights)? Because the school administrators had found zero tolerance to be neither popular nor effective, did they want to implement more zero-tolerance policies? Did they want more security guards and metal detectors?

Questions for Your Consideration:

1. What should be in a Safe Schools plan?

2. Should the request have been for a Safe Classrooms plan?

3. Have the superintendent and his administrative team identified all the necessary elements for such a plan or should other things be included?

4. What would it take to make this school district safer and also to satisfy the school board's request and the teachers' and parents' concerns?

 You can record your answers to these questions online on this book's Companion Web Site at *www.prenhall.com/manning*.

a classroom security checklist. Early warning signs allow educators to act responsibly and to get help for students before problems escalate. Early warning signs of violence include social withdrawal, excessive feelings of isolation and being alone, excessive feelings of rejection, being a victim of violence, feeling picked on and persecuted, low school interest and poor academic performance, expression of violence in writings and drawings, patterns of impulsive and chronic hitting and intimidating, history of discipline problems, past history of violent and aggressive behavior, prejudicial attitudes and intolerance for differences, drug and alcohol use, affiliation with gangs, inappropriate access to firearms, serious threats of violence (U.S. Department of Education, 1998b), low tolerance for frustration, poor coping skills, anger-management problems, alienation, signs of depression, drastic changes in behavior, lack of empathy, attitudes of superiority, fascination with violence, and negative role models (Schaefer-Schiumo & Patraka, 2003).

Written Intervention Plans

Before serious problems arise, educators should develop **written intervention plans** that establish a partnership with students, school, homes, and community and describe the effective prevention practices that have been taken. Included should be descriptions of intervention strategies educators can use to help troubled children; early interventions for students who are at risk of behavioral problems; and more intensive, individualized interventions and resources for children with severe behavioral problems or mental health needs.

The plan should include steps to be taken when early warning signs are observed, including a way for educators to inform parents and listen to their concerns while maintaining confidentiality and the parents' rights to privacy. Any plan also needs to educate students and families about the early warning signs of potentially violent behavior and how to respond with a contingency plan to be used in the aftermath of a tragedy. Finally, a plan should help students learn to become more responsible for their actions and should simplify the process for urgent assistance (U.S. Department of Education, 1998b).

Case Study 13–1 tells of a school board that challenged a superintendent to present a safe schools plan at an upcoming meeting. After you react to the Case Study, read the reactions of some school personnel in Voices of Educators: Reacting to Case Study 13–1.

Some educators use another effective security tool: the security checklist. Less involved than the intervention plan, the checklist reflects a school's unique conditions and might include such items as alternative education for some students, prenatal and postnatal care for pregnant students, and programs to celebrate the diversity in the school and community (Williams, 2001). Classroom educators can design a checklist for their individual classrooms. For example, educators can scrutinize their classrooms for conditions that might contribute to violence. Conditions might include hidden areas (e.g., freestanding bulletin boards), students sitting too close together, an overemphasis on competition, or desks arranged so students cannot always see the teacher (and vice versa). How Would You React 13–2 asks you to respond when a parent questions safety policies.

Voices of Educators

Reacting to Case Study 13–1

Here are selected responses by school personnel to Case Study 13–1:

- Not only must administrators, faculty, staff, and students must feel safe at school, but the parents and the community must know that every precaution has been taken to assure safety at school.
- The components mentioned in this case study (i.e., security guards, metal detectors, and zero-tolerance policies) have merit, but people are the most important.
- Change the culture of the school to one that assures mutual respect and emotional safety for everyone.
- The school board policies and the district's mission statement should support the Safe Schools policy, and the mission statement should be posted in every school and in every classroom.
- Have workshops to train all administrators, faculty, and staff on exactly what behavior is expected from educators and students.
- Develop uniform behavior standards for students and make sure all faculty and staff agree to follow them.
- Training for students should be at the beginning of the year and throughout the year to reinforce the guidelines.
- Use posters, announcements, and other reminders.
- Establish intervention programs that address anger management for students, peer mediation, and student discussion groups.
- Be sure to monitor the program and collect data to support it.

Questioning Safety Policies

Russell Sheldon asked for an appointment with Beverly Cox, a third-grade teacher at West Prairie Combined School, to discuss school safety issues. West Prairie Combined was located in a small, rural school district that had placed the elementary and middle school students in different sections of one building. Mr. Sheldon believed safety in the classroom and nearby halls was too lax. As he stated to Ms. Cox, "People come and go all the time. Every time I'm here, I see strangers, and any of these people could be carrying a gun. Sure, people have to sign in at the school entrance and get a name badge, but nobody really checks that they are who they say they are. Plus, those eighth-grade boys with their long hair and baggy clothes shouldn't be in the hall around my third-grader, Krystal. What are you doing about safety here? What are you doing to ensure that Krystal is safe in your classroom?"

1. Work with other students in your class and role-play responses to this scenario.
2. How might Ms. Cox respond?
3. What types of security measures would be appropriate to implement in her classroom?
4. How would you maintain security in your own classroom?
5. Would you recommend different plans for elementary, middle, and high school classes? Why?

CREATING SAFE CLASSROOMS AND SCHOOLS: EDUCATORS, STUDENTS, AND PARENTS

No one person or group can bear the responsibility for creating and maintaining safe classrooms. Instead, a collaborative effort must be made that includes as many people and perspectives as possible. In this section, you will read some of the ways educators, students, and parents can help classrooms become safe for all learners.

Working With Teachers

It is important for teachers to build a caring, supportive, and challenging classroom climate that will ensure effective social and emotional teaching and learning (Trends and issues: School safety and violence prevention, n.d.). That means teachers should help students develop social competencies, problem-prevention skills, and coping skills. By emphasizing prosocial attitudes and values about self, others, and work and by avoiding negative labeling and tracking, teachers should monitor student academic progress, behavior, and attitudes on a regular basis. Looking for ways to foster collaboration between home and classrooms, teachers can become nurturing role models who show support, warmth, mentoring, and responsiveness to student needs (Trends and issues: School safety and violence prevention, n.d.). Teachers also should encourage their school administrators to create and publicize safety initiative programs, especially those specific to classrooms.

Working With Students

Teachers should provide opportunities for students to assume responsibility for safer schools and to provide input and suggestions into district and school policies. Perhaps teachers can develop a student court system that is trained by local justice system experts or provide conflict-resolution materials and appropriate training. To ease the transition for newcomers, teachers can develop a buddy system in their classrooms in which current students help the new arrivals. Even something as simple as a classroom beautification campaign for the school and neighborhood using students as work crews can have a positive impact. Finally, teachers in some schools have established a student tip line, which provides an anonymous, nonthreatening way for students to report school crime (National School Safety Center, 1999).

Asking Our Children to "Spy and Rat"

Information is important in maintaining a safe school. However, some individuals see a fine line between providing information and spying. Before you read the following scenario, make a list of some of the things that you think a student should tell an educator. Are there things you believe are private and should not be passed on? What guidelines would you give to students to determine what things they should tell an adult? Now, read the following scenario and respond to the questions at the end.

The educators and counselors at Miller-Reynolds High School explained to students how they could contribute to everyone's safety by helping identify potentially dangerous students and situations. Three days later, an irate parent complained to the principal that she did not want her son to "spy and rat on others." She argued that school personnel should be able to identify and control violent students. In a disgruntled voice, the parent exclaimed, "You educators should accept responsibility for these problems rather than relying upon students."

1. What would you say to this parent?
2. Do you believe that student tip lines are beneficial or harmful? What advantages or disadvantages do they have?

The use of a student tip line is often controversial because some parents and educators do not want students placed in awkward situations. In How Would You React 13–3, a parent questions the use of a student tip line.

Working With Parents and Community Members

Although educators ultimately must accept responsibility for the safety of students in their classrooms, educators also can enlist the help of parents to promote safe classrooms. Parents should be encouraged to communicate with educators and to make special efforts to know their children's friends and their children's activities at and away from school. By talking with their children about acceptable methods of confrontation, parents can encourage children to report potentially dangerous situations to parents or teachers. Serving as a model and example for children, parents and community members can become familiar with the school's safe schools policy as well as an individual teacher's safe classroom policy (*www.yrbe.edu.on.ca/~bayh/policy-safe-school.html*). How Would You React 13–4 looks at a parent's report of a potentially violent student.

Reporting a Potentially Violent Student

As Ms. Thommen was walking down the hall to attend her tenth-grade son's required parent–teacher conference, she spied a boy of about 16, who appeared in her opinion to demonstrate a number of troubling characteristics. Mentioning her concern to Ms. Mahefsky, the teacher, during the conference, Ms. Thommen described the student as "dressed in a 'military fashion' and muttering something I think was obscene. He looked dark, brooding, and angry. I think he might assault someone." Ms. Mahefsky thought to herself, "Half the boys in this school fit that description. What does Ms. Thommen expect me to do about it? What if I do nothing and there really is a serious problem? What if there's a shooting? Will I be held responsible?"

1. What should Ms. Mahefsky say to Ms. Thommen?
2. What should she do about this student?
3. Respond to the concerns of Ms. Mahefsky and Ms. Thommen.

Table 13–1 Selected Classroom Management Theorists and Their Contributions to Safe Classrooms

Theorist	Proposals
Richard Curwin and Allen Mendler: *Discipline with Dignity*	Students learn how to be less violent, aggressive, and hostile and how to make better decisions.
	Educators model alternative expressions of anger and frustration, create and nurture community networks, and emphasize the importance of human dignity (Mendler Curwin, 1997).
Forrest Gathercoal *Judicious Discipline*	Students learn to respect others.
	Educators protect those around them and use the philosophical concepts of Judicious Discipline with other models (Gathercoal, 1997).
Alfie Kohn *Beyond Discipline*	Students care for each other and feel others care about them, feel valued and respected, begin to think in the plural, and feel physically and emotionally safe.
	Educators create a community (Kohn, 1996).
David Johnson and Roger Johnson *Three C's*	Educators recognize the violence and aggression facing schools, recognize the need for safe schools and teach cooperation, conflict resolution and civic values (Johnson & Johnson, 1995).
Jane Nelsen, Lynn Lott, and Stephen Glenn *Positive Discipline*	Students feel capable, genuinely needed, and able to influence their lives.
	Educators help students develop intrapersonal and interpersonal skills to get along with others (Nelsen, Lott, Glenn, 1997).

THEORISTS AND THEIR CONTRIBUTIONS TO SAFE CLASSROOMS

Many classroom management theorists did their work when violence and aggression were not a major concern. For example, the foundational theorists discussed in chapter 2 and other theorists such as Dreikurs, Ginott, and Jones wrote prior to the safe schools movement, when classrooms were considered safe except for the usual minor fighting and bullying that have always plagued schools. Table 13–1 looks at some of the more contemporary theorists who have addressed the issue of school violence and identified ways to make classrooms safe.

PEER MEDIATION AND CONFLICT RESOLUTION

Conflict between people is inevitable and normal. In fact, not all conflict is harmful or destructive. The difference between destructive and constructive conflict is the impact of the conflict on the participants. Unresolved conflicts can lead to poor academic achievement, low self-esteem, feelings of powerlessness, and general behavioral difficulties. It is fortunate that systematic *conflict-resolution* strategies can reduce in-school fighting, suspensions, disciplinary referrals, absenteeism, vandalism, and bullying. The most popular approaches to conflict resolution include a comprehensive violence-reduction program that incorporates proactive strategies, effective intervention approaches, and systematic collaboration between the schools and the communities they serve. With instruction in communication and cooperative problem solving skills, nonviolent approaches to conflict resolution can become standard operating procedure. School-based programs may include a combination of *conflict-resolution curricula, anger management training, peer mediation,* and the development of peaceable classrooms or schools (Chittooran & Hoenig, 2005).

Peer Mediation

Used to help two or more students resolve serious conflicts they cannot handle independently, **peer mediation** relies on an impartial third party, the peer mediator, to facilitate the problem-solving process. Peer mediation can be used to address a number of topics, such as jealously, the use of personal property, bullying, rumors, fights, and misunderstandings among students (Chittooran & Hoenig, 2005). By employing advanced communication, negotiation, and problem-solving skills, students can reach a mutually beneficial resolution. Mediators help people develop a better understanding of each other's positions, develop a relationship based on mutual respect, and encourage parties to reflect on one another's viewpoints so that they will be more willing to resolve their disputes (Brinson, Kottler, & Fisher, 2004).

How does the peer mediation process work? Students may request mediation to help them resolve a dispute or they may be referred by school personnel or families. In either case, the participants must voluntarily engage in the process. Students who are reluctant might be encouraged if they know the process will prevent harsher consequences. The materials needed for the process are minimal: a private room, a table, a couple of chairs, a timer, and writing materials.

Peer mediation sessions may be held before, during, or after school. The mediator records basic information about the conflict and its resolution and provides this information to the faculty coordinator, who monitors the effectiveness of the process. Chittooran and Hoenig (2005) described a process (see Management Tip 13–3) developed from others (Crawford & Bodine, 2001) that they think will work. However, they maintain that the process may be modified to suit a particular school or setting.

Conflict Resolution

In the same way that peers can mediate between other students when conflicts arise, teachers can use the techniques of conflict resolution to help students settle disputes without resorting to violence and aggression. **Conflict resolution** refers to the process of communication between two or more groups that are resolving a dispute. A mediator attempts to end the conflict and restore good relations between the groups. Participants are encouraged not to assign blame but to focus on understanding the origins of the dispute and finding common ground for consensus (Brinson, Kottler, & Fisher, 2004).

Management Tip 13-3

Using Peer Mediation

From the work of Chittooran and Hoenig (2005), we can identify steps to follow so that you can use peer mediation in your own classroom.

Open the session

* Have the students face each other with the mediator between them.
* The mediator should
  Make introductions,
  Clarify the purpose of the meeting,
  Explain the rules.
* The faculty coordinator should keep a record of the proceedings that will be shared only with the participants.

Identify the problem and gather information

* Give each student a specific amount of time to speak and describe the problem without interruptions.
* Allow the mediator to use summarization and clarification to help the students state their case.
* Encourage students to see the situation as a mutual problem.
* Have each person repeat, in his or her own words, what the other person said.

Develop goals and focus on common interests

* With the help of the mediator, the students should determine goals for the session.
* The students should agree on one set of common goals.
* There should be both short- and long-term goals so the students can experience success.

Generate options for solving the problem

* Students should brainstorm as many solutions as possible to the problem.
* A student should not judge or criticize another's ideas.
* The peer mediator may take notes and ask questions for clarification.

Evaluate options and choose a solution

* The students evaluate each option.
* The students decide on one option that best meets their needs or could work with some compromise.
* The peer mediator verbally summarizes the plan and asks the students for feedback regarding its potential for success.

Develop an agreement and commit to it

* The students develop a written agreement that includes
  A timeline,
  Roles and responsibilities,
  Evaluation procedures.
* All participants sign the agreement.
* No changes to the agreement can be made unless all participants agree.

Please go to www.prenhall.com/manning and click on the Management Tips for this chapter to complete management activities and find additional information on peer mediation.

Several models or theories discussed in earlier chapters of this book discuss conflict resolution. In addition, in Figures 13–5 and 13–6, you will find two additional approaches.

DEVELOPING YOUR PERSONAL PHILOSOPHY

In developing your own strategies for classroom management, you can adopt one of these conflict-resolution models or combine elements from several into your own approach. The important thing is to remember not to underestimate your students' abilities and motivation to engage in conflict resolution. Your job is to remain objective and to model how conflicts can be constructive and can lead to better understanding. Developing Your Personal Philosophy asks you to consider how you will incorporate ideas about safe classrooms and schools, the prevention of bullying and violence, and conflict resolution into your classroom management philosophy.

Providing safe schools and classrooms, eliminating bullying and violence, and teaching conflict resolution to students will take the work of many different groups, including

Figure 13–5 Beane's Eight Steps to Conflict Resolution

1. **Cool down.** Students should not try to resolve a conflict when they are angry. They need to meet later when they have had time to consider the situation.

2. **Describe the conflict.** Each student should describe what happened in his or her own words, with neither being considered right or wrong.

3. **Describe the cause of the conflict.** Each student should identify the specific events that occurred including what happened first, what happened next, and what turned the situation into a conflict.

4. **Describe the feelings raised by the conflict.** Each student should describe, in his or her own words, how he or she feels about what happened.

5. **Listen carefully and respectful while the other person talks.** Each student should listen to and try to understand the other point of view without interrupting.

6. **Brainstorm solutions to the conflict.** Students should identify as many ideas as they can for solving the problem. No one should make fun of anyone's ideas.

7. **Try your solution.** Students should consider how the possible solutions might work.

8. **If one solution does not get results, try another.** Students should continue to brainstorm solutions if the previously identified ones do not work.

Source: Developed from Beane, A. L. (2000, September). The bully-free classroom. *Scholastic Instructor,* 45.

Figure 13–6 Burnett's Four-Step Approach

1. **Identify the problem without blame.** Focus on the conflict rather than a particular student; use "I-messages;" and listen to each student define the problem.

2. **Brainstorm alternatives together.** Allow students to offer ideas for appropriate behavior and for solving the specific conflict.

3. **Agree on a solution.** Ask students to state which possible solution they think would most likely be best for all concerned.

4. **Evaluate the result.** Schedule a follow-up meeting for the next day, at which time everyone will review whether the suggested behaviors were followed. Even if no additional problems result, the meeting should be conducted so students can observe their own behavior, reflect on their discussion, and determine their own success.

Source: Burnett, E. M. G. (2000). Conflict resolution: Four steps worth considering. *Social Studies and the Young Learner, 12*(3), 20-23.

community members, parents, teachers, and administrators. Case Study 13–2 looks at three teachers as they discuss their role in providing safe schools and classrooms. After you react to the case study, read Voices of Educators: Reacting to Case Study 13–2 to find the response of educators.

Developing Your Personal Philosophy

Reflecting on Safe Classrooms

Ask yourself the following questions about developing safe schools and classrooms:

1. What theories or models discussed in this book can I use to promote safe classrooms? How?
2. Do I believe that it is the responsibility of educators to teach conflict resolution? If so, what model or method do I prefer?
3. How would I incorporate conflict resolution into my classroom?
4. What methods could I use to eliminate bullying in my classroom?
5. What do I believe about the issues of zero tolerance and profiling students? Do they have a place in my personal management plan?

CASE STUDY 13–2
A Teacher's Ideas on Safe Schools

As Kate Walker entered the teacher's lunchroom, she saw Jeremy Lamboda and Cassie Filippi engaged in what appeared to be a serious conversation. Immediately, Kate knew that these veteran teachers were discussing the new safe schools plan that had been presented to the faculty and staff of the Greenly Area School District the previous day at an after-school workshop. When Kate placed her tray on the table beside Cassie, Jeremy turned to her and asked, "Where do you stand on this whole safe schools issue?"

For a moment, Kate did not respond. Then she said, "Honestly, I don't know. Oh, sure, I agree that we need safe schools. Don't get me wrong, I dislike violence. But, I'm just not sure we're going about things the right way."

"What do you mean?" asked Cassie. "You were there at the meeting yesterday. And you know the kind of things that have happened in some school districts near here. Don't you agree that metal detectors are a way to keep guns and knives out of our classroom? And, don't you think the administrators have a responsibility for our safety?"

"You know I want a safe environment for everyone—teachers and students alike," Kate began, "but the plan was an administrative one."

"I know what you mean," Jeremy chimed in. "That's what I was trying to tell Cassie. That plan talked about uniform behavior standards for the district, intervention programs, and zero-tolerance policies. If Pete points a chicken finger at Makessa and says 'bang,' Pete's out of here—suspended for the rest of the year."

Cassie interrupted Jeremy. "Everyone needs to know that gun games are not acceptable. I don't mind enforcing district policies if it means eliminating violence in this school."

"There's more to it than what you two are fighting about," Kate interjected. "What's bothering me is that no one at the meeting yesterday indicated exactly what our roles as teachers should be in this whole safe school endeavor. Yes, we will have to enforce school policies. But I think that there's more that I can do to help create a safe environment in this school. I want this school to be a warm, welcoming place for students and teachers. I don't want it to look like a jail with guards, metal detectors, and safety police who are ready to pounce if someone isn't following the rules. I think there are things that I can do as a teacher to help students manage conflict and look for alternatives to violence."

Questions for Consideration:

1. What is the role of teachers in developing a safe school?
2. What things should the central administration do and what things should be left to individual classroom teachers?
3. How can Kate, Cassie, and Jeremy ensure that they and their students are working in safe classrooms?
4. How can they balance the ideal of a caring, supportive school and classroom climate with the pressure for safety for all students and teachers?

 You can record your answers to these questions online on this book's Companion Web Site at *www.prenhall.com/manning*.

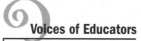

Voices of Educators

Reacting to Case Study 13–2

Here are some responses by teachers to Case Study 13–2:

- Administrators may create rules for safe schools, but the teachers and staff have to understand the rules and enforce them.
- There has to be two-way communication between administrators and their school security personnel, teachers, and students.
- Teachers are on the front line. I've had students come back to me long after they've move to another teacher just because they feel comfortable talking to me. I take the time to listen to students. I don't brush them off like some teachers do.
- The best way for these teachers to ensure that they and their students are working in safe classrooms is for them to watch everything around them. They need to keep their eyes and ears open for any changes that might signal a possible problem. They also need to be able to tell the difference between normal child's play and those actions that cross the line.
- Have a set of rules that are applied to everyone. That's the only way to have a safe school. But, I don't mean a zero-tolerance policy that expels the kid who points a banana at another student and jokingly says "I'm going to get you."
- You have to know what's happening outside school. Many school incidents actually start with something that happened off school grounds.

Please go to *www.prenhall.com/manning* and click on Concluding Remarks for this chapter to find more information.

CONCLUDING REMARKS

For many years, educators have coped with behavior problems such as students talking out of turn, goofing off, fighting, and bullying. Although most classrooms today are safe—in fact, safer than some neighborhoods where students live—many educators struggle with threats of violence and aggression. The safe schools movement is an effort of educators, parents, and community people to provide students with safe havens in which to learn. Some safe schools efforts are beyond the professional responsibilities of classroom teachers, but all educators can look to classroom management theorists and their models for suggestions that contribute to a physically and psychologically safe learning environment for all. "Reaching Out With Technology" on this book's Companion Web Site provides Internet resources that you can consult for additional information on promoting safe classrooms and schools.

Suggested Readings

Blum, R. W. (2005). A case for school connectedness. *Educational Leadership, 62*(7), 16–20. Blum suggests students are more likely to succeed, academically and behaviorally, when they feel connected to school.

Brunner, J., & Lewis, D. (2005). School safety's top ten. *Principal Leadership, 5*(9), 65–66. As the title suggests, this article is a list and brief discussion of strategies for assessing the safety and security of a school.

Bucher, K. T., & Manning, M. L. (2005). Creating safe schools. *The Clearing House* 79(1) 55–60. The authors look at the problems of providing schools that are intellectually as well as physically safe for both students and teachers.

Canfield, B. S., Ballard, M. B., Osmon, B. C., McCune, C. (2004). School and family counselors work together to reduce fighting at school. *Professional School Counseling, 8*(1), 40–46. Addressing the problem of fighting in urban middle schools, these authors provide a multifamily counseling program as an alternative to suspension programs.

Chittorran, M. M., & Hoenig, G. A. (2005). Mediating a better solution. *Principal Leadership, 5*(7), 11–15. These authors focus on peer mediation and suggest students become better problem solvers, decision makers, and communicators.

Gunzelmann, B. (2004). Hidden dangers within our schools: What are these safety problems and how can we fix them? *Educational Horizons, 83*(1), 66–76. Maintaining school safety is more than metal detectors and disaster plans, Gunzelmann discusses the essentials of a safe, healthy school climate.

Hernandez, T. J., & Seem, S. R. (2004). A safe school climate: A systemic approach and the school counselor. *Professional School Counseling, 7*(4), 256–262. Hernandez and Seem offer a conceptualization of school climate that contributing to school safety and provide implications for school counselors.

NCLB policies leave safe, orderly schools behind. (2005) *American Teacher, 89*(5), 6. This brief article maintains NCLB has a provision for safe schools, but some educators worry about implementation as it relates to school safety.

Schroeder, K. (2005). K–6 violence is global. *Education Digest, 70*(7), 71–73. Schroeder examines K–6 violence (mainly bullying, weapon use, and sexual harassment), the belief that "kids will be kids" (p. 71), and serious consequences that many victims face.

CHAPTER 14

Developing Your Personal Classroom Management Philosophy

Focusing Questions

After reading this chapter, you should be able to answer the following questions:

1. What is your personal classroom management philosophy, and how do your philosophical beliefs affect your everyday classroom management decisions?

2. What factors should educators consider as they develop their classroom management philosophy?

3. How can educators philosophically decide which student behaviors deserve to be addressed and which ones should be ignored?

4. How can teachers decide which definition of discipline (e.g., imposed discipline or self-discipline) best reflects their philosophical beliefs?

5. How can educators most effectively consider the commonly accepted classroom models (mainly the ones examined in this book) to decide philosophical foundations for their management practices?

6. Why should and how can educators seek collaborative assistance and advice from other stakeholders in classroom management efforts?

7. What other sources of information are available for readers as they develop a philosophy of classroom management that works for them?

Key Terms

> Imposed discipline
> Inclusion
> Taught discipline

This book has provided you with an opportunity to review a variety of classroom management models and theories. Now you need to decide whether you want to adopt one management model or eclectically select ideas from a combination of models to develop a personal classroom management philosophy. Most teachers reflect on their own beliefs about children and adolescents, their ideas about classroom management practices, and the practices of successful teachers. They then combine these ideas with a consideration of the specific behaviors they will need to address, the various definitions of discipline, their students' psychological and developmental needs, the goals of the safe schools movement, and commonly accepted management models, such as those examined in this text, to develop their own personal management philosophy. As you read through this chapter, examine your own philosophical perspectives to develop a personal philosophy of classroom management. To help, you may wish to use the "Voices of Educators," which is written by educators in response to the situations in the case studies as well as to some specific questions about classroom management. Then, in the next chapter, the experiences of practicing teachers will help you translate your philosophical position into application.

RATIONALE FOR DEVELOPING A PERSONAL PHILOSOPHY

As a result of our hundreds of visits to elementary, middle, and secondary schools, we have concluded that some educators have not engaged in a deliberate process to develop a personal philosophy of classroom management. They try one strategy, throw it out when it is not immediately effective, and move on to another. Some even move back and forth from one strategy to another, alternating between the autocratic and democratic classroom management methods within the same lesson and then wondering why classroom management is such a problem. We also have seen many educators who have developed carefully thought-out blueprints for their management practices. These effective classroom managers

- Use classroom management practices that reflect their philosophical beliefs,
- Think about their management practices and why they use them,
- Take into consideration the steadily increasing student diversity in the classroom,
- Provide actions to be used in the case of violent and aggressive behaviors to ensure safe schools,
- Keep in mind how students, parents, administrators, and other teachers will react to their plan,
- Make sure their management ideas are concrete and can be translated into practice.

Synthesis of Management Plan and Philosophical Beliefs

What kind of classroom manager do you want to be? Think back to Dreikurs, Grunwald, and Pepper's (1971) discussion of autocratic and democratic teachers. Do you recall how Coloroso (1994) labeled teachers as brickwall, jellyfish, and backbone? Dreikurs's and Coloroso's types of teachers reflect particular philosophical beliefs. For example, autocratic and brickwall teachers see themselves as adults who must control students who lack the ability to achieve self-discipline. In contrast, democratic and backbone teachers believe students can learn to discipline themselves. Somewhere in between are the jellyfish teachers, who appear to have neither the philosophical perspectives nor the desire to manage students.

If you are allowed the freedom to choose your own classroom management model or eclectically choose concepts from several models, you probably will be in a good position to have a management model that reflects your philosophical perspectives. Consider the range of models from the Canters's (1976, 1992) fairly rigid Assertive Discipline to Kounin's (1970) emphasis on teachers' instructional management. Do you feel comfortable using Skinner's behavior modification with its punishments and rewards, or are you inspired by Kohn's (1996) call to move beyond discipline?

If, on the other hand, you teach in a school that has adopted a specific classroom management model, you probably will have to adjust your philosophical thinking to meet the expectations of the model. However, even in a single-management-model school, your daily interactions with students will demonstrate your personal philosophical perspectives. Case Study 14–1 looks at Ms. Faletti, who taught in an elementary school that adopted a school-wide classroom management model. After reading the Case Study, you will find the reactions of some educators in Voices of Educators: Reacting to Case Study 14–1.

By now you may be asking how to go about developing your own management philosophy. Surprisingly, something that sounds as lofty as a philosophy can be relatively easy to

CASE STUDY 14–1
Dealing with a Schoolwide Model

Ms. Sharon Faletti, a fourth-grade teacher, taught in an elementary school that was known for its well-behaved students. Although the usual minor problems of students talking, walking around, and failing to do their work existed, the school had, so far, been free of violence and serious behavior problems. Either the students were good or the classroom management techniques were working. In fact, Ms. Tamika Story, the principal, required all teachers to use a specific behavior management model and had started the year with a series of workshops on the model and its use with consultant Dr. Felicia Ortega. As Ms. Story liked to say, "If we all adhere to the same classroom management system, children will see consistency from class to class."

Although Ms. Faletti remembered the workshops, she was not convinced that all teachers needed to adopt the same model rigidly. As she said, "We're all different—our management philosophies, our strategies, and our goals. Sure, we can make children behave with our adopted model, but with varying degrees of success. Plus, why shouldn't we be allowed to develop our own more personalized model that reflects our own philosophy? We should be able to look at the various models and choose among them to determine what works best for us."

Finally, a number of teachers, led by Ms. Faletti, went to Ms. Story to discuss this issue. The principal, although not overly pleased, gave the teachers permission to form a committee to look at the pros and cons of a "school-adopted model" over a "more personalized model." She asked Ms. Faletti to chair the committee.

After meeting several times, the committee developed the following list of pros and cons of a schoolwide classroom management model.

Advantages

1. Professional development in the management model can be provided to all teachers in the school.
2. Students will have consistent management expectations regardless of the teacher.
3. Teachers can collaborate with other teachers to refine management skills.

Disadvantages

1. Teachers often offer varying degrees of commitment to the model—some commit wholeheartedly, but others are less enthusiastic.
2. Teachers do not have the opportunity to consider various classroom management models and eclectically "personalize" their model.
3. Teachers have to use the model, regardless of whether students find it offensive or intrusive.

As the committee continued meeting, it became apparent that Ms. Faletti faced a dilemma. Although some teachers wanted a model based on their personal philosophy—one they could tweak when necessary—most teachers liked having a schoolwide model. Ms. Faletti could not see a compromise. If the principal and the majority of the teachers wanted a schoolwide model, she assumed she had no choice except to go along with them. As she said to herself, "Maybe I could change a few things, maybe change a few rules and use some flexibility in individual situations. No, I guess not; everyone is supposed to do the same. I just don't know. Maybe the only option is to transfer to another school."

Questions for Consideration

1. Is there a way Ms. Faletti can have a classroom model based on her personal philosophy in line with her philosophical beliefs and simultaneously adhere to the principal's expectations?
2. Could she legitimately use some flexibility in individual situations?
3. Is there a way she could be more eclectic and select some aspects of other theorists?

 You can record your answers to these questions online on this book's Companion Web Site at *www.prenhall.com/manning*.

develop, although it will take some time and thought. The first step is to determine how you feel about students, your role as a teacher, and the ultimate goals of your classroom management ideas. A number of items must be considered in reaching your conclusions, and Activity 14–1 contains a list of several questions to help you begin the process.

The Need for a Personally Effective Plan

You need to feel effective with whatever classroom management technique you adopt. Realistically speaking, what works for one teacher might not work for another.

Voices of Educators

Reacting to Case Study 14–1

After reading the case study, educators made the following comments:

- Teacher consistency and "buy-in" are big factors in the success of a schoolwide model.
- I've seen some training for a schoolwide model that is highly structured and without flexibility. It wouldn't work for me.
- Usually, there is some room for personalization to meet the needs of the students in your classroom and to align more closely with your own philosophy. I worked in a school that required teachers to "hire" students for classroom positions. But each teacher could design the jobs that fit his or her classroom.
- I've worked in a school that requires a classroom constitution with rules for schoolwide use, as well as for use in each classroom. Teachers have some flexibility to guide and develop goals in their own classrooms to match their personal philosophy and beliefs.
- The teachers in the scenario should ask to visit schools that have this model and talk with teachers in that school. E-mail works too.

Charlotta Kayama spoke softer and softer as her students grew louder. Without fail, her students also became quieter. Ms. Kayama was a teacher who could manage her class by softening her voice. We have seen other teachers try the same technique with the opposite results.

Elliott Purcell taught in a school that had adopted the Canters' Assertive Discipline. He liked it and had refined the model to a fine art. Kena Sample, an excellent student teacher, was placed with Mr. Purcell, but she did not like Assertive Discipline and never developed any degree of expertise with it.

Whenever we are in teachers' lounges and hear one teacher say to another, "Try my classroom management technique; it always works," we are skeptical. It is our belief that you have to decide for yourself what works for you and what you feel comfortable with. That is one reason we encourage an eclectic approach to decide what works most effectively. Remember, a teacher might be able to make students behave but might still feel ineffective or uncomfortable because of the management strategies that must be used. We asked a number of practicing teachers what they thought about developing a personal classroom management plan. Some of their responses are in Voices of Educators: Developing a Personal Management Philosophy.

The Need for a Plan That All Parties Consider Fair

Ms. Slate's class complained that she was unfair. Their comments included "She's mean," "A control freak," "She's got classroom pets and picks on the rest," and "Never listens to our side of the story." Everyone acquainted with Ms. Slate knew she could control her class. In fact, her principal once said, "I have no problems with Ms. Slate's class; she always makes the students behave." However, the students and some of the parents complained that she had favorites and used "heavy-handed tactics" such as sarcasm, ridicule, and autocratic demands to keep the rest under control.

Activity 14-1

Understanding Philosophical Beliefs

To help identify your philosophical beliefs about classroom management, ask yourself the following questions.

Beliefs About Students

1. Do I believe that students need to be "controlled and disciplined" or that they can be taught self-discipline?
2. Do I believe that students are basically good or are they naturally disruptive and therefore need to be molded and conditioned to behave appropriately?
3. Do I view students as equals or as subordinates?
4. Do I believe that establishing a democratic classroom and giving students responsibility means letting them take over the classroom?

Teachers' Roles

1. Do I see myself as an autocratic or a democratic teacher? A brickwall, jellyfish, or backbone teacher? An assertive teacher?
2. Do I see my management role as being a leadership process or a collaborative process with students, parents, and other professionals?
3. Do I believe that I should make all the rules and assign consequences, or do I believe that students should offer their input?
4. Do I want to "manage" or "discipline" my students? What do I perceive as the difference?
5. Do I believe that the time spent teaching classroom rules or developing rules with the students is time that could be better spent on instruction?

Classroom Management

1. Do I believe in rewards, punishments, bribes, and threats, and do I think these are necessary for effective classroom management?
2. Is the ultimate goal of my classroom management plan to manage to control the class for another day, to make everybody follow the rules, or to teach students self-discipline so they will discipline themselves?
3. Do I feel more comfortable adhering to the tenets of a school-adopted classroom management program, or do I want to have more freedom to choose my own classroom management practices?

We are concerned that many people did not think Ms. Slate's management philosophy was based on fairness and equitable treatment for all students, but we are equally concerned about the role model that she presented. As she demonstrated the opposite of equality, fairness, collaboration, and positive human relations, her students began to adopt many of the negative behaviors she modeled.

Advantages and Disadvantages of the Models

Although some classroom management models and theories almost purport to make miraculous changes in student behavior, it is realistic to say that all models and theories have their advantages and disadvantages. In our examination of each model in this book, we listed advantages and disadvantages in the respective chapters. Now, in Activity 14–2, we show how you might question the advantages and disadvantages of a few selected models in relation to your own philosophical perspectives.

Voices of Educators

Developing a Personal Management Philosophy

We posed the following question to a number of teachers: Why should a teacher develop a classroom management plan?

- To survive! To teach without a classroom management plan is unthinkable. If you do not have a plan, your students will.
- It is essential to have classroom procedures and rules to effectively teach. If students are not "on-task" because of disruptions, they are not learning. To develop my management plan, I used good common sense and based my plan on the ideas of respect for others and for property.
- An established routine is an absolute necessity for a functioning classroom. Each child is an individual with fears and concerns that have to be met. Their sense of security depends on understanding what is expected of them at all times.
- Some of the same rules [in a management plan] can work [for all teachers], but I do not believe that the same plan will work. Every teacher has a different personality and philosophy, and the level of students makes a big difference.

Activity 14-2

Comparing Theories and Models to Your Management Philosophy

As you begin to develop the philosophical basis for your own classroom management plan, consider the following general questions. Then, go back and review all the information that you recorded in the Developing Your Personal Philosophy sections in chapters 1 through 13.

General Questions to Consider

1. Do I believe that I can manage students' behaviors effectively and positively with this model or these practices?
2. Would I feel comfortable or would I feel constant anxiety or frustration using these ideas?
3. Does this model expect me to control students' behavior through rewards, punishments, bribes, and threats, and do I feel comfortable doing this?
4. Would I have to ask administrators and parents to intervene in efforts to maintain proper behavior if I used these ideas?
5. Would I have to use management techniques that I do not like?
6. What impression would I give students if I used this model in my classroom?

DEVELOPING A PERSONAL CLASSROOM MANAGEMENT PHILOSOPHY

Considering Which Problems to Address

When you develop your personal philosophy of classroom management, you need to consider the specific student behaviors you want to address in the plan. Do you want to respond to all behavior problems or just ones that interrupt the teaching/learning process? Are there problems you believe you can ignore? Table 14–1 illustrates three general categories of misbehaviors. As you develop your own philosophy of classroom management, you need to consider which misbehaviors your plan will address and which, if any, it will ignore.

Although minor misbehaviors can escalate into more serious problems, most teachers ignore them whenever possible.

> As one teacher explained: "I try to ignore a lot because I think it's better to address behaviors that actually interfere with my teaching. It's taken me a long time to come to this conclusion, but, now, I seem to know what behaviors to correct and which ones to ignore. Things like minor talking, a little walking around the room, and occasional goofing off don't bother me anymore. The students know the limits, but they know they have some freedom, too."

Rather than stopping the instructional momentum and losing students' attention, a teacher should try to ignore minor misbehaviors and proceed with the lesson. However, Redl and Wattenberg (1959), discussed in chapter 2, believe that misbehavior is often contagious. Once one student misbehaves and the teacher fails to provide an adequate response, other students misbehave because they assume the teacher is not going to take action. It takes talent and experience to determine which minor misbehaviors will probably not spread and which ones will escalate into more serious problems. Thus, the most effective managers usually consider each misbehavior to determine its seriousness rather than trying to address all misbehaviors. Unless the teacher believes a disruptive behavior is only temporary, it should be addressed before it interferes with teaching and learning. Finally, aggressive behaviors should always be dealt with firmly and decisively.

As you can see, trying to address all misbehaviors might be inviting disaster, but not addressing any misbehaviors creates an environment in which students fail to learn and are even physically and psychologically harmed. Case Study 14–2 looks at Mr. Vannostrand as he tries to determine which misbehaviors he can ignore and which ones to address. In Voices

Table 14–1 Levels of Misbehaviors

Levels of Misbehaviors	Examples
Minor Misbehaviors	While completing an in-class assignment, Eli asks Dunca for a pencil.
	During silent reading, Leah stops and stares out the window for a long time.
	In the middle of a lesson, Matt walks across the room and throws something in the wastebasket.
Disruptive Misbehaviors	Lynn calls out the answers all the time instead of raising her hand.
	Ty shoots paper wads at other students.
	Anita starts aimlessly walking around the room and stopping to talk to other students when she is supposed to be working on a project with her group.
Aggressive Misbehaviors	Trina pushes Sherena out of her chair and starts pulling Sherena's hair.
	Cade pulls a knife out of his pocket.
	Nelson calls Lakeisha "trash from the projects" and makes a crude gesture.

CASE STUDY 14–2
Identifying Misbehaviors That Need Attention

Mr. Stuart Vannostrand, a 10th-grade teacher, wanted to develop his own personal classroom management philosophy and model. Because he was uneasy about addressing every minor misbehavior, he wanted to identify those that would warrant his attention as well as the nondisruptive ones that he would ignore. When he mentioned his idea to some of his colleagues, they were skeptical and told him that it would be unfair for him to address some problems and ignore others. Most of the teachers in his school posted a fairly rigid set of rules and imposed penalties for all misbehaviors. To them, all behavior situations were clear cut. Students either broke the rule or they did not. If they broke the rule, they were punished. "You have to be consistent," one of his colleagues said. "You can't do all this deliberation. Spend your time teaching, and stop all this dallying around trying to figure out what misbehaviors need to be addressed—do something about all of them. That's the easiest thing to do."

Unwilling to give up his idea, Mr. Vannostrand tried to determine a way to differentiate between behavior problems to be addressed and ones to be ignored. As he jotted a few words and diagrams on his notepad, he pondered: What should I do if a student breaks a behavior rule, yet the misbehavior does not disturb anyone else? What should I do if a student breaks the same rule, and others begin to break the rule, too? For example, if Deon leans over to ask April a question about an assignment, should I remind him that it is quiet time? Then, what if Josh starts talking to Wansa about the basketball game last night and Sherina joins the conversation? How can I address one misbehavior and ignore the other? Although the misbehavior is the same, the result differs. Can I consider the effects of misbehaviors to determine my response? If Rohlin has a knife, then I have to address the problem. If he utters a relatively minor obscenity, do I have to say something? I realize I have to have a management philosophy, I just don't see why I should address every misbehavior. Wouldn't it be better to try to differentiate among behaviors to determine what to address and what to ignore?

Questions for Consideration

1. Are there times when one student could misbehave and Mr. Vannostrand should do nothing and other times when another student would misbehave and he would have to take action?

2. How much time will be involved with all the decision making, and is it worth spending this amount of time?

3. Does Mr. Vannostrand risk having students say he is unfair and inconsistent?

4. What models of classroom management featured in this book might Mr. Vannostrand want to consider?

 You can record your answers to these questions online on this book's Companion Web Site at *www.prenhall.com/manning*.

of Educators: Reacting to Case Study 14–2, some teachers provide their reactions to the Case Study. Then, Activity 14–3 helps you determine specific behaviors you want to address.

Discipline: Imposed or Taught?

As you develop your management philosophy, you also need to consider whether you believe discipline should be imposed or taught. This is a crucial point, because if you favor **imposed discipline**, then you must be willing to accept total responsibility for managing students' behavior. If, however, you believe in **taught discipline**, then you must work to teach discipline and to teach students to discipline themselves eventually. When imposing discipline, a teacher punishes students in order to convince them to demonstrate appropriate behavior.

"I will discipline Jodette for talking without raising her hand."

In contrast, a teacher who teaches discipline tries to help students learn or develop the self-discipline to demonstrate appropriate behavior.

"I will teach Jodette self-discipline so that she knows to always raise her hand before speaking."

You might remember this topic from chapter 4, which covered Rudolf Dreikurs's Democratic Teaching. In that chapter, we discussed how Dreikurs, Grunwald, and Pepper (1971, p. 21) thought "the teaching of discipline is an ongoing process, not something to resort to only in times of stress or misbehavior." The teacher who seeks only to impose discipline has a never-ending challenge; the teacher who seeks to teach discipline has hope that students will

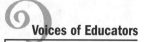

Reacting to Case Study 14–2

After reading the case study, educators made the following comments:

- Teachers need to respond to misbehavior. However, the best way to deal with class-room management problems is to prevent them. Well-behaved, productive classes are the result of the time and energy teachers devote to careful planning, meaningful activities, and a sense of fair play.
- It's important to establish an environment conducive to learning right at the begin-ning. That means discussing and developing, with students, needed classroom rules and consequences.
- Mr. Vannostrand should explain that he expects students to follow class rules but that he alters consequences depending on the situation. He should clarify his expecta-tions, using examples, and should show that to treat each person and situation *exactly* the same is not always fair. Most 10th-grade students will be able to understand and accept this concept. Although asking another student a question about the assign-ment during "quiet time" breaks one of his rules, it does not warrant the same con-sequences as an off-task conversation about a basketball game.
- The incident with Deon and April offers an opportunity for Mr. Vannostrand to demon-strate his classroom management style and begin to earn the respect of his students. Teenagers value teachers who are not afraid to confront problems, whether it is to help a student or to diffuse an explosive situation; they appreciate teachers whose priority is education, not rules.

learn self-discipline. However, the answer might not be so clear-cut. Teachers who want to teach discipline or teach students to discipline themselves might have to impose discipline until students learn self-discipline. In other words, instead of teachers facing an either-or situation, the reality is that students have varying degrees of self-discipline, perhaps even changing daily. Activity 14–4 asks you to consider whether you want to impose or teach discipline in your classroom.

Students' Psychological and Developmental Needs

Whether you decide to adopt one of the models in this book or eclectically select the "best" from a number of models, you need to consider how your management philosophy and prac-tices affect your students' psychological and developmental needs. Will your philosophy help students feel safe, physically and psychologically, from your actions, as well as the actions of other students? You also must let students know that you respect their diversity: cultural, gender, social class, and sexual orientation.

Although you should avoid embarrassing or ridiculing students into compliance, you also must use developmentally appropriate philosophical practices; management strategies appropriate for elementary or middle school students are probably inappropriate for high school students (and vice versa). Along with this, you must consider the powerful effects of peer pressure (negative and positive) on middle school and higher students and remember the disastrous effects that can occur when students are harassed, bullied, ridiculed, and threat-ened on a daily basis. Although it can be difficult at times, you must work to leave students'

Activity 14–3

Determining Specific Misbehaviors to Address

Make a list of misbehaviors you might expect to see in your classroom. Then use the following questions to categorize them. Which are misbehaviors you need to address and which, if any, can you ignore?

1. What seems to be the goal of the misbehavior?
2. What is the result of the misbehavior?
3. Does the misbehavior directly affect or annoy someone?
4. Is a student being physically or psychologically harmed (e.g., fight is beginning, someone is being called names, or someone is being threatened)?
5. Does it appear that the misbehavior is temporary?
6. Does it appear that other students might copycat the misbehavior?
7. Is it a violation of a stated rule or should the student just know better?
8. Will the correction of the misbehavior cause more disruption than the actual problem?

Activity 14–4

Deciding Whether to Teach or Impose Discipline

Read the following questions and consider how you might respond to each of them. Then be prepared to explain where you stand on teaching or imposing discipline.

1. Do I believe that because I am the teacher/adult, I have a responsibility to discipline them?
2. Do I believe students have the ability and motivation to learn self-discipline?
3. Could I teach students to discipline themselves even if I wanted to?
4. Can I impose discipline (and therefore be an autocratic teacher) until students learn self-discipline?
5. Will I be perceived as a jellyfish (Coloroso, 1994) if I try to avoid imposing discipline?
6. Will I be perceived as a brickwall (Coloroso, 1994) if I try to impose discipline?
7. Will students' behavior grow worse during the process of moving from "imposing" discipline to "teaching" discipline?

self-esteem intact, regardless of their misbehaviors. Finally, you always must consider your students' cognitive, psychological, and physical developmental characteristics and then examine how your classroom management practices (and the underlying philosophical beliefs) affect students' many developmental and psychological needs.

Case Study 14–3 looks at Dr. Kellerstrass, a principal who thinks a kindergarten teacher is failing to provide appropriate classroom management practices that meet the developmental and psychological needs of her students and asks some questions about how you would handle the situation. Then, in Voices of Educators: Reacting to Case Study 14–3, educators comment on the case study.

Considering the Challenges of Inclusion

Inclusion, or the teaching and managing of special needs students in regular classroom settings, should also be considered as you develop your management philosophy. First, you need to explore honestly your beliefs about educating and managing special needs students in regular or general education classes. In addition, you should consider how your management responsibilities will change as you have increasingly diverse student populations in your classes. Your philosophical deliberations should address the academic and the behavioral needs of students with disabilities (Gable, Hendrickson, Tonelson, & Van Acker, 2000).

CASE STUDY 14–3
Questioning a Teacher's Management Style

Dr. Marissa Kellerstrass, a new principal, thought that Ms. Laverne Sallo, a primary school teacher, used management techniques that failed to consider the developmental and psychological needs of her kindergartners and that were more appropriate for students 4 or 5 years older. For example, Dr. Kellerstrass was concerned that Ms. Sallo tried to keep her 5-year-olds too quiet and seated for too long. The principal also believed that Ms. Sallo did not give her students enough opportunities to be creative and spontaneous in their learning. In one meeting with Ms. Sallo, Dr. Kellerstrass explained, "You keep your students seated and quiet for too long. These are 5-year-olds. They should be given more opportunities to move around, explore their world, and develop self-discipline."

In reply, Mrs. Sallo said, "True, but I'm afraid to give them too much freedom; they are too much trouble to get calmed down again. You know, they're such a rowdy group at times. I'm afraid you might walk in the room and the children might be going bonkers. What if you did an impromptu evaluation and they were loud? What if I tried to get them back in their seats and they wouldn't go?"

Dr. Kellerstrass tried to help Ms. Sallo understand about 5-year-olds' development and the activities they needed. "Your children need to socialize, experience freedom of movement, learn self-discipline, make decisions about their behavior, move around to the various learning centers, and talk quietly among themselves. Please reconsider your philosophical beliefs about classroom management and children's developmental and psychological needs."

After the meeting, Ms. Sallo thought about the conversation for a long time. She had to admit that the principal was correct in think-ing that she did not have a management philosophy that was compatible with kindergartners' development. However, she also knew that she had difficulty managing her kindergarten class. She had always had management problems, even during her student teaching. In fact, she chose to teach kindergarten because she feared she could not get older students to behave. Now she faced another predicament: Her principal did not like her management philosophy and style. With her annual evaluations at stake, she knew she had to take some action to show Dr. Kellerstrass that she was at least trying.

Questions for Consideration

1. Is it possible for Ms. Sallo to let her kindergartners talk a little and walk around and still get them back on-task when she wants them to be?

2. What are some of the developmental characteristics and psychological needs of kindergartners that she would need to consider?

3. What management techniques are appropriate for addressing these characteristics and needs?

4. How can Ms. Sallo balance being too firm with being too nice?

5. What can she do to meet Dr. Kellerstrass's expectation of considering the developmental and psychological needs of her students and, at the same time, making the children behave?

 You can record your answers to these questions online on this book's Companion Web Site at *www.prenhall.com/manning*.

Voices of Educators

Reacting to Case Study 14–3

Educators made the following responses to the case study:

- To meet the developmental needs of kindergartners, you have to give them choices of activities. They need to socialize, make decisions about their own behavior, and have choices and limits provided so that they can develop self-discipline and begin to think for themselves.
- Ms. Sallo has to understand that when children are actively engaged, they can sound loud or seem unruly at first glance. However, if you look closely, you'll see children talking about their learning and learning through play.
- Let Ms. Sallo pay several visits to developmentally appropriate kindergarten classrooms so she can observe center time, transitions, and direct instruction.
- New teachers have to establish classroom management procedures the first week of school and then follow through on a consistent basis.
- Kindergartners need lots of practice with things like lining up, walking quietly in the hall, reading aloud, calendar time, cleaning up, moving between centers, etc. For example, centers should be introduced slowly, modeled, and practiced at the beginning of the year so that students understand what exactly is to be done at each center. Classroom management takes less time at the end when you spend more time in the beginning.

Activity 14–5

Exploring Your Beliefs About Inclusion

Explore your beliefs about inclusion by responding to the following questions:

1. Do I believe that inclusion is the best way to educate special needs students?
2. Do I agree with the philosophical assumptions suggested by Gable et al. (2000)?
3. If I do not agree, how can I best meet the challenge so I can stay in compliance with Individuals with Disabilities Education Act?
4. How do I feel about special needs learners who will be educated in regular classrooms?
5. Can I manage special needs learners in a caring and professional manner?
6. What special management methods should I employ as I work with these children and adolescents?

Positive student–teacher relationships and quality academic instruction are key factors that help all students achieve (Osher, Catledge, Osward, Sutherland, Artiles, and Coutinho, 2004). According to Gable et al. (2000), to meet the behavioral needs of all students, you must accept the beliefs that all students learn best

- In an environment that reflects a unified approach to positive disciplinary practices, with emphasis on early intervention so that minor difficulties are resolved before they escalate and become major problems,
- In an environment in which schoolwide and classroom academic and behavioral supports are routinely provided,
- When discipline is addressed through instruction, with appropriate behavior taught in a routine and systematic manner,
- In an environment in which administrative leadership fosters a school, home, and community partnership for promoting positive school outcomes for all students.

Thus, as you develop your classroom management philosophy, you need to consider the impact that inclusion will have on the realities of your situation. It will be important for you to resolve these philosophical considerations prior to developing your classroom management plan. Ask yourself the questions in Activity 14–5.

Developing a Personal Philosophy

We favor an eclectic approach to classroom management, in which educators pick and choose from a number of management models and theories as they develop their personal

Table 14-2 An Eclectic Approach: Selecting From Various Models

Theory/Model	Concepts to Reflect in Our Personal Philosophy
Kounin: Instructional Management (Kounin, 1970)	Classroom management must include instructional management. Teacher's behavior affects students' behavior.
Coloroso: Inner Discipline (Coloroso, 1983; 1994)	Students are worth the effort and should be treated with respect and dignity. Teachers should abide by the Golden Rule.
Canter and Canter: Assertive Discipline (Canter, 1974; Canter & Canter, 1976)	Both teachers and students have rights. Teachers should insist upon students demonstrating responsible behavior.
Dreikurs: Democratic Teaching (Dreikurs and Grey, 1968)	Teachers should use logical consequences instead of punishments. Teachers should be democratic rather than autocratic.
Ginott: Congruent Communication (Ginott, 1965; 1969)	Teachers accept and acknowledge students. Teachers avoid you-messages.
Curwin and Mendler: Discipline with Dignity (Curwin & Mendler, 1980)	Classrooms should be student-centered. Teachers avoid authoritarian stances.
Jones: Positive Classroom Management (Jones, 1987)	Management strategies should be simple, easy to use, and "cheap" (Jones, 1987, p. 25). Teachers must have exemplary planning and instruction.
Freiberg: Consistency Management (Freiberg, 2000)	Students should be self-disciplined. Teachers should have student-centered classrooms.
Gathercoal: Judicious Discipline (Gathercoal, 1997)	Teachers should demonstrate professional ethics, provide democratic classrooms, and provide behavior guidelines.
Kohn: Beyond Discipline (Kohn, 1996)	Teachers should not base their management decisions upon negative ideas about students. Educators need to develop a sense of community in the school.
Evertson and Harris: Managing Learning-Centered Classrooms (Evertson, Emmer, & Worsham, 2000)	Teachers should plan for the first of the year so that students know exactly what to do. Teachers should categorize misbehaviors to identify those needing minor, moderate, and extensive interventions.

Voices of Educators

Developing a Personal Plan

We asked a number of educators the following question: How would you go about developing a management plan for your classroom? Here are a few responses.

- To develop a plan, consider first what you and your students need to make the most effective use of time. How can the plan be made positive but have consequences for those who do not follow the rules?
- Use common sense and the advice of others. Be consistent, be firm, be fair. Respect is the key.
- In my mind there is a list of dos and do-nots. The dos include

  Be fair and consistent,

  Have a good sense of humor in the classroom,

  Call parents for support,

  Be calm (students want to see you blow up),

  Admit when you are wrong and laugh about it,

  Remember you are the adult and a role model.

  The do-nots are

  Do not be like the students and get an attitude,

  Do not hold grudges,

  Do not show favoritism,

  Do not take things personally.

  I do my dos and do not do my do-nots, and that is why I believe I have had a very good rapport with my students. It has taken me awhile in my 13 years of teaching to get this far and use my personality to help with the discipline in the classroom. It helps a great deal that I am a happy person with a good sense of humor. My students know that I really enjoy teaching because I have fun.
- All grade levels require a well-ordered classroom. The most effective upper-grade teachers appear to have effective management systems firmly in place. My advice to new teachers about developing a classroom management plan is to consult the other teachers on their grade level and to use the other teachers' systems as much as possible until there is time to develop their own plan.

philosophies on which to base their classroom management strategies. What makes this particularly difficult is that we can decide only for ourselves what we think works most effectively. We are not able to decide what works for another teacher. Thus, you will need to consider each topic discussed in this chapter and identify your own philosophical precepts (e.g., perspectives toward students, students' and teachers' roles, and whether discipline should be taught or imposed, to name a few examples) to determine what you want to adopt from the various models and theories.

What do we like? What aspects of the models in this book reflect our own thinking? Because space will not permit a detailed listing of each of the models and all of the aspects we think reflect our philosophy, we have provided some examples in Table 14–2. All the other theorists and models discussed in this book can also be of help in the development of a personal philosophy of classroom management. Once you have examined your philosophical beliefs, review the models and identify the concepts in each that reflect and support your ideas. To help you, we asked some practicing teachers how they developed their classroom management plans. A few answers are in Voices of Educators, Developing a Personal Plan.

SEEKING COLLABORATIVE ASSISTANCE AND ADVICE

All too often, educators see classroom management as a singular or isolated effort in which teachers are assigned a class but given little professional assistance in managing it. Some teachers might have the help of subject-area and instructional specialists, but most schools expect teachers to have a well-developed classroom management philosophy as well as workable management strategies. Often, teachers fend for themselves and hope their students are well behaved, and they hope their classroom management strategies work. However, as you read in Voices of Educators, Developing a Personal Plan, experienced teachers often recommend that new teachers seek the advice of others in developing their management plan.

Activity 14–6

Interviewing Other Educators

The following are some questions that you might ask and some topics to cover when you interview a practicing educator about classroom management. Prior to interviewing the individual, consider what you want to gain from your interview and add your own questions.

1. What is your grade level? Are you in an urban, suburban, or rural school? How many years have you taught?
2. Do you believe that discipline should be imposed or taught? (*Note:* You might have to explain what you mean by these two terms, so review the terms prior to your interview).
3. How have behavior problems changed since you began teaching? Has student behavior improved or grown worse?
4. What are the most common behavior problems in your classroom?
5. What do you think are several causes of discipline problems in your school? Are they caused by problems in the home, at school, or in society in general?
6. Do you believe that schools should adopt schoolwide models of discipline or that should teachers be allowed to select their own management practices? What is your school's policy concerning allowing individual teachers to select their own classroom management practices? Is there a particular management model that you prefer? If so, which one and why? What factors do you look for in selecting a management model?
7. What student-parent-teacher-administrator collaborative efforts do you have to promote positive classroom management?
8. How do parental attitudes promote or impede student discipline?
9. Does your school or school division have a written safe-school policy? Do you feel safe in your school, in your classroom, in the halls, and on the school grounds? Why? What could you as a classroom teacher do to make children feel physically and psychologically safe?
10. Has your school provided inservice training sessions that focus on school safety, avoiding school tragedies, and reacting and coping with tragedies?
11. What security measures does your school have? Do you use security guards, closed-circuit television cameras, metal detectors, or security alarm buttons? What other security measures do you believe schools should use?
12. What management advice do you have for beginning teachers or experienced teachers who are seeking new ideas?

Unfortunately, we have known teachers who considered a career change after only a year or two because they felt the demands of classroom management were too great and because they thought other professionals neither understood the problems they faced nor wanted to help. Rather than feeling isolated or overwhelmed with behavior problems, teachers need to collaborate with others. In doing so, they can see that other school professionals do understand the challenges of classroom management and are willing to offer advice and expertise.

CASE STUDY 14—4
Seeking Advice and Collaboration

After 5 years of using a schoolwide management model, the teachers and administrators at Carver Middle School decided to allow individual teachers to choose their own management strategies. Some of the teachers quickly chose specific management models and theorists, but other teachers elected to develop more eclectic management strategies based on their own personal beliefs and preferences.

Ms. Andrea Zeichner, a seventh-grade teacher, was a member of the second group and had two main goals for her plan. First, she wanted her plan to reflect her personal attitudes and thoughts about students and the classroom. Because she was ultimately responsible for the success of her management effort, Ms. Zeichner knew that she did not want to be autocratic or mean spirited. What she wanted was a plan that would show respect for students, assure their physical and psychological safety, convey a sense of trust and dignity, and provide a positive and caring classroom. Ms. Zeichner also wanted a plan that would reflect the views of others, including the students, their parents, and other educators in the school. She had a vision of incorporating everyone's ideas into a single plan for her classroom. Thus, she made the following lists of questions to ask each group.

Students

1. What do you want your classroom to be like?
2. What rewards, rules, and consequences do you want? If you do not want rewards, rules, and consequences, what type of management system do you suggest?
3. What freedoms and restrictions do you believe are necessary?
4. What will it take for you to feel physically and psychologically safe?
5. What suggestions do you have to make our classroom management workable and fair?

Administrators and Other School Professionals (library media specialists, counselors, speech pathologists, and other support professionals)

1. What type of management plan or management strategies do you think will work most effectively in our middle school?
2. How can I develop a management plan that reflects the developmental needs of the students as well as the school's overall goals and mission statement?

3. Do you agree with the practice of rewards, rules, and consequences? If not, what do you suggest that will result in an equitable and democratic management system?
4. What other factors should be considered as I develop my classroom management plan?
5. What can I do to promote safe schools where students feel physically and psychologically safe?

Parents

1. What behavior goals and expectations do you have for your child while he or she is in school?
2. What kinds of classroom management strategies would you like to see in your child's classroom?
3. Do you agree with the practice of rewards, rules, and consequences for your child? If not, what do you suggest that will result in an equitable and democratic management system?
4. What other suggestions do you have as we develop a classroom management system for your child?
5. What can we do to promote safe schools where students feel physically and psychologically safe?

Questions for Consideration

1. Analyze Ms. Zeichner's plan for developing her classroom management system. Is it realistic or idealistic to seek input from all of these groups?
2. Is she asking the right questions?
3. Are other ways available to find the information that she is seeking?
4. Should Ms. Zeichner even try to develop a classroom management plan of her own or should her plan be similar to those used by other members of her seventh-grade team?
5. How can Ms. Zeichner best accomplish her goals?
6. What models discussed in this text might she examine?

 You can record your answers to these questions online on this book's Companion Web Site at *www.prenhall.com/manning*.

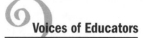

Voices of Educators

Reacting to Case Study 14–4

After reading Case Study 14–4, educators provided the following responses:

- Ms. Zeichner is unrealistic. If she surveys everyone suggested in the study, she'll be faced with an insurmountable amount of paperwork.
- It would be interesting to see what people say, but in reality, it's the teacher who's in the classroom with the students. Ultimately, she is the one who has to make decisions with respect to rules and the management required to enforce them.
- Having taught with a schoolwide management model for 5 years, Ms. Zeichner knows what works and what does not. She should use what works and make changes to those things that do not.
- Because she's working with a team of teachers, she needs to have a plan that is consistent with what others on her team are doing. Consistency in discipline is important for middle school students.
- This teacher needs to include regular communication with parents in terms of keeping them aware of what is happening in the classroom as it relates to their own child.

While realizing that the practices that work for some teachers might not work for others (hence the need for a personal philosophy of classroom management), they can learn new and innovative methods of managing students and can see that, especially in middle schools or where teachers are teamed for instruction, classroom management can be a collaborative rather than an isolated effort. In working with others, teachers also can see that the various constituencies have differing opinions on the challenges of managing students, such as views about the responsibilities of students, the roles of teachers, the definitions of discipline, and the goals of classroom management. Activity 14–6 provides a beginning list of questions that you can use to interview other educators about classroom management.

Case Study 14–4 considers Ms. Andrea Zeichner's efforts to collaborate by seeking the advice of students, educators, other school professionals, parents, and families to develop her classroom strategies. After you react to her situation, examine Voices of Educators, Reacting to Case Study 14–4.

CONCLUDING REMARKS

Please go to *www.prenhall.com/manning* and click on Concluding Remarks for this chapter to find more information.

Educators need to develop a personal philosophy of classroom management, regardless of the grade they teach or the management problems they face. Their philosophy can include any number of aspects, such as definitions of discipline, roles of teachers, behavior problems faced, and the goals of classroom management. We lean toward an eclectic approach or selecting the best from each model, but we encourage all educators to rely on their professional expertise as they develop a personal philosophy that they think will work for them. The Internet sites listed in "Reaching Out With Technology" on this book's Companion Web Site have additional information and resources on developing a classroom management philosophy. Once developed, the philosophy should become the basis for their classroom management strategies, with practices that reflect their philosophical positions.

Suggested Readings

Blum, R. W. (2005). A case for school connectedness. *Educational Leadership, 62*(7), 16–20. Blum maintains that students feeling connected to school are more likely to succeed academically and behaviorally.

Cookson, P. W. (2005). A community of teachers. *Teaching PreK–8, 35*(7), 12, 14. Cookson explains an effort to help create a community of teachers that supported each other and helped each other to improve classroom practices.

Finn, J. D., & Pannozzo, G. M. (2004). Classroom organization and student behavior in kindergarten. *The Journal of Educational Research, 98*(2), 79–92. The authors examine the conditions that promote or discourage engagement in the kindergarten classroom.

Lane, B. (2005). Dealing with rumors, secrets, and lies: Tools for aggression for middle school girls. *Middle School Journal, 36*(3), 41–47. Lane looks at bullying as social aggression and offers an excellent list of suggestions for dealing with girls' aggressive behaviors.

Lieberman, A., & Miller, L. (2005). Teachers as leaders. *The Educational Forum, 69*(2), 151–162. Lieberman and Miller look at the challenges facing schools: being asked to do more with less, dealing with management issues, and meeting the needs of diverse students.

Mano, S. (2005). Moving away from the authoritarian classroom. *Change, 37*(3), 50–57. The authoritarian stance of many teachers has resulted in the breakdown of trust in student–teacher relationships.

McCloud, S. (2005). From chaos to consistency. *Educational Leadership, 62*(5), 46–49. The author describes a school that changed its culture from chaotic to calm using the KIDS (Kentucky Instructional Discipline and Support) model developed by Randy Sprick.

Szente, J., Massey, C., & Hoot, J. L. (2005). Eyes in the back of your head: Cameras for classroom observation. *Learning and Leading with Technology, 32*(5), 18–21. This article describes how cameras allowed for improved instruction and student learning, teacher reflection, parent involvement, and documentation of student learning.

CHAPTER 15

Applying a Management Philosophy in Your Classroom

Focusing Questions

After reading this chapter, you should be able to answer the following questions:

1. How can I translate my personal philosophy of classroom management into effective and practical management practices and strategies?

2. How can I use human relations skills to contribute to my management effectiveness as I collaborate with students, parents, and administrators?

3. What factors should I consider as I build a positive classroom climate and instill a sense of community, one that will make students feel physically and psychologically safe?

4. How can I emphasize self-discipline and cooperation rather than impose discipline and control?

5. How can I treat students as individuals with unique behavior problems rather than making assumptions based on the class as a whole?

6. How can I most effectively understand and address students' differences, especially their cultural, gender, social class, and other differences?

7. What sources of information are available as I translate my philosophical beliefs into management practice?

Key Terms

Class meetings
Classroom community
Classroom management plan
Human relations skills
Inclusion

Now that you have considered your philosophy of classroom management, you need to think about how you will implement your philosophical beliefs and turn them into a management plan. As most educators will affirm, it is a big step from philosophy and theory to actual practice. The process can be challenging, but the results of developing and implementing your own classroom management plan will benefit you and your students. Just like the management plan itself, the move from philosophy to practice varies from teacher to teacher and depends on the use of human relations skills and the ability to build a civil classroom community, communicate with parents, and teach discipline and cooperation to all students.

APPLYING YOUR CLASSROOM MANAGEMENT SYSTEM

The first chapters in this book presented many classroom management models and theories; then, chapter 13 looked at the concepts of safe schools, and chapter 14 asked you to develop your personal philosophy of classroom management. Now, based upon this information, you need to begin to make the transition from theory to practice.

Personalizing your Classroom Management System

Although some teachers prefer the security of a school-adopted classroom management model, other teachers like to implement classroom management strategies that work for them and that reflect their philosophical beliefs. Still others are able to use their own ideas while working in a school with a schoolwide or grade-level management plan. To see how practicing teachers felt about this issue, we asked a number of experienced teachers for their views on personalizing a management system. Their responses are in Voices of Educators: Personalizing a Management System.

As you move from philosophy to practice, you must examine ways to develop effective human relations skills, build a sense of classroom community, teach self-discipline and cooperation, and communicate and collaborate with parents. Likewise, you must understand and plan for students' many differences—developmental, cultural, gender, and social class. In doing so, you have to keep in mind the realities of life and the fact that live students in a classroom are different from cardboard students on the page of a textbook. Case Study 15–1 looks at the difficulty Ms. Ocha experienced when she tried to translate her philosophical beliefs into practice. Responding to Ms. Ocha's situation, in Voices of Educators: Reacting to Case Study 15–1, educators provide their comments.

Developing Human Relations Skills

Like Ms. Ocha, all educators need to realize that classroom management involves working with live human beings. Thus, effective **human relations skills** need to be used in every classroom. Perhaps the best example of good human relations is a teacher who follows Coloroso's idea (1983, 1994) and applies the Golden Rule, in which teachers treat students as they would like to be treated. Good human relations skills also can include the ability to

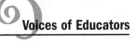

Voices of Educators

Personalizing a Management System

The following are the responses of experienced teachers to the question: Can the same management plan work for all teachers?

- No, the same plan will not work for everyone. Everyone has different strengths/weaknesses. What one teacher can do with a look or a tone of voice, another may have to do with consequences. Some may be able to use humor; others may not.
- Yes, the same plan can work. Fair, consistent classroom management applies to all disciplines, all levels, all students.
- Yes, the same plan can work, as long as the goal of using time wisely for teaching and learning is the same.
- My management system is one that I've developed over a number of years and it works for me! I taught first grade for 10 years and this is my second year teaching second grade. My system works well for both grade levels. Although some people may say that I have too many routines and procedures, I am just as serious as I can be about having a classroom that is safe, secure, and run in an orderly manner.

CASE STUDY 15–1
Translating Philosophical Beliefs Into Practice

Ms. Ocha, a first-grade teacher, was experiencing difficulty translating her philosophical beliefs into workable practices. As she explained to another first-grade teacher: "I know what I want, but moving from philosophy to practice is really difficult. I want a democratic classroom and freedom without rules, but the children just will not cooperate. In fact, they seem to throw up obstacles to derail my plan by fighting, calling each other names, and generally acting up. Two or three even bully others. I just don't know what to do. How can I implement a caring environment when my students don't care for each other? Plus, I'm sorry to admit it, but I do get upset at times. I mean, what else can I do when they try to hurt each other, walk around the room for no good reason, and call each other names? I can't believe first graders are doing this.

That night, Ms. Ocha tried again to list on paper what she wanted her class to be like. Then, she tried to determine the problem in moving from her philosophical ideal into actual practice. She wrote, "I want my children to

- Work in a positive environment that is free from undue criticism and unfavorable judgment,
- Collaborate with other children in an atmosphere free of competition and some children winning at the expense of others,
- Feel they are safe from bullies, harassment, sarcasm, and ridicule,
- Feel they are in a caring environment, or "community," where the teacher cares for and respects children and children care for and respect each other,
- Work in a classroom environment that is free from rewards, punishments, and bribes,
- Work in a classroom that promotes self-esteem and self-worth, both as children and as students."

Then, Ms. Ocha thought about how she could translate her philosophical beliefs into practical application. She decided she could

- Demonstrate more patience and understanding; she remembered how she had snapped at Cesar for speaking out of turn,
- Teach the behaviors by taking class time to teach the children how she wanted them to behave,
- Model respect, positiveness, caring, and collaboration so students would see what she was trying to teach,
- Speak individually with students who bully and harass others in an attempt to change their negative behaviors,
- Speak with the counselor, who might be able to suggest resources or even conduct a class on how to treat others,
- Speak with the library media specialist about books on "civility" that she could read to her class.

Questions for Consideration

1. Is it possible for Ms. Ocha to implement all of her philosophical ideals in her classroom?
2. How realistic are her ideas?
3. Why does such a gap exist between what she expects and the way her students act?
4. Will Ms. Ocha's ideas for practical applications be helpful?
5. What other suggestions can you give to help Ms. Ocha translate her philosophical ideals into practical applications?

 You can record your answers to these questions online on this book's Companion Web Site at *www.prenhall.com/manning*.

respond appropriately when someone is having a bad day, to say something positive instead of offering a negative response, or not to say anything at all and to convey emotions and concern in a nonverbal way. "The point of classroom management [should be] to ensure a productive environment in which children are challenged, respected, and able to grow" (Ullucci, 2005, p. 41). Activity 15–1 asks you to identify the human relations skills you could use in a variety of classroom situations.

Building the Right Climate

Just as teachers need human relations skills, schools and classrooms need to have strong, positive cultures in which educators share a sense of purpose; collegiality, improvement, and hard work are valued; and rituals and traditions are used to celebrate student accomplishments,

Voices of Educators

Reacting to Case Study 15–1

The following are the responses of experienced teachers to Case Study 15–1.

- Poor Ms. Ocha! I commend her expectations, but she needs to get in touch with reality and modify her fantastically unrealistic goals. They are certainly not achievable as long as teachers are dealing with real live little human beings, who will never be capable of achieving the perfect harmony Ms. Ocha is dreaming about.
- This teacher needs rules! And, she needs to teach them to her students.
- Even first graders need to know that actions have consequences and part of life is accepting responsibility for our own actions.
- I object to her belief that children should work in an atmosphere free from competition. Life does involve judgment and competition, and children need to understand that.
- This teacher has some good ideas about what she needs to do. She can't forget that her job is to teach students how to be what she wants them to be.
- I like Ms. Ocha's strategies for improving the environment of her classroom and applaud her positive goals.
- She should learn to be happy with small successes and not frustrate herself by trying to change human nature and achieve perfect harmony in a first-grade classroom.

teacher innovations, and parent commitment. If feelings of success, joy, and humor are present, there is usually a shared sense of what is important, a shared sense of caring and concern, and a shared commitment to help students learn (Peterson & Deal, 1998). When teachers develop a caring classroom culture, students can be taught how to behave and to treat others with dignity. Students should know that teachers want to help them and should realize the importance of more cooperation and fewer punishments.

> David Rollins, an experienced teacher, decided to work on creating a positive culture in his classroom. With the help of an advisory committee consisting of students, parents, and the school's administrators, Mr. Rollins assessed current student behavior in his classroom and identified behaviors to be changed and those to be ignored. After discussing student diversity and the safe schools movement, Mr. Rollins and the committee came up with a set of lofty but attainable goals to improve student behavior. Without overwhelming Mr. Rollins and his students, the committee also helped him identify an effective way to assess changes in student behavior and to measure the progress that students made toward developing self-discipline.

Creating a Sense of Community

In addition to creating a positive classroom culture, effective classroom managers also create a sense of **classroom community.** Westheimer and Kahne (1993, p. 325) defined the term community as "a process marked by interaction and deliberation among individuals

Using Human Relations Skills

Give specific examples of ways that you could use each of the following human relations skills in your own classroom:

1. Convey warmth and positive feelings toward students
2. Demonstrate or model positive treatment of others
3. Accept students and their strengths and weaknesses
4. Convey appreciation of students' various differences
5. Offer constructive criticism
6. Encourage success in behavior
7. Avoid finding fault and blame unless absolutely necessary
8. Provide students with hope and optimism
9. Disagree without being argumentative or blaming others

who share common interests and commitment to common goals." Graves (1992, p. 64) defined the term community as "an inherently cooperative, cohesive, and self-reflective group entity whose members work on a regular and face-to-face basis toward common goals while respecting a variety of perspectives, values, and life styles."

In a genuine school community, people should feel an attachment to the community and a sense of duty to work toward the welfare of the school community as well as the community at large (Sergiovanni, 1994; Obenchain & Abernathy, 2003). While providing students with opportunities to learn and interact in a humane, respectful, and psychologically safe learning environment, teachers want a safe and supportive community that promotes harmony and interpersonal relations among students and reflects positive verbal interactions. Such a school community provides teachers and students with opportunities to express opinions, listen to others with empathy, and support others in a nonthreatening situation. In addition, it helps eliminate student cliques and other sources of conflict (Batiuk, Boland & Wilcox, 2004). Ideally, the existence of this community should lessen conflicts between educators and students, reduce discipline referrals, and reduce confrontations among students. Although rubrics exist (Rubin, 2004) to evaluate school climate, the challenge is how to develop such a community. Activity 15–2 offers several strategies, based on the work of Canning (1993) and Graves (1992), for building a sense of community in a classroom.

Selecting Classroom Rules

In creating a classroom management system for a classroom community, you need to decide whether you want classroom rules for your students. Before you decide, remember that Kohn (1996) cautioned against rules in his call for teachers to move beyond discipline. If you decide

Activity 15-2

Building a Community in the Classroom

To build a sense of community within a classroom, teachers can

- Identify things the class can do together,
- Help each member identify his or her place within the class,
- Ensure that discussions are inclusionary rather than exclusionary,
- Provide everyone with opportunities to participate,
- Do not force a member to voice an opinion.

What other things might you do to create a sense of community within your classroom? What obstacles might you face? Is creating a sense of community an unrealistic goal for some teachers? Are there some situations in which it might be difficult to create a sense of community?

that you do not want to make and enforce rules, you might depend, instead, on the ability of students to discipline themselves for the overall welfare of the class.

We respect Kohn's (1996) ideas and think students ultimately should accept responsibility for their behavior, but our experiences tell us to think more realistically. We believe that some classroom rules will be necessary from the first day of school until students learn the self-discipline necessary to demonstrate appropriate behavior. In each classroom, students need to know what the rules (behavior expectations) are and that the rules will be applied fairly. In addition, the presence of rules does not mean that classrooms are not democratic. In classrooms where time was devoted early in the school to organization and teacher-managed activities, more time was spent later in the year on child-managed activities (Cameron, Connnor, & Morrison, 2005).

What rules should teachers select? Should they have rules posted the first day, prior to students arriving? Should they delay and have students offer suggested rules? Should they wait to see how the students behave prior to making and posting rules? These are good questions and deserve conscientious attention. In fact, we posed these questions to a number of educators. Their responses are in Voices of Educators: Developing Rules.

We believe that teachers need to develop their own rules for the beginning of school, at least until the students can be involved in making rules or until they learn self-discipline. It is to everyone's benefit for students to behave appropriately and avoid infringing on others' rights and property. Basic rules that are necessary for the welfare of all students should be posted and discussed the first day of school and, if necessary, taught during the first several days of school. Within the first weeks of school, teachers should give students an opportunity to suggest other rules that they consider important for the general operation of the classroom and for students' safety, well-being, and academic achievement.

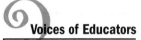
Voices of Educators

Developing Rules

We asked a number of practicing teachers whether they involve their students in creating rules in their classroom. Here are a few of their responses:

- Yes I do involve students. If students have "ownership" of the rules, if they made an investment in creating the class rules, they are more likely to follow them.
- No, I don't involve my students in establishing my management system. I already know what works and what doesn't, and I am not willing to go through what doesn't just so they can see for themselves. It is always easier to lighten up later than to get stricter.
- Students should know what is expected of them by teachers, classmates, and parents. Thus, in addition to my own rules, I usually allow students to give me the three rules they think are most important. I also send parents a questionnaire asking what they expect their child to accomplish, how we can best meet that accomplishment, and what they are willing to do to make sure it happens. I review this at all conferences with parents.
- No, I don't involve the students in establishing rules. I have before and the students gave pretty much the same rules as I would. I just do not want to take class time for something that can take a few minutes instead of practically a whole bell.
- I teach young students, so I have a set of rules and procedures that I've developed over a number of years. I start the year with my basic rules, and they are usually well established by the end of September.
- I establish my rules before school begins. A handout is given to every student and explained by me the first few days of school. The student and parent/guardian are required to sign the classroom expectations indicating they have read and understand them. Some of my rules and classroom procedures consist of the following:

  Respect all others and their property.
  Raise your hand and wait to be called upon if you wish to speak.
  Speak courteously and politely to others.
  Remain in your seat unless permission has been granted by your teacher.

Before making rules for your class, you might want to review the ideas of Gathercoal (2001) found in chapter 11 of this book, especially his ideas about rules and compelling state interests. Setting a positive tone (listing the things students should do rather than the things they should not do), rules should, whenever possible, be developed before the misbehavior occurs. However, making the rules is not enough. An effective teacher also needs to develop a process for communicating the rules to students as well as parents or guardians, teaching the rules, reviewing them periodically, and revising them as needed.

Along with rules, you must consider the consequences when the rules are broken. Review your philosophical beliefs and the ideas of the classroom management theorists discussed in this book. Will you use rewards when rules are followed or a check-mark system when rules are bro-

Voices of Educators

Considering Consequences

We asked a number of educators about the misbehaviors they saw in their classrooms and how they dealt with them. Here are their replies.

- The usual things I see are daydreaming, playing with things in their desks, and constant talking instead of time on-task. I keep a clipboard with a class list and chart. Students who are noticed "on-task" and following the rules get + (plus) marks, those caught not on task or breaking class rules get 2s (minus marks). Three is the big number. Three +s equal a reward. Three 2s equal the beginning of consequences. My scale is the following:

  3 minus marks—Note home with loss of one privilege

  4 minus marks—Behavior essay

  5 minus marks—Immediate phone call

  6 minus marks—Office visit

- I can usually tell if students are doing something other than what they are supposed to be doing by the way they look down at their laps. They may be reading or writing a letter. I usually give them my "evil eye" and they get back on-task. Sometimes I walk over to them and they get back on-task. If they have done it before, I just warn them that the next time I catch them, they will receive a detention.

- I have posted a behavior chart divided into three sections. The left section represents the happy face, the center section has the worried face, and the right side has a sad face. Every student in my class has a number. Students who misbehave move their number progressively to the right on the chart. When their number is under the sad face, they go to time-out in the room or miss part of their recess time. I rarely take away all of recess because that leaves the child with nothing to work for.

- The most common thing I see is students doing tasks that do not apply to my instruction (writing notes, doing homework, etc.). I have them clear their desks of everything—that is a great way to focus attention.

- The most common things I encounter are talking, not having supplies, and daydreaming. I gently but firmly let the students know their behaviors are unacceptable and give them a chance to change them. For repeat offenders, I let the natural consequences occur. For severe cases, I contact the parent or an administrator.

ken? Will you have a hierarchy of responses? Will you examine the reason for the misbehavior before identifying a consequence? In Voices of Educators: Considering Consequences, several teachers briefly comment on the misbehaviors they see and the consequences they use.

Conducting Class Meetings

An excellent time to discuss rules and expectations is at a class meeting. Several classroom management theorists discussed in this book advocated the use of **class meetings:** Glasser (1969); Albert (1995); Johnson and Johnson (1987); Nelsen, Lott, and Glenn (1997);

and Gathercoal (2001). You might recall that Gathercoal mentioned the key elements of democratic meetings, and Nelsen, Lott, and Glenn suggested the eight building blocks of class meetings.

Emphasizing, Ignoring, and Addressing Issues

Even when you have rules in your classroom, you will be faced with a dilemma of whether to ignore minor infractions or to address the behavior whenever a rule is broken. Some teachers place an emphasis on positive behaviors rather than on negative behaviors. This approach reflects the ideas of Skinner's behavior modification and Redl and Wattenberg's group dynamics. By ignoring minor misbehaviors and praising positive behaviors, these teachers hope that negative behaviors will lessen and positive behaviors will increase. When students see other students demonstrate positive behavior and receive rewards or reinforcement, then they also will start to demonstrate positive behavior.

Ignoring negative behaviors does not mean ignoring serious misbehaviors, especially misbehaviors that can result in physical and psychological damage to students. Teachers never should ignore threats, acts of violence or potential violence, weapons, racial slurs, accusations about others' sexual orientation, or any misbehavior that could cause physical or psychological damage. In addition, teachers should not ignore misbehaviors that disrupt the teaching/learning process and students' learning. Nor should they ignore misbehaviors that have the potential for becoming contagious. The hardest part is knowing what to ignore and what might become contagious. This is a skill that takes time to develop. Teachers have to know their classes so well that they know which behaviors might spread and which students might be the instigators of trouble. Just remember that ignoring the

Activity 15–3

Reacting to Positive and Negative Behaviors

For each of the following actions, first identify whether the action is positive or negative. Then, indicate how you would respond if the action occurred in a classroom on the level you want to teach. Would you ignore any of these actions? Be sure that your response is developmentally appropriate.

- Alma raises her hand to answer a question.
- Lanita complains that you are unfair for giving homework on Fridays.
- Lucious calls Martin a "sissy" and says Martin acts like a girl.
- Chad accidentally knocks Tabatha's books to the floor and then helps her pick them up.
- Rumor has it that Quentin, a boy in your class, bullies other children on the school bus.
- Luis sees a knife in Burton's backpack and tells you, even though Burton has not taken the knife out.
- Duffy keeps drumming his pencil on the desk in an attempt to annoy you.
- Francisco and Earl have a few disgruntled words, but nothing significant happens.
- Three students in a cooperative learning group are working collaboratively and are on task.
- Sherita quietly helps Jorge find the right page number in the book as you explain an assignment.
- Patti tries to trap you in a last-worder situation.
- Melinda hurries to get her assignment notebook out of her desk and her books accidentally crash to the floor.
- Toby calls Raul a "homo" and says he probably has AIDS.

negative should never mean ignoring behaviors that could result in physical or psychological harm. Activity 15–3 presents some situations and asks you to determine how the teacher should react.

Communicating With Parents

"I hope you can do something with him; his mom and I can't. But then discipline is your job, not mine." These words were said to a kindergarten teacher as a father dropped his son off at the classroom door on the first day of school. Some parents and guardians think their responsibility stops when the child leaves for school. They view classroom management and discipline as the teachers' responsibility. Fortunately, all parents and guardians do not share that opinion.

> When Mr. Owens brought Marcia to school, he said to the teacher, "This is my granddaughter. Please let me know if Marcia does not behave or if she gets in any trouble. I'm behind you, you know."

Well-informed parents or guardians can be significant assets to teachers and overall classroom management efforts. Some parents or guardians even might want to have an active role in classroom management programs and might be willing to serve on classroom management committees to review management policies and to know consequences for misbehavior.

Communication with parents and guardians is important. Parents and guardians who know the teachers' expectations are more supportive. Particularly effective teachers send letters and classroom management expectations to parents or guardians during the first few days of school. Figure 15–1 lists some items that can be included. Parents and guardians then sign to show they have read and understand the teacher's behavior expectations. Although all parents and guardians probably will not read the letter and expectations, it is still a good idea to provide the opportunity.

Teaching Discipline and Cooperation

Some teachers try to change from autocratic (control and demanding practices) to more democratic practices. This does not mean, however, that they become what Dreikurs (1968) called permissive or what Coloroso (1983, 1994) called jellyfish. When teachers try to provide a democratic classroom environment, they teach and model self-discipline, cooperation, and collaboration. This is often not an easy task to accomplish, because teachers also have to maintain an orderly learning environment in which students demonstrate proper behavior and feel safe. Because some students are accustomed to autocratic teachers who demand strict obedience, convey the rules, and apply consequences for misbehavior, the change to

---

Teachers should communicate the following types of management information to parents and guardians:

- The overall behavior goals of the school and class
- The specific behavior expectations for the particular class
- The consequences for behavior
- The times when a student misbehaves that the teacher will contact an administrator
- The times when a student misbehaves that the teacher will contact the parents and guardians
- The best times and places for the parents and guardians to contact the teacher
- The ways the parents or guardians can help promote safe schools and well-managed classrooms

Figure 15–1
Management Information for Parents

CASE STUDY 15–2
Sensing Frustration with Applying Management Techniques

During his student-teaching semester, Mr. Tucker Rahman, a middle school teacher, developed the philosophy of classroom management that he planned to implement during his first year of teaching. Rather than being autocratic like his cooperating teacher, he wanted to teach cooperation, have weekly class meetings, create community in his classroom, and communicate with parents. However, by December of his first year of teaching seventh grade in an urban middle school, he was finding a tremendous gap between his philosophy and actual practice. In fact, he was afraid that he might become an autocratic "ruler" rather than the "manager" he had planned to be.

Although Mr. Rahman wanted to teach cooperation, he found that his seventh-grade students were anything but cooperative. In fact, he found that teaching cooperation was difficult or impossible with some students who were accustomed to autocratic teachers who ruled sternly. "Some of them don't know how to cooperate; they seem to think that an adversarial relationship should exist between students and their teacher," he said in dismay.

The weekly class meetings ended in failure. The students refused to participate in meaningful discussions. They were rude to each other, offered accusatory remarks, wisecracked, and did not have a clue about how to act in a civil manner. "I really wanted those class meetings to work," Mr. Rahman said, "but after the third week, I thought I should invest my energies in other areas. Maybe someday I'll try it again."

When Mr. Rahman tried to create a sense of community, he had equally dismal results. Instead of caring and respecting each other, students were hostile, clownish, and discourteous, with many trying to one-up the others. "I made a mistake by putting my full name on the door. I thought it would make me seem more human. Now, some students even call me F###er Rahman behind my back. I'm supposed to teach a sense of community and caring to this bunch?"

The final straw was his lack of success in communicating with parents. He moaned: "Parents won't respond, won't collaborate with me, and won't help me teach their children. Very few come to progress report meetings each 9 weeks, and even fewer attend monthly parent–teacher meetings."

With all his frustrations during his first 4 months of teaching, Mr. Rahman wondered how long he would last in the profession. Each day as he drove home, he relived his school day, questioned his philosophy, and second-guessed the decisions he had made that day. "Is it the students or is it me?" he asked himself. "Why can't I get these students to act civilly? Why can't I get the parents to cooperate? What else can I try that I have not already tried?"

Questions for Consideration

1. Evaluate Mr. Rahman's actions during his first 4 months.
2. Why has he met with such limited success in implementing his ideas?
3. Must he become an autocratic ruler to survive as a teacher?
4. If not, what must he do to turn his philosophical beliefs into practical applications in his middle school classroom?
5. Would Mr. Rahman have experienced the same problems in a suburban or rural school?
6. How might this scenario have changed if Mr. Rahman had taught in an elementary school? A high school?

 You can record your answers to these questions online on this book's Companion Web Site at *www.prenhall.com/manning*.

a democratic classroom requires a change of mindset for teachers and students. Case Study 15–2 explains the frustration Mr. Rahman experienced as he tried to apply his management techniques. Then, in Voices of Educators: Reacting to Case Study 15–2, educators respond to Mr. Rahman.

Individual Students and Their Differences

No matter what classroom management plan you adopt, you must consider individual students' differences. This important step is often overlooked. Perez (1994) maintained that American public schools have never welcomed student differences enthusiastically, and educators have, in fact, sometimes tried to remove differences that they saw as barriers to more equal access to opportunities outside the school. Instead, Perez suggested that schools should view diversity not as a problem but as an opportunity for every student to experience other people and their differences.

As a result, effective classroom managers often have to figure out how they can match instructional behaviors and management strategies most effectively with students' motivation; self-esteem; and gender, cultural, and developmental characteristics. Some students

Voices of Educators

Reacting to Case Study 15–2

Here are the reactions of educators to Mr. Rahman's situation.

- Mr. Rahman has good goals, but he made a mistake in thinking that he could not accomplish them in the kind of classroom that he called autocratic.
- Students at the middle level are experienced enough in the workings of a school that they know the academic expectations: Complete all work to the best of one's ability in order to succeed. Socially, however, they are just beginning to grow up and need lots of help.
- Structure is important even in the middle school. And, structure does not make a dictatorship. Rules and procedures are important. Otherwise, students just run wild.
- By implementing weekly class meetings and trying creating a sense of community within the classroom, Mr. Rahman was asking these students to blindly leap into a democratic style of classroom management, one that was probably completely foreign to the majority of them. He needed to teach them what the expectations were.
- Mr. Rahman not only wanted these students to commit to his style and prosper from it, but he also wanted them to be appreciative of his progressive thinking and willingness to share control. Students simply do not have the background knowledge and experience required to perform as Mr. Rahman hoped at the middle school level without a great deal of modeling and preparation.

---

are motivated to excel in school and behave accordingly, but other students are less motivated or are disinterested in schoolwork and see misbehavior as an escape from the "chores" of school. Similarly, some (but not necessarily all) boys prefer competitive activities that could lead to classroom management problems, and some (but not necessarily all) girls prefer collaborative activities that can be less disruptive. Do keep in mind that although socialized gender differences exist, many girls like to compete and many boys like to collaborate.

Also remember that the same misbehavior can occur for different reasons. Students who mature later might misbehave to gain attention or seek power, and those who mature earlier might misbehave to prove their adulthood. Although students with lower self-esteem might misbehave to gain attention [remember Dreikurs's (1968) goal of inadequacy], students with high self-esteem might be sufficiently confident to misbehave to gain attention. Because of stereotypes, students in some cultures could be labeled or perceived as loud or boisterous, and students in another group could be seen as quieter and more reserved. However, it is important to remember that diversity exists within groups as well as between them and that it is imperative to avoid stereotypes. For example, a teacher should not expect all members of a cultural group or gender to act the same way. Only by recognizing their own cultural predispositions toward management and understanding the cultural backgrounds of students and the behavioral pressures of society, can teachers provide appropriate management strategies for all cultural or gender groups (Weinstein, Tomlinson-Clarke, & Curran, 2004).

As you implement your management plan, you need to keep in mind student differences. To help you identify the differences among your own students, you can ask the following questions:

Motivation

- Is the student genuinely motivated or feigning motivation to stay out of trouble?
- Is the student intrinsically motivated or is extrinsic motivation necessary?
- Is there a relationship between the student's motivation (or efforts) and achievement, or is the student experiencing only frustration and therefore misbehaving?
- Do your classroom management strategies seem to motivate students to misbehave or only make behavior worse?

Self-Esteem

- Does the student have positive self-esteem?
- Does the self-esteem vary with educational activities or behavior situations?
- How does the student's self-esteem affect his or her behavior?
- Do your classroom management strategies promote self-esteem or do they denigrate self-esteem, thus making student behavior worse?

Gender and Culture

- Are girls and boys allowed to engage in competitive and collaborative activities, depending on which they choose?
- Do classroom management strategies treat boys and girls equitably, without gender stereotypes?
- Are cultures treated equitably without perceived expectations that some students will be well behaved and others, rowdy?
- Do your management strategies take into consideration cultural differences and preferences?

Development

- Does the student's rate of development affect his or her behavior?
- Is there evidence of significant developmental differences (e.g., psychosocial development lagging physical development)?
- Does the student's development affect his or her self-esteem, which in turn affects behavior?

Inclusion and Learners with Special Needs

As **inclusion** brings more learners with special needs into the general classroom, you need to consider the impact that this will have on your philosophical beliefs and classroom management practices. A common misconception is that teachers must rely on complex and intrusive procedures to deal with special needs learners. In fact, the majority of these students will respond positively to standard classroom management strategies (e.g., group contingencies, teacher proximity, clear expectations, and teacher praise) (Gable, Hendrickson, Tonelson, & Van Acker, 2000).

However, in addition to the standard strategies, several others are especially valuable when teaching in an inclusion classroom. Peer-mediated instruction and interventions (PMII) are a set of alternative teaching arrangements in which students serve as instructional assistants for classmates. This peer teaching can be direct (e.g., tutoring) or indirect (e.g., modeling, encouraging) and can focus on academic or interpersonal outcomes (Maheady, Harper, & Mallette, 2001).

Another classroom management method is the "Good Student Game" (Babyak, Luze, & Kamps, 2000), a tool that uses a game format to help students monitor appropriate classroom behaviors, such as staying seated and working quietly. The game is too complex to describe here; however, in general, teachers define target behaviors that they would like to see improved. Then they set the criterion for winning the game, establish reinforcers, teach students how to play the game, divide the class into teams, and write the team names on the board. Teachers put a mark under the name of the students' team when a student breaks a rule. At the end of the game, any team with fewer marks than the preestablished criterion wins, and winning teams receive reinforcers. In the "Good Student Game," students have opportunities to observe, evaluate, and record their own behaviors.

According to IDEA, the development of an intervention or management plan for a special needs learner is accomplished through a team problem-solving process known as functional behavioral assessment (FBA). Most educators realize that various social and environmental events influence appropriate and inappropriate student behavior. Functional behavioral assessment identifies those antecedent events (e.g., the teacher asks Paige to answer a question) that set the occasion (e.g., Paige makes a vulgar comment) for subsequent events (e.g., the teacher gets upset and asks another student) that likely maintain a misbehavior. In this example, the teacher is less likely to call on Paige again; therefore, Paige has learned that she can get rid of something she does not like to do by misbehaving. If the teacher realizes this, either the teacher or the team can devise strategies that allow the student to achieve the desired consequences without resorting to disruptive acts (Gable et al., 2000).

Alexakos (2001) suggests that one way of promoting positive behavior in inclusive classrooms is to create a learning environment that nurtures and supports all students. A sense of belonging, relevance of tasks, hands-on experiences, and fun contribute to classroom interest. In classrooms where teachers show interest in students' needs, students are more likely to ask for help. In addition, the physical environment (e.g., the physical space) can help eliminate or reduce stress, anxiety, and disorder.

Students with mild disabilities might be less accepted by peers and in danger of becoming "invisible" (Alexakos, 2001, p. 43). To help all students feel included (and thus improve classroom behavior), teachers can ask students at the beginning of the year to complete personal inventory cards that identify their likes and dislikes. These interests can be incorporated into lessons, establishing positive personal connections.

The instructional strategies that you use can have an impact on the classroom learning environments. Students in inclusive classrooms (as well as all classrooms) need opportunities to interact with each other and to engage in shared inquiry and discovery in their efforts to solve problems and complete tasks. The use of cooperative learning groups helps all students see the benefits of bringing together people with diverse backgrounds (e.g., disabilities and special needs) to solve problems as they listen, talk, read, and write together to achieve common goals. In the process, everyone becomes accountable because individual performance affects group outcomes (Montgomery, 2001).

Addressing Off-Task and Disruptive Behaviors

Most teachers deal daily with students who demonstrate off-task behaviors. As you might recall, Frederic Jones in his book *Positive Classroom Discipline* (1987, p. 27) found that most behavior problems are of a lesser degree, or what he called *small disruptions* (Jones's italics). You can review his findings in chapter 8 of this book, but in general he found that students are off task between 45% and 55% of the time (Jones, 1973). Thus, any classroom management plan must provide ways to address these common misbehaviors.

Off-task and minor disruptive behaviors can have a number of negative consequences, especially if the off-task students disturb other students who want to learn and stay on-task or if they disturb the teacher who is trying to teach. Thus, off-task behaviors are significant problems for many educators, and keeping students on-task can be time consuming and challenging. Something as simple as a change of classroom setting can have a significant impact on off-task behaviors (Rimm-Kaufman, La Paro, and Downer, 2005). In this chapter, you already have read the comments of some educators (Voices of Educators: Considering Consequences) about the ways they handle minor misbehaviors and the consequences they use. Case Study 15–3 tells about Ms. Bazemore, who must deal with off-task behaviors. In Voices of Educators: Reacting to Case Study 15–3, educators respond to Ms. Bazemore.

Dealing With Violence and Violent Behaviors

In chapter 1 and more extensively in chapter 13, we discussed the violence that is affecting our schools and the safe schools movement. In the future, educators will continue to deal with bullying, aggression, and violent behaviors. Do remember though as Jones (1987, p. 27) explained, 95% of classroom disruptions are "nickel and dime" misbehaviors of students goofing off and taking a break from their work. For information on resolving conflicts, dealing with bullies, and coping with the more serious but infinitely less common violent behaviors in some school, we refer you to chapter 13 in this book.

CASE STUDY 15–3
Dealing with Off-Task Behaviors

As a ninth-grade teacher, Ms. Celestine Bazemore thought the biggest problem she faced was her students being off-task. "It's not the fighters and bullies that give me problems. It's the students who just sit and do nothing productive that really bother me," she repeatedly said. "Students look out the window, daydream, play around, goof off, and distract each other from learning. They don't actively misbehave; they just don't do what they're suppose to do. Some feign sickness to get out of work; others only make a halfhearted effort to complete assignments. Sure," she continued, "I've tried commonly accepted techniques such as looking the students in the eye, standing close to them, and reminding them to get back on task. I even spoke with them in small groups and individually about the need to keep working productively, to listen to me, and to take a more active interest in their schoolwork. I've explained that they're in high school now and they needed to think about their future. However, nothing worked for long. Some of the students worked for awhile; but others never made a serious effort. I've tried small cooperative groups, hoping individuals in the group would have some success motivating others to take an active role in learning activities. But that didn't work for most of my students."

Then, at a professional conference she was attending, Ms. Bazemore went to a management techniques session that focused on productive time on task. As she listened to the presentation by Dr. Chela Kwon, Ms. Bazemore learned that at least some of the problems with her students might begin with her. Dr. Kwon explained that classroom management techniques include more than just behavior strategies. Effective management techniques also include teachers' teaching techniques (e.g., lesson plans, instructional pace, instructional level, and efforts to motivate). Dr. Kwon suggested that teachers should

- Adapt lessons to learners' interests and talents,
- Do more direct teaching—standing in front of the class and proving direct instruction,
- Provide work at the learners' levels—neither under-challenging nor over-challenging,
- Provide work at the appropriate instructional pace, so learners would not get bored.

Ms. Bazemore left the conference with several thoughts in mind. "I'm still convinced they are unmotivated and perhaps downright lazy, but I do need to look at what I do. Maybe I have been trying the wrong approach. I mean, it seems logical that my instructional techniques influence my students just as my behavior management strategies do."

Questions for Consideration

1. What role does instruction play in a classroom management plan?
2. Are teaching techniques as important as behavior-management techniques?
3. What other instructional techniques should Ms. Bazemore consider?
4. What else might Ms. Bazemore consider in addition to her instructional techniques to motivate her students and keep them on task?

 You can record your answers to these questions online on this book's Companion Web Site at *www.prenhall.com/manning*.

Voices of Educators

Reacting to Case Study 15–3

Here are the reactions of educators to Ms. Bazemore's situation.

- A well-planned and delivered lesson can do much to end off-task behaviors.
- Ms. Bazemore is in a corner. Her instructional methods and her students' behaviors have been long established. An overnight change cannot happen in her class, and it is too late for the old adage "don't smile until Christmas" to work. I never bought into that idea, however. I recommend doing five things in the beginning of the school year to prepare students for the optimal use of instructional time, and smiling is allowed through (almost) all of them.

  1. Use 10 minutes of instructional time to teach classroom procedures for the first several weeks of school; establish a routine from the beginning.
  2. Define expectations and establish consequences early—from the first day of school. Students need to know that for an ACTION there will be a REACTION and that as they choose a BEHAVIOR, they also choose a CONSEQUENCE.
  3. Identify learning styles and achievement levels the first week of school.
  4. Decide for yourself (from the beginning) what behaviors you will tolerate and what behaviors you will not.
  5. Make many phone calls the first month of school.

- Ms. Bazemore needs to consider other instructional techniques, such as working with partners before working in larger groups.
- Try rubrics; students love to know exactly what is expected of them and often "work up" to the rubric.
- Vary activities. Use two or three activities per bell instead of one long lecture or one singular classwork assignment.
- Have students responsible for doing SOMETHING during instruction—have them manipulate materials, record ideas and notes, write answers.
- Put all of the students' names on note cards and draw these randomly; participation is then mandatory, and the teacher can assign a weekly participation grade.
- Ms. Bazemore needs to give frequent feedback; in the beginning of the year, it helps to give graded feedback every day. Students will know that they can succeed, yet they will also know that not doing work has repercussions.
- Occasionally, I offer a free homework pass or allow the students to have lunch in the classroom.
- Teacher attitude and enthusiasm go a long way in motivating students—much more so than external rewards.

PUTTING YOUR MANAGEMENT PLAN TOGETHER

Now that you have had an opportunity to review management theories and to reflect on your own philosophy of classroom management, it is time for you to put everything together into your own personal classroom management system. Activity 15–4 is designed to help

Activity 15–4

Developing Your Personal Classroom Management Plan

Following are some things you will want to include in your personal classroom management plan. We have identified a few of the questions that you might ask in each category as you develop your plan. For other ideas, you can review some of the Management Tips found throughout this book or on the Internet sites listed in each chapter. In addition, you should consider your responses to the activities and the Developing Your Personal Philosophy sections of this book. When you are done, you should have an opening day plan that can be modified as you go along.

My Classroom Management Plan

Philosophy of Management

- In one or two sentences, what is my philosophy of classroom management?

Behavior Expectations

- What behavior do I expect from my students? How can I convey that to my students?

Pre-School Checkoff

- What things will I need to do before school begins each year?

Classroom Slogan or Motto

- What will it be (i.e., Respect, Cooperate, Participate)? Will I develop this or ask for student input?

Classroom Arrangement

- How can I arrange my classroom most effectively (i.e., placement of desks for students and teachers; location of bulletin boards, chalkboard, whiteboard, other permanent fixtures)?

Class Rules

- What rules will I have to begin the school year? Will I ask for student input for all, some, or none of the rules?

Hierarchy or Consequences for Rule Infractions

- What will I do when a student breaks a rule? Will I have a hierarchy of consequences?

Motivational Strategies

- What strategies will I use to motivate my students (i.e., tickets or marbles in a jar)? Will I rely on intrinsic or extrinsic motivation?

Management Procedures and Routines

- What procedures will I use in my classroom (i.e., beginning the class, ending the class, distributing materials, collecting materials and assignments, assigning student helpers or assistants)? How often will I change the assignments?

Instructional Planning

- What lesson planning format will I use? What instructional strategies will I rely on? What, if any, of the instructional techniques of Kounin will I use?
- What strategies will I use to
  Develop a positive classroom management culture and climate,
  Build a community in my classroom,
  Communicate with parents and guardians,
  Teach self-discipline and cooperation,
  Teach rules and procedures to my students,
  Deal with individual students and their differences,
  Prevent discipline problems,
  Support my discipline program (i.e., physical proximity, withitness),
  Correct discipline problems (i.e., conflict resolution, zero tolerance),
  Work with inclusion students in my classroom,
  Provide a safe classroom for myself and my students?

Voices of Educators

Advising Beginning Teachers

We asked a number of experienced teachers what advice about classroom management they would give beginning teachers. Here are a few of their comments.

- Respect your students.
- Develop a philosophy, but don't be afraid to adjust it over time. Think everything through to the most minor detail, and don't assume your students will know or do certain things. Ask them or tell them.
- Classroom management is a number 1 priority. Consistency makes it work and team-work (teacher, students, and parents[/guardian]) is the only way it can be successful.
- Be fair and consistent with the rules you establish. Do not hold grudges or show favoritism toward the students. Try to always be calm and talk to the students. Have a sense of humor. Admit when you are wrong and apologize if you make a mistake about disciplining a child for something he did not do. Do not be afraid to call parents for their support.
- Plan, plan, plan! And don't be afraid to ask other teachers for their advice.

you begin that process. In addition to the questions we have listed, you also should consider personal questions—ones that you consider relevant for the students and the grades you plan to teach. A good management plan requires review, evaluation, and modification throughout the year and throughout your career as a professional educator.

CONCLUDING REMARKS

Please go to
www.prenhall.com/manning
and click on Concluding
Remarks for this chapter to
find more information.

Applying effective classroom management strategies requires more than acting on intuition or a whim. Educators with successful and effective classroom management programs usually have a personalized philosophy of classroom management goals and strategies. They use these philosophical perspectives as the basis of their classroom management program. As successful educators can attest, an effective classroom management program requires specifics, such as effective human relations skills with students and parents, the willingness and ability to build a positive class environment, and the ability to establish rules and conduct class meetings. Sadly, effective classroom managers also must deal with difficult challenges, namely, violent and aggressive behaviors, that are often beyond the purview of classroom management models and efforts. Lest you think classroom management is too great a challenge, we asked some experienced teachers what advice they would give to beginning teachers. These comments are contained in Voices of Educators: Advising Beginning Teachers. For more information on classroom management, we encourage you to consult the Internet sites listed in "Reaching Out With Technology" on this book's Companion Web Site and the sources listed in the Suggested Readings.

Suggested Readings

Bafumo, M. E. (2005). Impacting achievement. *Teaching PreK–8, 35*(5), 8. Bafumo describes three teacher factors (e.g., instructional strategies, classroom management, and curriculum design) that make a measurable difference in student achievement.

Barbetta, P. M., Norona, K. L., & Bicard, D. F. (2005). Classroom behavior management: A dozen common mistakes and what to do instead. *Preventing School Failure, 49*(3), 11–19. As the title suggests, this article discuss mistakes committed frequently at many grade levels and in all types of learning environments.

Christie, K. (2005). Chasing the bullies away. *Phi Delta Kappan, 86*(10), 725–726. Christie maintains the most effective approach to bullying hinges on a commitment to action on the part of school staff members, some of whom ignore the problem.

Day-Vines, N. L., & Day-Hairston, B. O. (2005). Culturally congruent strategies for addressing the behavioral needs of urban African American male adolescents. *Professional School Counseling, 8*(3), 236–243. These authors discuss the problems faced by urban African American males, possible causes, and ways to address their needs

Desiderio, M. F., & Mullennix, C. (2005). Two behavior management systems, one classroom: Can elementary students adapt? *The Educational Forum, 69*(4), 383–391. These authors discuss a cooperating teacher who used the Canters' Assertive Discipline and a student teacher who used her own management system; students responded to both teachers in expected ways.

Protheroe, N. (2005). A schoolwide approach to discipline. *Principal, 84*(5), 41–44. Protheroe thinks schoolwide discipline programs are more likely to be effective than classroom-by-classroom approaches.

Spitalli, S. J. (2005). The don'ts of student discipline. *The Education Digest, 70*(5), 28–31. This author discusses ten disciplinary strategies that teachers should avoid.

Glossary

1-minute student managers Students assume classroom management positions, freeing the teacher for instructional activities by assuming responsibility for routine classroom tasks.

Accountability The teacher holds all members of the class responsible for their learning and behavior.

Active listening A belief fostered by Thomas Gordon, it says that teachers must genuinely hear and understand the comments, concerns, and behaviors of students.

Advance preparation Organizing and managing classrooms for effective instruction is advance preparation and planning from the first day of school.

Appreciative praise Considered productive by Ginott, this type praise deals only with the students' efforts and accomplishments.

Assertive confrontation Teachers sometimes need to use assertive confrontation, a method that offers seven rules for a fair fight and a productive confrontation

Assertive style This style is used by teachers who clearly and specifically place limits and rewards or consequences on students and make their expectations known.

Attention getting One of Dreikurs's four goals of misbehavior, this is when students feel they are worthless and often misbehave to get the attention they want.

Autocratic teacher In contrast to permissive teachers and democratic teachers, autocratic teachers rule with an "iron fist," demanding obedience at all times in a controlled environment and allowing students little freedom. This hands-on teacher has rigid expectations and demands immediate obedience.

Backbone teacher By emphasizing democracy through learned experiences, backbone teachers advocate creative, constructive, and responsible activity; have simply and clearly defined rules; use natural or reasonable con-

sequences; motivate students to be all they can be; and teach students how to think.

Backup systems These plans (e.g., classroom policy, school rules, and law enforcement and juvenile justice) are in place for correcting continuing and more severe misbehaviors.

Barriers These are disrespectful and discouraging behaviors.

Behavior modification (sometimes called operant conditioning or stimulus-response theory) The belief that positive reinforcement or a reward should follow positive behavior.

Body language The way a teacher stands and acts that conveys skill and confidence in classroom management.

Brickwall teacher A teacher who restricts and controls others; he or she is all powerful; the student is the subordinate.

Broken-record response According to the Canters, this is a response to misbehavior in which the teacher repeats the same or a similar request for compliance a maximum of three times before invoking the consequence.

Builders These are respectful and encouraging behaviors.

Bullying Physical or psychological intimidation that occurs repeatedly over time and creates an ongoing pattern of harassment and abuse.

Capable Students feel confident and capable of achieving appropriate behavior and achieving academically.

Cheap Instead of referring to financial costs, "cheap" refers to management techniques that are simple and require the least planning time and paperwork.

Choice Theory A theory by William Glasser, it holds that students have specific human needs and motives and should accept responsibility for their behavior.

Citizens Active decision makers who feel they are an integral part of the classroom are called citizens.

Civic values The common goals and values that help define appropriate behavior in a community are civic values.

Class meetings These are meetings in which classroom conflicts are resolved peacefully in a democratic forum of students and the teacher.

Class rules According to the Canters, rules should be age and grade-level appropriate and specific and should clearly spell out the behavior expectation.

Classroom community This is a school community in which people feel an attachment to the community and a sense of duty to work toward the welfare of the community

Classroom management This involves strategies that teachers use to assure physical and psychological safety in the classroom; techniques for changing student misbehaviors and for teaching self-discipline; methods to assure an orderly progression of events during the school day; and instructional techniques that contribute to students' positive behaviors.

Classroom management plan This is an organized plan that is based on philosophical foundations of discipline and spells out the management activities and practices in a classroom.

Classroom structures Structures are the rules, procedures, and physical arrangement of the classroom.

Code of conduct Students (and sometimes teachers) develop a code that governs their behavior and attitudes in the classroom; different than a list of rules in the sense that a code is broader and guides students toward behaviors they adopted.

Code of ethics Rules, guidelines, and expectations that consist of a few principles that guide behavior comprise a code of ethics.

Communities A place in which students feel cared about and are encouraged to care about each other; they experience a sense of being valued and respected; the children matter to one another and to the teacher. They have come to think in the plural: They feel connected to one another; they are part of an "us." And, as a result of all this, they feel safe in their classes, not only physically but emotionally. (Kohn, 1996a, p. 101–102)

Compelling state interests These are the basis for classroom rules: health and safety, property loss and damage, legitimate educational purpose, and serious disruption.

Conflict resolution A model of solving conflicts that focuses on productive ways to handle conflict, without aggression or passivity; it may include a conference with the parents or guardian or the development of an individual behavior contract with the student.

Connect Students feel connected or have workable relationships with other students as well as the teacher and administrator.

Consequences Punishments that result from misbehaviors are consequences.

Consistency Not be confused with rigidity, consistency provides a sense of continuity of actions and expectations for students and teachers.

Constitution Sometimes referred to as a *contract,* this is the product of the teacher and students, working together, to develop rules that reflect both classroom rules and the standards identified by the school as a whole.

Contribute Students feel capable of making a contribution to the behavior and well-being of the class.

Control theory This is an earlier name for the Choice Theory of William Glasser.

Cooperation Cooperation is the need for students, teachers, administrators, and community members to work toward mutual goals.

Cooperative learning This is the instructional use of small groups so that students work together to maximize their own and each other's learning.

Corporal punishment This is physical punishment that, according to most classroom management theorists, is ineffective and accomplishes "nothing that cannot be achieved better by some other method"(Redl & Wattenberg, 1959, p. 375).

Dangles The teacher continues to find materials, reviews lesson plans, and talks with individual students when the class as a whole is ready for instruction.

Desists The teacher engages in a effort to stop a misbehavior.

Democratic classrooms These are classrooms in which students know that their human rights are secure

Democratic teacher A hands-joined teacher encourages students to help devise classroom rules and their logical consequences as well as helps students feel psychologically safe in the classroom environment.

Direct bullying These are actions such as teasing, taunting, threatening, hitting, and stealing.

Discipline as self-control This is a belief by Thomas Gordon that the ultimate responsibility for discipline lies within the individual students who have to accept responsibility for changing their behavior.

Discipline hierarchy This is a plan that informs students of consequences and the order in which they will be imposed.

Diversity Differences among students that teachers must consider as they identify appropriate classroom management strategies; these differences include (but are not limited to) culture, gender, ethnicity, social class, and development.

Empathic Understanding This is a technique favored by Thomas Gordon in which a teacher learns about individual students, their specific needs, and their interests and abilities in order to tailor curricular and instructional decisions toward individual students.

Empowering perceptions These include three perceptions: perceptions of personal capabilities (teachers create a safe climate where students can experiment with learning and behavior without judgments about success or failure); perceptions of significance in primary relationships (teachers listen to the feelings, thoughts, and ideas of students and take them seriously); perceptions of the personal power of influence in life (teachers give students the opportunity to contribute in useful ways, and help them accept their power to create positive and negative environments).

Encouragement In contrast to praise, teachers should use encouragement to boost confidence and self-esteem and less praise, because students can become dependent on the praise.

Environmental design This school design contributes to safe classrooms and schools.

Essential skills These consist of intrapersonal skills (students gain understanding of their emotions and behaviors by hearing feedback from their classmates); interpersonal skills (students develop interpersonal skills through dialogue and sharing, listening and empathizing, cooperation, negotiation, and conflict resolution); systemic skills (students respond to the limits and consequences of everyday life with responsibility, adaptability, flexibility, and integrity because they do not experience punishment or disapproval); and judgment skills (students develop judgment skills when they have opportunities and encouragement to practice making decisions in an environment that emphasizes learning from mistakes rather punishment).

Evaluative praise Considered destructive by Ginott, this type of praise deals with the students' character and personality.

Extrinsic bribes The opposite of internal motivation, it may consist of things such as a homework pass, token, or sticker.

Feelings of inadequacy One of Dreikurs's four goals of misbehavior, students who harbor feelings of hopelessness and inferiority might misbehave to compensate for their inadequacy.

Flip-flops The teacher is engaged in one activity and then returns to a previous activity that the students thought they had finished.

Foundational theorists These are theorists in the study of student behavior and classroom management, including B. F. Skinner, Fritz Redl and William Wattenberg, William Glasser, and Thomas Gordon.

Fragmentation The teacher engages in a type of slowdown, e.g., the teacher breaks down an activity into subparts that could be taught as a single unit.

Front loading One of the first things that happens in a classroom is that students develop a class set of expected behaviors. The students focus on the Bill of Rights and the legal compelling interests and then help define what these concepts mean in various teaching and learning situations.

General rules These describe teachers' goals and objectives—their hopes and aspirations for classroom management during the coming year. Rather than dictating behavior, they establish a tone in the class, raise expectations, express the teacher's values and typically deal with good behavior and good work habits.

Group alerting The teacher obtains and holds the attention of the class, both at the beginning of a lesson and as the activities change within a lesson.

Group dynamics "Group life in the classroom" (Redl & Wattenberg, 1959, p. 262): an understanding that individual behavior affects group behavior and vice versa.

Group focus The teacher keeps the attention of all members of the class at all times, which assists in maintaining an efficient classroom and reducing student misbehavior.

Healthy classrooms Classrooms in which students trust their abilities and their environments, see benefits of improving behavior, and make significant and meaningful decisions, and teachers and students work collaboratively and cooperatively.

Hostile style According to Canter and Canter, this is a teacher's style that uses an aversive approach, including shouting, threats, sarcasm.

Human relation skills These are interpersonal skills that a teacher uses to work with and manage the students in a classroom.

I-messages Teachers use these statements to express how they feel about a given behavior or how it affects them. For example, effective teachers use statements such as "I'm frustrated by all the talking in this room."

Imposed discipline Teachers assume responsibility for managing students' behavior. Punishments are used.

Inclusion This is a policy of educating a learner with special needs in the school and, whenever possible, in the class that the child would have attended if she or he did not have the disabling condition.

Indirect bullying These actions cause a student to be socially isolated through exclusion.

Ineffective things These behaviors, techniques, and decisions are those that teachers continue to demonstrate that do not work or achieve the desired purpose.

Influence As opposed to control, teachers try to influence students to demonstrate appropriate classroom behaviors.

Internal motivation The opposite of external motivation; for example, taking self-satisfaction in having appropriate behavior is internal motivation.

Interventions Either **minor** interventions, **moderate** interventions, or **extensive** interventions; instead of having the same punishments for all misbehaviors, teachers must determine the severity of the behavior offense and then determine the needed intervention.

Jellyfish teacher– teachers are wishy-washy, are inconsistent about classroom management, and allow anarchy and chaos. Without recognizable structure and rules, they are arbitrary and inconsistent with rules and punishments, use minilectures and putdowns, use threats and bribes, and allow emotions to rule students and their behaviors.

Jerkiness The teacher fails to develop a consistent flow of instruction, thus causing students to feel lesson momentum jerks from slow to fast (also see *thrust.*)

Judicious consequences Consequences must be commensurate with the violation and must be compatible with the needs and interests of the student and the school community.

Justice Concerned primarily with due process and deals with basic government fairness; students have the same right to fair and reasonable rules as citizens in the nation have to be governed by fair and reasonable laws.

Logical consequences In contrast to rewards and punishments, Dreikurs suggests teachers use logical consequences that result from the misbehaviors.

Long-term efforts These efforts hope to change students' attitudes and mindsets to a point where they will not want to repeat (nor see a reason to do so) a misbehavior in the future.

Limit setting These are a set of physical moves performed by the teacher that signal the student to stop specific behaviors.

Movement management The teacher keeps lessons and groups engaged at an appropriate pace, with smooth transitions and varying activities.

Natural and reasonable consequences Real-world consequences or interventions deal with the reality of the situation rather than the power and control of the adult doing so.

Negative consequence According to Canter and Canter, this is an unpleasant consequence or penalty system having increasingly severe sanctions that follows negative behavior.

New Disciplines These are the newer classroom management models and theories that, although not behaviorist in nature, are similar to behaviorist models.

Nonassertive style This style is used by ineffective teachers who fail to establish clear standards of behavior or who fail to follow through on threats with appropriate actions.

Obedience According to Mendler (1992, p. 36), this means "do not question and certainly do not be different." Obedience also implies a hierarchical structure in which one or several powerful individuals dictate the terms of behavior for everyone else.

Operant Conditioning (or Behavior Modification) This name is used to refer to the theories of B. G. Skinner, which hold that human behavior can be dramatically improved through the use of scientific application of behavioral principles.

Overdwelling The teacher dwells on a issue and engages in a stream of talk clearly longer than the time needed for students' understanding.

Overlapping The teacher supervises and attends to more than one group or activity at the same time.

Ownership Students learn that they are capable of taking ownership of their behaviors and full responsibility for the problems their behaviors create, not because of fear, but because it is the right thing to do.

Peer mediation This is a technique used to help two or more students resolve serious conflicts they cannot handle independently.

Permissive teacher Hands-off teachers usually let the students do what they want to do and depend upon their judgment to do what is best for them and other students without clear guidance from the teacher.

Pleasure–pain principle According to Redl and Wattenberg, a teacher uses the pleasure–pain principle to deliberately provide experiences to produce pleasant to unpleasant feelings. The hope is that a pleasant experience will induce an individual to repeat a desirable behavior, and an unpleasant experience will make the individual want to avoid repeating that unwanted behavior.

Positive Reinforcement A theory of B. F. Skinner, which holds that proper and immediate reinforcement (a favorite food, compliment, or other reward) strengthens the likelihood that appropriate behavior will reoccur; he also found that behavior can be shaped by providing a reinforcing stimulus just after a desired behavior happens.

Power seeking One of Dreikurs's four goals of misbehavior; power-seeking students attempt to prove their power by defying the teacher and doing whatever they want.

Praise In contrast to encouragement, when praise is used, if students do not or cannot continue the behavior or record of achievement, they begin to think they are of less worth.

Preferred activity time (PAT) This involves allocation (both giving and taking away) of time for appropriate and inappropriate behaviors.

Problem Ownership A theory of Thomas Gordon; it holds that educators must get the message to students that the behavior problem rests with the individual students and they will have to accept responsibility for changing their own behavior.

Profiling Checklists of behaviors and personal characteristics associated with youths who have perpetuated violence are used to predict an individual student's potential for acting out in a violent manner.

Proximity This is the distance a teacher stands from a student, in an effort to let the misbehaving student know his or her inappropriate behavior is recognized by the teacher.

Quality schools This term used by William Glasser refers to schools that have positive academic and behavior results.

Reality Appraisal A theory by Fritz Redl and William Wattenberg, it holds that teachers must help students understand whether their actions are guided by intelligence and conscience or by fear or prejudice. To guide students, educators should appeal to students' sense of fairness and also see the consequences of their behaviors.

Reconciliation This is the process of healing, with the offender honoring the restitution plan and making a commitment to live up to the resolution.

Resolution Determining a way not to let the behavior happen again; in other words, how can students accept what they have done and see its implications for a new beginning?

Responsibility According to Mendler (1992, p. 37), this means "make the best decision you possibly can with the information you have available." Within a responsibility model of discipline, students accumulate information, see the options available to them, learn to anticipate consequences, and then choose the path they feel is in the best interest of themselves and others.

Restitution This involves fixing what the student did and repairing the physical damage (if any) and the personal damage.

Revenge One of Dreikurs's four goals of misbehavior; students who are seeking revenge want to hurt someone else and believe that revenge is important for their own self-esteem.

Ripple effect The teacher corrects one student or calls attention to one student for his or her misbehavior (called a *desist*) and it "ripples" to other students, causing them to behave better.

RSVP approach These consequences are reasonable, simple, valuable (as a learning tool), and practical.

Safe school This is a place where the business of education can be conducted in a welcoming environment free of intimidation, violence, and fear.

Safe schools movement This movement is supported by individuals, professional associations, and governmental agencies and places a priority on making schools safe for students and educators by focusing on the problem of violence and proposing possible remedies.

Sane messages These messages address the students' behavior rather than the students' character.

Satiation The students have focused on one learning aspect too long and begin to lose interest, make more mistakes, and misbehave.

School-based risk factors These are items such as poor design of school space, overcrowding, lack of caring, insensitivity toward multicultural factors, student alienation, rejection of at-risk students by teachers and peers, and anger and resentment at school routines and demands for conformity.

Security technologies These are items such as smart cards, metal detectors and wands, alarm systems, and closed-circuit television.

Sense of community This is a feeling of togetherness, where all students (both elementary and secondary), teachers, and administrators know each other and create a climate for intellectual development and shared educational purpose.

Severe clause This part of the Canters' discipline hierarchy provides a way to remove students from the classroom if they pose a threat to others.

Short-term efforts Efforts to provide a quick fix for behavior problems; the goal is to stop the behavior at that particular time, but it does little to prevent the student or another student from repeating the same behavior again.

Significant Seven These are the **essential skills** and **empowering perceptions.**

Situational Assistance This theory by Redl and Wattenberg holds that if a student has lost his or her self-control, a teacher steps in with situational assistance to help the student regain control.

Slowdowns The teacher, when teaching, moves too slowly and stops instruction too often. Thus, the students lose interest or learning momentum.

Social contracts In this arrangement, teachers and students work together to define acceptable and unacceptable behavior and consequences for breaking the agreed-upon rule.

Specific rules These rules train a class to do *what* you want them to do and *when* you want them to do it.

Stimulus bound The teacher has the students engaged in a lesson and then something attracts her or his attention; she or he loses the instructional focus and momentum while dealing with the other issue.

Target behaviors Educators decide to address these behaviors because they violate class or school policy or interfere with teachers teaching or students learning. Addressing all misbehaviors is not an efficient use of instructional time.

Taught discipline Teachers work to teach students to discipline themselves.

Thrust The teacher teaches too slowly or too fast or switches back and forth, thus failing to acquire and hold an appropriate momentum for students to learn.

Tourists Passive onlookers lack feelings of genuine participation in classroom activities

Truncation The teacher engages in a dangle, yet fails to resume the original, dropped activity.

Violence These behaviors range from threats of physical violence to physical assaults and homicide and contribute to an unsafe school.

Warning signs These are indicators that could be used to prevent violent behaviors.

Withitness The teacher perceives everything in all areas of the classroom at all times.

Written intervention plans This document describes the effective prevention practices that will be taken to help troubled children, educates students and parents, and includes steps to be taken when early warning signs are observed or when a tragedy has occurred.

You-messages These messages attack a students' personality and character, as contrasted with I-messages.

Zero-tolerance policies These rules provide strict consequences, without regard for individual circumstances and individual consideration.

References

Adler, A. (1927). *Practice and theory of individual psychology.* New York: Harcourt, Brace, & World.

Adler, A. (1930). *The education of children.* New York: Vail-Ballou Press.

Albert, L. (1989). *A teacher's guide to cooperative discipline.* Circle Pines, MN: American Guidance Service.

Albert, L. (1995). Discipline: Is it a dirty word? *Learning 24*(2), 43–46.

Albert, L. (1997). How to talk to parents about their child's behavior. *Instructor, 107*(1), 62–63.

Alexakos, K. (2001). Inclusive classrooms. *The Science Teacher, 68*(3), 40–43.

Angell, A. V. (2004). Making peace in elementary classrooms: A case for class meetings. *Theory and Research in Social Education, 32*(1), 98–104.

Babyak, A. E., Luze, G. J., & Kamps, D. M. (2000). The Good Student Game: Behavior management for diverse classrooms. *Intervention in School and Clinic, 35*(4), 216–223.

Bailey, K. A. (2001). Legal implications of profiling students for violence. *Psychology in the Schools, 38*(2), 141–156.

Banks, R. (1997). *Bullying in schools.* Champaign: University of Illinois at Urbana-Champaign.

Batiuk, M. D., Boland, J. A., & Wilcox, N. (2004). Project trust: Breaking down barriers between middle school children. *Adolescence, 39*(155), 533–538.

Batsche, G. M., & Knoff, H. M. (1994). Bullies and their victims: Understanding a pervasive problem in the schools. *Psychology Review, 23*(2), 165–174.

Beane, A. L. (2000, September). The bully-free classroom. *Scholastic Instructor, 110*(2), 43–45.

Behind the surge in girl crime. (2004, Sept. 15). *The Christian Science Monitor,* 16.

Bertone, S., Meard, J., Flavier, E., Euzet, J. P., & Durand, M. (2002). Undisciplined actions and teacher-student transactions during two physical education lessons. *European Physical Education Review, 8*(2), 99–117.

Beychok, T. (2003, May 1). Unhappy teenagers (Book Review). *Psychiatric Times,* 69.

Bluestein, J. (2000, September). Create a caring classroom. *Scholastic Instructor,* 35–37.

Blum, R. W. (2005). A case for school connectedness. *Educational Leadership, 62*(7), 16–20.

Bosch, K. A. (1999). *Planning classroom management for change.* Arlington Heights, IL: Skylight.

Brandt, R. (1995). Punished by rewards: A conversation with Alfie Kohn. *Educational Leadership, 53*(1), 13–16.

Brinson, J. A., Kottler, J. A., & Fisher, T. A. (2004). Cross-cultural conflict resolution in the schools: Some practical intervention strategies for counselors. *Journal of Counseling and Development, 82*(3), 294–301.

Brophy, J. E., & Everston, C. (1976). *Learning from teaching: A developmental perspective.* Boston: Allyn and Bacon.

Brophy J. E., & Evertson, C. (1981). *Student characteristics and teaching.* New York: Longman.

Browning, L., Davis, B., & Resta, V. (2000). What do you mean "Think before I act"?: Conflict resolution with choices. *Journal of Research in Childhood Education, 14*(2), 232–238.

Brunner, J., & Lewis, D. (2005). School safety's top ten. *Principal Leadership, 5*(9), 65–66.

Bucher, K. T., & Manning, M. L. (2005). Creating safe schools. *The Clearing House, 79*(1), 55–60.

Burnett, E. M. G. (2000). Conflict resolution: Four steps worth considering. *Social Studies and the Young Learner, 12*(3), 20–23.

Cameron, C. E., Connor, C. M., & Morrison, F. J. (2005). Effects of variation in teacher organization on classroom functioning. *Journal of School Psychology, 43*(1), 61–85.

Canfield, B. S., Ballard, M. B., Osmon, B. C., & McCune, C. (2004). School and family counselors work together to reduce fighting at school. *Professional School Counseling, 8*(1), 40–46.

Canning, C. (1993). Preparing for diversity: A social technology for multicultural community building. *The Educational Forum, 57,* 371–385.

Canter, L. (1974). *The ways and hows of working with behavior problems in the classroom.* San Rafael, CA: Academic Therapy Press.

Canter, L. (1988). Let the educator beware: A response to Curwin and Mender. *Educational Leadership, 46*(2), 71–73.

Canter, L. (1989a). Assertive Discipline—More than names on the board and marbles in a jar. *Phi Delta Kappan, 71*(1), 57–61.

Canter, L. (1989b). Assertive Discipline: A response. *Teachers College Record, 90*(4), 631–638.

Canter, L., & Canter, M. (1976). *Assertive Discipline: A take-charge approach for today's educators.* Santa Monica, CA: Lee Canter & Associates.

Canter, L., & Canter, M. (1992). *Assertive Discipline: Positive behavior management for today's classrooms.* Santa Monica, CA: Lee Canter & Associates.

Canter, L., & Canter, M. (1993). *Succeeding with difficult students: New strategies for reaching your most challenging students.* Santa Monica, CA: Lee Canter & Associates.

Canter, L., & Canter, M. (2001). *Assertive Discipline: Positive behavior management for today's classroom* (3rd ed.). Los Angeles: Canter & Associates.

Carson, R. N. (1996). Reaction to presidential address of Ronald Butchart. *Educational Studies, 27*(3), 207–216.

Casella, R. (2003). Zero tolerance policy in schools: Rationale, consequences, and alternatives. *Teachers' College Record, 105*(5), 872–892.

Chemlynski, C.(1996). Discipline as teaching. *The Education Digest, 62*(3), 42–44.

Chittorran, M. M., & Hoenig, G. A. (2005). Mediating a better solution. *Principal Leadership, 5*(7), 11–15.

Clark, K. (2003). Bringing back compassion, counseling, and mental health: Featured presenter Dr. William Glasser discusses Choice Theory, the New Reality Therapy with Annals. *Annals of the American Psychotherapy Association, 6*(2), 4–10.

Coloroso, B. (1983). *Discipline: Winning at teaching.* Littleton, CO: Kids Are Worth It.

Coloroso, B. (1994). *Kids are worth it: Giving your child the gift of Inner Discipline.* New York: Morrow.

Coloroso, B. (1997). Discipline that makes the grade. *Learning, 25*(4), 44–46.

Coloroso, B. (2000a). *Parenting through crisis: Helping kids in times of loss, grief, and change.* New York: HarperResource.

Coloroso, B. (2000b). *Parenting with wit and wisdom in times of chaos and loss.* Toronto: Penguin.

Coloroso, B. (2002). *The bully, the bullied, and the bystander.* New York: Harper-Resource.

Crawford, D. K., & Bodine, R. J. (2001). Conflict resolution education: Preparing youth for the future. *Juvenile Justice, 8*(1), 21–29.

Crothers, L. M., & Leveinson, E. M. (2004). Assessment of bullying: A review of methods and instruments. *Journal of Counseling and Development, 82,* 496–503.

Curran, M. E. (2003), Linguistic diversity and classroom management. *Theory into Practice, 42*(4), 334–340.

Curwin, R. L., & Mendler, A. N. (1980). *The discipline book: A complete guide to school and classroom management.* Reston, VA: Reston Publishing Company.

Curwin, R. L., & Mendler, A. N. (1988). Packaged discipline programs: Let the buyer beware. *Educational Leadership, 46*(2), 68–71.

Curwin, R. L., & Mendler, A. N. (1989). We repeat, let the educator beware: A response to Canter. *Educational Leadership, 46*(6), 83.

Curwin, R. L., & Mendler, A. N. (1997a). *As tough as necessary: Countering violence, aggression, and hostility in our schools.* Alexandria, VA: Association for Supervision and Curriculum Development.

Curwin, R. L., & Mendler, A. N. (1997b). Discipline With Dignity: Beyond obedience. *The Education Digest, 63*(4), 11–14.

Curwin, R. L., & Mendler, A. N. (1999). Zero tolerance for zero tolerance. *Phi Delta Kappan, 81*(2), 119–120.

Curwin, R. L., & Mendler, A. N. (2001). *Discipline With Dignity.* Upper Saddle River, NJ: Merrill Education/ASCD College Textbook Series.

Dake, J. A., Price, J. H., & Telljohann, S. K. (2003). Teacher perceptions and practices regarding school bullying prevention. *The Journal of School Health, 73*(9), 347–355.

Deci, E. L., & Ryan, R. M. (1990). A motivational approach to self: Integration in personality. In R. Dienstbier (Ed.), *Nebraska Symposium on Motivation, 38.* Lincoln, NE: University of Nebraska Press.

Dinkmeyer, D., & Dreikurs, R. (1963). *Encouraging children to learn.* Upper Saddle River, NJ: Prentice Hall.

Ditzhazy, H. E. R., & Burton, E. M. (2003). Bullying: A perennial school problem. *The Delta Kappa Gamma Bulletin, 70*(1), 43–48, 62.

Dreikurs, R. (1957). *Psychology in the classroom.* New York: Harper & Row.

Dreikurs, R. (1964). *Children: The challenge.* New York: Harper & Row.

Dreikurs, R. (1968). *Children: The challenge* (2nd ed.). New York: Harper & Row.

Dreikurs, R., & Grey, L. G. (1968). *Logical consequences: A new approach to discipline.* New York: Dutton.

Dreikurs, R., Grunwald, B. B., & Pepper, F. C. (1971). *Maintaining sanity in the classroom: Illustrated teaching techniques.* New York: Harper & Row.

Edwards, C. H. (2000). The moral dimensions of teaching and classroom management. *American Secondary Education, 28*(3), 20–25.

Elkind, D. (1992). How to criticize so teens will listen. *Parents Magazine, 67*(10), 222–223.

Emmer, E. T., Evertson, C., & Worsham, M. E. (2006). *Classroom management for middle and high school teachers.* Boston: Pearson/A and B.

Encourage student successes with trips to the couch. (2004). *Curriculum Review, 44*(2), 6.

Ervin, R. A., Ehrhardt, K. E., & Poling, A. (2001). Functional assessment: Old wine in new bottles. *School Psychology Bulletin, 30*(2), 173–179.

Evertson, C. (1985). Training teachers in classroom management: An experimental study in secondary school classrooms. *Journal of Educational Research, 79*(1), 51–58.

Evertson, C. (1987). Creating conditions for learning: From research to practice. *Theory Into Practice, 26*(1), 44–50.

Evertson, C. (1989). Improving elementary classroom management: A school-based training program for beginning the year. *Journal of Educational Research, 83*(2), 82–90.

Evertson, C., Emmer, E. T., Sanford, J. P., & Clements, B. S. (1983). Improving classroom management: An experiment in elementary school classrooms. *The Elementary School Journal, 84*(2), 172–188.

Evertson, C., Emmer, E. T., & Worsham, M. E. (2000). *Classroom management for elementary teachers* (5th ed.). Boston: Allyn & Bacon.

Evertson, C., & Harris, A. (1992). What we know about managing classrooms. *Educational Leadership 49*(7), 74–78.

Evertson, C., & Smithey, M. W. (2000). Mentoring effects on proteges classroom practice: An experimental field study. *Journal of Educational Research, 93*(5), 294–304.

Fashola, O. S., & Slavin, R. E. (1998). Schoolwide reform models: What works? *Phi Delta Kappan, 79*(5), 370–379.

Feinberg, T. (2003). Bullying prevention and intervention. *Principal Leadership, 4*(1), 10–14.

Feldman, S. (2004). Bullying prevention. *Teaching PreK–8, 34*(6), 6.

Finn, J. D., & Pannozzo, G. M. (2004). Classroom organization and student behavior in kindergarten. *The Journal of Educational Research, 98*(2), 79–92.

Flecknoe, M. (2004). Challenging the orthodoxies: Putting a spoke in the vicious cycle. *Educational Management Administration & Leadership, 32*(4), 405–422.

Freiberg, H. J. (1996). From tourists to citizens. *Educational Leadership, 54*(1), 32–36.

Freiberg, H. J. (1999). Consistency Management and Cooperative Discipline: From tourists to citizens in the classroom. In H. J. Freiberg (Ed.), *Beyond behaviorism: Changing the classroom management paradigm* (pp. 75–97). Boston: Allyn & Bacon.

Freiberg, H. J. (2000). Carl Rogers: His enduring message. In H. J. Freiberg (Ed.). *Perceiving, behaving, becoming: Lessons learned.* (pp. 35–51). Alexandria, VA: ASCD.

Freiberg, H. J. (2002). Essential skills for new teachers. *Educational Leadership, 59*(6), 56–60.

Freiberg, H. J., & Driscoll, A. (2000). *Universal teaching strategies* (3rd ed.). Boston: Allyn & Bacon.

Freiberg, H. J., Prokosch, N., Treister, E. S., Stein, T., & Opuni, K. A. (1989). Turning around at-risk schools through Consistency Management. *Journal of Negro Education, 58*(3), 372–382.

Gable, R. A., Hendrickson, J. M., Tonelson, S. W., & Van Acker, R. (2000). Changing disciplinary and instructional practices in the middle school to address IDEA. *The Clearing House, 73*(4), 205–208.

Gartrell, D. (2001). Replacing time-out: Part one—Using guidance to build an encouraging classroom. *Young Children, 56*(6), 8–11.

Gathercoal, F. (1990). Judicious Discipline. *The Education Digest, 55*(6), 20–24.

Gathercoal, F. (1997). *Judicious Discipline* (4th ed.). San Francisco: Caddo Gap Press.

Gathercoal, F. (1998). Judicious Discipline. In R. E. Butchart, & B. McEwan (Eds.), *Classroom discipline in American schools: Problems and possibilities for democratic education* (pp. 197–216). Albany, NY: State University of New York Press.

Gathercoal, P. (2000, April). Conducting democratic class meetings. Paper presented at the American Educational Research Association, New Orleans, LA.

Gathercoal, F. (2001). *Judicious Discipline* (5th ed.). San Francisco: Caddo Gap Press.

Gathercoal, P., & Crowell, R. (2000). Judicious Discipline. *Kappa Delta Pi Record, 36*(4), 173–177.

Gathercoal, P., & Nimmo, V. (2001). *Judicious (Character Education) Discipline.* Paper presented at the Annual Meeting of the AERA, Settle, 10–14 April. ERIC ED 453 124.

Ginott, H. (1965). *Between parent and child.* New York: Avon.

Ginott, H. (1969). *Between parent and teenager.* New York: Macmillan.

Ginott, H. (1972a). *Teacher and child.* New York: Macmillan.

Ginott, H. (1972b). I am angry! I am appalled! I am furious! *Today's Education, 61*(8), 23–24.

Ginott, H. (1973). Driving children sane. *Today's Education, 62* (7), 20–25.

Give poor parenting a time-out. (2002). *U.S. Catholic, 67*(5), 12–17.

Glasser, W. (1965). *Reality therapy: A new approach to psychiatry.* New York: Harper & Row.

Glasser, W. (1969). *Schools without failure.* New York: Harper & Row.

Glasser, W. (1985). *Control theory in the classroom.* New York: Harper & Row.

Glasser, W. (1986). Discipline has never been the problem and isn't the problem now. *Theory Into Practice, 24* (4), 241–246.

Glasser, W. (1992). *The quality school: Managing students without coercion.* New York: HarperPerennial.

Glasser, W. (1993). *The quality school teacher.* New York: HarperPerennial.

Glasser, W. (1997). A new look at school failure and school success. *Phi Delta Kappan, 78*(8), 597–602.

Gordon, R. L. (1997). How novice teachers can succeed with adolescents. *Educational Leadership, 5*(7), 56–58.

Gordon, T. (1970). *Parent effectiveness training: The no-lose way to raise responsible children.* New York: Wyden Books.

Gordon, T. (1974). *T.E.T.: Teacher effectiveness training.* New York: Wyden Books.

Gordon, T. (1989). *Teaching children self-discipline: Promoting self-discipline in children.* New York: Penguin.

Graves, L. N. (1992). Cooperative learning communities: Context for a new vision of education and society. *Journal of Education, 174,* 57–79.

Green, L. (2005, February 28). Fighting back against bullies: A recent survey of Sarasota County's schools finds more than half of middle schoolers were bullied. *Sarasota Herald Tribune,* p. BV1.

Grossman, H. (2004). *Classroom behavior management for diverse and inclusive schools.* New York: Rowman & Littlefield.

Grossman, H. (2005). The case for individualizing behavior management approaches in inclusive classrooms. *Emotional and Behavioural Difficulties, 10*(1), 17–32.

Guetzloe, E., & Rockwell, S. (1998). Fight, flight or better choices: Teaching nonviolent responses to young children. *Preventing School Failure, 42*(4), 154–159.

Gunzelmann, B. (2004). Hidden dangers within our schools: What are these safety problems and how can we fix them? *Educational Horizons, 83*(1), 66–76.

Hernandez, T. J., & Seem, S. R. (2004). A safe school climate: A systemic approach and the school counselor. *Professional School Counseling, 7*(4), 256–262.

Hodgkinson, H. (2000/2001). Educational demographics: What teachers should know. *Educational Leadership, 58*(4), 6–11.

The INTASC Standards. (n.d.). Retrieved June 8, 2004, from NCPublicSchool.org Web site: http://www.dpi.state.nc.us/pbl/pblintasc.htm.

Johnson, D., & Johnson, R. (1987a). *Learning together and alone: Cooperative, competitive, and individualistic learning.* Upper Saddle River, NJ: Prentice Hall.

Johnson, D., & Johnson, R. (1987b). The three C's of safe schools. *Educational Leadership, 55*(2), 8–14.

Johnson, D., & Johnson, R. (1989). *Cooperation and competition: Theory and research.* Edina, MN: Interaction Book Company.

Johnson, D., & Johnson, R. (1989/1990). Social skills for successful group work. *Educational Leadership, 47*(4), 29–33.

Johnson, D., & Johnson, R. (1993). Gifted students illustrate what isn't cooperative learning. *Educational Leadership, 50*(6), 60–62.

Johnson, D., & Johnson, R. (1995a). Why violence prevention programs don't work—and what does. *Educational Leadership, 52*(5), 63–66.

Johnson, D., & Johnson, R. (1995b). *Reducing school violence through conflict resolution.* Alexandria, VA: Association for Supervision and Curriculum Development.

Johnson, D., & Johnson, R. (1999). The three C's of school and classroom management. In H. Jerome Freiberg (Ed.), *Beyond behaviorism: Changing the classroom management paradigm* (pp. 119–144). Boston: Allyn & Bacon.

Johnson, D., & Johnson, R. (2004). Implementing the "Teaching Students to be Peacemakers Program." *Theory into Practice, 43*(1), 68–79.

Johnson, D., & McLeod, S. (2004/2005). Get answers: Using student response systems to see students' thinking. *Learning and Leading with Technology, 32*(4), 18–23.

Jones, F. H. (1973). The gentle art of classroom discipline. *Principal, 53*(3), 26–32.

Jones, F. H. (1987a). *Positive classroom discipline.* New York: McGraw-Hill.

Jones, F. H. (1987b). *Positive classroom instruction.* New York: McGraw-Hill.

Jones, F. H. (1996). Did not! Did, too! *Learning 24*(6), 24–26.

Jones, F. H. (with Jones, P., & Jones, J.). (2000) *Tools for teaching.* Santa Cruz, CA: Fredric H. Jones & Associates.

Kehle, T. J., Bray, M. A., Theodore, L. A., Jenson, W. R., & Clark, E. (2000). A multi-component intervention designed to reduce disruptive classroom behavior. *Psychology in the Schools, 37*(5), 475–481.

Keiper, R. W. (2004). Peacemaking. *Kappa Delta Pi Record, 40*(2), 91.

Kingery, P. M., & Coggeshall, M. B. (2001). Surveillance of school violence, injury, and disciplinary actions. *Psychology in the Schools, 38*(2), 117–126.

Kohn, A. (1986). *No contest: The case against competition.* Boston: Houghton Mifflin.

Kohn, A. (1993). *Punished by rewards: The trouble with gold stars, incentive plans, A's, praise, and other bribes.* Boston: Houghton Mifflin.

Kohn, A. (1993). Rewards versus learning: A response to Paul Chance. *Phi Delta Kappan, 74*(10), 783–790.

Kohn, A. (1994, December). The risk of rewards. *ERIC Digest* (December 1994): EDO-PS-94-14, 1–4.

Kohn, A. (1995). Discipline is the problem—not the solution. *Learning, 24*(3), 34.

Kohn, A. (1996a). *Beyond discipline: From compliance to community.* Alexandria, VA: Association for Supervision and Curriculum Development.

Kohn, A. (1996b). What to look for in a classroom. *Educational Leadership 54*(1), 54–55.

Kohn, A. (1997). How not to teach values: A critical look at character education. *Phi Delta Kappan, 78*(6), 428–439.

Kohn, A. (1997, September 3). Students don't "work"—they learn. *Education Week*, 60+.

Kohn, A. (1999). Constant frustration and occasional violence: The legacy of American high schools. *American School Board Journal, 186*(9), 20–24.

Kohn, A. (2004a). Challenging students—And how to have more of them. *Phi Delta Kappan, 86* (3), 184–194.

Kohn, A. (2004b). Rebuilding school culture to make schools safer. *The Education Digest, 70*(3), 23–30.

Kohn, A. (2004c). *What does it mean to be well educated: And more essays on standards, grading, and other follies.* Boston, MA: Beacon Press.

Kounin, J. S. (1970). *Discipline and group management in classrooms.* New York: Holt, Rinehart, and Winston.

Landau, B. M., & Gathercoal, P. (2000). Creating peaceful classrooms: Judicious Discipline and class meetings. *Phi Delta Kappan, 81*(6), 450–454.

Landreth, G. L. (2002). Therapeutic limit setting in the play therapy relationship. Professional Psychology: *Research and Practice, 33*(6), 529–535.

Lathan, A. S. (1998). Rules and learning. *Educational Leadership, 56*(1), 82–83.

Liepe-Levinson, K., & Levinson, M. H. (2005). A general semantics approach to school-age bullying. *ETC: A Review of General Semantics, 62*(1), 4–17.

Lumsden, L. (2000). Profiling students for violence. *ERIC Digest 139.* Eugene: University of Oregon, College of Education.

Maag, J. W. (2001). Rewarded by punishment: Reflections on the disuse of positive reinforcement in schools. *Exceptional Children, 67*(2), 173–186.

Mabie, G. E. (2003). Making schools safe for the 21st century: An interview with Ronald D. Stephens. *The Educational Forum, 67,* 156–162.

Maheady, L., Harper, G. F., & Mallette, B. (2001). Peer-mediated instruction and interventions and students with mild disabilities. *Remedial and Special Education, 22*(1), 4–14.

Maier, H. W. (2001). Pioneer House: Reflections of working with Redl and Wineman in 1947. *Reclaiming Children and Youth, 10*(2), 71–77.

Manning, M. L., & Baruth, L. G. (2004). *Multicultural education of children and adolescents.* Boston: Allyn & Bacon.

Mano, S. (2005). Moving away from the authoritarian classroom. *Change, 37*(3), 50–57.

Martini-Scully, D., Bray, M. A., & Kehle, T. J. (2000). A packaged intervention to reduce disruptive behaviors in general education students. *Psychology in the Schools, 37*(2), 149–166.

McAndrews, T. (2001). Zero-tolerance policies. *ERIC Digest 146.* University of Oregon: College of Education.

McCormack, S. (1989). Response to Render, Padilla, and Krank: But practitioners say it works. *Educational Leadership, 46*(6), 77–78.

McEwan, B. (2000). *The art of classroom management: Effective practices for building equitable learning communities.* Columbus, OH: Merrill/Prentice Hall.

McEwan, B., Gathercoal, P., & Nimmo, V. (1999). Application of Judicious Discipline. In H. J. Freiberg (Ed.), *Beyond behaviorism: Changing the classroom management paradigm* (pp. 98–118). Boston: Allyn & Bacon.

Mendler, A. N. (1992). *What do I do when . . . How to achieve Discipline With Dignity in the classroom.* Bloomington, IN: National Educational Service.

Mendler, A. N. (1993). Discipline With Dignity in the classroom: Seven principles. *The Education Digest, 58*(7), 4–9.

Mendler, A. N. (1994). Teaching hard-to-reach youth. *Reclaiming Children and Youth: Journal of Emotional and Behavioral Problems, 3*(2), 23–24.

Mendler, A. N. (1995). Classroom counteraggression. *Reclaiming Children and Youth: Journal of Emotional and Behavioral Problems, 4*(1), 16–17.

Mendler, A. N. (2002). Connecting with students to limit high-risk behaviors. *Reclaiming Children and Youth: Journal of Emotional and Behavioral Problems, 11*(3), 162–163.

Mendler, A. N., & Curwin, R. L. (1983). *Taking charge in the classroom: A practical guide to effective discipline.* Reston, VA: Reston Publishing Company.

Mendler, A. N., & Curwin, R. L. (1997). Toward the peaceful school. *Reclaiming Children and Youth: Journal of Emotional and Behavior Problems, 5*(4), 226–228.

Mendler, A. N., & Mendler, B. (1995). Humor and discipline. *Reclaiming Children and Youth: Journal of Emotional and Behavioral Problems, 4*(3), 16–18.

Merrow, J. (2004). Safety and excellence. *Educational Horizons, 83*(1), 19–32.

Montgomery, W. (2001). Creating culturally responsive, inclusive classrooms. *Teaching Exceptional Children, 33*(4), 4–9.

Morris, R. C. (1996). Contrasting disciplinary models in education. *Thresholds in Education, 22*(4), 7–13.

Morrison, G. M. (2001). Predicting violence from school misbehavior: Promises and perils. *Psychology in the Schools, 38*(2), 173–186.

Morse, W. C. (2001). A half century of children who hate: Insights from Fritz Redl. *Reclaiming Children and Youth: Journal of Emotional and Behavioral Problems, 10*(2), 75–84.

National Center for Education Statistics. (2003). *Crime and safety in America's public schools: Selected findings from the school survey on crime and safety.* Washington, DC: U.S. Dept. Of Education.

National Education Association. (1998). NEA action sheet. www.nea.org/issues/safeschol/safeacsh.html.

National School Safety Center. (1999). *Working together to create safe schools.* Westlake Village, CA: Author.

NCLB policies leave safe, orderly schools behind. *American Teacher, 89*(5), 6.

Nelsen, J., Lott, L., & Glenn, H. S. (1997). *Positive discipline in the classroom.* Rocklin, CA: Prima.

Newman-Carlson, D., & Horne, A. M. (2004). Bully Busters: A psychoeducational intervention for reducing bullying behavior. *Journal of Counseling and Development, 82*(3), 259–267.

Obenchain, K. M., & Abernathy, T. V. (2003). 20 ways to . . . build community and empower students. *Intervention in School and Clinic, 39*(1), 55–60.

Olweus, D. (1993). *Bullying at school: What we know and what we can do.* Cambridge, MA: Blackwell.

Osher, D., Catledge, G., Osward, D., Sutherland, K. S., Artiles, A. J., and Coutinho, M. (2004). Cultural and linguistic competency and disproportionate representation. In R. B. Rutherford, Jr., M. M. Quinn, and S. Mathur (Eds.). *Handbook of Research in Behavioral Disorders.* (pp. 54–77). New York: Guilford Press.

Palardy, J. M. (1996). Taking another look at behavior modification and Assertive Discipline. *NASSP Bulletin, 80*(581), 66–70.

Perez, S. A. (1994). Responding differently to diversity. *Childhood Education, 70,* 151–153.

Petersen, K. D., & Deal, T. E. (1998). How leaders influence the culture of schools. *Educational Leadership, 56*(1), 28–30.

Peterson, R. L., & Skiba, R. (2001). Creating climates that prevent school violence. *The Clearing House, 74*(3), 155–163.

Plucker, J. A. (2000). Positive approaches to preventing school violence: Peace building in schools and communities. *NASSP Bulletin, 84*(614), 1–4.

Pryor, D. B., & Tollerud, T. R. (1999). Applications of Adlerian principles in school settings. *Professional School Counseling, 2*(4), 299–304.

Putnam, J., Markovchick, K., Johnson, D., & Johnson, R. (1996). Cooperative learning and peer acceptance of students with learning disabilities. *The Journal of Social Psychology, 136*(6), 741–753.

Redl, F., & Wattenberg, W. W. (1959). *Mental hygiene in teaching* (2nd ed.). New York: Harcourt, Brace, & World.

Redl, F., & Wineman, D. (1952). *Controls from within.* Glencoe, IL: Free Press.

Render, G. F., Padilla, J. M., & Krank, H. M. (1989). What research really shows about Assertive Discipline. *Educational Leadership, 46*(6), 72–75.

Rife, S. L. (2004, November 11). Author talks about bullies. *Sarasota Herald Tribune,* p. E1.

Rimm-Kaufman, S. E., La Paro, K. M., Downer, J. (2005), The contribution of classroom setting and quality of instruction to children's behavior in kindergarten classrooms. *The Elementary School Journal, 105*(4), 377–394.

Roebuck, E. (2002). Beat the drum lightly: Reflections on Ginott. *Music Educator's Journal, 88*(5), 40–44, 53.

Rogers, C., & Freiberg, H. J. (1994). *Freedom to learn* (3rd ed.). Columbus, OH: Merrill.

Rubin, R. (2004). Building a comprehensive discipline system and strengthening school climate. *Reclaiming Children and Youth: Journal of Emotional and Behavioral Problems, 13*(3), 162–168.

Ruiz, M. R. (1995). B. F. Skinner's radical behaviorism: Historical misconstructions and grounds for feminist reconstructions. *Psychology of Women Quarterly, 19*(2), 161–179.

Rutherford, A. (2000). Radical behaviorism and psychology's public. B. F. Skinner in the popular press: 1934–1990. *History of Psychology, 3*(4), 371–395.

Sanders, D. (1987). Cultural conflicts: An important factor in the academic failure of American Indian students. *Journal of Multicultural Counseling and Development, 78,* 22–31.

Sanders, D. (2001). A caring alternative to suspension. *The Education Digest, 66*(7), 51–54.

Scelfo, J. (2003). Family: facing bullies. *Newsweek, 141*(5), 64.

Schaefer-Schiumo, K., & Patraka, A. (2003). The effectiveness of the Warning Signs Program in educating youth about violence prevention: A study with urban high school students. *Professional School Counseling, 7*(1), 1–8.

Schmidt, J. J. (1989). A professional stance for positive discipline—Promoting learning. *NASSP Bulletin, 73,* 14–20.

Schneider, T. (2001a). Safer schools through environmental design. *ERIC Digest 144.* University of Oregon: College of Education.

Schneider, T. (2001b). Newer technologies for school security. *ERIC Digest 145.* University of Oregon: College of Education.

School-safety rankings—or just black marks? (2003, August 20). *The Christian Science Monitor,* 1.

Schroeder, K. (2005). K–6 violence is global. *Education Digest, 70*(7), 71–73.

Sergiovanni, T. J. (1994). *Building community in schools.* San Francisco: Jossey-Bass.

Sheviakov, G. V., & Redl, F. (1956). *Discipline for today's children and youth.* Washington, DC: Association for Supervision and Curriculum Development.

Skinner, B. F. (1948). *Walden two.* New York: Macmillan.

Skinner, B. F. (1971). *Beyond freedom and dignity.* New York: Knopf.

Smith, M. (2001). Creating community in the classroom. *Kappa Delta Pi Record, 37*(3), 111–115.

Solutions for handling 117 misbehaviors. Retrieved November 1, 2001. from http://www.disciplinehelp.com/parent/list.cfm?cause=All.

Soodak, L. C. (2003). Classroom management in inclusive settings. *Theory into Practice, 42*(4), 327–333.

Staddon, J. (1995). On responsibility and punishment. *The Atlantic Monthly, 275*(2), 88–94.

Stanley, P. H., Juhnke, G. A., & Purkey, W. W. (2004). Using an invitational theory of practice to create safe and successful schools. *Journal of Counseling and Development, 82*(3), 302–309.

Tomczyk, K. (2000). Prevention, not punishment. *American School Board Journal, 187*(5), 60–61.

Trends and issues: School safety and violence prevention. Retrieved April 17, 2001, from eric.uoregon.edu/trends_issues/safety/index.html.

Ullucci, K. (2005). Picking battles, finding joy: Creating community in the "uncontrolled" classroom. *Multicultural Education 12*(3), 41–77.

U.S. Department of Education. (1998a). *Preventing bullying: A manual for schools and communities.* Washington, DC: Author.

U.S. Department of Education. (1998b). *Early warning timely response: A guide to safe schools.* Washington, DC: Author.

Van Acker, R. (1994). Dealing with conflict and aggression in the classroom: What skills do teachers need? *Teacher Education and Special Education, 16,* 23–33.

Vargas, J. S., & Chance, P. (2002, May/June). The depths of genius. *Psychology Today,* 52–55.

Verdugo, R. (2002). Race-ethnicity, social class, and zero tolerance policies: The cultural and structural wars. *Education and Urban Society, 35*(1), 50–75.

Walsh, J., & Reina, C. M. (2004). Learning the hard way. *Principal Leadership, 5*(4), 36–40.

Wattenberg, W. (1967). *All men are created equal.* Detroit: Wayne State University Press.

Wattenberg, W. (1973). *The adolescent years.* New York: Harcourt Brace.

Wattenberg, W. (1977). The ecology of classroom behavior. *Theory Into Practice, 26*(4), 256–261.

Weinstein, C. S. (1999). Reflections on best practices and promising programs: Beyond assertive classroom discipline. In H. J. Freiberg (Ed.), *Beyond behaviorism: Changing the classroom management paradigm* (pp. 147–163). Boston: Allyn & Bacon.

Weinstein, C. S., Tomlinson-Clark, S., & Curran, M. (2004). Toward a conception of culturally responsive classroom management. *Journal of Teacher Education, 55*(1), 25–38.

Wemlinger, C. (2004). Classroom behavior management for diverse and inclusive schools. *Teachers College Record, 106*(12), 2381–2384.

Westheimer, J., & Kahne, J. (1993). Building school communities: An experience-based model. *Phi Delta Kappan, 75*(4), 324–328.

Williams, K. (2001). A school security check-list. *American School Board Journal, 188* (3), 35.

Willis, S. (1996). Managing today's classroom: Finding alternatives to control and compliance. *ASCD Education Update, 38*(6), 1–7.

Wolfgang, C. H. (1995). *Solving discipline problems: Methods and models for today's teachers* (3rd ed.). Boston: Allyn & Bacon.

Name Index

Subject Index